Thinking as Sport and Dance
Learn the Power of Creative Thinking

Gary Anthony Catona

iUniverse, Inc.
New York   Bloomington

Thinking as Sport and Dance
Learn the Power of Creative Thinking

iUniverse books may be ordered through booksellers or by contacting:

iUniverse
1663 Liberty Drive
Bloomington, IN 47403
www.iuniverse.com
1-800-Authors (1-800-288-4677)

ISBN: 978-0-595-43374-2 (pbk)
ISBN: 978-0-595-68225-6(cloth)
ISBN: 978-0-595-87700-3 (ebk)

Printed in the United States of America

iUniverse rev. date: 8/14/09

In loving memory of my parents Anthony and Caroline Catona and my dear brother Jack Catona

Acknowledgments

I am grateful and indebted to so many people, both living and dead, that it's difficult to single out a group of people as being the most important in writing this book. But certainly the list must include my dear parents, Anthony and Caroline Catona, whose endless love and generosity enabled me to pursue my dreams; Ron Ignatuk, my best friend from childhood up through my university years, who urged me to attend college; psychoanalyst and author Erich Fromm, who was the first thinker to stimulate my interest in psychology and human nature; Bob Cox, professor of phenomenology, who was the first person to encourage me to pursue studies in philosophy; Professor Alphonso Lingis, who was my philosophical mentor when I was a graduate student at Pennsylvania State University; Professor Joseph Kockelmans, who instructed me in the philosophy of science; Dr. Fabrizio Mancinelli, professor of classical studies and former Vatican Museum curator in Rome, Italy, who ignited my interest in Greek, Roman, and Italian culture; biologist Ernst Mayr, whose book, *The Growth of Biological Thought* reoriented my thinking about Darwinian evolution and science generally.

As far as the great philosophers are concerned, Friedrich Nietzsche stands out as the thinker who influenced me the most; Plato, Aristotle, David Hume, Arthur Schopenhauer, Edmund Husserl, Martin Heidegger, and Jean-Paul Sartre were also important influences on my thinking.

I would like to thank Luke McGowan for his editorial critiques and suggestions regarding the biological subject matter in the book as well as for his overall organizational contributions. My editors at Iuniverse also deserve a great deal of credit for their edits and suggestions. I have special love and affection for Channe Gallagher, whose enthusiastic support during the writing of *Thinking as Sport and Dance* made the experience that much more enjoyable; I am also very grateful for her word-processing skills. Finally, I'd like to thank the countless philosophical conversationalists who challenged and criticized me throughout the years—without their input this book would not have been possible.

Contents

Introduction 1

Thinking as Sport and Dance was an accidental book. Ever since I received a master's degree in philosophy from Pennsylvania State University, I had always intended to write philosophy books *someday*, but my career and ambitions as a voice builder/singing teacher had largely dominated my attention. Since I developed a voice-building system in the late 1980s, my primary focus has been to establish my system as the dominant model for building the singing and speaking voice. To that end, I have been working both alone and with associates to bring my ambitions to fruition. There is no question that I am making significant progress, but challenging obstacles still stand in the way. Achieving a reversal in thinking with respect to any topic or activity is very difficult, especially if one aims to change deeply embedded cultural practices. It's certainly true that old habits die hard, but it's equally true that old ways of thinking die even harder. Traditional ways of teaching singing and treating vocal disorders are deeply entrenched cultural practices that have remained stuck in the past, despite the clear evidence that the received wisdom in both fields is far from wise.

My goal to have my voice-building system become the standard model in the fields of voice teaching and voice rehabilitation, caused me to put everything else on hold, including writing philosophy books. Nonetheless, my heartfelt love for philosophy has never been absent from my daily life. My family and friends will attest to my endless obsession for debate and discussion. The desire to put my thoughts down on paper grew steadily over the past few years, and finally, while touring with different students, an idea started to come to light. On long bus rides across the United States and Europe, and during sleepless plane flights across vast oceans and continents, I had many occasions to talk with band members, singers, and musicians about a wide range of subjects, including science, philosophy, history, politics, and religion.

I was delighted to find that my comrades had genuine interest in these subjects even though they were not their usual areas of concern. I hatched the idea for *Thinking as Sport and Dance* during these times, when our discussions would pop up spontaneously, and I found myself speaking extemporaneously about a wide range of subjects to attentive ears and hungry minds.

The experience of conversing philosophically with my traveling companions was eye opening; and our manner of discussion—spontaneous, random, and unstructured—was also very engaging and even exciting. There was something natural and liberating about moving freely from topic to topic without directly controlling the movement of ideas—and surprisingly, this relaxed discourse proved to be very effective in coaxing people to speak their minds with passion and insight; and rarely was there the sense that our discussions were not relevant. Explaining Plato's theory of forms, for example, or discussing the weirdness of quantum physics is not light fare, and yet these closet truth seekers were often there with me all the way, arguing their positions with conviction, asking intelligent questions, and giving their very best to get to the crux of the matter. What really intrigued me about these conversations was the degree to which they prodded all of us to think, and do so as clearly and creatively as we were able.

But the birth of the idea for *Thinking as Sport and Dance* had another dimension to it. Human beings must think—this is a fact of human nature. We are not guided thoughtlessly through our daily activities by inborn instincts, but rather we must use our minds to make daily decisions; to plan for the future; to investigate and understand the world around us; and to build, organize, and manage our lives. Once we fully realize our virtual dependence on thinking, then the quality and effectiveness of our thinking should be of serious interest.

Yet thinking is routinely misused, degraded, and disrespected in our world, even in America. And why? Because thinking as a value is not nurtured in our popular culture and is not cultivated in our educational systems. Scientific thinking, on the other hand, is certainly embraced by some segments of society, especially when it's connected to technology. This may be so, but most people still have little understanding of the process of rational argumentation and debate or the methods that scientists employ to arrive at scientific understanding.

But even scientific thinking is necessarily limited to the areas of science. Many people have argued, though, that scientific thinking is the *only* proper way to use our minds—but this belief is sheer foolishness for the simple reason that most of human life vibrates along nonscientific pathways. Scientific thinking is thoroughly inappropriate when I am trying to decide on the values and goals toward which my life should be devoted, for instance; or as a way to ponder my feelings and ideas of love, friendship, or joy; or in understanding moments of personal or spiritual insight; or, generally, as a way to navigate through the many complex situations that normally arise on a daily basis. Scientific thinking was designed to describe and, ideally, to *quantify*—assign numerical value to—what is true about the world around us, and particularly, to discover the laws, principles, regularities, and symmetries that determine and shape it. This is true not only for the physical and biological sciences, but also for the social and psychological sciences.

The object of much of our ordinary thinking, by contrast, are *unquantifiable* feelings, desires, moods, ideas, judgments, and perspectives and to address them adequately, we must employ our minds in creative ways that often have little in common with the quest for scientific truth. It's for these reasons that thinking, as applied to nonscientific areas, is more of an *art form* than a strictly rational science: there are no absolutely reliable theories, mathematical formulas, or roadmaps to guide us effortlessly and painlessly through our lives and answer all our questions and concerns. So we must learn to think artfully.

After many years of considering writing a philosophy book, I was finally inspired to do so thanks to my many accidental, philosophical conversations. It also seemed appropriate to compose this book in the spirit of these discussions—where thoughts, beliefs, theories, insights, and questions would often spring suddenly into being, and were bandied about in an unstructured and nonlinear way. Following this methodology, I proceeded to write down—stream-of-consciousness style—whatever entered my mind, with little concern for overall organization or continuity between sections. Surprisingly, this unplanned format soon produced a momentum of its own, and I found myself moving from topic to topic with ease, and even manifesting original thought in the process. Although this method is an unorthodox approach for writing a philosophy book, the creative freedom that I experienced in following this free-flowing writing style could only be described as philosophically exhilarating.

In covering the many subjects in this work, I was careful to check references in recording dates and names, and I always confirmed factual (especially historical) information of which I was unsure. I was also careful to give credit to other thinkers when I used their ideas and statements, and I often refer to their seminal works. The book does not contain footnotes, bibliography, or an index; this decision was based upon my interest in remaining true to spontaneous manner of thinking that had inspired and produced this work. I have, though, arranged the book into chapters and subsections to give the reader a feel for the general flow of topics and ideas.

The title of my book came to me one morning as I was running (jogging) around my neighborhood in West Hollywood, California. I was musing on possible titles for this unusual work and it soon became clear that the title would have to capture the book's stylistic idiosyncrasies as well as reflect the substance of the work itself. The problem was that my book addresses so many topics that no title could ever faithfully reflect its actual contents. I began to reflect back on the numerous debates and discussions that I had as a graduate student in philosophy, and on the unscripted philosophizing that I had enjoyed with friends and strangers over the years, and realized that these conversations were defined by two different ways of thinking. One was analytical, probing, and dispassionate, where we deployed the cold knife of reason to dissect and defeat all oppositions. The other approach was what I would describe as *warm-hearted*, where the ideas and passions of the various participants would unite harmoniously to celebrate the arrival of new ideas or the unraveling of intellectual knots that were constraining our thinking. Then it struck me, a very fortunate metaphor that is fantastically rich with meanings that served my purposes well: *Thinking as Sport and Dance!*

The central metaphors of "sport" and "dance" reflect two very distinct but complementary ways of thinking. In the first case, artful thinking is like a sport—it's goal-orientated, analytical, rule bound, and confrontational. We play sports to win, and a good sportsperson will think very rationally to discover the best ways and strategies to prevail, while keeping in mind that his actions are guided by clearly defined, inflexible rules. Sports are often very confrontational and aggressive and, in many athletic competitions, such as boxing, football, and tennis, success is thoroughly dependent upon being exceptionally confrontational and aggressive. Sports, at least professional sports, also require a "team effort," where different individuals with diverse skills and capacities (coaches, trainers, medical experts, fellow players, organizers) all work together to maximize the chances for players, or a team, to achieve victory.

Rational inquiry also has many of the characteristics of sports and necessarily so. To get to the truth of the matter, for example, ideas often have to do battle with each other or must overcome stern philosophical opposition by sheer force of logic. The history of philosophy and science, in fact, could be seen as centuries-long sports competitions, wherein certain ideas, beliefs, and theories win out over others and are celebrated for their victories, while other go down in defeat and have to retreat into the depressing locker rooms of irrelevance. Finally, the pursuit of rational understanding is often a joint effort that incorporates the diverse, creative accomplishments of many truth seekers—both past and present, whose ideas and critiques serve as guideposts and correctives along the path to victory—that is to say, to genuine knowledge!

Besides pursuing knowledge with the attitude of a dedicated sportsperson, artful thinkers could also engage reality in the spirit of dance, where thinking becomes intuitive, playful, and harmonious. We dance for the sheer fun of it. This means that the joy that the dancer seeks is not a goal toward which she aims, but rather is an abiding pleasure that the dancer experiences at every moment of the dance. Dancing also requires a *letting-go* of our thinking faculty, rather than an analytical use of it. We don't think when we dance—we *un-think*, and simply "go with it" and allow our natural movements and rhythms to take over. Dancing, finally, is a coming together of partners rather than, as in sports, a confrontation of opponents—in dance, in other words, we embrace our partner and do our best to harmonize his or her movements with our own.

Some of the greatest moments in thinking occur when we let our minds dance, when there is no philosophical struggle to wage or logical obstacles to overcome, in order to arrive at a deeper understanding of something; this is the meaning of *insight*. Insight can be both a solitary occurrence or can include fellow truth seekers on the same path to knowledge and understanding. In the all-embracing light of insight, thoughtful harmony and balance bring together all philosophical interlocutors, as each person keeps in perfect step with the other—they think as one, because their ideas are dancing to the same music!

Thinking, at its best, emerges when the mind of an athlete and that of the dancer live together competitively and playfully in the same mind. When this happens, the result is beautiful thought-performances. I wrote *Thinking as Sport and Dance* with this ideal in mind.

Casanova's Apology: An
Allegory in Dialogue

2

Various coaches and gondolas arrive at an extravagant Venetian villa of art patron Joseph Smith, circa 1750. Each person's name is announced as he or she enters the household. Besides noted Venetians, there are in attendance visitors from other cities in Italy and Europe. The purpose of the gathering is a dinner party in celebration of Lent. During dinner there is lively discussion until Joseph Smith rises to speak.

Joseph Smith. Honored guests, I want to thank you all for attending my little party to celebrate one of our most sacred times of the year. I am delighted that good fortune has befallen me this evening, for I see in your midst some of our most illustrious citizens. Permit me to introduce a few of them to you. To my left is the most wonderful artist in the civilized world, maestro Canaletto, whose timeless paintings have glorified our fair city throughout the world. Seated next to him is the incomparable singer of our time, Giovanni Carestini, whose voice has enthralled the most demanding audiences all across Europe. Across from him sits another maestro of supreme rank, Europe's greatest playwright, Carlo Goldoni, whose bold and honest depictions of the real world have revolutionized theatre in Italy. In front of me is seated the most venerated Bishop Luca Moscini—the master of ceremonies for this evening. Seated on the Bishop's left is the gracious queen of Venice, Madame Helene, whose talents in the realm of amorous delights are the symbol for Venice's international reputation as a city unequalled in the world for love.

A masked man and two lovely companions arrive and interrupt the dinner. They walk over to their assigned seats and sit down. The man removes his mask and exposes his real identity—it's Giacomo Casanova, the infamous lover and adventurer. Casanova rises and speaks.

Casanova. My deepest apologies to all of you, especially to you, Joseph, for our late arrival. I could hardly secure a gondola.

Joseph Smith. Think nothing of it, my good friend; we're just glad that you are here. My honored guests, I am very pleased to introduce to you one of Venice's deepest sources of pride, Giacomo Casanova—master of literature, theatre, philosophy, languages, law, religion, medicine, and music, and last, but certainly not least, our greatest maestro of love!

Casanova, (*standing*). Thank you for your kind words, Joseph. My dear and loyal friend, your celebrated reputation as Venice's greatest party host has been tremendously enhanced with this fabulous festival. As usual, you have not failed to enchant us with irresistible seductions.

(He samples an item of food and some wine).

This delectable food and wine could be served at the table of Dionysus. Here among your honored guests are the noblest citizens in Venice (*he salutes them*); the most gifted artists and musicians in Europe (*he salutes them*); and, to the exquisite pleasure of all sentient beings, the most sublime women in all the world (*he salutes the women, who giggle*). God the almighty should be present at this remarkable gathering. I was praying that the Almighty would make an appearance, but with this divine presence (*gesturing toward the women*), for what more could a simple mortal ask? A toast to you, dear Joseph, to God, and, of course, to the goddesses.

Joseph Smith. God is always welcome at my home. In fact, I thought that you, Giacomo, have come as his personal representative—this seems only natural, given your reputation among us mortals.

Casanova, (*gesticulating to the heavens*). Come to think of it, I do feel especially powerful and intelligent this evening. In fact, just today—

Luca, (*interrupting*). Please, Giacomo. I beg your pardon; it's Lent, we should be mindful to avoid offending our Lord Jesus Christ. Please sit down so we can proceed with the evening.

Casanova, (*sitting down*). Of course, my apologies, Bishop; all due respect to our Savior!

Madame Helene, (*privately*). Sweet Casanova, I have not seen you in such a long time. I have missed the pleasure of your company. Where have you been?

Casanova. I've been very busy, my dear Helene, in France.

Madame Helene. What did you find there that kept you away for so long? Trouble … a woman? Or both?

Casanova. I was doing important research. The French taught me new ways in the art of love.

Madame Helene. Is not the Venetian way enough?

Casanova. The Venetian way of love is sufficient for many, but I am a philosopher of love, always pursuing a deeper understanding of its nature. In France, I learned that passion has more dimensions than I had thought. A true lover must know all the forms and fine subtleties of lovemaking in order to serve a woman more fully, to ensure that she feels as though she is being touched by the hand of God.

Madame Helene. Bravo … Being your first teacher in love, I would be curious to know more about the subtleties you're talking about. Oh, I heard a rumor about you and the French duke. Is it true?

Casanova. Indeed. He invited me to his lovely chateau to give violin lessons to his wife. As it turned out, he wanted me to make love to her, as well, while he watched. Each night I was required to perform my noble duties. What the Duke didn't know was that I was also sleeping with his mistress, his stepdaughter, and his young sister. I must say that between performing my musical obligations and living up to everyone's unreasonable expectations, I found the whole ordeal very exhausting. A weaker constitution certainly would have faltered. But, all in all, it was quite enjoyable—and lucrative, I might add. And I was invited back whenever I return to Paris.

Madame Helene. You are much too scandalous, Giacomo; take care that your actions don't cost you your head.

Casanova. Thank you for your genuine concern, my sweet, but living well and living safely don't always go hand-in-hand. Nonetheless, since Lent is upon us, I have been moved to make a difficult resolution. The voice of Venus is beckoning me with great force to satisfy my erotic appetites, but I have vowed to forego my own personal pleasure altogether, in order to focus on serving women more completely. And I am willing to do my best and sacrifice everything to that end!

Madame Helene. Oh how very noble—or should I say, Christian—of you, Giacomo. I am sure the Almighty will appreciate the extent of your painful sacrifice.

Casanova. Madame, it may be hard for you to believe, but I am a religious man.

Madame Helene. On the contrary, I have heard you call out God's name on quite a few occasions.

Casanova. And you prayed right along with me, perhaps a little louder.

Luca, (*eavesdropping*). You two must cease talking about such indecent topics; it's Lent—

Madame Helene, (*interrupting and teasing*). Sweet Casanova. How does a woman say no to you?

Casanova, (*index finger pointed to the heavens*). Women are the true manna from heaven. So the question should be, how to say no to a woman?

Carestini, (*eavesdropping and speaking loudly*). Maestro, your incredible life should be told in an opera, and I would like to sing the part of the amazing Casanova!

Casanova, (*standing and garnering all the attention*). I am truly flattered that a genius like yourself would make such a suggestion, although I find it rather charming that a castrato would like to play the role of a great lover. For how do you convince a fair maiden that great love could be complete with so much missing?

Carestini, (*crosses his legs and giggles*). You know, Giacomo, that nothing is really missing; I have only been altered somewhat, and it's hardly noticeable. Besides, no one has ever complained.

Casanova. A woman's imagination is much richer than ours—even a little alteration is often more than they will tolerate. Perhaps your blinding desires have distorted your perceptions, my good man. We also must never underestimate a women's aptitude for deploying good discretion in dealing with their lovers.

Joseph Smith. I think that you have a good idea, Maestro Carestini. I should commission Albinoni to compose the music and you, Carlo, to write the libretto.

Madam Helene. Which castrato will play me?

Joseph Smith. I wish the great bass Massini to play me.

Luca. Stop this outrage! An opera about this heathen? This is an insult to all that is moral and decent. Your perverse ideas about love and your idiotic boasting are bad enough, but you dare to mention God's name in the same breath? You are repulsive, and I will not allow you—

Casanova, (*interrupting loudly*). God created women to be loved, adored, and served. If Adam gave his rib to create woman, why can't I give all my powers to glorify them as the most perfect act of creation? For if God does exist, God is more the likeness of a woman than a man!

Luca. I will hear no more of this blasphemy!

Casanova. By submitting to a woman, not only do we come to know the soul of a woman better, we come to know God better, too.

Luca. How dare you question the existence of God! How dare you say that God is a woman!

Joseph Smith. Calm down, Luca. Calm down. Giacomo is only having some fun with you. You are the master of ceremony, so why don't you decide how we are to be entertained this evening?

Luca, (*taking time to regain his composure, he is staring at Casanova, who continues standing*). You are right, Joseph. Forgive me. Let me proceed, then. If it is acceptable to you, I would like to begin this evening with a little humor and instruction by allowing our beloved Casanova to defend his good reputation, especially at this period of Lent when all of us should take the time to reflect deeply on our spiritual condition. The amazing Casanova has honored us with his presence; it would be foolish to waste such an opportunity to engage our most celebrated guest. It will all be in good spirits, I assure you.

Joseph Smith. Ah, my treasured friend Giacomo seems to be stealing the evening; what a surprise!

(*Joseph laughs, indicating that this is typical*).

But given the wonderful entertainment value that the both of you have provided so far, I hardly think that my guests could refuse such an offer. So, with Giacomo's consent and with that of my fantastic guests, please carry on, Luca. I am sure that he could handle anything that you might throw at him.

Luca. Thank you, Joseph, and with your permission, Giacomo?

(Luca pauses and waits for Casanova's consent; Casanova smiles and nods in agreement).

Ladies and gentleman, the golden years of my life have ushered in important changes. In particular, I now find it easier to speak my mind more honestly and to confront difficult situations with, let's say, more directness and ardor. I feel rather rambunctious tonight, and so I would like, if permitted, to speak quite openly with our celebrated vagabond, Giacomo Casanova. I think that this special occasion deserves a little entertainment, and I can't think of a better way than to have the infamous lover give a brief account of his life. We don't have to fear, I think, that such an exposition might prove embarrassing to him, since affections, life embarrassment, and shame don't seem to be basic to his emotional constitution. Besides, I doubt that our beloved adventurer would pass up the chance to talk about himself. Maestro, we know that you view yourself as an enlightened man filled with worldly wisdom. Would you do us the honor and speak openly to us about your life, your accomplishments, and your work?

If you would pardon my candor, Giacomo, how do you justify your profligate life, given over to shameful indulgence in sensual pleasure, and your gross, careless, and callous erotic misdoings? How do you justify years of guiltless hedonism with no concern for Christian morality or for basic human decency? As a wandering gigolo, what legacy have you left us? What should our children think when they learn of Casanova, the great Italian lover, who loved only himself? You have plundered your way through the world, robbing souls and seducing the hearts of innocent and vulnerable women. You recognize no law above your own, only the dictates of those insatiable appetites within you. You know only "I need," "I want"—and to hell with the rest of humanity. How do you answer these charges, Casanova?

(Luca is now standing and is very emotional).

Casanova. Calm down, Luca, lest you injure yourself—

Luca, *interrupting*. Please talk to us, Casanova, but don't try to beguile and seduce us with your silvery tongue and well-seasoned charm. We all have seen the slow deterioration of our beloved Italy; our culture, once the world's richest, is now dying because of moral bankruptcy and widespread corruption, and you, my dear Casanova, are a glaring symbol of this fiasco: amoral and self-serving. What do you have to say for yourself?

(Casanova sits quietly and is lost in thought, while others at the table encourage him to answer the charges. After a few moments, he cheerfully responds).

Casanova. Years ago I learned to disregard these rather exorbitant charges, as I have heard them many times, and, to be quite frank, defending myself has always bored me and wasted my precious time, time taken away from pursuing other—let us say—more pleasurable activities. However, I have become more generous with age, and so, dear Luca, I will not deny you the chance this evening to have some pleasure at my expense. For heaven knows that in old age pleasure becomes more and more of a memory than a preoccupation, and, in your case, I fear that you have neither. I rarely deny myself an intriguing adventure. In fact, I have always prided myself on being something of a daredevil. To indulge you this evening could be rather dangerous, like flirting with suicide, for having to face oneself honestly in front of one's friends and contemporaries could prove to be fatal. Nonetheless, I may likely extract some pleasure—if only masochistic—from this experience, so I am eager to get started. *(Casanova laughs and then addresses the crowd.)* Although Luca boasts a deep understanding of my life, character, and accomplishments, he has, in truth, greatly distorted the basic facts.

Joseph Smith. Carry on, Giacomo, carry on!

Madame Helene. I could speak personally about some of his accomplishments, which I know from, let us say, firsthand experience *(she clears her throat suggestively)*, so to speak. Now, about Giacomo's character ... Well, I don't think I should say too much about that, because—

(Casanova interrupts Madame Helene, pokes her in her side, and tickles her; they both laugh).

JOSEPH SMITH. Yes, it's those sorts of accomplishments that we are all very eager to explore here.

Casanova, *(becoming momentarily very solemn.)* It seems that this honorable Italian has painted a rather gloomy picture of my life, when, in fact, there has been radiant sunshine throughout. I daresay that life has bestowed upon me many of its sweetest fruits—from a magnetic countenance irresistible even to my most unforgiving enemies, to an instinctive appreciation for exotic foods and drink most tantalizing to the palate, to a rare eye for aesthetic nuance that never fails to notice the beauty that hides even in the most unlikely places. Nor have I yearned for a more powerful philosophical facility, and I have been blessed with a fertile and playful imagination that has never ceased to create for me many fantastic delights. My musical sensibilities and aptitudes are also far from meager, for I play the violin excellently, and I am a highly valued music critic. My command of the sword is of such uncommon excellence that the finest swordsmen in Venice typically move from my path in deference when they see my coming their way, and my talents as a horseman are often the fodder of lively conversation. My tongue commands a number of languages, and I have engaged some of the most remarkable minds and artists of our time in intimate and revealing conversation. I am a writer of first rank, as some of you will, doubtless, one day discover. And my opinions on art, culture, and society are esteemed by our most distinguished cultural critics. I am sought out by men of letters, often for the final word on a variety of topics, both mundane and profound.

One of the creator's greatest gifts to me is that I have been granted a strong and vibrant constitution, as well as a warm, charming, and at times even humorous nature quite appealing to a rich variety of people—from kings and scholars to prostitutes and thieves. And if you look closely, my friends, you will see that the sum of my life's interests and activities have a common thread—all have given me immeasurable pleasure. If you question how I managed achieve so much given the necessary ingredient of sacrifice in all accomplishments, be not deceived—I have always been able to create much joy in all my sacrifices. Some of you may also wonder about my claims to being a man of God in light of my rather colorful obsession with the things of this world. Well, it seems to me that a wise and prudent god would not have devised a world possessing so many heavenly delights and blissful experiences had he not intended mankind to enjoy them fully. To shun these divine gifts, I believe, is what is really iniquitous and a blasphemy to our perfect benefactor; to experience them passionately, on the other hand, is to know something of God's munificent nature and is the best way to pay homage to our creator. If I have a tragic flaw, it is this: that I have loved life too much, and I have often lain prostrate before its intoxicating forces!

Early on, I had an awesome revelation: that each person is a solitary being, alone, left to his or her natural and acquired devices to arrive at some level of worldly happiness. I myself have not indulged in that typical Christian pastime of always looking to an ideal world to discover the reason for being alive. Passionate expression in this world has been my earthly salvation and has led me to a natural acceptance, and even unconditional love, of life. That I find the fairer sex so congenial to my nature is due, in no small measure, to the amorous sentiments that I find so easy to arouse in them. Because I am a warm and compassionate man by nature, an astute psychologist, and a tender conversationalist—I have been able to win over many fragile as well as obstinate hearts—and may I say in all humility that I have known moments of such transcendent ecstasy that I am confident that only a select handful of mortals have ever known the same.

The rapturous intertwining of heated bodies is not mere hedonistic overindulgence, my friends—although I find everything about a lovely maiden delectable. (*Casanova breathes in and smiles with sensual pleasure and sighs.*) Even her feminine scents—shameful and odious to some—are to me of the sweetest essence, a delightful fragrance that never fails to astonish my senses. Early on I discovered a deep secret locked quietly in a precious maiden's heart: that you glorify her most when you make her feel intensely her erotic core. To be able to satisfy her exotic needs and extravagant fantasies is a high and noble art, my good people—one that calls on a man's most formidable physical and spiritual powers.

To know women in this way is to be in possession of sacred knowledge, like having a golden key reserved only for those passionate spirits who are able unlock the magical door to the eternally feminine and plunge deeply—without restriction or shame—into the lush pleasures of her voluptuous being, which is man's being, the womb of life. It's a dangerous adventure, and those who enter fully into this subterranean world may not return the same. How to command, and how to surrender? How to take without asking, and how to give without permission? How to reveal the deepest secrets of one's own heart, and how to embrace the darkness of love? To acquire these answers, one must leave behind much of what one knows; for this is the only way to experience life anew, to be born again. And I am one who knows, for I have been reborn countless times—indeed, I am the child eternal!

It may have surprised you that I have thought very deeply about my life. I have come to know my instincts well, and I have a natural faith in them. Their fulfillment, I believe, is a human being's only chance for genuine happiness; an enlightened man has learned to live in harmony with his instincts by allowing them requisite expression, if not in raw form, then in more artful fashions, perhaps dressed up in the garbs of philosophy, statesmanship, or spirituality. How is one to forge a meaningful life of pleasure? That, my fellow truth seekers, is the greatest challenge, one that requires the practiced art of honest self-reflection and creative experimentation with one's instincts.

Luca is right! Seduction has been my life's main indulgence. But isn't seduction the very process that moves the living world? Why do plump and succulent fruits hang so deliciously from their branches? Can we so easily turn from them? And I am not alone: the mating rituals of animals, birds, fish, and insects all attest to the erotic craving of life—the inescapable desire to seduce and to be seduced!

Should I boast a fundamental separation from nature even as I see so much of myself in my fellow creatures? I say absolutely not! My body, my senses, my whole being craves union with life. I want desperately to dance the dance of life and rejoice in nature's procreative energies. The way of nature is the way of God, and I am God's abiding servant.

You may find it puzzling, perhaps even paradoxical, that my life, so absorbed in amorous attachments, has been so rich in personal, social, and professional accomplishments of all kinds, and that I have come to have intimate knowledge of many aspects of this strange and multifarious world. Be not dismayed at this apparent incongruity at the very base of my being, for what appear to be mutually distinct worlds that are separated by radically different motives and actions are, in truth, one world. In me, the life force flows quite naturally from the realm of love to various and sundry expressions of creativity, to the thirst for knowledge. You see, erotic overflow is not only the fountain from which all life drinks and is nourished; it's also the force that guides and sustains the whole universe.

Again, I concede to Luca: you are right! The follies of love are irresistible to me. But have I ever failed to enchant? I have caressed many feminine flowers—fair and brutish, young and old, of lofty mind and spirit, and even the morally depraved—and in all cases, their gratitude has never failed to overwhelm. You give most to what claims your passions, and for me, I have been held spellbound by a woman's infinite charms. I've had little choice but to serve her with all my heart and with all my strength. That I have been blessed with such spectacularly energetic health that permits me to glorify a maiden many times in one night is surely no mere coincidence—it speaks of the wisdom of our perfect creator, for whom all things have a purpose.

I see how I could be judged as a rogue, and, at times, I have been one. But, by all means, don't condemn me! Don't despise Casanova, for he really has benefited you greatly and has done you all a tremendous service! If I provoked your disgust, indignation, contempt, pity, or laughter, then good—it's thrilling to feel deeply, and furthermore, now all of you know yourselves better—what you hate, desire, or perhaps love—because of me. If this is so, should you not thank me for steering your hearts and minds in such lucrative directions? Should you not have second thoughts before you cast me so heartlessly out of paradise?

Luca. My abject apology to you, most honorable Giacomo, the remarkable humanitarian and devoted Christian, most noble in mind and spirit, whose many gifts have glorified humanity and God. Ha! Just as I expected, you did not fail to entertain, to seduce—in fact, you have outdone yourself with this dazzling display! But your fanciful and patently absurd apology has just exposed, better than I ever could, the perverse state of your soul. Here you are shamelessly boasting about your sordid indiscretions and dubious accomplishments and humiliating yourself with illusions of romantic grandeur, when what really stands behind your words and actions is a despicable compulsion to degrade women for your own pleasure. Then you have the audacity to suggest to this illustrious gathering that your behavior has divine sanction? Your own words and excuses, although cleverly contrived and convincing to the naïve mind, are, in fact, the most appalling proof of your twisted spirit. What dark and devious force has taken hold of you, my son?

My dear philosopher, can't you see that after years of living, you have nothing—neither spiritual wisdom nor good reputation? That your happiness is a fraud? That you have deceived yourself into believing that your life has real meaning and joy? Can't you see that you have sacrificed knowing true, spiritual love for its vacuous and demonic surrogate: lust; that you will grow old and die alone; and that posterity will look back upon you with sad eyes and see only a pretentious and pathetic buffoon? My pitiful friend, you have nothing, because you gave nothing. I know the truth of my words cuts like a dagger, but there is no way out for you, Giacomo. You must face the tragedy of your life and stop running from the light of God!

(Casanova sits silently looking down to his lap and appears to be contrite. Luca, who believes that he has landed a decisive blow, continues).

But I have good news, Giacomo: it is not too late! Tonight, before our friends and contemporaries, if you were to admit that given the chance to live your life again, you would have chosen a more decent and honorable road, and if you humbly confess your wretched spiritual condition before the Lord God, Casanova, we will applaud you—in fact, you should applaud yourself. And then all of us will embrace you. Remember the thief on the cross at our Lord's crucifixion? Remember how in his last hour he was forgiven his sins by giving himself to the Lord Jesus Christ? So with you, Giacomo; if you tell us that you wish that it could have been different, that you from now on will, in fact, *be* different and change your heart, then it will be the beginning of a new life, a life blessed by God himself! Be forthcoming, my son, and be neither afraid nor ashamed. We all share your misery and reach out to you. So please, denounce your evil life and embrace God, our Father, through his son Jesus Christ!

Casanova, *(with great conviction)*. You know, my friends I am a self-reflective man. Lately I have been musing about what it would have been like to have lived a different, perhaps more conventional, lifestyle. In fact, recently, in Venice, I met a wonderful priest, a certain Padre Flavio, who impressed me greatly with his grace, style, his unconditional acceptance of life, and his passionate commitment to truth and justice. And I thought, as foolish as it may sound, that perhaps the priesthood would have been an intriguing choice for me—a devoted life of inner spiritual intensity, passionately devoted to God and to the betterment of humanity. I thought that with my native talents, I possibly could have been a veritable holy man—perhaps traveling throughout Europe spearheading an exciting revival. *Padre Giacomo Casanova*—I think I like the sound of that!

Can you imagine how wondrous my work could have been? Given the spiritual emptiness of countless people, my achievements could have had world-historical importance! Feeding the hungry, aiding the sick, providing solace to the suffering, and rescuing ignominious lives from eternal damnation; by God, I can almost feel the power now!

Casanova is now standing with his hands raised toward the heavens, as he stares longingly into the emptiness of space, moving his head from side to side as if he's in a heavenly trance. At that moment, there are cheers and explosive applause from many seated at the table and from others standing. Casanova slowly awakens from his trance-like state and begins applauding and shaking hands with his enthusiastic devotees. At that moment, a riot commences as Luca and his supporters express their outrage at what they perceive as just another of Casanova's ruses; a screaming match begins between both parties that quickly escalates to the point of physical violence and even swords are drawn. Casanova is amused by the developments, as an overzealous Casanova supporter, who is facing Luca nose-to-nose, soundly squelches Luca's objections. Both Joseph Smith and Madame Helene are standing together and are holding each other up, as they are close to collapsing onto the floor from uncontrollable laughter. Luca, who is standing, is in shock, and a look of helplessness overtakes him; he suddenly falls down into his chair in defeat. Casanova cheerfully walks over to him, playfully slaps him on his back, kisses him on his forehead, and then walks into a crowd of adoring fans.

end.

3

Voice, Existence, and Human Nature

3.1

The voice is a dynamic process in which breath and tones intermingle to express emotions, ideas, mindsets, moods, attitudes, and intentions. This definition could apply to almost all forms of vocal expression, from crying to opera singing. But some vocal sounds, such as sneezing and hiccups, are reflexive biological responses to specific physical imbalances and do not originate in mental, emotional, or psychological states.

Human voice lives at the threshold between what is most familiar, distinct, and certain and what is remote, ambiguous, and mysterious. Your voice speaks your identity and announces to the world that it is *you* who are present and not someone else. In the mere sound of your name, a personal identity emerges that sets you apart from all other human beings. And yet even as your name is sounded and your identity is fixed, an uncanny shift occurs: if I try to fix my mind on what is unique about you and then try to express it in words, your identity fades into the fuzzy world of the vague and inexplicable. The best I can come up with are general categories that could apply to countless others.

What is truly particular about you defies linguistic description. You are there in your voice. I hear it, know it, I even sense it, but I can't quite put the personal identity that I hear in the sound of your voice into language. In these instances, pre-reflective, unspoken understanding is better able to grasp personal selfhood than thoughtful, linguistic description. To mix a metaphor: the sound of a voice is a direct window into the soul, even though one's vision is progressively obscured the more one tries to peer inside and talk about it. But how could mere sound waves disclose something essential about us? How could the textures and colors of your voice reveal a uniquely recognizable person?

The quality and character of our speech—our idiosyncratic phrasing, choice of words, personal ways of configuring words and blending vowel and consonant sounds together, particular ways of releasing and retaining breath during speaking, distinctive pitch movements and volume fluctuations—all contribute to the individuality of our voices. But what makes the elements of speaking become a voice, "come alive" and point to an unmistakable identity, is how they are emotionalized through the vocal colors and textures of our voices.

Both vocal color and texture modulate to varying degrees of intensity as the voice rises, falls, and vibrates in specific ways. The typical ways in which your voice behaves and expresses emotions during word production, along with your unique vocal colors and textures, gives your voice and speech a consistent and persistent identity. Vocal color and texture are the essence of vocal identity. Let's look at this more closely.

Consider your voice in normal speech. Say aloud, for instance, "I think that singing is a beautiful form of expression." In this voiced phrase, one can clearly hear your distinctive identity shine through, one that points to a one-of-a-kind-person. Now, repeat the same phrase, but this time, just *whisper* it. You'll notice that, although your pitch and volume fluctuations, personal phrasing patterns, and even your emotional expressions are very close to those in your original spoken utterance, "you" are, nonetheless, conspicuously absent. What was most essential about the identity of the voice has vanished.

Consider a child's coloring book—one with empty figures to be colored in with crayons. On one page you see the simple sketch of a popular vista in Yellowstone National Park, with the outlines of mountains, valleys, clouds, perhaps a log cabin, and a lake in the distance. Although the bare-bone figures and landscapes are recognizable for what they are individually, the viewer has a difficult time seeing them as a necessary and integral part of the national park. But the difference is even deeper.

If we casually gaze at the denuded picture, we will notice that the vacuous configurations effectively shut down our imagination and emotions; they don't inspire our longing for nature; they don't elicit the melancholy memory and feeling of the days of our youth when we used to go camping with our families; they don't elicit our wonder at the sight of what is beautiful; they do not invite us to imagine how the fresh mountain air must smell, how exhilarating the lake's pure, crystal-clear water must feel, and so on. On the other hand, simply add a few wistful strokes of white texture to the clouds, glistening aqua blue to the lake, grainy brown to the cabin, verdant hues to the valleys, and then you will begin to know, recognize, and imaginatively experience the vital life portrayed in the picture.

Similarly, one's vocal colors and textures fill in and give identifiable substance to one's voice. Words, phrases, pitch, volume fluctuations, and breathing patterns are general structures of vocal communication that have no necessary connection to individual people. But when a person's uniquely colored vocal tones and textures are heard, then personal emotional states of mind, attitudes, and intentions come into existence for the listener to experience. One's vocal sound, in other words, contains the essential person—a truly astonishing fact!

3.2

When we hear a voice directed at us, we experience a person's unique identity searching for recognition.

3.3

Communication is the great theme of human existence—it is an instinct; a passion; a learned behavior; a biological imperative; a spiritual state; and a personal, social, psychological, and historical necessity.

3.4

Non-primate communication is, to a great extent, the sending and receiving of *thoughtless* signals, whose meanings are, in the main, rigidly preset by genetic-driven biological necessity. Contrast this form of communication—what I call "mutual signal stimulation"—with the typical communication process of human beings, where spontaneously emerging meanings, structured in logical thinking, comprise the essential mode of communication. Human beings, by virtue of the thinking process, *interpret* these meanings or ideas and don't simply respond to them passively and automatically—that is, instinctively, to precognitive signals—although mutual signal-stimulation also plays a part in human communication. Human beings must thoughtfully (however rapidly) interpret the ideas that enter their consciousness, because it's only through this activity that the goal of communication can be reached: understanding. Communication and understanding, in fact, necessarily imply one another.

But understanding for human beings can occur only after ideas pass through the meaning-filters of the particular cultures in which they live. That human communication, unlike nonprimate communication, breaks down so easily and regularly is conclusive evidence that ideas possess an inherent contingency: ideas are unstable, malleable realities that move freely, and even unpredictably, through the open atmosphere of human consciousness without necessarily meaning anything, or anything *definite*, at all—that is, unless they are embraced by the power of logical thinking and defined in understandable ways. Then there will be something definite and meaningful to communicate, and hopefully there will also be another who will understand.

3.5

Culture is non-genetic—that is, *meaning-full*—information communicated from minds to minds, from one generation to the next.

3.6

Most life forms are controlled or manipulated by inborn rules and programs for behaving—they are genetically "hardwired." The benefits of being hardwired consist in the success (in terms of survival and reproductive fitness) that such pre-programming confers on life forms in relatively manageable and predictable physical environments. These hardwired genetic programs operate well in environs where probable beneficial outcomes can be anticipated.

Newly born alligators, for instance, thoughtlessly scurry to the safety of water. And the sexual behavior of many animals is performed in standardized ritualistic forms—they just "do it." Nature has provided them with spontaneous mechanisms and behavior patterns that promote survival strategies. For the majority of animals, no additional information is necessary.

3.7

Despite our biological connection to all life, human beings have emerged from the womb of nature and have moved away from its initial, comprehensive protection and guidance. The primitive biological mechanisms and inherited patterns of behavior that once served as guides from birth to reproduction to death were fatally weakened with the emergence of Homo sapiens. The reasons for this atrophying of purely animal instincts has to do with the limitations these standardized, repetitious patterns of behavior placed on newly evolving humans, who were desperately trying to survive and reproduce in an ever-changing, and often life-threatening, environment.

A life guided by set, rigid patterns of behavior, however convenient in a safe and stable world, can wreak fatal havoc in an unpredictable, ominous environment. Rigid behavior patterns lack the creative responsiveness and resourcefulness to act quickly and favorably to unexpected challenges, such as sudden changes in weather or surprising advances from new predators. As a result, countless inflexible life forms passed out of existence and were replaced by new and improved ones, ones that evolved the instinctive flexibility to adapt successfully to daily, life-threatening situations in order to pass on their genes to subsequent generations.

The increasing size or sophistication of Homo sapiens' brain led to the evolution of language, rational figuring, social intelligence, and new survival strategies, which, in turn, affected the further development of the brain. Bipedal walking, which freed humans to use their hands in novel ways (e.g., carrying, hand-communication, and hunting), also contributed significantly to the increased capacity for human survival and reproduction. What these changes really mean was that Homo sapiens were increasingly able to respond creatively to the difficult and complex challenges of everyday life. Creative thinking, which led to adaptive strategizing, was, in fact, nature's most aggressive solution to the problem of human survival. But, for early humanity, there was more to creativity than thinking creatively. Rather than seeing creativity only as a practical tool to be used, in conscious and rational ways, to resolve on-the-spot survival problems, it was, even more basically, the mode of being for evolving, early humans. This meant that the primitive human, as a total organism—physically (from the molecular to the neurological level), intellectually (in the realm of logical thinking), psychologically (consciously and unconsciously)—was constantly evolving in creative ways—and often invisibly—to maximize the chances for survival and reproduction. In this sense, creativity for early humans was a multidimensional process that necessarily interpenetrated many aspects of their physical, intellectual, and psychological makeup. That humans are "social animals," for example, meant that that creative, social intelligence (which requires high levels of creativity and rational thinking) had to evolve very early in the history of humanity.

Speaking of the place of rational thinking in the life of primitive humanity, rationality itself meant more than mechanical, conscious figuring; it also expressed itself in different ways. Conscious, rational thinking can be an exceptionally sluggish and dangerous process in emergency situations, where split-second decisions often make the difference between survival and annihilation. It is for this reason that the capacity for rapid and dramatic decision-making had to evolve, which, oddly enough, was accomplished through bypassing conscious, rational thinking altogether. It's not clear, however, whether the capacity for instant but unconscious thinking and spit-second decision-making (e.g., quickly running from a predator or thoughtlessly striking a debilitating or lethal blow to an enemy) is a new human response mechanism, an old instinct that has been carried over from humanity's animal ancestry, or a creative combination of the two. Whatever it is, it certainly realizes an important goal of rational figuring, to the extent that it is typically an orderly response that increases the chances for survival.

3.8

If I wanted to determine the time the sun rises on a particular day, I could simply wake up very early in the early morning and wait for the sun to come up. If my watch says 5:30 am when I first see the rising sun, then I can be confident that I am observing an occurrence that I played no part in producing. I merely recorded an event that happened outside in the world: the sun rose; I saw it and made note of it. If I had overslept that morning, the sun would have risen anyway at 5:30 am. This is a good example of using thinking in an *objective* way—that is, in a way that is independent of my personal or subjective influence, desires, or biases. This is essentially how much of scientific thinking operates.

By contrast, if I want to know the meaning of my life, or why happiness is so elusive, or how to live well in light of the inevitability of my own death, do I also employ objective thinking in the same sense? Am I, in fact, seeking answers that are independent of my own personal influences, desires, or biases—objective, scientific answers? The success that the sciences have had in accumulating objective knowledge is one of humanity's most astounding accomplishments, one that has transformed the world countless times over. Nonetheless, gaining knowledge that is independent of one's subjective influences, desires, and biases is little help in a quest that is and must be subjective through and through, one that is completely empowered by my personal desires, and one that is biased, from beginning to end, in favor of discovering answers that satisfy me alone.

What I am really seeking in this case is the understanding that will illuminate my awareness of my personal existence and intensify my day-to-day sense of being alive. Bits of knowledge that rest inertly in my mind like so many lifeless marbles in a ceramic bowl are not what I am after. I want the kind of understanding that rattles my mind, opens my eyes, and compels me see my life in a new light; understanding that energizes my body and quickens the tempo of all my actions; understanding that motivates, uplifts, and propels me forward into my future with passion and purpose. Unlike gaining objective knowledge, understanding of this kind is only revealed from the inside, so to speak, from thinking to myself about what it is like to feel, think, and act in this mysterious world, and from undergoing the emotional, intellectual, and psychological gravity that this experience generates. And what do I gain from this form of interior inquiry and existential undergoing? Clear and distinct answers to my questions? No. Knowledge that is measurable, provable, and reliable? No. What I receive is *insight*—a new and deeper way of seeing into what concerns me most. Insight is knowledge that emerges effortlessly from thoughtful reflection and cannot be not teased out or captured by aggressive, objective investigations. Insight, instead, rises to my awareness and floats into my consciousness; it's a coming into focus, a coming together of formally disconnected parts. An insight makes sense, and the very moment that it does, I can be shocked and even astonished, because it seemingly came out of nowhere. Insight comes to *me*, and not me to it.

Most mysteriously, despite the transformative quality of great insights, they do not provide the final answers to my deepest questions or deliver the definitive knowledge I sought. *Insight, by contrast, makes the questions more profound and the possible answers more seductive and thrilling.* As much as this form of knowledge can be analyzed rationally and forced to meet the standard of logical consistency, in the final analysis, it's not logical thinking that is its power, but what it does to me: I simply let my mind and imagination luxuriate in the knowing energy of insight. And as a result, I am different somehow: I see more, and what I see is more interesting, deeper, and brighter than before. Insight is a form of knowledge that is never final or exhaustive, because every emergence of this form of knowledge always reveals even more of what I don't know. And in the end, I am grateful for so much insight, so much luminosity, even though its glow is hopelessly limited—eternally finite.

3.10

One of the great contributions made by philosophers is their discovery that naming or defining something grants that thing the status of existence—whether in the mind or in the external world.

3.11

Humans need to know because they are finite, and they know it. Animals don't need to know, because although they are finite, they don't know it. God doesn't need to know, because he is infinite and knows. Both animals and God have no need for philosophy. The onerous burden to know rests solely on humankind. Perhaps the animals are between God and the angels!

3.12

A chair has four legs, a seat, a backrest, and two armrests and is usually made of wood or metal. A unicorn resembles a horse but has the additional attribute of a horn protruding from the middle of its forehead. Both the chair and the unicorn have been defined—and so they have attained the status of existence. The difference is that a chair has tactile substance that is perceptible to our senses, is measurable and analyzable; it also occupies space and is present in the outside world at precise moments in measurable time. In addition, it's available for other people to experience and investigate in the same way. The unicorn, by contrast, exists in a purely imaginative form, with no tactile, space/time—occupying substance and hence is not available for observation by other people. Both exist, but in two different forms: in fantasy and in the outside world. That both realms can overlap at moments of emotional, intellectual, and psychological drama has caused not a little confusion and havoc.

This account does little, however, to dispel the specter of solipsism—the idea that all experience is the creation and projection of the experiencing person and that there is no independently existing, outside world that could ever be experienced. Unfortunately, solipsism is still a logical possibility. And this is why the belief that the outside world exists independent of one person's subjective experience is necessarily humanity's greatest article of faith. Observing mentally deranged individuals who live as though their fanciful, subjective reality is reality, and observing the disastrous results, at least gives us some solace that our faith-based distinction between subjective and objective reality is justified. But in the end, it's simple faith just the same.

3.13

Another crucial philosophical discovery is that the meaning of something is not identical to the material thing itself. When I view the chair before me, what I really observe are two distinct kinds of items: there is a physical, tactile structure in space and time with a specific configuration—it is hard, curved, measurable, stable, and observable by anyone who is looking at it.

And in addition to this physical structure, there is also what I *call* a chair. The "chairness" of this thing is a meaning I attach to the physical object. That is, the meaning or idea of a chair is not necessarily connected to the physical structure I see before me. A primitive tribesman, for instance, could easily look upon this physical object and not see a chair at all but instead see, perhaps, a religious symbol or something to be broken down and used for firewood. The material thing itself and the meaning that is typically attached to it are clearly not one and the same. But what brings the physical items and their meanings together? Is the experience of meaning always the result of humans projecting meaning onto the items, actions, and happenings in the outside world?

3.14

What are mental properties? Are they physical qualities that can be objectively analyzed? Are they the direct expression of brain activity? Or are they of an entirely different order of existence altogether that have no direct connection to the physical brain? Or perhaps they are of a different order but somehow are also dependent on, related to, integrated with, and the result of, brain activity. And how would such answers be sought in the first place? Philosophical and scientific investigators all agree that a major problem with mind/body issues is that one cannot peer inside another's brain and observe what is occurring between brain activity and corresponding mental occurrences. Mental realities are not physical items with objective properties that can be investigated and quantified by outside observers but instead are nonmaterial, private, experiential "meaning-states" that are present only to the experiencing subject. If a brain surgeon were to enter into brain tissue during a subject's experience of the color blue or during the subject's feelings of sexual arousal, for instance, the most the surgeon could hope to accomplish in his investigation would be to give an accurate physical description of the neural activity during these mental states. The surgeon could never see or feel what the subject is actually experiencing.

3.15

The connection of meaning-states—which can be as spontaneous and brief as a passing thought or emotion—to the physical brain relates similarly to that of the meaning of things in the outside world and the physical items to which they are attached. A meaning-form that is attached to this or that physical item in the outside world is a nonphysical aspect of that object, and—as in the case of mental states—it cannot be investigated and quantified with typical scientific methods. My idea is that subjective meaning-states and the objective meaning-forms that saturate and define the physical items in the outside world are of one and the same nature and possess the same nonphysical status. By observing the associations between meaning-forms and the physical items to which they are connected in the outside world, we can see a faithful reflection of what is occurring internally between the physical brain and the meaning-states that it produces. I call this "mind/body" association "integrated dualism theory" (IDT).

The bare, physical items in the world are far from inert. In fact, particle physicists tell us that there is an astounding degree of activity that occurs between and among the various particles and forces of energy at the atomic and subatomic levels, levels unperceivable to our survival-based senses and minds. Clearly, the wonder of nuclear power and technology, as well as the horrifying violence of atomic weaponry, have shown us that there is more to physical reality than what meets the naïve eye. One of the most dazzling discoveries of modern physics is that everything in the universe is composed of the same basic physical and chemical ingredients. This means that the human body, including the brain, is made up of star matter, for instance, and that the stars themselves are composed of brain matter that has been cooked up and energetically reorganized through subatomic processes in such a way to enable them to generate light, the very same light that travels each day over ninety-three billion miles to Earth to sustain life.

Brain scientists supplied additional angel dust to the cosmic mix when they discovered that the brain has even more in common with the material universe than its physical and chemical composition: both the brain and the universe reflect a sort of symphony of chaos at their atomic basis that ultimately arrives at levels of astonishing order and breathtaking energy management. In fact, the more scientists investigate the foundations of the natural world, the more they realize how interconnected the universe is. Quantum physics, for example, which studies the atomic and subatomic universe, has revealed undreamed-of principles, symmetries, and connections at the quantum plane that have forced modern physicists to redefine physical reality in a radically new way.

For instance, in the atomic and subatomic world, cause and effect gives way to "probability." Substance gives way to energy waves that fluctuate in and out of existence. And different events that are separated—even by millions of miles—give way to a experimentally verified proposition called "quantum entanglement." This proposition argues that the two events, although spatially separate, are, in fact, directly and immediately connected (e.g., when one object moves from this way to that, the other object instantaneously does the same, even though they may be separated my millions of miles). Scientists are still struggling to comprehend these science fiction—like revelations, and it's certainly likely that as the mysterious knots of the universe begin to unravel, even more wonders will be unearthed. Of course, the idea that everything in the universe is essentially interconnected makes logical sense when we consider that for most scientists, every aspect of the present universe evolved from a common physical source some thirteen billion years ago, which scientists believe to be the moment of the "Big Bang"—the most compelling scientific theory to date for the universe's origin.

The question naturally arises as to the extent to which the physical universe is interconnected. Which phenomenal breakthroughs are yet to be discovered through the relentless probe of philosophical and scientific exploration? And what if we reveal, say, that the human brain and the material universe are united in even more bizarre ways? Is the human brain the sole producer of meaning-forms? *Or could the natural world— both in its biological and purely physical expressions—be their original, and perhaps most creative, source, with every aspect of the universe creating meaning-forms from its own particular point of view?* This could only mean that that the universe, as a whole, thinks! Then the question, "What is the meaning of life?" would be ill suited to our new understanding of physical reality and would need to be replaced by another, more telling question: "What are the meanings of the universe?" And the answers, like the universe itself, would easily be endless.

Of course, scientists and philosophers alike would justifiably scoff at such ideas and consider them preposterous, to say the least; after all, this would mean considering the possibility of disregarding much of what science thinks it knows about the physical world along with the mathematics that describes and reveals it. The very foundation of science is based on the idea that there are measurable differences in natural reality and that different aspects of it have different appearances, functions, and actions. The task of science is to catalogue all these differences and determine how they are interrelated by discovering the physical laws and principles that determine their relationships. Mathematic is a critical tool in this process, especially in physics. Doesn't the act of thinking presuppose a brain that thinks, precisely because science has discovered that a particular item—a brain—functions in a way that is different from all other items in nature? As far as science can tell, asteroids, snowflakes, molecules, and electrons, to name a few, don't possess humanlike brains or anything close to them. Thinking for these items is clearly impossible, at least as we presently understand thinking. Without a doubt, no one has discovered the sort of evidence, or put forth the compelling arguments, that scientists and philosophers require to take the idea of a thinking universe seriously and there is no doubt that this notion may turn out to be nothing more than the mad and idiotic ravings of an imagination that has lost its way.

Although science is bravely and ingeniously pushing back the veil of ignorance and is exposing many wonders of the universe, it still suffers from its own radical limitations. Scientific advancement is tricky, for scientists and philosophers have to strike a delicate balance: they need to be skeptical yet open-minded, challenging but not dismissive, and protective of what they think they know but enthusiastic about the possibility of uncovering new ideas that may overturn previously held scientific doctrines. This has happened more than once in scientific history; in modern times general relativity theory and quantum physics were first considered to be assaults not only on common sense but also on scientific and philosophical sense. But as the evidence in their favor grew, the credibility of these radical ideas grew, as well. Today they are themselves integral components of the modern, scientific worldview.

A universe in which each aspect of it thinks and produces meaning-forms may be an outrageous idea, but it's not necessarily an impossible one. It's a possible, logical extension of the observation that all that we see around us appears to be interconnected—and increasingly so. What this notion would require to be taken seriously is credible evidence, and we have to wait and see if it ever arrives as science probes more deeply into the physical and energetic basis of reality. And what are we to watch for? Which questions should guide our thinking? A few come to mind: Maybe there are deeper laws, symmetries, and principles to thinking that are typical of the universe as a whole. Maybe all movement, even in its most elemental and material/energetic form, produces forms of thinking—meaning-forms—that we are unable to recognize at our present level of philosophical and scientific understanding. Maybe meaning-forms are the necessary nonphysical complements to "quantum fluctuations" that pop in out of existence. Perhaps meaning-forms are visible only to their original sources—to their own particular perspectives—and are invisible to all other observers. In this latter view, a dust particle may think and produce its own meaning-forms that are naturally invisible to human beings or bacteria, for instance. And vice versa.

All these "perhaps" and "maybes" are just words and seem to resemble New Age metaphysical fantasies more than legitimate questions in physical science. But such speculations are great fun, nonetheless, and they may even have some truth to them. If this highly fantastic tale does turn out to be yet another step closer to *what is*, then both the ancient, mythical vision of the oneness of all reality as well as the fascinating idea that the universe, as a whole, is alive, thoughtful, and meaning-ful, would have to be absorbed into the ever-growing body of scientific and philosophical knowledge, even as the body itself undergoes substantial reshaping.

3.16

Normal perception is notoriously obtuse. Human perceptual and conceptual faculties evolved to aid in the survival and reproduction of the human species and were not formed to provide an accurate, precise assessment of objective reality. The reason for the unscientific quality of our sensory and mental capacities is simple enough: human life (all biological life) was able to evolve without it. In other words, human evolution did not require precise, accurate, and objective knowledge in order to succeed. General approximations of reality worked very well for the human species, and this is exactly what the five senses and the human mind provide. Our senses and natural intellect reduce, limit, distort, and integrate the raw data of experience for purposes of efficiency. In short, human perception and intellect reduce complexity to simplicity, because this is what has proved to work in the human struggle for survival and reproduction. It is also true that too much information and knowledge can be dangerous for a species that is often concerned with split-second survival strategies. Perceiving the precise anatomical details of a hungry lion that is about to pounce on you is not necessary information. Perceiving "big" and conceiving "dangerous" are necessary and tell you all you need to know to act quickly to ensure your survival.

3.17

One of the most influential philosophical ideas and one that is particular to Western culture is that mathematical reasoning is the key to understanding the world, human beings, and the universe. The methodological rigor of mathematics has served as a philosophical guide and ideal for Western thinking, in both scientific and nonscientific pursuits of knowledge, from the very outset of Western thinking in ancient Greece. In science, especially in physics, chemistry, and astronomy, mathematics is the primary tool of investigating physical reality. In fact, the physical universe, as far as scientists can tell, is actually structured in the languages of mathematics. Even philosophy itself—which is largely a language-based, knowledge-pursuing process—has been seduced by mathematics, even though mathematical-based philosophy has been dubious at best. This is true despite philosophy having benefited enormously from trying to live up to the scientific ideals of rational proof, precision, clarity, and inner consistency.

3.18

Of all the great philosophical breakthroughs that have defined the history of Western philosophy, one of the most critical was the realization that the presence of something and its meaning are not necessarily connected. That there is a disjunct between the items, actions, and processes of experience and their meanings has profound implications: this experiential discontinuity means that there is a *lack of necessity* right in the middle of human experience. As a result, one of the goals of human culture is to overcome this discontinuity, and to make everyday experience more cohesive and, by extension, more reliable. It is for this reason that humanity's great ideas, ideals, and guiding themes—such as oneness, harmony, unity, integration, holism, brotherhood, and universalism—have had such a hold on the human imagination.

3.19

Science is obsessed with the issue of unity. Scientists are searching for the one theory (or at the very least, a bare minimum of mutually harmonious theories) that will explain all the processes of nature, including human nature and human culture. Although many bright people think that such comprehensive theories are wishful thinking, many notable physicists truly believe that, at least in physics, a "grand-uniform theory"—one set of equations that integrates and explains all the laws and forces of nature—is the ultimate goal of physics.

Western History, the Bio-ontological Shift, Darwin, Survival, and Knowledge

4

4.1

It is fascinating to ponder the profound psychological impact that the Roman Empire had on its citizens and on Western civilization as a whole. With the Roman Empire, the modern notion of "civilization" itself made its first modest appearance—in the sense of many diverse peoples and ethnicities from different parts of the world all unified by a common language Latin, one set of universal laws, shared values and customs and a common vision of what it meant to be Roman. The simple idea of Rome as the world was itself a unifying power, a guiding ideal that was new in history. To be Roman meant to be a part of a vast, worldwide, cultural network, in which all citizens shared all the practical (legal protection) and spiritual (part of a greater reality) benefits of being participants in what they considered the greatest civilizing force in human history.

The spirit of the people at their best was embodied in the Roman ideal of Roman *virtu'*—to be tough, noble, reliable, loyal, and unshakable in commitment. This virtue was not only a standard by which Roman character was measured, but it was the trademark, so to speak, that Romans stamped on all their most impressive accomplishments, whether it was their unstoppable military strength, their remarkably modern legal system, or their unprecedented skill as builders and engineers. When gazing upon the massively commanding Pantheon, the awe-inspiring Coliseum, or the ingeniously designed and executed aqueducts, for example, one cannot help but *feel* what was distinctly Roman and understand immediately what these works conveyed to all those who ever viewed them: power, permanence, unity, nobility, pride, ingenuity, and virility. And when we consider that the small city of Rome controlled most of the known world, it is no wonder that its citizens believed that Rome *was* the world and that to be Roman was to have dominion over it.

Roman culture was not restricted to a city-state, country, or group of privileged people; rather, Roman civilization was the culture of the world—available, in principle, to all humans extant on Earth. Unfortunately, in practice, the many flaws and limitations of Roman civilization—such as the unmanageable vastness of the empire, horrible leadership, dissipation of the Roman character, economic decline, the inability cope well with natural disasters, and relentless barbarian incursions—eventually led to its descent and ultimate demise. When the Western empire fell in 476 CE, the unifying coherence of the Roman world fell into disarray. The foundation of the empire—the particular Greek-Roman synthesis that was Western civilization itself—was lost. The sense of helplessness and despair that fell over the Romanized world was due in no small measure to the fact that, to the people of the Empire, the end of Rome meant the literal end of the world. This is likely one of the reasons why the Empire lasted as long as it did—its citizens were desperately struggling to avert what they believed was the actual termination of the world itself. The Dark Ages fell upon the Western world, and the people—confused, distraught, and traumatized—scrambled to survive as best they could. With the help of the Roman Catholic Church, they were able to bring some order back to their turbulent world.

One reason why the Roman Church was such a tremendous power in the Dark and Middle Ages was that it represented the unity and stability that once defined the Roman world. One could argue that the Roman Church was in so many ways the Roman Empire—in different form, to be sure, but similar in effect. The Roman Church responded forcefully to the desperate pleas of a lost world frantically trying to rediscover the guiding cultural light that went out when the Empire fell and struggling to reinvent itself. The Roman Church, grounded in many Roman traditions, including speaking Latin, was the last remnant of the old Roman Empire. The church, in this sense, was the last great Roman achievement; and remaining true-to-form, the church was Roman from top to bottom: stable, ordered, all-powerful, and all encompassing.

Although Europe finally began shaping up—with individual countries, cultures, and languages slowly taking form—the unifying glory that was once Rome continued to haunt the Western mentality. Napoleon and Hitler, for instance, strove to create their own empires. Napoleon went so far as to crown himself "Emperor" and viewed himself as the last in a long line of Roman emperors. Hitler waged war on all of Europe and dreamed of bringing it all together, Roman style, under his Nazi regime.

4.2

Thoughts, emotions, moods, states of mind, creativity, wonder, ecstasy, and happiness; human culture, human history, mythology, religion, philosophy, science, art; love, loneliness, anxiety, hatred, compassion, and human experience itself—all are the natural by-products of a species that has lost its way, a species that has moved away from nature's rigid control and ultimately taken up residence in a world of its own making—human culture. I call this general movement from nature to human culture the "bio-ontological shift." This term means, literally, a change in the very nature of biological existence.

The term "ontology" is typically defined as the "study of being" or existence. A car and a tree, for example, don't exist in the same way. A car was created by human technology to fulfill specific human needs and is made of lifeless materials such as metal, aluminum, plastic, leather, and rubber. Cars also need to be sustained by human care and maintenance. Furthermore, cars don't die; they simply become worn out with age, or nonfunctional if they are not cared for on a regular basis.

A tree, by contrast, grows naturally from the earth, is made exclusively of living materials, and does not exist inherently for the sake of meeting human needs, although humans use trees for various technological products, such as paper. Trees also are not ambulatory but remain rooted firmly in the earth, and they don't need to be cared for by humans to thrive well; they also don't die a biological death. Cars and trees clearly exist in different ways—that is, *ontologically*, they are different.

The bio-ontological shift is the final evolutionary process that gave birth to humanity. From a biological perspective, this phase is just another in a long series of natural developments in the lush bush of life, but from the perspective of a humanity reflecting back on its animal past, the transition to human existence appears to be sort of a fracture in nature, a disconnect in the natural order of things. Life, beginning with the rise of humanity, certainly started existing in a new way, a way that could conveniently be described as primarily a cultured-based existence as contrasted to its former nature-based existence. This is true, even though some nonhuman life utilizes imitation as a teaching tool, and some nonhuman primates even seem to possess a crude form of culture transfer. Nonetheless, the effects of imitation and cultural learning are minimal in animal life as compared to the pre-programmed instructions that are naturally and powerfully in place. With human beings, the opposite situation is true: cultural existence dominates the very meaning of human life at the expense of strong, instinct-guided behavior. It is the transition to this relatively new manner of cultural existence that I have tried to capture in the idea of the bio-ontological shift. And what is at the basis of this new way of existing that opened the way to the creation of human culture?

A new form of nature—human nature—emerged in the wake of the bio-ontological shift, and with it arose what I call the "three psycho/emotional ecstasies"—three kinds of awareness that forced the very first humans to look to and reflect on the outside world. The psycho/emotional ecstasies are isolation, ignorance, and powerlessness; these in turn brought forth three corresponding compulsions that I call the "three meta-cravings", which are overpowering urges that raise human beings above their animal past and give form, movement, and direction to human life. The meta-cravings are the need to unite with an unchanging and reliable frame of reference, the need to answer deeply felt questions about the meaning of life, and the need for purposeful action. Both the psycho/emotional ecstasies and their corresponding meta-cravings are the natural expression of the bio-ontological shift and represent what is most distinctive about human nature and human existence—they define, in other words, the *ontology* of human life. What do they signify?

- *Isolation and Unity*

With the emergence of humankind, there occurred for the first time in the history of evolution a form of life that was largely without predetermined, genetically structured programs for survival in the world. The primitive "closeness with nature" that exists with respect to other life forms was absent in Homo sapiens. "Primitive closeness" may not be philosophically or scientifically precise, but it nonetheless carries forth the important idea that with the rise of, and shifting to, humanity, there was a movement away from, or at the very least a dramatic weakening of, the biological programming that ensured *automatically* activated survival strategies. The very meaning of human existence can only be understood within the context of the dramatic weakening of nature's deterministic grip. The result was that humans felt isolated from nature. Whether or not the human species is, in fact, isolated in this sense is a contentious issue—for how could life forms that developed out of nature be isolated from it?

This question, however, is quite beside the point. The more important issue is that with the unfolding of the bio-ontological shift, primitive humans felt isolated from the natural world. Compared to life forms whose lives are controlled mostly by thoughtless, genetic programming, humans now had the onerous burden of having to think before acting. While genetic programming enacts very specific, inflexible instructions as to how to behave, thinking, by comparison, is very flexible and presents humans with *possible* ways of choosing and behaving. There is certainly learning among certain nonhuman life as well as primitive, culture transferal; there are also clear indications that some species, particularly nonhuman primates, utilize a degree of thought before acting. Nonetheless, the idea of that the actions of nonhuman primates are *thoughtful* and that reflective thinking precedes their behavior is far-fetched. Rather, the primary motivators for their behaviors remain spontaneous reactions both to internal, unlearned, genetic programming as well as cues from their environment. For humans, the situation in the world is dramatically different. The feeling of isolation that resulted from the bio-ontological shift had the double effect of drawing primitive humans inward while, at the same time, forcing them look outward to the world for the purpose of reuniting with it. Thus, trying to unite with a stable frame of reference—for instance, God, an ideology, a "cause," an occupation, or a political party—is the attempt to regain a seamless connection with nature—an effort, in effect, to try to derail the bio-ontological shift.

• *Ignorance and Knowledge*

The bio-ontological shift also brought into the natural world a conscious, thoughtful being who used thinking as the primary tool for survival, independent of, and mostly oblivious to, instinctive control of any sort. This new process functioned by surveying the natural and human-made landscape, and employing the multifaceted powers of reasoning—analyzing, calculating, and predicting—to determine the best ways to survive in an extremely hazardous world. But the work of thinking automatically implies both a primal ignorance with respect to critical information in order to live and the need for thinking to address this ignorance. With the requirement for thinking arose the "interrogative mood"—that is, the questioning attitude. In no uncertain terms, primitive humans needed survival questions answered in order to survive: Where can I find shelter? How am I going to hunt this dangerous animal for food and clothing? How am I going to defeat this enemy? Without these kinds of questions being answered, and answered correctly and quickly, survival for early humankind would have been perpetually at risk—and it constantly was. Evolutionary anthropologists tell us that, in fact, several primitive human species went extinct tens of thousands of years ago, and it was probably the case that these species were not sufficiently good at answering important survival questions.

Besides answering survival questions, however, there were other kinds of questions that became profoundly important to the human race and were extraordinary difficult to answer. The bio-ontological shift forced humankind into the challenging position of having to pose and answer *meaning questions*; and the answers had to be good ones—answers that told humans of their place in the general scheme of things; answers that gave significance and direction to the actions of daily living; answers that quelled the deep-seated fear of death and what happens afterward; answers that gave moral counsel; answers that described the origin of the universe and everything that's in it; answers that gave solace in the face of cruelty and suffering; answers that justified the injustice that is often heaped upon blameless, innocent victims; answers that helped humans make sense of the fearsome, often lethal, forces of nature; and answers that spoke to the wonder of being alive. And where could such answers be found? The human imagination responded heroically to the calling by producing repositories of knowledge: mythology, art, and religion, and ultimately, philosophy and science.

- *Powerlessness and Action*

At times we look with envy upon the other life forms that populate our planet, such as insects, birds, and fish, and marvel that they appear to possess almost unlimited energy: they act with purpose and drive and strive relentlessly to reach goals about which they seem to have little doubt—marching over treacherous terrain in flawless symmetry to hunt for food, flying over whole continents and oceans to find more agreeable weather, or swimming blindly upstream for countless miles to lay eggs in the same waters in which they themselves were born. They carry out these tasks thoughtlessly, as it were, without hesitation or uncertainly, as though these creatures intuit unambiguous instructions for purposeful action.

With the human species, the bio-ontological shift eliminated this sort of genetically programmed behavior instructions and resulted in a form of life thoroughly bereft of inborn short- or long-term plans of action. And this loss of nature's direct guidance caused new kinds of problems to emerge: Homo sapiens had to deal with the problem of not knowing precisely what to do to survive, and even beyond confronting basic survival issues, they also had to grapple with the complex problem of knowing what to do with their lives after pure survival needs were met. In both cases, they were equipped only with thinking as their guide.

"Not knowing what to do" had little meaning before the rise of the human species; plants have no need for knowledge, since *doing* is not a part of plant life, and animals' behavior is still largely (although, in some instances, not exclusively) guided by their genetic makeup. Human beings, by stark contrast, had to act completely on their own, which meant they had to think about, and initiate, their own actions. Determining which actions were best to ensure survival in a murderous world was extraordinarily difficult for primitive humans, since thought-based action was for them something new and untested. It's impossible to imagine the massive loss of primitive human life that had to follow from the countless unintentional and experimental mistakes committed by early humankind. But early human beings discovered that they had to do more than simply survive; they had to *live lives.* There was, in short, life after survival, and it consisted of addressing and answering meaning questions. How did humanity ultimately answer the two principal questions of survival and meaning?

Early humans found themselves not only with the freedom to choose among many possible ways of thinking and acting but also with the capacity to carry out these new responsibilities creatively— that is, by devising their own self-styled schemes and solutions. *Creative thought, then, was humankind's ingenious solution.* Nonhuman primates have also been observed using creative solutions to practical problems, such as using tree branches as a sort of spoon to scoop up insects for consumption. But once again, nonhuman primates were not essentially creatively orientated; if they were, they also would have had a dynamically rich culture that evolved quickly over time, and this is obviously not the case. The nature of human creativity will become clear after considering three new challenges that presented themselves to humankind, challenges that tackled the questions of survival and meaning. I describe them as the *call-to-action questions*: Which actions are necessary and appropriate for my life? How do I do what I should do? To which ends do I act?

At stake with regard to the call-to-action questions is power. What is power? Power is the natural release of energy when something is on the move. But it's much more than that. Power is the ultimate confirmation that action is happening; that something is doing; that a doer is doing; that something is being done; that something new is being created; that an obstacle is being confronted; that a struggle is underway; that a conflict is reaching a climax; that a block is being exploded; that a secure foundation is being established; that a frame of reference is being constructed; that an identity is being fixed; that a victory is at hand; and that a destiny is being realized. *Action produces power, and power creates centers from which further action bursts forth.* This classic relationship between action and power has special significance to the emergence of humankind. Because the bio-ontological shift deprived Homo sapiens of preprogrammed strategies of action, it's a natural condition of humans to suffer from varying degrees of power deprivation. The inconsistent, sporadic, ill-conceived, and poorly executed actions that define much of human behavior clearly reflect an ever-changing, unreliable experience of power. And what is the consequence? Restlessly shifting, mutually conflicting centers of power that destabilize human experience and either deplete or energize the power reserves that are needed for further action. It's no wonder that human nature is so unpredictable—listless at one moment and obsessively focused in another. It's also no surprise that human beings are constantly seeking stable power centers to which they can become attached.

Action immediately gives birth to power. Power is directly spawned from action. A person who does not act is powerless. A person who acts, even badly or immorally, is still a person of power; the more action, the more power; the greater and more effective the action, the greater the power that follows. From the perspective of expanding power, it matters little what a human being does, how he does it, or even why he does it—as long as whatever he does, he maximizes his actions in doing so. Power, however, does not necessarily follow only from *physical* effort or force. One could also possess a powerful mind or a powerful character, but even in these cases a powerful mind always follows from having a highly active mind, which produces powerful ideas, and a powerful character is the natural expression of a person who habitually acts with resolve, focus, and purpose. Finally, action does not necessarily have to be overt for it to produce power; action could just as easily be the invisible ground or source of what is visibly powerful. Silence could be very powerful, for example. So could restraint, simplicity, effortlessness, and elegance.

Human beings, unlike other life forms, are not naturally programmed to be action-driven. This is why the call-to-action questions must be answered, and answered well, if humans ever hope to acquire the power that they desire and require. This is a simple fact of nature—human nature—as defined by the bio-ontological shift.

4.3

In a world where ignorance, failure, instability, and suffering are normal human experiences, science and technology offer themselves as comforting repositories of knowledge, reliability, pleasure, and promise. The whole of modern technological life—cars, computers, the various networks of communication, and business and medicine—is based on the astounding reliability of scientific knowledge and provides profound psychological relief to a problematic humanity. But science and technology are more than ways of understanding, manipulating, and rebuilding nature; they also represent a worldview—a way of approaching and understanding the totality of human life. There is no doubt that science and technology are humanity's best effort to date to address at least two of the three meta-cravings: the need to unite with an unchanging and reliable frame of reference and the need for purposeful action. Meaning-of-life questions, by contrast, typically transcend the boundaries of science and technology and require philosophical attention. It is fascinating to note that both science and technology are sort of a *return to nature* in the sense that in their stability, reliability, and predictability they are reminiscent of a former ontology—the ontology of animal life under nature's wide-ranging guidance. Is it any wonder that the human race is obsessed with science and particularly with technology?

4.4

The history of philosophy in the West has been the history of one philosophical system competing with another to discover what is necessarily and ultimately *true* about nature, the world, and humankind. After thousands of years of philosophizing, not any one philosopher or philosophical system has emerged victorious. The failure of philosophy to discover unequivocal truth has, for many, thrown into question the very purpose and value of the philosophical enterprise. Others have redirected the philosophical mind and argued that its primary service is in the scientific enterprise, as the handmaiden of science.

Still others remind us that philosophy is not simply a discipline or subject matter, but additionally, and most importantly, a *human dimension* that is part and parcel of all that we do in the realm of conscious thought and action. They argue that it is only through the philosophical attitude that human beings can legitimately confront and inquire into "what is the case." They argue that it is the deepest means by which a human being can interface with the stark realities of being a finite, mortal being in an infinitely large universe that provides no conclusive, facile, and unambiguous answers to the most important questions of human existence. Indeed, asking questions and seeking answers is not simply an intellectual exercise reserved for philosophers and scientists; it is a fundamental mode of psychological and spiritual being, both privately and in the world. It is simply a matter of how good or bad you are at doing it.

4.5

In no uncertain terms, science has effectively kicked God out of the physical universe—and for many, this beating has killed God altogether. Science is a decidedly atheistic activity; no mention of God or "divine powers" is required to do science. Yet some scientists, like the late evolutionary biologist Stephen Jay Gould, argue that science and religion can coexist in harmonious, mutual respect once we clearly delineate the territories that each occupies—science for descriptions of the physical universe and biological life, and religion for issues of ethics, for moral teachings, and for all things spiritual. It is always painful to observe a brilliant, resourceful, and inventive mind such as Gould's eviscerate itself by indulging in shoddy reasoning and disingenuous argumentation. Science here and religion over there—now isn't that nice and tidy! Most people, even those without Gould's intellect and skills, know that religion does and *must* make claims about topics that are scientific in nature. The Bible is full of them: creation stories, the nature of human nature, the age of the earth and the universe, how the earth was formed, the relation of the earth to the sun, and even the value of reason and philosophy. And science itself, especially evolutionary biology, enters Gould's hallowed region of religion with investigations into, to name a few, the nature of morality, sexuality, and aesthetic preference, utilizing the Darwinian notion of natural selection.

And how can physicists dance around the idea that they have shown that randomness and chance are central to the movement of the universe, that perhaps the universe itself may have just popped into existence through a quantum fluctuation (or two) with no need for there being a first (or second) cause? Does this not relate to religious issues? Of course it does, and Gould had to know this, as he would have known, better than most, that biology cannot be enclosed in a sealed philosophical box or "magisterial" realm. Why Gould felt compelled to try to rescue religion from science with such feeble arguments will have to remain a mystery. That thinkers of Gould's brilliance and stature argue for such ridiculous positions is both fascinating and frustrating, and invites the curious investigator even further into the realms of psychology and philosophy.

4.6

Many scientists and philosophers argue that philosophy itself—as a way of arriving at the truths of human existence—has been an unequivocal failure. Like religion, it promised much but has fallen pathetically short. In many instances, philosophy has moved from being an enterprise that pursues truth or objective understanding about the important *meaning issues* in life to being a practical tool in science, where philosophy's essential function is to provide clear, concise language that enables scientists to formulate and communicate their ideas. Philosophy has also been relegated to a branch of linguistics. In this sense, philosophy is merely "talk about talk"—that is, it is a way to investigate the meaning, structure, and limits of language, with no intrinsic value as a way to understand human reality. In short, philosophy corresponds only to itself and has no meaningful relation to objective reality. Has philosophy failed so miserably that it's philosophically useless? The posing of this question is just one example of how absurd this position really is—for an essential purpose of philosophy is enter into the core of difficult or contentious issues and expose inconsistencies, irrational positions, misguided lines of thinking, as well as to reveal, uncover, and develop ideas and rational strategies that are more truthful and faithful to our basic premises. There can be no doubt that philosophy has not fulfilled its mission of discovering absolute, unchanging truth. But the real mistake is in asking philosophy for what it cannot provide. This has been a persistent problem throughout its history.

But philosophy has also been on the path of self-discovery, and understanding what it *cannot* do is also a major philosophical advance—as important, in fact, as revealing something new. In this sense, philosophy, like all human endeavors, is a work in progress. It's both humorously and tragically ironic that the thinkers who derive pleasure in debunking philosophy use philosophy to do so. They have failed to realize one of the most basic tenets of human nature: philosophy is here to stay as long as the human mind is finite—that is, as long as thinking is humanity's principal way of getting on in the world.

4.7

With the publication of Charles Darwin's *On the Origin of Species* in 1859, there occurred a philosophical and cultural convulsion that was an ideal complement to the "Copernican Revolution" two hundred years earlier. In that instance, Galileo Galilei (1564–1642) gave credible (although inconclusive) evidence for the idea that the sun and not the earth was the center of the solar system. In both instances, fervently held beliefs about the nature of the universe and humankind were exploded, and biblical interpretations of the universe were overturned. Darwin's ideas, however, were even more radical than those of Copernicus and Galileo because they revolutionized our understanding of life on earth, including human life.

Although the biblical passages that argue for an earth-centered solar system exposed the Bible as a poor source for astronomical understanding, the Bible suffered a more severe blow, in fact the decisive one, with the biological evidence that all life on the earth descended from a common source; that all life is interconnected; that all life evolved out of earlier species; and that the origin of life was a random, biochemical process that occurred billions of years ago, perhaps in some murky, primordial goop or chemical "bubble," where accidental events, galvanized by cosmic events, churned up the beginnings of life. Biology has also shown that it is logically and empirically unnecessary to believe that human life was created or guided by the so-called will of God or some divine plan.

Darwin's theory of "natural selection" gives compelling support to the idea that life on earth has evolved over the period of billions of years, through *natural* processes. Darwin's theory also argues that all life forms are caught up in a constant struggle to survive. Because food is scarce, populations tend to increase, and environmental challenges are extremely severe (and include unpredictable ecological changes, disease, and predators), the life forms that are unable to adjust successfully simply perish—they die off. And those life forms that do survive become the parents of new generations of offspring and so it goes, generation after generation. Darwin believed that species change into other species when segments of one species are forced, by environmental challenges, either to evolve into a new species or perish. Natural selection is, in this way, a decidedly negative, destructive process that has no ultimate goal, and is not necessarily progressive. It simply weeds out all forms of life that are unable to cope successfully with survival pressures. Finally, the most radical implication of Darwin's theory is that the emergence of human beings, rather than being a result of some "special creation" by the God of the Bible, is better explained by natural selection, and that Homo sapiens is just a highly developed ape, with the same origin as all life on Earth some four billion years ago.

Darwin's theory has itself evolved since Darwin's day, and particularly, the science of genetics was created, which offered the much-needed grounding and mechanisms for natural selection. Darwin's essential ideas, nevertheless, remain untouched and in fact, have been further substantiated not only in genetics, but also in comparative anatomy, geology, physics, cosmology, and psychology. The convergence of confirming evidence is so strong for his theory that only someone who is severely biased against it could deny its explanatory power.

Christian apologists who argue for a divine plan behind evolution—a so-called "theistic evolution"—have to account for the fact that 99.9 percent of all species that have ever lived have perished. Some divine plan! What a cruel way for a loving God to express his loving nature! If we are to refrain from making these sorts of judgments about God, then what are we to think of the Bible, which often references God's qualities? He is clearly depicted in both the Old and New Testaments, for instance, as jealous, angry, loving, and compassionate. What are we to make of these characterizations? Are we not to conclude anything at all about God? Then what's the point of reading the Bible in the first place?

If one were to look only to the natural world and clearly comprehend the unspeakable brutality that defined the evolution of life on earth, what sort of God might the person infer was responsible? A sadistic monster could be the only conclusion. And if one were to look only to the Bible and try earnestly to discover what it says about the creation of life, would one ever find in its hallowed pages the theory of evolution? Of course not. And this is why no prophet, no savior, no spirit-filled disciple, and no theologian ever extracted the theory from the Bible. It's simply not there, and beyond that, the Bible actually proclaims the opposite: in other words, it cites special creations and permanent, unchanging species. It's also quite funny to think that the perfect "Word of God" would have left out such vital information as the evolutionary nature of life on Earth and then had to wait thousands of years for a simple, imperfect mortal—an *agnostic*, no less—to correct it. Aren't these inconsistencies obvious even to the childish mind? If humankind were to hold similar standards of credibility in other areas of cultural life, like medicine, astronomy, or history, we would hardly have advanced out of the Middle Ages.

Detractors of evolution often proclaim that evolution is merely a "theory" and therefore does not deserve to be considered as a scientific fact. This position shows a misunderstanding of the meaning of scientific theories. A theory in science is not a speculative idea, a tentative explanation, or even a hypothesis (a prediction that needs to be tested and verified by others). Rather, a scientific theory that is accepted by the scientific community is a well-supported and comprehensive interpretation of physical events that has successfully stood up against numerous tests and rigorous scrutiny by many scientists. Gravitation is a theory, and so is the idea that germs cause physical illness. Would anyone dare to deny the fact of gravitation or germs because they are only theories? Evolution enjoys the same degree of credibility among leading scientists as these theories. In fact, the theory of evolution is so well established that it represents the very foundation upon which the whole of biology is based. We wouldn't have vaccines or pesticides, for example, without Darwin's theory of natural selection leading the way

But could a scientific theory turn out to be misguided? Of course, but typically when a long-standing theory has been found inadequate, it's usually modified—and not abandoned altogether—to accommodate new findings. The most notable theory reformulation occurred when Einstein's theory of relativity caused Sir Isaac Newton's ideas of about space, time, matter, and gravity to be reinterpreted and dramatically reduced in areas of application. Science's self-correcting nature is one of its greatest strengths. Scientists, at least the best ones, are committed to maintaining the highest standards of intellectual honesty. If a theory is found lacking, then they have to choose then either to modify it or abandon it completely. In the final analysis, a theory, regardless of how much evidence is accumulated in its favor, will always remain only a theory. A theory is not a law or sacred idea, and, in principle, is not beyond refutation. Rather, it is the best-supported position that scientists have established, given the available evidence. With the growth of scientific thought, everything can change as new evidence is gathered. In the case of the theory of evolution, we come upon one of science's greatest success stories. Science has never put forth a theory with so much riding on its shoulders or one that has yielded so many productive results.

4.8

Human history has been mostly a comedy and tragedy of errors, with a good number of significant advances along the way. It appears to be no small miracle that humanity has survived thus far—one is tempted to say that of all the arguments advanced in favor of God's existence, the survival of the human race is perhaps the most compelling. But this argument is not a serious one and was never intended to be. The real reason for humanity's continued survival is that its errors, crimes, and catastrophes have been localized in groups, territories, and countries or isolated on continents. However, with the development of modern technology, and the subsequent creation of weapons of mass and ecological destruction, local blunders, miscalculations, desperate measures, and indifferent behaviors now have a reach that is truly worldwide. Indeed, with the ongoing exploration of outer space, it seems only a matter of time until this ominous element of the human legacy will be felt cosmos wide. Today, many in the world community are anxiously holding their collective breath just waiting to see how it will all turn out.

5

Nonlinear Improbables, God, and the Historical Unfolding of the Secular World

5.1

History tells the sad story of endless repetitions of humanity's foibles. But why should this be so? Why do human beings repeat behaviors that have proven, time and time again, to be stupid, destructive, or horrific? Actually, we are asking two different questions. One is an historical one regarding the behavior of the human race over the course of many thousands of years; the other refers to the individual, and the unfortunate decisions and actions that are part of a single lifetime.

Our individual lives seem to be living testimonies to the much-quoted idea that "We don't learn from our experiences." Do I need to chronicle all the tragic stupidities, absurd decisions, destructive emotional outbursts, and misguided existential turns that plague all our lives—most of which, if not exact repetitions of familiar patterns, are minor variations on them? And if you think that you are alone in having to deal with the above, then just consider that a high percentage of your fellow humans spend exorbitant amounts of time and money receiving psychological counseling, purchasing self-help books, following New Age philosophies and practices like yoga and meditation, and, last but not least, indulging in reality-altering habits. Many of us, in fact, believe that much in our lives has gone terribly wrong and that we are in extreme need of remedies for our many failures, failures that are often self-generated

But are we not overstating the case? However familiar the old maxim is to all of us, at closer inspection, we should realize that our right decisions, judgments, and behaviors far outweigh the bad ones. If this were not true, few of us would survive for very long, at least at an acceptable quality of life. It is simply the case that the consequences of a small number of repeat stupidities and offenses often magnify, in our minds, their actual effects in our lives.

Speaking of small numbers, I have coined a principle that I call "nonlinear improbables" to note the observation that, on very rare occasions, simple occurrences can have unexpectedly profound consequences, far greater than common-sense reasoning would ever predict. I am reminded of the famous fifteenth-century Italian composer Jean Baptiste Lully, creator of French opera, who, while conducting an opera one day with his famous staff, accidentally struck his toe when he forcefully pounded his staff to the floor at a particularity dramatic moment in the opera. Besides the pain and embarrassment that he suffered at the moment of impact, who would have guessed that this little injury to his toe would quickly turn gangrenous, eventually ending in the composer's painful death? This is an unusually poignant example of a nonlinear improbable, but there are even more impressive ones.

Approximately four billion years ago, a random combination of chemical elements came together, by accident, and were vitalized by cosmic and earthly forces in just the right environmental conditions for "replicating molecules" to form. These, the first stirrings of life, produced countless variations. One of these variations led to the evolution of bacteria, which became the only life form on Earth for about a billion years, before another accidental variation began evolving into what would eventually become the fertile and variegated "bush of life." Life then began spreading and diversifying wildly across the face of the earth, up until the present time, when one curious member of the tiny, accidental variation that we call humankind sits at a computer typing these words. Now, how's that for an impressively unexpected improbable? The origin of life is one of the two grandest examples of nonlinear improbables—the other is the origin of the universe.

Actually, from the perspective of the birth of the universe, some thirteen billion years ago, and the creation of life on Earth about four billion years ago, everything that exists today is a nonlinear improbable. The complex relationship between linear probables, like ordering a small, nonfat coffee drink and getting one, and nonlinear improbables, is a fascinating one. This connection deserves a great deal of attention and investigation. Nonlinear improbables play a large role on both the micro and macro scale and can have both positive and negative consequences. But even the effects of unfortunate decisions and actions in our lives—whether linear or nonlinear—are usually not powerful enough to offset our good and beneficial choices and actions.

We generally mislead the balance between the fortunate and unfortunate episodes in our lives, because we tend to focus more on our negative actions and their consequences, rather than on the positive and fruitful ones. Additionally, it appears that our natures are such that the psychological/emotional—and sometimes even physical—pain that we suffer from foolish decisions and behaviors is of greater intensity and duration than the moments of pleasure that follow our good efforts. Actually, most of our days are comprised of choices and behaviors that maintain the status quo, which, if we were honest, is largely in our favor.

The general point is that despite the many repeat offenses that we commit against others and ourselves, we can and do make the proper adjustments that break unpleasant psychological/emotional cycles and destructive thinking and behavior patterns. The fact that countless numbers of people have turned their lives around is conclusive proof that the past is not necessarily destiny and that individual histories do chronicle wonderful surprises. But what about human history? Why hasn't the human race turned itself around? Perhaps the human community—given its enormous population, incompatible cultural diversity, and economic disparity—is essentially unmanageable. Maybe it's simply too late for radical change!

Some convincing arguments suggest that humanity may be heading for a tragic ending, in fact to extinction, because of repeating behavior patterns that are pernicious to biological life, especially human life. Could the ultimate irony turn out to be that just as one nonlinear improbable gave birth to life, another one ends it? Or perhaps it's only human life that is at risk. Could a local, irrational political decision in the Middle East or the Far East precipitate a deadly chain reaction that results in one of the greatest "extinction events" in the history of life on Earth? Will bacterial life then return in full force and reclaim complete dominion over planet Earth? Sounds improbable, but we know that story.

Common sense suggests that if one average person can dramatically improve the quality of his life by breaking negative patterns of thinking and behaving, then a large number of individual persons in the world community should be able to do the same, and then all of us could look to the future with renewed hope and expectation. Unfortunately, there are a number of reasons why this rosy prospect is profoundly unrealistic, including that the world is composed of many different cultures, some of which are mutually antagonistic. Despite the most optimistic assessment, it is virtually impossible to harmonize highly conflicting worldviews.

Human beings are born into the world without knowing anything. It is also true that nonhuman life forms are born ignorant. In their case, however, knowledge, as an indispensable tool and guide for survival, is only partly necessary, because nature has provided them with genetically programmed ways of behaving and responding to the challenges in their environment. Human beings, by contrast, have two strikes against them from the start: not only are they ignorant, but they also can never rely on strict, genetic programs to guide them through the obstacle course of life. Rather, they must rely on culture as their teacher and guide. And even the residual instincts and cravings that rudely remind human beings of their bestial origins are not much good, since humans can never return to their largely instinctive, preconscious past and live close to nature, as their prehistoric, nonhuman ancestors once did. This would require divesting human beings of their cultural essence, which is not possible; to be human is to be a cultural being—the two are inseparable.

5.2

The basic problem of any culture centers on issues of information and knowledge and, more to the point, how to acquire the *right* information and knowledge. Information is the accumulation of facts of experience, and knowledge is the understanding that is gained from organizing these facts, seeing their meaningful relationships, and inferring their significance. The ultimate purpose of culture, then, is to pass to human beings, through whatever means available, the information and knowledge that will ensure their survival and potential for reproduction, as well as to provide a *world of meaning* in which they can think and act productively and harmoniously with other human beings. Each generation is responsible for gathering the right facts and gaining necessary understanding in order to promote cultural life. This is no easy task. A major source of the problem is that each generation has to start from scratch, so to speak, and acquire anew the information and knowledge that the previous generations garnered; information and knowledge are not carried through genes. One of the great responsibilities of any culture, therefore, is the transfer of information and knowledge from one generation to the next. This is the meaning of education.

Information and knowledge are always subject to interpretation. This is unavoidable, because human beings always only have partial information and limited knowledge; because both exist in unlimited supply, we will always face corrections as we acquire more information and gain more knowledge. Additionally, human beings are naturally *perspectival*—that is, any gain of information or knowledge is always from a limited, finite viewpoint. This means that humans could never, even in principle, gain the "full picture" of any subject. Information and knowledge are also subject to interpolation, distortion, and bias and run the risk of being eliminated altogether, either accidentally or purposefully. Humankind's cultural *transference mechanisms*, in other words, could never be absolutely sufficient to ensure that each generation acquires reliable and truthful information and knowledge. This is one of the frustrating aspects of being human. The best we can do is try our best to pass on the most accurate information and the most reliable knowledge that we possess. But another issue is even more frustrating.

The problem of the unavoidable deficiencies in information and knowledge transferal from one generation to the next is aggravated by the profound disagreement between the world's cultures as to what constitutes information and knowledge. We live in an asymmetric cultural universe, in which there are competing definitions of reality, knowledge, and morality. Without a general consensus in these three critical areas of cultural life—what a fact is, what knowledge is, and what is right and wrong behavior—extreme conflict between cultures is unavoidable. And the recorded history of humankind has chronicled this truth very faithfully. At the heart of many of the conflicts between cultures are religious differences.

All religions are rooted in, and are guided by, supernatural beliefs of one kind or another. The three monotheistic religions are grounded in the belief in an invisible, perfect, moral, just, and good creator-God who maintains a personal and loving relationship with each person and with humanity as a whole. The creator-God also plays an integral part in human history and human destiny (both individually and collectively). For their part, humans are commanded to love their creator with unbounded devotion and enthusiasm, to be willing to make every required sacrifice to him, and to live from day to day in strict accordance with the spiritual principles, commandments, and guidelines as they are outlined in divinely inspired scriptures. According to the faithful, the "Word of God," is where the voice of God can be clearly heard, if one's heart is open and willing.

From the perspective of a conservative, observant Jew, a fundamentalist Christian, or a traditional Muslim, facts and knowledge have a clear meaning. To begin with, reality for the true monotheist is *eternal*; it withstands the ravages of time; it is unchangeable, because it is perfect—whatever does change loses its essence and therefore can never be perfect. Earthy existence is a realm of change, of things coming into being and passing out of being. It's the arena of death. This is why a fact, for the monotheist, can have real meaning only in a perfect realm of the spirit, of true reality, where there is no change.

It makes sense, then, to the monotheist that facts must be otherworldly. Here are the facts as devout monotheists understand them: the eternal reality of a transcendent God (Judaism, Christianity, Islam); God's omniscience, omnipotence, omnipresence, and moral perfection (Judaism, Christianity, Islam); faith both as an act of devotion to God and as an abiding attitude in spiritual life (Judaism, Christianity, Islam); a spiritually lost and fallen humanity (Judaism, Christianity, Islam); grace understood as God's gift of salvation to a sinful humanity (Christianity); God's masculine gender (Judaism, Christianity, Islam); humanity as God's greatest creation (Judaism, Christianity, Islam); the privileged, spiritual status of humankind (Judaism, Christianity, Islam); the need of humanity to reconcile itself to God for its sinfulness (Judaism, Christianity, Islam); Jesus as God in the flesh (Christianity); the life, death, and resurrection of Jesus for the sins of humanity (Christianity); the spiritual requirement of women to submit to the authority of their husbands (Judaism, Christianity, Islam); men as being more qualified than women to address the spiritual needs of the community of believers (Judaism, Christianity, Islam); the existence of an immaterial soul (Judaism, Christianity, Islam); heaven (Judaism, Christianity, Islam); hell (Christianity, Islam), angels (Judaism, Christianity, Islam); demons (Christianity, Islam); the devil (Christianity, Islam); salvation (Christianity, Islam); the supernatural power of prayer, ritual, and sacrifice (Judaism, Christianity, Islam); the supernatural status of sin (Judaism, Christianity, Islam); and evil (Christianity, Islam); the sinful nature of any indulgence in sensual passion and gratification outside of God-sanctioned arrangements (Judaism, Christianity, Islam); the foolish and depraved state of the humanity's rational faculty independent of God's guidance (Judaism, Christianity, Islam); life after death (Judaism, Christianity, Islam); the lower spiritual stature of the things of *this* world (some denominations of Judaism, Christianity, Islam); nonbelievers as spiritually lost (Judaism, Christianity, Islam); that there will be a dramatic end of human history when the "Messiah" returns to defeat God's enemies and to gather together the faithful (Judaism, Christianity, Islam); the divine status of Torah (Judaism, Christianity, Islam), the Bible as a whole (Christianity, Islam), and the Koran (Islam).

Monotheistic facts are not available to our senses for empirical observation and verification; nor can they be logically inferred from the natural world. Rather, the devout Jew, Christian and Muslim must believe in the facts of monotheism on faith. The understanding that follows from integrating these religious facts produces a philosophical worldview that determines what one views as good and bad and true and false; what one values and devalues; the goals that one ought to pursue; and how one is to treat other people, including those who don't subscribe to the same spiritual beliefs.

What is right and wrong behavior? What is the ground for moral behavior? Is it religious, or secular, or a combination of both? Moral views, in fact, depend on ideas about reality. If this world is metaphysically unimportant, and if what is real is understood as what one views as eternal and transcendent, then right and wrong behavior would follow accordingly. The strong desire for and pursuit of material goods, for instance, would be viewed as wrong, because it reflects too much interest in this world, when all of one's energies should be focused on the higher, transcendent reality—the only true, unchanging reality. In this view, one should live a meager existence and wait patiently for the next, higher one. On the other hand, if one believes that this world is the only true reality, then moral behavior could be based on incentives that promote creating worldly happiness and material wealth—this is a secular-based morality.

5.3

Secularism is a philosophical worldview that interprets reality, promotes moral values, and fosters thinking, acting, and decision-making from naturalistic—nonsupernatural, nonreligious—perspectives. Its tool is rational thinking as applied to the reality of natural experience. Secular values are decidedly this-worldly (as opposed to otherworldly) and hold that the proper and effective use of natural reason includes the pursuit of knowledge and happiness; the solution of humanity's social, political, economic, and ecological ills; and the way to improve the moral condition of mankind. The scientific methods of the natural sciences typically guide and color secular thought, although philosophy, literature, and art are also celebrated to be of great value in uncovering and expressing areas of human experience that are not available to usual scientific study and understanding.

Secular thought has always been a part of Western culture, beginning with the ancient Greek tradition of the rational pursuit of truth, knowledge, and wisdom. What was revolutionary about this cultural direction was that, unlike all civilizations before it and many after it, in most instances the Greeks believed that human beings had the ability, through the power of reason alone, to figure out the verities of existence.

The ancient Greeks believed in the existence of many gods and often made sacrifices to them in hopes of winning their favor, and the Greeks also consulted oracles for answers to questions of dire importance. But these superstitious customs were based on the desire to achieve ends, and to find answers, that could never be accomplished and discovered by reason alone, such as the outcome of an upcoming battle or the results of a momentous political decision. One might say that the ancient Greeks left reason behind only as a last resort, whenever they thought that its limitations had been reached. But the Greeks loved reason with a passion and even defined the essence of a human being as *rational*. The truth is that the gods were more like big brothers to the Greeks than a Yahweh-like, transcendent, perfect deity who looks down suspiciously upon his sin-laden creation with a judgmental eye. In fact, although the gods were immortal, they possessed many of the same vices and earthly interests as their mortal counterparts and could often be found consorting with them.

The Greek pursuit of knowledge, truth, and wisdom took different forms that varied in degrees of abstraction. The Greeks were enamored of mathematics and placed great emphasis on *measuring* as a profound way to discover truths about the physical universe. And they also looked to the "mathematical model" as the standard that all pursuers of knowledge and wisdom should strive to emulate. In this sense, the requirements of precision, clarity, logical rigor, and inner consistency became the guides for Greek thought (and modern science). Even philosophy, the language-based pursuit of truth, was, in the mouth of Socrates or in the hands of Plato and Aristotle, devoted to logical rigor and consistency. This was so even when it was poetically expressed, as in Plato's works.

It's no coincidence that the ancient Athenians invented democracy. The "rule of the people" follows naturally from a citizenry who hold thinking in such high esteem. In fact, a true democracy requires a populace that has the capacity to think and decide for itself, to apply reason to the practical and complex realities of living in a large community of people. Greek democracy also makes a clear statement about the inherent worth and dignity of the people who determine how they are to be ruled. Why put the well-being of the whole community in its own hands, in the hands of the people? Because for the Greeks, human beings have both the natural right and the capacity to determine what is best for them. At the same time, Greek democracy was far from perfect. Women were not permitted to vote and, in general, were not on equal footing with men. And slavery was a fully accepted institution; the slaves were viewed, and often treated, as subhuman. And the Greeks viewed non-Greeks as "barbarians"—something other and lower than fully human. Nonetheless, the Greeks represented the most radical cultural transformation in recorded history, one that was to become the destiny of all of Europe, if not the whole world.

And the ancient Greeks didn't stop with philosophy, logic, mathematics, science, and democracy. In virtually every area of cultural life, the ancient Greeks made profound and lasting contributions: unsurpassed works of art and architecture, the invention of drama and unmatched works in epic poetry, the art of governing, the idea of the rule of law, the scientific study of history, the humane treatment of medical patients as outlined in the Hippocratic oath, and the mathematical structure of music. The notion of mind-body balance that we hear so much about today began with the Greeks. "Become all that you can be" was a Greek idea, as was the tradition of athletic competition to demonstrate excellence (e.g., the Olympics). In fact, the idea of excellence (*arête*) itself infused and motivated the Greeks in all areas of cultural life. Even our classical ideals of beauty—balance, harmony, grace, elegance, simplicity, and proportion—were of Greek origin and informed all of their works of art and architecture, and these ideals have done the same for the rest of Western civilization for over two thousand years.

We can see with the ancient Greeks the beginnings of secular thought and its impact on the life of a people and their culture. Although the Greeks were polytheistic, their version of spirituality was decidedly of this world. Actually, it is misleading even to imply the notion of spirituality, since their religiosity had very little impact on how they lived their lives. Reason and passion commingled in the Greek soul in the most astonishing ways, giving birth to the mind and soul of what is best in the Western world and forever pointing the way to the future of humankind, reminding us of the startling heights to which human beings can climb, and showing us the power and glory of the human mind. This is true despite the deep injustices that even greatness can willingly perpetrate.

The ancient Greeks laid the foundation of Western civilization by fertilizing its cultural soul with precious ideas and ideals that served as its guiding themes and strategies. These ideas and programs were to have a long, and at times tortured, history as they made their way down through the ages through both oral and written traditions, cultivating the Western mind and often mutating into variations of their original. The Romans, for instance, took the rule of law idea, developed it in their Romanized version of Greek Stoicism, and extended it to include not only a city-state but also a vast empire. In effect, they *created* Western civilization, in which many different peoples lived as Romans, sharing a common culture and receiving the many benefits that existed therein.

Early Christianity also absorbed Greek ideas, reframed them in a religious context, and then claimed them as their own: a nonmaterial soul that survives death; the sacrificial lamb; the resurrection; the virgin birth; God as the "logos," the underlying, *rational* structure of the universe; the idea of a nonmaterial realm of perfection—these are some of the Greek ideas that Christians absorbed into their doctrine.

After ancient Greece was conquered in 146 BCE, its pagan/secular culture became incarnated in the body politic of its conquerors—the Romans. In some instances, the Romans absorbed Greek ideas and traditions directly, as in the case of the Greek gods, and in others instances, the Romans modified or transformed them to serve their particular needs, character, and culture. These changes can be seen in the Roman adoption of Stoicism and in their warfare, engineering, architecture, social planning, administration, law, art, and literature. In all these instances, the Romans were innovators, but Greek ideas and traditions were critical ingredients in all areas of Roman culture. It's not surprising, then, that the Romans had utter reverence for Greeks and often used them as teachers and mentors; Romans even traveled to Athens—especially to Plato's Academy—to study philosophy and other Greek subjects. In the final analysis, secular ideas passed through the Roman cultural filter in excellent, unsullied condition, but not before they took an unexpected and dangerous detour in the fourth century CE when Rome, in one of the pivotal moments in history, turned its back on its pagan past and established a small but rapidly growing, Jewish sect called Christianity as the principle religion of its vast empire.

Rome fell in the fifth century, but its most powerful contribution to the Western world, the Roman Catholic Church, survived very much intact, and its influence picked up where the empire had left off. Although the former empire was in frantic disarray, the Roman Church became the new unifying force in the Western world, and for the next eleven hundred years or so, pagan and Christian ideas gradually came together in a mighty, if uneasy, alliance. Despite the all-powerful control that the church had over virtually all areas of cultural life in the Middle Ages, one finds many so-called Christian ideas and traditions that were actually pagan-based. For example, the sacrifice and resurrection of gods, praying and kneeling to the spirits and statues, and communion, in which the body and blood of a god are ritualistically eaten and drunk—these are just some of the many practices that were borrowed from pagan Greece and Rome, and perhaps from other lands like Persia, Syria, and, Egypt, and incorporated into Christianity. Even the dates for the birth (December) and death (between late March and late April) of Christ were dates for pagan holidays that Emperor Constantine conveniently changed into Christian ones.

At the very beginning of Christian rule, there was, as yet, no completed and edited Bible that could serve as a reliable, doctrinal information source. Rather, there were various ideas, practices, and rituals that were imperfectly woven together and gave Christians only a *sense* of what it was to be a Christian. But many crucial questions still needed to be answered. The most important one dealt with the nature of Jesus himself. That there was only *one* God and not many was something on which all Christians could agree. Or could they? Christians certainly believed in Jesus Christ, but, ironically, it was far from clear *who* it was that they believed in—was he the "Son of God," or was he actually God in the *flesh*, as some Christians believed? There seemed to be evidence to support both positions. After all, scripture and tradition tell us that Jesus called himself the "Son of God" and never said unequivocally that he was, in fact, God. And if Jesus were God, this would mean that he gave birth to himself and even prayed to himself! That would make no sense. And there was much more that seemed senseless.

How could a perfect God live and suffer like a mortal human being while remaining perfect? How could an eternal, unchanging God *become* his own son and still retain his essence? Jesus clearly was made of flesh and blood, so how could he also have been made of the same substance as God, who is nonphysical? And how could the infinite and immortal God die? Persons holding the position that Jesus was both God and human are forced to admit that this view is an assault on logic and even on common sense.

But if Jesus was not God, it would mean that Christians would be required to worship not one God, but both God *and* Jesus, who wasn't divine. Wouldn't this be just another version of the old paganism? And if Jesus was only a spiritual man or even just similar to God spiritually, then what was all the fuss about? After all, Jesus still couldn't have been perfect, only God is perfect. And how could an imperfect man—however spiritual—be the "light of the world" and be our Lord and Savior?

Such logical and doctrinal inconsistencies plagued the young church and resulted in radical confrontations, actual riots, between the Arians and the Athanasists. The Arians believed that "there was a time when the son was not"—that God and Jesus were *not* the same. Conversely, the Athanasists believed that God and Jesus were made of the same substance and were "coeternal"—that Jesus and God always existed together. The conflict became so divisive that Emperor Constantine convened the Council of Nicea in 325 to resolve the issue (along with other important doctrinal issues). Over three hundred bishops from all over the empire came together to debate openly the merits and demerits of both views, and the emperor himself—to the delight of the bishops—served as referee and judge between the two hostile camps. By this time, a version of the four Gospels had been completed and was available during the conference for referencing. Ultimately, Constantine decided in favor of the Athanasists and proclaimed—coining his own special word—that God and Jesus were *homoousios*, Greek for "of the same substance." Despite his decision, the conflict went on, and support for both views continued through several more councils, but eventually, after Christianity finally became the official state religion at the century's end, the balance began shifting permanently in favor of homoousios.

As the Roman Empire grew to immense proportions, it became more and more difficult to manage effectively. By the third century CE, social, political, economic, and military chaos was threatening the very foundations of Roman civilization. To regain a measure of control of the Roman world, Emperor Diocletian (who ruled from 284 to 305) decided to divide the empire in half and established another capital in the Eastern frontier of the empire (in present-day Turkey). This was the beginning of the Byzantine Empire, which lasted for over a thousand years until 1453, when the Ottoman Turks assumed control. This rebalancing of the Roman power had profound consequences, not the least of which was the continuation of the Roman Empire (as many would agree) and its civilization (as all would agree) far beyond its demise in the West, although now it was to have a distinctly Eastern flavor and orientation.

In 324, Emperor Constantine constructed a new capital in the Eastern Empire that he named Constantinople (present-day Istanbul). It was from this "New Rome" that he would rule the whole empire with godlike power and authority, far from political rivals. But the Roman Empire, in general, fell on even more difficult times, with recurrent barbarian invasions, plagues, revolts, political corruption, incompetent emperors, and famines all over the Roman world. It was a wonder that the empire lasted as long as it did. Men of insight knew that the end was near. It was clear that the empire—tired, and disheartened—was about to collapse. In the West, at least, Roman civilization was doomed.

When the Western Roman Empire eventually fell to Germanic invaders in 476, chaos overtook the Western Roman world, and the peace, order, and stability that were Rome's great contributions to civilization—*Pax Romana*—became but a distant memory, at least in the Western empire. But still, all was not lost in the West. The Roman Church survived the barbarian invasions and the disintegration of the empire. The Romans, possessed by both panic and despair, ran to the Roman Church for solace, protection, and counsel. It was at this time that paganism, as a viable belief system for the Romans, began a slow but steady decline. Ultimately, pagan ideas and practices survived only to the extent that they could be disguised and inconspicuously absorbed into Christian doctrine. The ascendancy of Eastern Christianity beginning in the fourth century made the neutralizing of overt pagan culture likewise inevitable.

Despite growing doctrinal differences between the Eastern Greek Orthodox Church and Western Roman Catholicism, there was one issue about which there was no disagreement: pagan thought and traditions—at least so named—must be expunged from Christian culture at all costs. The first order of business for Catholic clergy in the West became the destruction of statuary, relics, shrines, and pagan temples (some of which were transformed into Christian temples), as well as the burning of classical manuscripts and libraries containing the immortal works of Greece and Rome's geniuses.

In the East, the Christian emperor Justinian (527–565) similarly went on a rampage to purge the Byzantine Empire of any hint of pagan culture, including closing pagan schools—among them Plato's highly venerated School of Athens. In 529, Justinian literally *imposed* Christianity on Constantinople, making any display of pagan worship or devotion a punishable crime. Persecution of pagans and Jews in the Eastern and Western empires, in fact, became commonplace. It was during this time that state-sponsored religious intolerance began gaining unprecedented power and influence in the affairs of humankind.

The Christian war against all things pagan resulted in an incalculable loss of Western cultural treasures—from original works in philosophy, mathematics, astronomy, natural science, medicine, politics, and history to masterpieces in literature, drama, and art. In the West, the annihilation of classical thought was almost complete. Ironically, the little that was saved was due, in large part, to Benedictine monks in monasteries writing out passionate refutations to noted pagan works. Scholars have also discovered Christian devotional works that were inscribed on ancient parchments that still contained imperfectly erased writings on Greek and Roman thought.

It was the Eastern Empire, however, that saved from cultural extinction the majority of what we do have of the Western classical heritage. When Justinian outlawed pagan education and closed the School of Athens, students fled to more tolerant areas of the empire, such as Spain, and carried with them the major works of classical antiquity. For the next several centuries, the Arabs took up the role of custodians of classical culture. In ninth-century Al Andulus, Spain, for instance, the Arabic Moors integrated Arabic and Greco-Roman culture to produce an extraordinary culture of tolerance, learning, sophistication, and accomplishment. The Arabs themselves were rich in ingenuity and made significant contributions in many fields, one of the most important of which was the invention of algebra. The Moors in Cordova, and then in Toledo, carried forward the blazing torch of knowledge for Western humanity and produced wonderful books of classical learning. They also created libraries in which the intellectual gold from the Greek and Roman civilizations was preserved.

In 1085, Toledo was taken over by Christian invaders, who were overwhelmed by the civilization they found there. To the Europeans, it was as though they had discovered a new Atlantis; then began extensive incursions into Spain where Europeans hungry for knowledge began absorbing all that the Arabs had preserved and created. The Europeans industriously exported to the rest of Europe the immortal contributions of classical and Arabic civilizations. During this time, Arabic and Jewish scholars, such as the Spanish/Arabic scholar Averroes, and the Jewish physician/philosopher Maimonides, were busy translating from Greek and Arabic into Latin the works of Plato, Aristotle, Euclid, Hippocrates, Galen, and Arabic authors. These translated works would eventually illuminate the benighted medieval mind and give birth to the Italian Renaissance, the Enlightenment, and the modern world.

The Italian Renaissance—literally, "rebirth"—was a pagan revival. That the rebirth of pagan civilization occurred first in Italy in the fifteenth century should not come as a great surprise. As the seat of the great Roman Empire, Italy had always exerted a hypnotic power over the rest of Europe and especially over the Italians themselves. Many have looked back on the Roman Empire, at its height, as a veritable Golden Age—a civilization that brought together in stunning balance the ancient Greek and Roman cultures. For two hundred years—the longest stretch of relative peace in world history—Pax Romana (Roman peace) stabilized the known world. In their heart of hearts, the Italians yearned to rule the world once again—and they also longed to be the most civilized culture on Earth.

It was only natural for the Italians of the Middle Ages to have felt themselves to be the direct descendants of the Romans. One might even revert to unscientific ideas and terminology and suggest that the Italians never got the Romans out of their *blood*. They can hardly be blamed for this cultural, self-indulgence; outside of the many Roman traditions that were still rigorously observed (artistic practices, for instance), and the countless ways that ancient Rome informed their everyday life (including dietary habits), Italy was—and still is—a veritable virtual-reality experience of the most magnificent empire of antiquity. From the top to the bottom of the Italian boot, we find mind-boggling aqueducts, awe-inspiring buildings, opulent villas, heroic statues, sophisticated classical architecture, breathtaking fountains, endless roads heading in every direction—all these items attesting to the glory that was once Rome. Living within Italian culture of the Middle Ages, and directly absorbing the Roman achievement on a daily basis, it was impossible to banish paganism from the Italian mind. It seemed as though it was only a matter of time until Greece and Rome would make a triumphant return, and the Italians eventually got the historical nod when the pagan literature of Greece and Rome—after having been retrieved from near oblivion by the Moors in Spain—electrified fourteenth and fifteenth-century Italy, and the pagan spirit reappeared in brilliant form.

But it wasn't as though the Renaissance arose all at once out of the darkness of the Middle Ages. In fact, there was much creative preparation during that time, which had a decisive influence on the flowering of Italian culture of the fifteenth century. During the Middle Ages, the Catholic Church did its very best to control every aspect of an individual's personal and public life, but it could not control the influx and circulation of the Greek and Roman ideas that were whizzing around Europe, due to the new translations from the Greek and Arabic languages. Given this fact, the church had no choice but to attempt to fit these ideas into the Christian doctrine wherever possible. Plato's idea that there is a nonphysical soul that survives the death of each person is a good example of a pagan idea that Christianity appropriated and made into its own.

Most spectacular, however, was the influence of the Greek philosopher Aristotle (384–322 BCE). In particular, Aristotle's philosophy is a sort of grandiose manifesto for the secular life, in which he defined reason as a human being's most distinctive quality and placed *this world* as the sole object of man's concern and investigation. This is true even though he believed in a supreme architect of the universe; but Aristotle's god was not a personal one to whom one prayed and with whom one communed. Rather, his was an aloof deity that had little to do with the day-to-day affairs of human beings.

Aristotle was the first philosopher of earthly happiness (*eudaimonia*) and believed that happiness was a natural accompaniment of living a life devoted to achieving—by the disciplined and balanced use of reason—excellence in all endeavors. It is in excellently practiced contemplation, in fact, that the greatest happiness—the greatest "Good"—can be sustained. Aristotle was to have an immeasurably profound influence on the emergence of the Italian Renaissance, the Enlightenment, and, by extension, the modern world.

5.4

The Italian churchman, theologian, and Scholastic philosopher Thomas Aquinas (1225–1274) was the thinker who, unintentionally, let the secular cat out of the religious bag. He achieved this momentous feat by integrating into one huge (yet incomplete) treatise of intimidating accomplishment—the *Summa Theologica*—the main body of Christian doctrine and the philosophy of Aristotle. Aquinas laid down a rational foundation for Christianity and made this foundation consistent with philosophical principles. But this stunning accomplishment had unintended consequences: what Aquinas concocted, quite naïvely, was a Trojan Horse strategy, with the Catholic Church itself as the unwitting victim.

Aquinas embodied two contradictory philosophical orientations: he was a devout Catholic who believed in the unquestioned authority of the Bible and Catholic tradition, but he was also strongly secular in his passion for the rational understanding of existence. Other religious figures before him, such as Saint Anselm of Canterbury (1033–1109), had appealed to reason in discussions of religious issues, but only as a way to clarify what had already been accepted on faith—not as a valid, independent way to acquire knowledge in itself.

Aquinas also had great contemporaries, such as the scientifically minded Roger Bacon (1214–1292), who pushed forward the cause of science, and William of Ockham (1288–1348), the great logician noted for his "Ockham's Razor," the logical principle that one should strive to explain, or account for, something with the *fewest* number of principles without sacrificing what is the true and important. And there was John Duns Scotus (1265–1308), a staunch Aristotelian-minded theologian who addressed a number of theological, logical, and philosophical issues and whose critiques had a great impact on the church.

Bacon's effort was frustrated by his inability to convince the church of the value of his scientific work, and he was eventually imprisoned for antagonizing his religious brethren. Ockham used his great logical skills to argue *against* Aquinas' mission of marrying of faith and reason, but, in the end, he had nothing revolutionary to offer. Scotus, although a deft and original theologian, was not systematic in his thinking, and his obscure and difficult works were more an attack on and dissection of theological, logical, and philosophical issues than a constructive reworking of them.

Aquinas was radically different from all three of these thinkers. He not only possessed a brilliant intellect of encyclopedic proportions, but he was also one of the truly great *systematic* thinkers in history. He was also a venerated teacher and lecturer. Although the more conservative religious order of the Dominicans refused to accept Aquinas' affirmative embrace of reason (the universities in Paris and Oxford banned his ideas), ultimately his influence was to be decisive in the church. He married two very complex traditions—Aristotelian and Christian—with such seductive intellectual dexterity that it was impossible for the church not to embrace his work enthusiastically. In short, he demonstrated to the church how and why reason is a valuable tool for both earthly and spiritual knowledge, and how they could and should work together harmoniously to reach a common goal: *the truth*. It was his unshakable stand for the power and integrity of rational thinking—in the very midst of a devout Christendom—that made Aquinas one of the truly great, pivotal figures in Western history.

Despite Aquinas' position as a foundational figure of the Catholic Church, his commitment to philosophical reasoning and investigation was close to an obsession. But it was Aristotle's philosophy, and how he could modify it for his own Christian purposes that were the true object of his obsession. Unlike other Scholastic theologians, he was unwilling to relegate reason to the inferior status of simply being the feeble "handmaiden of religion." Rather, he believed that the rational faculty itself had the capacity to discover real truth about the world. That is, he believed that contrary to the prevailing Christian wisdom, human beings *could* obtain real knowledge about earthly reality through reason. In addition, Aquinas was also unwilling to castigate the senses as a distortion of, or a misrepresentation of, reality. In his view, the senses supply reliable data about the real world.

However, Aquinas argued that when dealing with the truths and mysteries of spiritual reality, reason alone was no longer adequate to the task, but required faith and revelation. Aquinas' great mission, then, was to negotiate the boundaries between reason and faith and to make their relationship mutually supportive in the overall quest for the truth of existence, whether earthly or spiritual.

Aristotle, or as Aquinas liked to refer to him, "The Philosopher," was the ideal philosophical mentor for Aquinas. Unlike Plato, whose metaphysics was grounded in alleged transcendent realms of nonmaterial perfection, Aristotle's focus was on the world of everyday existence and the truths that can be discovered within. In this sense, Aristotle's philosophy did not directly step on Christian toes, so to speak, because it was not orientated toward trying to understand or describe supposedly transcendent and nonphysical realities. This made it easier for Aquinas to weld Aristotle's earthly ideas with Christianity's spiritual truths.

Aristotle was also preoccupied with the question of how reason functions in discovering the truths of the world, and he invented an important branch of logic—Aristotelian logic—as a sort of ABCs of proper reasoning. Aquinas seized upon Aristotle's ideas and philosophical methods and modified them so they were in accord with Christian principles. The result was an ingenious synthesis of Christian and Aristotelian/Aquinian ideas that was to have an incalculable influence on both Christian and secular thought. One enormous consequence, for example, was that by laying a rational basis for Christianity, Aquinas argued for the *literal* reading of scripture, as against metaphorical interpretations. Aquinas' position had a profound effect on biblical interpretation and ultimately made the Bible vulnerable to critical analysis, a position that turned out to be very destructive to the traditional status of the Bible as the inerrant, divinely inspired Word of God.

In his famous idea "Five Proofs for God's Existence," from his *Summa Theologica*, Aquinas tried to demonstrate that God's existence could be logically deduced from the simple experience of the world and the universe. In one of his five proofs, "The Cosmological Argument," he argued something alone these lines: the Bible maintains that God's fingerprints are everywhere to be seen in the world around us. This, the sheer revelatory presence of God's handiwork, was the starting point for Aquinas, a first premise, if you will. He then deduced from the *visible* things of the universe—employing a variation on one of Aristotle's positions—that every thing that exists is in motion; that each thing in motion has a preceding cause; that *that* cause is also in motion; that this motion also had to have a prior cause that was also in motion; and so forth and so on, all the way back in cosmological time to the very beginning of the universe, where there had to have been an uncaused *first motion*, or "Unmoved Mover." For Aquinas, this Unmoved Mover is God. Aquinas employed this sort of Aristotelian reasoning in all five proofs, using reason to lend support to, justify, and, in some cases, even help explain spiritual reality.

Aquinas' work was the culmination of the Scholastic philosophical movement that began in the eleventh century with Saint Anselm's interest in clarifying through reason what was already known to be true through faith. (Saint Augustine initiated an earlier synthetic tradition in the fifth century by combining faith with mystical versions of Plato.) Initially, the Scholastic movement combined Aristotle's logic and philosophy with faith in such a way as to retain reason as a helpless servant of religion. Aquinas, by contrast, elevated the status of reason and made it a significant, if ultimately inadequate, tool for acquiring truth and knowledge.

The average twenty-first-century Westerner is so thoroughly inculcated with secular and scientific thinking that it's hard for him to realize the truly revolutionary and audacious nature of Aquinas' philosophical strategy. The Middle Ages (approximately 500 CE to 1400 CE) was a very superstitious time, during which much of the Christian population sincerely believed that the devil, demons, witches, and evil forces inhabited the real world and often preyed on spiritually vulnerable people. These bogeymen were thought to be able to steal people's souls and even force them into criminally deviant behavior such as performing sexual acts outside of church-sanctioned marriage or seducing people into the study of black magic. Mental illness and all sorts of physical disorders were frequently attributed to demon possession, which often resulted in unspeakably cruel attempts for a cure. Most horrific was the church policy of abducting young girls and women suspected of being witches and torturing them to try to extract confessions and then putting them to death, regardless of the result of the interrogation. It should not be surprising to discover that during the Middle Ages relatively few Western citizens could read and write; that the Romans, by comparison, were a very literate people; and that the average life expectancy in Europe during most of the Middle Ages was in the teens. In this cultural environment, it was hardly possible for a rational approach to life to thrive in any meaningful way.

During this time the church was committed to controlling the private and public lives of Christians, and this involved a sort of mind control insofar as independent, critical thinking was not cultivated, nor was using reason as a tool for investigation. Such rational interests and activities were viewed as tragically misguided or were more often seen as the handiwork of the devil. What was required of Christians was strict adherence to the church's principles and doctrines without questioning the legitimacy of what was being demanded. In other words, Christians were required to believe the so-called truths of Christianity by simple, unquestioned *faith*. True believers should never demand reasons or evidence for revealed truth but must put reason aside and simply believe.

As the Middle Ages progressed toward the fourteenth century, however, it became more and more difficult for the church to constrain the European mind in a religious straitjacket. Arabic translations of a number of ancient Greek and Roman works had already begun circulating throughout Europe and influencing notable figures. Aristotle's ideas, in particular, began surfacing, and attempts to keep them in check by religious censorship were beginning to fail. We already mentioned Saint Anselm, who in the eleventh century was peddling Aristotelian ideas in offering to true believers well-reasoned arguments in the service of the church. His famous "ontological argument," for instance, concludes that God exists because, by definition, he is perfect, and perfection necessarily implies existence; therefore God *must* exist. There we see Anselm present an ingeniously reasoned, step-by-step, *deductive* (Aristotelian) argument for God's existence. But he was quick to add that this argument was designed only for those who already believed in God on faith, as a way to give intellectual clarity and comfort to the believer, and should in no way be seen as a serious attempt to prove that God exists. For Anselm, human reason—echoing Saint Augustine from the fifth century CE—was inadequate and prideful and should be looked upon with suspicion. It doesn't require great insight to conclude that this apology for reason was disingenuous at best and demonstrates that the medieval mind was beginning to awaken from its thoughtless slumber.

The secular breakthrough that Europe so desperately needed—and toward which it had been gradually moving—finally occurred in the thirteenth century, in the very womb of the Christian Church itself, in the person of Saint Thomas Aquinas, who inadvertently laid the secular seeds for Europe's reawakening. And he did so right before the watchful eyes of the church! But what does "secular" even mean in this context? And what were the seeds?

Remember, the original Christian campaign to stamp out paganism at all costs meant eliminating the things that pagan culture valued, which included not only their gods but also their obsession—really the Greek obsession—with rational thinking. In the typical Christian mindset of the true believer, paganism and rationality were inseparable. Rationality was associated with the pagan love of the things of this world, including the desire for sensual pleasure and the interest in pursuing earthly happiness; these interests were abhorrent to Medieval, Christian sensibilities and contradicted the accepted interpretation of Christian doctrine, which was decidedly otherworldly and exclusively faith based. In fact, pagan values, to the devout Christian of the Middle Ages, came directly from Satan himself.

You can see here another dimension of Aquinas' startling accomplishment. He convinced the Christian Church, after many centuries of tradition, to disassociate paganism from reason and to affirm reason—even though the form of rationality that Aquinas advocated came right from the heartland of paganism itself, from ancient Greece, and from its most distinguished representative, Aristotle. The church's acceptance of Aquinas' arguments was a tribute to the power of his synthesis. The church was moved to conclude that reason was *good* and that it could be a great ally to religion if it was employed with spiritual wisdom and holy guidance. Keep in mind that earlier versions of Scholasticism did not promote reason as a legitimate means to acquire knowledge and truth in itself. It was Aquinas who pushed the theological envelope—by promoting the elevated status of reason—and, as a result, he restored a significant degree of integrity to reason.

But there is a caveat. Although Aristotelian/Aquinian thinking became an integral part of Christianity and reintroduced rationality as a *good* for the church, rational thinking was still kept tightly packed within the narrow constraints of Christian doctrine. Reason was granted a degree of freedom unprecedented in the church, but this is not to say that the rational mind was truly liberated. It was not. It was still in the service of the church, and the clergy was very careful about which areas it permitted reason to probe. As a result, even Aquinas' Scholasticism was a stagnant philosophy and has been deservedly criticized for its lack of creative imagination and its obsession with logic, semantics, and insignificant theological issues. This was as far as the church permitted rational thinking to go. So, as revolutionary as Aquinas' work was, it was still only a beginning. Nonetheless, we can see the transformative upshot of Aquinas' accomplishment: he rehabilitated reason and unintentionally sent it on its way to fertilize European cultural soil. The result of this was the eventual birth of the secularism of the Italian Renaissance, the breakup of the church in the Reformation, the profound secularism of the Enlightenment, and the cultural liberalism of the modern world.

It is important to understand the close connections between paganism and secularism. This relationship can become confusing, because we normally define secular as "nonreligious" or "not grounded in supernaturalism," yet the pagan Greeks and Romans *did* believe in the gods, though they were also committed to rationality (much more so the Greeks than the Romans). So what is the connection between paganism and the secularism of the Greeks and Romans?

To the extent that the ancients conducted their daily lives largely without relying on the gods for guidance, had little understanding of what we would normally call faith, and held reason-based views and belief systems to be essential, we should conclude that, for all intents and purposes, the ancient Greeks and Romans were essentially secular. This is true even though the Greeks and Romans believed in gods, made frequent sacrifices to them, and even held religious holidays in their honor. Unlike the God of monotheism, the Greek and Roman gods possessed mortal-like traits and vices and were hardly divine examples of moral perfection. Neither were they all-knowing or all-powerful. The Greeks acknowledged the existence of the gods and made token gestures to them primarily because it was always good to have the gods on their side, especially during difficult times, such as wartime. Otherwise, the gods were of little interest. The same was true for the Romans. Consider the fact that polytheism neither possessed sacred scriptures nor included what one might consider a priesthood; that the pagans did not pray to the gods and lived without trying to live up to elevated spiritual principles invented by a perfect deity (or deities); that the pagans *affirmed* their lives and did not view themselves as being—by nature—morally defective and in need of divine forgiveness and redemption; that they were passionately absorbed in the things and pleasures of this world; and finally, that despite occasionally seeking advice from oracles, they (especially the Greeks) were committed to the pursuit of knowledge through reason. In light of all this, it is difficult to see the Greeks and Romans as religious by typical Christian standards.

The Italian Renaissance appeared to have emerged out of nowhere. At least this was a common bias held by those who failed to understand that the Middle Ages (actually, the High Middle Ages—1000 to 1400 CE) was not a stagnant, culturally barren lapse in Western history. Rather, it was a time when pagan values went "underground," so to speak, but remained active in working and nourishing the cultural soil from which the Italian Renaissance would spring—the greatest pagan flowering since ancient Greece. Nor were the Middle Ages devoid of significant achievement. We already spoke about the amazing Arabic Renaissance in Medieval Spain, during which truly great work was done in mathematics, science, philosophy, literature, and art. But in Europe by the late 14th century, the evidence of a new awakening was everywhere to be found.

The classical culture that the Spanish Arabs—the Moors—had transferred to Europe eventually took root in new universities, in which the medieval mind began cooking up the political, social, and economic recipes for what would come to define the modern age. Trade and commerce began in earnest after 1000 CE, which made cities like Venice rich and laid an early foundation for modern business life. The first document ever crafted in which a king agreed to a series of power concessions—the Magna Carta—was written in England in 1215, setting the stage for modern liberal theories of government. The art and architecture that developed during the High Middle Ages was profoundly innovative and influential. An example of this is the Gothic style of architecture in thirteenth-century France—the "architecture of light." Italian poet Dante Alighieri (1265–1321) wrote what is generally considered the greatest and most influential poem ever written. *The*

Divine Comedy (written not in Latin as was the tradition, but in Italian) brought together in one awe-inspiring work all the philosophical, religious, and scientific orientations of the Middle Ages. Through its ingenious prose, comprehensive scholarship, audacious insights into the human condition, and new passageways into literary art, Dante helped till the medieval soil from which modern humanism would grow. And, of course, geniuses like Aquinas and Bacon championed the cause of reason and science. In virtually every area of culture, the High Middle Ages was both creatively expressive as well as decisive for the emergence of the modern world.

6

Pagan Rebirth, Christian Humanism, and Philosophical Roots in Greece

6.1

When we think about the Italian Renaissance (circa 1420–1600), we typically focus on the achievements of geniuses like Michelangelo, Leonardo, Raphael, and Brunelleschi in art and architecture; Petrarch and Boccaccio in literature; Machiavelli in philosophy and politics; and Galileo in science. However, the rebirth was deeper than great achievements by geniuses. It was a victory for *pagan values*, the same values that galvanized the ancient Greeks and the Romans at their best. One could say that the Italian Renaissance represented one of the precious few moments in human history when raw human potential and cultural conditions inter-energized each other, maximizing the realization of individual human potential and cultural nurturing. The result was not simply the reemergence of the past in the sense of bringing to life what was best about the cultures of Greece and Rome, but was, more dramatically, the emergence of new and revolutionary ideas, programs, and strategies that both built on and, in many instances, transcended all that came before them.

The philosophy that came to life during the Italian Renaissance is often called "humanism," a worldview that places the human perspective—represented by a diverse mix of ancient pagan and Christian values—at the center of all thought. As time went on, the specifically religious elements in humanism began fading as increasingly secular strands came more into focus. From this perspective, one must see the Renaissance humanists as transitional figures that were suspended, however uncomfortably, between two worlds: the pagan and the Christian. The first humanists, in fact, were Christians who fell in love with the literature and languages of Greece and Rome and incorporated their pagan values into Christianity. The result was a *paganized* Christianity, one fraught with tensions and inconsistencies. That paganism and Christianity represent diametrically opposed worldviews and value systems was no obstacle to the early humanists, however. Their spirit was so optimistic, so filled with wonder, joy, and promise that it appears they chose not to see what seems obvious to the critical eye. But for some, the insurmountable problems with the pagan-Christian fellowship could not be ignored. We can see the Christian-pagan tension at work, for instance, in sculptor/painter/architect/poet Michelangelo, who was a devoted Christian, but who, nevertheless, was not able to harmonize his devout Christian beliefs with his artistic commitment to the pagan values that he expressed in his art. As a result, he was racked with religious uncertainty throughout his life.

Where Aquinas worked exclusively to reestablish the honor and power of rationality, the humanists were also absorbed in the *world of beauty*, the beauty that they found in literature, art, and nature, in the things of this world and in humankind. In other words, their newly discovered passion was for the aesthetic, with beauty as such. For the humanists, reason and beauty were the opposite sides of the same coin. Their project, then, was to project their newly discovered pagan vision into the Christian mindset.

One of the great legacies of Renaissance humanist tradition was that it argued for the power, integrity, and expression of individuality. In fact, one can say that the humanists reintroduced the notion of the *individual* into the modern world. Although the High Middle Ages was moving more toward modern ideas of selfhood, it was still mired in medieval traditions that did not recognize the autonomous individual. Promoting one's individuality, from a Christian perspective, was still thought to be sinful, prideful, and shameful. In the medieval feudal system, wherein overlords bought and sold serfs like lowly slaves, personal anonymity was inevitable.

The Renaissance humanists restored human dignity to the individual and endorsed a human-centered philosophy based on the following grounds: human beings are not inherently fallen, ignoble, sinful, and in need of salvation to merit great worth; rather—being the highest of God's creations—they are naturally beautiful, noble, good, and filled with godlike qualities such as reason, freedom, and creativity. What humans do, think, and create has great value and importance, because humans have divinity in them.

Italian philosopher Giovanni Pico della Mirandola (1463–1494) fully embodied the humanist perspective, and in his *Oration on the Dignity of Man* he laid out a sort of manifesto for Renaissance humanism. As a philosopher, Pico saw himself as a syncretist, that is, as a thinker who was committed to the massive undertaking of bringing together, in one unified whole, the truths of all philosophies and religions in the world. He believed that, in the end, all points of view, and all philosophical and religious systems, contain truth. Pico's commitment to assembling such an awesome edifice of knowledge—Christian, non-Christian, and pagan—is not just a testimony to his rare gifts as an intellect and scholar, but it also reflects Pico's own audacious belief that human beings *should* possess such ambitions. In fact, in Pico's view, all humans possess the divine powers of reason, creativity, and self-expression; and unlike the rest of God's creation, human beings are not fixed or determined to be one kind of thing, but rather are blessed with absolute freedom and the power of self-creation. The possibilities for human self-creation are, in fact, limitless.

It's not coincidental that such ideas sound remarkably modern. In the nineteenth century, existential thinkers like Kierkegaard and Nietzsche took the notions of individuality, freedom and creativity as foundation stones for their philosophies. The idea of creative self-expression was particularly dear to Nietzsche, who argued that the belief in God has lost all credibility, and, as a result, the individual has no choice but to rely on his own creative powers to find meaning and purpose for his life. Nietzsche had a particular fondness for artistic and philosophical creativity and fervently endorsed a life committed to such ideals. The similarity between Pico's religious humanism and Nietzsche's atheistic views is not simply ironic; it illuminates the paradox that has persisted in religious philosophy ever since Aquinas' marriage of reason and faith in the thirteenth century and the subsequent birth of Renaissance humanism in the fourteenth century. The source of this tension is clear enough: a worldview that admonishes living only for the afterlife, while encouraging the joyful acceptance and engagement of the values of this one, is impossible to realize.

In other words, no amount of enthusiasm for Christian humanism can erase the radical differences between a life committed to fundamental Christian principles of faith, on the one hand, and one devoted to the power and prestige of reason, worldly affirmation, and creative self-expression, on the other. Not, at least, without distorting either perspective beyond recognition. Pico, for instance, considered himself a devout Christian, and yet he held and promoted beliefs—such as the inherent goodness, beauty, and dignity of humankind—that ran counter to typical Christian principles. After all, if humankind is, *by nature*, good and distinguished by divine gifts like reason and creativity, what did the "Fall" in Genesis really mean? And why were Christ's life, death, and resurrection necessary? Isn't each individual, according to standard Christian dogma, inherently sinful and in desperate need for salvation? And isn't this world the domain of the devil, filled with disgusting temptations (sins of the flesh), and unworthy of our interest? And isn't the love of beauty, especially when associated with the things of the world, a sign of spiritual depravity? And doesn't worldly ambition of any kind take the focus away from the only real good: the transcendent reality of God? And, finally, isn't the love of self among the worst—if not *the* worst—of all sins?

These are familiar Christian beliefs that find significant biblical support, and yet they are not what Pico had in mind when he conceived of uniting Christianity with all other philosophies and religions to make one, truth-filled whole. What Pico really had in mind was an existential philosophy fully devoted to pagan values together with a reconstructed Christianity—a version of Christianity that didn't resemble in the least what one finds in the New Testament.

Be that as it may, the spirit that fueled Pico's enthusiasm for a transformed humanity seized control of an entire culture and sent an astonishing number of remarkable individuals into fits of creative frenzy, during which they produced works of amazing genius in all areas of culture. "Individuals" is the operative word. The Italian Renaissance is often viewed as a time when the modern "individual" was born, when the creative genius—powerful, charismatic, willful, and possessing boundless talent and ambition—began to dominate art, literature, politics, science, and philosophy. Actually, the emergence of modern individuality, like all aspects of the Italian Renaissance, began in the late Middle Ages. The Christianity of the early Middle Ages was passionately anti-individual. It was considered sinful to draw attention to oneself, because the sole purpose in this life was to glorify God, not oneself, nor the fruits of one's labors. Artists, for example, didn't sign their paintings, because it would draw attention to them and away from God.

Laying the foundation for Christian life in faith was an ingenious way for the early church to ensure that true believers remained steadfast in their personal devotion, while still suppressing their sense of individuality (after all, individuality typically breeds resistance). This is because faith, as a way of supporting one's religious life, is essentially a passive state of mind, an unconditional acceptance of what is being asked. The essence of faith is to believe that something to be true, not only without having evidence, but also without thinking about it in an honest and critical way. For the faithful, God does all the thinking; it's what God thinks that matters, not what I think. It's *"thy* will be done," as the prayer goes.

Thinking for oneself is a sort of spiritual disruption, a form of rebellion against the will of God. The true believer must abide passively, patiently, and thoughtlessly *in faith*. The true believer waits. Patience is a great virtue in traditional Christianity. Faith works against a sense of individuality, because it inclines the devout to focus only on God whom the Christian believes will think and judge, and even provide guidance, on his or her behalf.

Reasoning, by strong contrast, is self-assertive, aggressive, and proactive; it highlights the individual who is doing the reasoning as the *source* of what is being thought. Reasoning is naturally self-promoting. It is individuality at its most extreme.

But with the reassertion of reason by Aquinas and others as a viable tool for both secular and religious uses, it became impossible for the church to dismiss individuality as an illegitimate existential category and living reality. After all, one reasons, analyzes, and comes to logical conclusions. These are distinctly individual acts that are strongly self-referential. The thinker reasons in his mind, and this internal activity makes it very difficult for even the staunchest anti-individualist to argue for the anonymity of the reasoning individual. By comparison, it was much easier for the church to suppress the individuality of, say, a painter, because he works *externally* on canvas, wall, or ceiling, and the viewer's interest is naturally directed to the work of art and not to the painter himself.

During the High Middle Ages, the Roman Catholic Church endorsed rational thinking as a viable tool for expressing and understanding the basic truths of Christianity, but it unintentionally unleashed a cultural force over which it had little control. The church gambled that it could exploit reason for its own doctrinal justifications—and lost. What began as a highly restrained concession to the rational side of paganism resulted in the gradual birthing of individualism over the course of the twelfth, thirteenth, and fourteenth centuries—that, in turn, exploded into the radical individualism of the Italian Renaissance, the breakup of the church in the Reformation, and finally the Age of Reason—the Enlightenment. But it was in the Italian Renaissance that paganism and Christianity met, face to face, in their greatest, most profound battle. The fallout from this confrontation was to decide no less than the future of Christianity and Western civilization itself.

It is a mistake to see the emergence of the Italian Renaissance simply as the direct result of religious and philosophical influences in the culture of the Middle Ages without considering other social, political, and economic factors. The formation of Europe's nation states, for example, and the rapidly developing world of commerce in places like northern Italy were integral to the dynamically changing culture of the late Middle Ages and also helped in the rebirth of pagan values.

The invention of the printing press in 1450 by the German Johannes Gutenberg had a profound effect on Western culture. Before the printing press, books numbered in the thousands; only a few years after the printing press's invention, books quickly numbered in the millions. Now the Bible, the texts of the ancient Greeks and Romans, and the works of the Renaissance humanists could be read by millions of Europeans. And, of course, the availability of reading materials fostered the creation of educational institutions, such as universities, to meet the demand for greater literacy and knowledge.

"New worlds" were also discovered thanks to the courage and greed of explorers like Columbus. European cultural horizons underwent a dramatic broadening as the lure of new and exciting civilizations heightened the European appetite for all things foreign.

At bottom, however, was the particular kind of culture that finally began emerging in the Renaissance. It was galvanized by pagan ideals, ideals that gave meaning and purpose to the new countries of Europe and provided good reasons to believe that rich and productive economies; the acquisition of knowledge; and the adventure into the unknown were each absolute goods for humanity. But what was it about this new humanist philosophy that was so captivating and inspirational? If the renewed respect for, and belief in, reason was the initial catalyst for the humanism of the Renaissance, what was it about the rehabilitated status of reason that was so transforming? The answer lies in the very nature of thinking itself.

The rational mind is *future* orientated, forever renewing and reshuffling itself; it has many goals but never a final one; it is constantly deconstructing and reconstructing itself in an attempt to answer an infinite number of questions, clarify issues, resolve conflicts, find solutions, adapt to new situations, uncover meaning, make distinctions, and discover new ways of thinking. The rational mind is eternally optimistic because it is forever open ended; it believes in itself with an undying passion. Thinking always produces *more* thinking, and so, at least in principle, thinking is always on the road of progress. Herein lies the core of humanistic spirituality.

Behind all the great works of the Renaissance and driving all political, social, and economic engines, was the optimism of reason transformed into a tireless passion for beauty and artistic perfection, philosophical and scientific certainty, economic prosperity and full-throttled— individual—self-realization. Renaissance humanism, in effect, was a *transfigured paganism*, guided by the tireless spirit of reason, with the creative imagination of the individual serving as the primary wellspring of inspiration. The incredible outpouring of creative genius during the Renaissance was the ultimate testimony to this transfigured paganism.

Who, then, was the modern individual of the Renaissance? He was the one who asked himself: "Why am I here on Earth?" and answered: "To realize and cultivate my own natural talents to the highest degree possible; to discover and create beauty in the world; to think for myself; to forge a way through this life that is truly my own; and to live life with gusto." It was during the Italian Renaissance that paganism began to free itself from the shackles of religion, and genuine secular thought finally began to see the light of day.

We noted earlier that the Italian Renaissance did not spring out of a cultural vacuum but was the natural progression of a number of cultural orientations in the Middle Ages. We talked about the importance of Aristotle's revised philosophy being absorbed into the medieval church thanks to Aquinas and others and the general impact that pagan ideas began to have on the intellectual life of the Middle Ages. We also mentioned the social, political, and economic factors that seeded the cultural soil of the fourteenth century. This helped set the stage for the breakthrough in humanism that finally occurred in the early fourteenth century. Perhaps the real spark that ignited the vast wildfire that was to become the Renaissance was the discovery of original manuscripts from ancient Greece and Rome. It's clear that the pagan literary traditions provided the spiritual food for the voracious humanistic hunger that was growing as the High Middle Ages drew to a close. One person in particular had an insatiable appetite for pagan cultures, and through his poetic brilliance and scholarly accomplishments, he inaugurated the humanism movement that we call the Italian Renaissance. This person was Italian poet and scholar Francesco Petrarch (1304–1374).

Petrarch holds many honors: he was the greatest scholar of his age; the founder of modern humanism; the initiator of a period of search for and discovery of pagan books; the first to foster serious interest in exploring ancient works of art; the first modern poet; the inventor of the sonnet; and the inventor of the language of the modern poetry of Europe. He was also the originator and master of elegant Italian poetry. Petrarch devoted himself to collecting ancient books and found letters of the Roman philosopher and orator Cicero in 1345 and even organized a library of two hundred volumes of various manuscripts. As a scholar, he criticized Scholasticism and had a particular fondness for Plato, which Petrarch tried to integrate with Christianity. Although he wrote an immense amount of scholarship in Latin, he was most famous for his heartfelt love poetry; this he wrote in Italian to Laura, a girl he apparently met but with whom he never had a relationship—and it's also possible that Laura was a fictional character.

Giovanni Boccaccio (1313–1375) was a friend and disciple of Petrarch and shared his passion for all things pagan. Many consider Boccaccio the real father of Italian prose. He was the first Italian in seven centuries to read classical Greek, and he wrote scholarly works in Latin. He is duly honored for raising modern languages to the high level of the ancient Greek and Latin. Following in Petrarch's footsteps, he also carried out a revival in learning. He is most famous for his masterpiece in prose, *The Decameron,* which consists of one hundred tales, told by ten people (seven ladies and three gentlemen) over the course of ten days—hence the title *Decameron,* which literally means "ten days" in Greek. The ten people are sequestered in a villa outside of Naples to escape the plague during the Middle Ages. Each person takes turns telling stories to inform and entertain the others. Boccaccio's work is ripe in pagan sensibilities; beauty, pleasure, and fun often color the stories. The author explored the feelings, passions, and vices of all classes from the most depraved to the noblest; challenged religious hypocrisy and narrow-minded moralizing; and focused the reader's attention on the virtues of effective action and having a good character. Boccaccio also sounded the great secular theme that human beings must accept the natural limitations of existence and live heroically without seeking divine assistance.

The net result of both Petrarch and Boccaccio's teachings and writings was a veritable call to action for a culture already poised for radical self-transformation. It's not surprising that Renaissance humanism quickly became an awesome cultural force all over Europe. Soon, other humanists joined in to advance the humanist cause— including the Dutchmen Desiderius Erasmus (1466–1538) and Rudolphus Agricola (1413–1485); the Englishman Sir Thomas More (1478–1535); and more skeptical thinkers like French essayist Michel de Montaigne (1533–1592) and the Italian political philosopher Niccolo Machiavelli (1469–1527).

Erasmus' devotion to classical culture motivated him to attack the stupidities and injustices of the church, particularly its antiquated Scholastic tradition. His rational critiques of the church were to have an enormous impact on Martin Luther and, consequently, contributed to the breakup of the church in the Reformation and ultimately to the formation of modern Europe. He was so in love with the ancient pagan literature that he encouraged his students to engage literary topics in a rigorously rational terms and he also wanted his students to study secular topics such as archeology and astronomy.

Machiavelli blazed a new trail by exposing what he viewed to be the hard facts about the nature of political power—how it is gained and maintained through clever, deceptive, and, often, amoral leadership. He argued that politics, and even the morality of leaders, needs to be *utilitarian,* because what is good in leadership is what works to retain political control and stability. According to him, the histories of states and civilizations are likewise dictated by the same basic rules and principles of political leadership. Machiavelli's naturalistic cause and effect analyses and the prescriptions in his masterpiece *The Prince* represented the first authentic example of secular/scientific thinking applied to politics. Unlike all other thinkers before him, he did not appeal to religion or utopian/philosophical ideals in his blunt, factual descriptions of politics and history. One could argue that the modern scientific spirit was fully manifested in the person of Machiavelli and that, along with his fellow countrymen Leonardo da Vinci and Galileo, he carried the torch for science into the modern world.

Finally, Frenchman Michel de Montaigne was a humanistic skeptic who directed his thinking inward to "reflect" on himself and the world. In practicing this quasi-Cartesian technique of inquisitive self-reflection, he invented the modern literary essay. In his *Essays* (*essai* is French for "attempt"), he had a try at self-discovery. Why only a try? Because he questioned the capacity of the rational mind to arrive at true knowledge. His famous quip, "What do I know?" sums up very well his skeptical view of the purely rational pursuit of knowledge. Instead, he proposed the essay as a sort of unstructured stream-of-consciousness thought process in which one talks freely and spontaneously about one's thoughts, feelings, and observations on particular topics. Montaigne wrote many essays on a vast array of subjects, from the purpose of a thumb, to how to educate children, to the nature of cannibalism. Although Montaigne's critiques questioned the value and capability of pure, rational thinking, they represented a remarkable advance for secular thought, because they demonstrated the ability of reason to take itself to task—to question itself—which is the hallmark of authentic scientific thinking. Montaigne's style of essaying had a profound influence on such Western philosophers as Descartes and Nietzsche and such literary figures as Shakespeare.

6.2

The Reformation in the sixteenth century was much more than a religious rebellion within and against the Roman Catholic Church. It was the logical consequence of a secular cultural movement that began to question authority and think for itself. The idea that secular, cultural currents incited the Reformation may sound puzzling, even though the Reformation was aimed at recovering an earlier, more fundamental version of Christianity. On the surface, in fact, it appeared simply to be a radical religious uprising sustained by those Christians who pointed an accusatory finger at the corrupt church and argued that it had become too "worldly." But it was more fundamentally the newly awakened craving to think for oneself as applied to Christianity. By becoming more personal, in other words, Christianity became more *individual* with the Reformation. The pope and the saints were no longer the indispensable links to spiritual truth. The reformed Christian could read the word of God and allow God to speak directly to him.

It didn't help the Catholic cause that the church flaunted clearly absurd practices, such as "selling indulgences" to Christians, which meant that for a financial contribution to the church, a believer could buy his or her way into the good graces of God and be forgiven for sins. With a large enough contribution, the believer could wipe away *all* sins—past, present, and future—to win salvation once and for all. With new translations of the Old and New Testaments in the original Hebrew and Greek, it became clear to biblical scholars that selling indulgences, and other core Catholic teachings and traditions stood in scriptural and logical contradiction to the Bible. The emergence of a new brand of humanist scholars was an important sign of the times and soon turned the Christian world on its head, and led directly and indirectly to a seemingly endless shedding of blood, all in the name of various interpretations of the Bible.

The notorious instigator of the Reformation, Martin Luther (1483–1546), appeared to be a throwback to an earlier time in the history of the church, to the fourth century, when the reigning authority was Saint Augustine. Saint Augustine promoted the doctrine that humanity is irreparably "fallen"—that, because of the sins Adam and Eve committed in the Garden of Eden, human beings are condemned to a life of sin and separation from God. Most importantly, the doctrine holds that there is absolutely nothing we can do on our own to improve our depraved spiritual condition. Our only hope is through God, who—by his loving gift of "Grace"—sent himself down to Earth in the person of Jesus Christ to live like a human (but without sin), to suffer, die for our sins, and finally to be resurrected to "new life." And therein, Christianity says, lies humanity's *only* chance for salvation.

Salvation will be awarded to those who believe, by simple faith, in the gift of Christ's life, death, and resurrection for the sins of the human race. This is the "Gospel of Jesus Christ." It is only through this personal surrender to God's will—in other words, the acceptance of his Gospel—that a person can become pure in God's eyes, achieve spiritual union with him, and live forever with him in "heaven" after death. This particular (medieval) installment of Christianity is what Luther was arguing for, and it's clearly a far cry from Pico's version of humanist Christianity. Further, it certainly was not the official view held by Catholic Church during the Renaissance.

It was with the nature of sin and salvation that Luther began stirring the pot of religious discontent. The fact that the church had given itself over so conspicuously to corrupt practices like selling indulgences helped to make Luther's case even more compelling. The Christian humanists did Martin Luther a great service by learning to read the Gospels in the original Hebrew and Greek, translating them into native tongues, and exposing what appeared to be irreconcilable contradictions between Catholic tradition and the "expressed word of God" in the Bible. The Catholic emphasis on "good works," for example, as foundational to salvation, seemed to Luther and his followers a total affront to God's recipe for salvation, and was, as far as the protesters were concerned, spiritually misguided and decadent.

Luther also argued that the church obscured the fundamental relationship between God and his believers. In keeping with the salvation story as presented in the Gospels, what is required of the true believer is to have a personal relationship with God through Christ and not one mediated by the pope, the Virgin Mary, the saints, or priests. The Christian must fall back on his or her own conscience and communicate *directly* to God through prayer. He or she must ask for forgiveness, and believe without reservation in God's plan for salvation through Christ.

Initially, Luther viewed himself as a devout Catholic monk who simply wanted to live according to the Gospels. When he was severely rebuffed and chastised by the church for arguing strongly for his ideas, Luther responded with a vengeance by committing himself heart and soul to bringing about a radical reform in Christianity. Yet, even as a reformer, his aim remained what it always had been: the restoration of what he considered to be true Christianity, one based on the simple message of the Gospels. The church's traditions of selling indulgences and salvation based on good works were to him clear signs that the church had been for some time on the path of secularism. It became obvious to him that the Catholic clergy, including the pope, was more concerned with political control and power than with tending to the business of salvation and following rigorously the word of God.

Luther was an advanced student of theology and law, and he also studied pagan thinkers such as the Romans Cicero and Virgil. When he finally abandoned his humanist leanings and training and devoted himself exclusively to Christianity, he could not very well leave behind what he gained intellectually from his humanist studies. In fact, one could say that his attacks on what he viewed to be the secularism of the church were, in themselves, secular themselves; they were based on logical analysis and criticism of the various inconsistencies and contradictions of the Catholic dogma in relation to the Bible. Luther inaugurated the beginning of biblical criticism that would have a sorry history in Christianity and result in the horrors of war, political and social chaos, and the destruction of many lives, all in the name of the same God. Ultimately, Luther's secular attack on the irrational practices of Catholicism resulted in the spiritual evisceration of Christianity.

Luther's revolution soon spread throughout Germany and ultimately took on monumental proportions as all of Europe was drawn into various religious conflicts. Wars that lasted many years broke out within and between nations. One was the Thirty Years' War (1618–1648), which was in part the result of religious conflict. It engulfed all of Europe and wrought immense destruction.

From the vantage point of modern times, it is perhaps more accurate to say that there were a series of reformations, not simply one involving a particular dissenting, religious persuasion. Other Reformation leaders, such as the Frenchman John Calvin (1509–1564) in Geneva and the Swiss Ulrich Zwingli (1484–1531), jumped on the Reformation bandwagon in attacking the Catholic Church for many of the same reasons that Luther did, although they had their own views on what they thought was "the truth" about Christianity. Calvin, most famously, promoted the doctrine of "predestination," which says that God knows, in advance, who will and who will not be "saved," and that there is at any given time on Earth a small group of the "elect" who are "predetermined" to go to heaven, while the vast majority are literally hell-bound. Zwingli's concern was to remain as observant of the Bible as possible, and he worked to simplify Christian services, eliminate all icons and statuary, and promote the translation of the Bible into native languages.

A horrific result of the Reformation schisms was Christians spilling the blood of other Christians over conflicting biblical interpretations. Wiping out vast portions of European populations in the name of the God of love, peace, and compassion became a way of life during the time of the reformations.

Equally ironic was that Luther's return to aspects of medieval Christianity was actually a secular gesture, to the extent that sixteenth-century Protestantism placed the ultimate weight of salvation squarely on shoulders of the *individual*. The individual's thoughts, his choices and commitments, his interpretations of the Bible were to be the foundation of his Christian life. The pope and priests, in other words, no longer held a monopoly on the meaning of scripture, which was, instead, to be found and interpreted by individual effort. This is not to say that the individual did not have guidance. Christ (and by extension—the "Holy Spirit," which is *one* with God and Christ) was now the sole guide for all things spiritual. The intimate relationship between the solitary person and God (through Christ) was to be the only bond that assured a life of true spirituality for Luther's new brand of Christianity—"Protestantism." In this view, the Protestant Church functioned as a sort of "support system" for individuals, offering inspiration and solace to Christians as they strived to help to keep the essential Christian truths, priorities, and principles clearly in mind.

But for a Christian to assume personal responsibility for his spiritual life required new skills and aptitudes that Christians during the Middle Ages did not possess: reading, writing, and at least a rudimentary understanding of logical reasoning and argument. Since the rise of Scholasticism during the Middle Ages, the church worked earnestly to incorporate Greek rationality into Christianity, and Catholic theologians became accomplished in reading, writing, and semantics. They also used Aristotelian logic as an important religious tool. On the other hand, the general population remained illiterate and, as a result, stayed dependent on the church for guidance in all spiritual matters. That the Catholic Mass was conducted in Latin only increased the dependency of the illiterate masses on the holy pronouncements of the pope (who, according to Catholic dogma, is considered infallible) and his ordained clergy.

But now the Protestant population could no longer afford to remain illiterate; too much was riding on their shoulders—namely, the whole of their religious life. With the Bible now being presented in the native languages of Europe, Protestants had the responsibility to learn to read their Bible and interpret its meaning. And, of course, learning how to read and think logically meant that education became a necessary component of a good Christian life. As a result, courses in reading, writing, religion, and even mathematics began to be offered to the growing "middle class" of sixteenth-century, Protestant Europe. As we can see, secularism was making great advances.

The European reawakening to its pagan past that began in the Late Middle Ages and culminated in the Italian Renaissance also fueled the Reformation. Despite the return to a more literal and austere interpretation of Christianity, the Reformation embraced paganism in much the same way that the Scholastics had done in previous centuries: selectively and with great care not to expose its pagan roots. Once again, faith and reason had to try to get along in this mismatch of a relationship, but as we saw with the Italian humanist Pico, a great deal of enthusiasm and clever twisting of logic can go a long way in quelling the anxieties and uncertainties of the religious mind. Unfortunately, the result was far from peaceful.

Aside from the bitter wars and loss of life because of religious disputes, Christianity itself lost its inner cohesion and unity with the Reformation and deteriorated into antagonistic factions, all claiming to possess the Christian truth. Lutheranism, Calvinism, Zwinglism, Anglicanism, and the countless spin-offs, from Anabaptists to the Mennonites, all claimed to know the truth, although the disagreements were deep and irreconcilable. The major problem for Reformation Christianity (to this day) is that the various factions could not *all* possibly be right. One of the fundamental principles of Christianity is that there is only one truth (To quote Jesus, "I am The Way, The Truth, and the Life") and not *many*. At least with Catholicism—despite its doctrinal inconsistencies and absurdities—there was only one truth for *all* Christians: the truth as the pope saw it. As unsatisfying as this position was to reformers, it was more consistent with the "one truth" message of the Gospels.

Thinking critically for oneself is not an inherently peaceful activity. In fact, it is conflict-orientated. Critical thinking wrestles with ideas and disruptive feelings; it strives for resolution but thrives on disagreement, challenge, and confrontation; it craves the heat of dialectic battle; it's inherently critical and judgmental, because, in order to be successful, it must always be on guard for logical fallacies, contradictions, inconsistencies, mistaken reasoning, and invalid arguments—not to mention thoughtlessly and unconsciously held assumptions that don't support the ideas in question. Thinking critically is successful when it neutralizes the bad ideas it runs into on its path to a deeper, more comprehensive understanding. It's fruitful when it's being driven forward by the necessity of remaining logical and consistent with itself and reality, and when it is fueled by the principles of honesty and intellectual integrity at all costs, even at the cost of personal loss and disgrace. Where critical thinking fails at these requirements is where understanding ceases—that is, where thinking becomes dogmatic and frequently irrational.

The Reformation leaders had no idea of the trouble that they were creating for Christianity when they engineered the break with the Catholic Church. By encouraging Christians to read and interpret the Bible for themselves, and to resist the pronounced "truth" as presented by the Roman Catholic Church, the reformers set Christianity on the road to critical thinking, a road that would lead to one religious catastrophe after another, to cultural and political chaos, and ultimately to a dramatic loss of the credibility of Christianity as a spiritual orientation, a repository of truth, or even as a viable institution. We could easily argue that the increasing secularism that we see dominating most of modern Europe is, at least in part, the logical consequence of Luther's break with the Catholic church.

How did critical thinking lead to this disaster for Christianity? In the last paragraph, I said that the Reformation set Christianity "on the road to critical thinking." This idea means that Roman Catholicism did not require analytical thinking in order to be a true believer; it also suggests that the Reformation movements, although they were movements toward critical thinking, were still, largely, characterized by non-thinking. Why is this so?

Critical thinking is not a freely given gift of the intellect; instead, it arises out of the mental and emotional confusion and conflict that begins first in youth—as the immature mind struggles to come to terms with, and make logical sense out of, everyday experience— and continues throughout an entire life. Critical thinking, in other words, is an *emergent* process. To think is to be committed to trying to understand the truth of what is being considered. It is for this reason that rigorously logical thinking is a retreat from the irrational and from the narrow-mindedness of dogma.

Critical thinking is also open to change if it falls out of logical harmony and balance; it's rooted in the *intention* of the thinking person. Does the thinking person really desire to know the truth? Or are there other agendas at play, such as using the appearance of thinking to justify irrational positions (i.e., Nazi racism, or rationalizing to protect one's fragile ego)? If the answer is the former, then thinking is possible.

At the same time, even the most committed thinking is never pure, never without *un-thought* or irrational components, because thinking always suffers from its own limitations and from the *unconscious* forces that influence it. And, of course, thinking may be misguided and simply wrong because of mistaken judgments or poor reasoning. This is true for individuals as well as for traditions and even cultures.

As far as the thinking in Catholic and Reformation Christianity were concerned, it was an anxious mix of thinking and unthinking. The

Catholics during the Middle Ages were concerned were encouraged not to think for themselves, but rather to accept, without questioning (without thinking), the living word of God as interpreted by his divine representative, the pope.

Reformation Christianity, by contrast, focused on the personal relationship between the believer and God, without intermediary interpreters, and, as a result, it put the burden of interpretation squarely on the shoulders of the individual believer (although with guidance and support from appointed ministers and preachers). Although the transition to personal responsibility for arriving at Christian meaning and truth might appear to qualify as critical thinking, it was actually only a gesture in the right direction.

The problem for the Christian believer who had been liberated from the dogma of Catholicism was that analytical thinking was not possible without throwing into question the very foundational ideas of Christianity itself, which had always been accepted on faith to be true. Ironically, the thinking process that began within Christianity (first in Protestantism and then in Catholicism) was what ultimately weakened Christianity and made it vulnerable to attack externally from philosophers and scientists and led to its collapse as a legitimate spiritual institution and belief system. The various conflicting factions that characterized reformed Christianity represented the first phase of its decline.

With the emergence of Protestantism, the ideas of Jesus Christ became the subject of mutually conflicting interpretations. Something had to give. Critical thinking demanded it. Christianity either had to return to the universal, one truth—based Christianity of Roman Catholicism or it had to be selectively broken down and reconstructed, and made more "reasonable."

The breaking up of Catholic Christianity into conflicting Protestant denominations was a natural consequence of giving believers the freedom of biblical interpretation. This is not to say that Protestant Christians became "thinkers"—far from it. In fact, some factions fell even more deeply into superstition and irrationalism. To illustrate, many early Protestants believed that demons populated the world, and many women accused of being witches were tortured and put to death. Nonetheless, the Protestant flights into excessive irrationalism were a natural consequence of the religious imagination discharging itself unchecked once the shackles of Catholic intellectual oppression were loosened. Logically coherent thinking always passes through irrational phases before it becomes increasingly rational.

The mutually antagonistic Protestant denominations, irrational religious beliefs, outrageous religious practices, religious wars, and the religion-inspired social and political chaos in and between nations— these were the birth pangs of modern, secular consciousness. But within the context of the various Christian belief systems (Catholic and Protestant alike), this birthing was doomed from the start. The reason for this failure is clear: *genuine critical thinking within the Gospel-based Christian mindset is never possible.* Once a Christian arrives at legitimate thinking, faith—thoughtless devotion to a supernatural reality such as God and the abandonment of one's self-centered desires and passions— is neutralized. In effect, he or she is no longer a Christian, proclamations to the contrary notwithstanding. It is not uncommon, in fact, for one to move back and forth between both Christian and secular mindsets (which is, in itself, evidence that one is not a Christian). For instance, the Italian scientist Galileo (1564–1642) is often credited with being the first modern scientist because of his devotion to scientific theory, mathematical descriptions of observed phenomena, and repeatable, meticulously performed, empirical experimentation. He did all this without appeal to God, the Bible, or religious authority, despite the fact that he was also a devout Catholic. In reality, he thoughtlessly suspended his Catholicism when he performed his science and typically returned to it when he was through.

Galileo was able to balance these two worlds as long as they appeared to have nothing to do with each other; in fact, this was his stated position. But he got into trouble when religious authorities perceived that his science had religious implications—for example, when Galileo argued, and offered some evidence for, the Copernican view that the sun, and not the earth, was the center of the solar system, a view that was inconsistent with scripture. In this case, the religious authorities were correct to challenge the scientist, especially because he could not provide conclusive proof that Copernicus' theory was right. The real problem, however, was that Galileo, the *thinking* scientist, stepped on the toes of Galileo, the non-thinking Christian. Conflicts of this type are typical not only with religious people, but also within cultures and traditions. One could say that to the degree that Christianity began to think, it left behind its religious underpinnings by the same measure. In this sense, Christianity, by trying to think authentically, was betraying its religious tradition. As far as Galileo was concerned, it is surely questionable whether he really was a true believer to begin with, despite his comments to the contrary. He was simply too secular in his sensibilities and orientations, and his science—a truly godless exercise in reason—seems to have been the real object of his passions.

The destructive assault on Christianity by critical thinking (even if it was less than fully genuine)—leveled primarily by Christian scholars and humanists—had profound consequences. Within the Protestant tradition itself, the Bible became the object of scholarly analysis and criticism. And, as it turned out, biblical criticism eviscerated the Bible's soul and reduced it to just another fatally flawed document from the standpoint of philosophical and moral consistency, authentic authorship, and historical accuracy. From this view, reformed Christianity committed a sort of suicide—and Catholicism didn't fare any better. The old idea that Catholicism possessed the truth of Christianity slowly began losing credibility and eventually was seen as a self-serving myth. At minimum, the philosophical ravaging of Christianity by rational analysis made more consistent and reasonable worldviews, such Darwinian evolution, that much more believable.

Luther and others attacked Catholicism because the church was thought to have betrayed its original commitment to true Christianity by becoming progressively more secular, more "worldly." In this context, the allegations of worldliness did not mean that the church had started promoting pagan virtues, like thinking or individualism, among believers. Rather, it meant that the church had become increasingly more oriented toward what Luther viewed to be the non-spiritual values of financial interests, political power, and the pursuit of earthly pleasures.

Ironically, Protestantism initiated a form of secularization of Christianity that did cultivate greater individualism, and some movements toward genuine thinking—all, of course, within a Christian framework. Interestingly, these Protestant principles and activities were, at their root, concessions to the Italian Renaissance's humanist tradition of placing each human being as the central interpreting agent. As such, the humanist strand that insinuated itself into Protestant values further accelerated Christianity's decline as a believable worldview.

The Protestant movement toward thinking was aimed at taking Christianity to a higher level of spirituality, but it had the ultimate result of undermining and weakening both Catholicism and Protestantism. The only beneficiary was secularism, which gained greatly in strength and prestige.

6.3

Europe's rediscovery of its pagan roots during the Renaissance had set the stage for its transformation. This radical change took many forms. The assault of Reformation Christianity on Roman Catholicism, which, as we've seen, made additional room for individualism and thinking to flourish, was just one example of this change. The general religious, social, and political upheaval that followed was cataclysmic. However, there was another side to the emergence of secular thinking during the Renaissance that was to prove equally transformative.

Human beings are a curious species. Their curiosity is rooted in their natural ignorance. This is a serious deficit for a species whose very survival depends on *knowing* how to survive. But beyond gaining what I call "survival-knowledge," humans also want to know *why* survival is important. And this is why questions of "meaning" and the pursuit of metaphysical truth have concerned the human race from the start. For most of human history, people sought meaning and metaphysical truth in religion and myth. This is true even though the importance of religion and myth to the world's cultures has fluctuated dramatically throughout human history. In some cases, their influence has been dominant, as in the early European Middle Ages, and in other cases, their relevance was only peripheral, as in the case of the European Enlightenment in the eighteenth century. But other cultural activities born out of humanity's burning curiosity to know were of an entirely different nature than religion and myth: philosophy and science.

The meaning of philosophy has always been in flux over the course of Western history. The word's origin is Greek and means "love of wisdom," but this idea does not help us much in capturing the essence of what philosophy is, for "wisdom" is also an elusive idea and has had different meanings in different traditions and cultures. The same can be said about the meaning of "love." Nonetheless, we can make some unambiguous observations about the nature and definition of philosophy.

On the one hand, philosophy is a "subject matter"—that is, one can study philosophical topics and learn what the "Great Philosophers" thought about them. And if you're taking a class in philosophy, you will undoubtedly be expected to offer your own personal views about philosophical issues and even challenge the positions of the great philosophers. What did Plato say about the meaning of "good"? What proof is there that God exists? How do we distinguish between subjective and objective reality? How do we know for sure that we know something? Is democracy the best form of government in light of human nature? What is the essence of human nature? Why is something beautiful? Can there be justice in an unjust world? What is evil? What is free will? These are the sorts of questions that defined philosophy for over 2,400 years. Today, by contrast, philosophy—actually academic philosophy—has, in many ways, turned away from traditional philosophical categories such as metaphysics (the study of reality), ethics (the study of moral values), aesthetics (the study of beauty and art), and epistemology (the study of knowledge), and is concerned with the study of *language*, focusing largely on the structure, meaning, and function of language in human cultures. But in both the traditional and modern versions, philosophy, as subject matter, can be like studying any other subject, such as history or chemistry, where information needs to be learned, and possibly recited, and *creatively* expounded on.

On the other hand, besides being a subject for study, philosophy also has a human dimension—an aspect of human nature that is evidenced by the simple fact that humans are naturally ignorant creatures who, nevertheless, require knowledge and meaning to live. Philosophy in this sense is the need, desire, and passion to know; it is, in one regard, the "philosophical instinct" manifested in asking questions. But philosophy is not simply asking questions: *it is the very source from which these questions arise in the first place*. This source, this openness to the infinite mysteries of life and the passion to understand them, is the philosophical dimension. It is from this *lived sense* of "I don't know, but I need to know" that the human dimension comes to the fore and sets the intellectual stage for asking genuine philosophical questions. But there is a caveat.

The answers that one seeks must be *logical* ones to qualify as genuinely philosophical—that is, they must be rational responses to the questions being asked. This is why religious answers to philosophical questions are not philosophical responses. Religious answers have their alleged validity in revelation or faith (faith in the infallibility of the Bible, for instance) and not in rational justification or logical consistency. "Because it says so in the Bible" or "Because that's the way God wanted it" do not qualify as philosophical answers, because logic is not a standard by which one accepts or rejects answers of this sort.

In the final analysis, philosophy suffers because it could never achieve what it aims for: full and exhaustive knowledge of all reality. This is the natural consequence of an unalterable truth of human reality: the human mind is finite, and—under all circumstances—it can only obtain partial knowledge and understanding, regardless of how much knowledge and understanding it has accumulated or will ever accumulate. Nonetheless, the allure of possibly attaining a deeper and more comprehensive grasp of reality is the most thrilling aspect of pursuing philosophy. And the same is true for philosophy's closest relative—its child, science.

It is often said that modern culture is "scientific." When one considers that science employs secular reasoning to try to uncover the truths of the universe, it's clear that science and philosophy have a great deal in common. So why would we not be inclined to say that modern culture is also "philosophical"? In fact, the first philosophers in Western history—the ancient Greek Pre-Socratics (who lived mostly between about 621–370 BCE, before Socrates)—were scientifically minded and did practice what has often been called "natural philosophy."

6.4

The mathematician Thales (624–546 BCE) argued that everything derives from "water," and he introduced into Western culture the idea of "deductive reasoning" (arguing in such a way that one's conclusion follows logically from basic premises). Pythagoras (582–507 BCE), another mathematician (and mystic), discovered, among other scientific/mathematical principles, the "Pythagorean Theorem"—the square of the longest side of a right triangle is equal to the sum of the square of the other two sides. Pythagoras believed that reality could be reduced to numbers.

There were also the "atomists" Leucippus and Democritus (460–370 BCE), who argued that reality is basically composed of what they called "atoms," anticipating modern physics. Heraclites (500 BCE) argued that it is logically and empirically evident that everything is in "flux." He was reputed to have said that a "man couldn't step into the same river twice," because the river is in constant movement and therefore is always a different river. Parmenides (510 BCE) opposed Heraclites by arguing that all movement is illusionary, that reality is *one* and necessarily unchanging. If something "is," then it isn't something else; identity implies unchanging. A changing identity, in other words, is a contradiction in terms. Anaximenes (585–525 BCE) contributed the notion that air is the most basic element of the universe. Empedocles (490–430 BCE) synthesized the ideas of other pre-Socratics, arguing that four elements make up the universe: earth, air, fire, and water. He also believed that the universe moves in cycles and is the arena where opposite forces of attraction and division are constantly engaged in a cosmic battle, the outcome of which fluctuates and is the motor force behind the eternally cyclical universe.

Anaxagoras (500–428 BCE) argued that, contrary to the atomists, the universe is "infinitely divisible." He also made the bold assertion that the universe must have a separate, unifying principle, or Mind (*Nous*), from which everything emanates, including all change. He argued, in effect, that the universe reflects the work of an intelligent mind, but he offered little explanation as to the identity or nature of this mind.

The Pre-Socratic, natural philosophers were distinguished by two characteristics: they raised rational questions about the nature of the physical world (such as what is the world made of and how does the universe function); they also attempted to answer these questions by the use of mathematics, logic, and empirical observation. This is true even though scientific views were frequently blended with unscientific ones. For example, Pythagoras held mystical views like reincarnation, and Empedocles believed that *Love* and *Strife* were real, conflicting forces in the physical universe that determined its overall makeup. The natural philosophers contributed philosophically by addressing fundamental questions; they wondered about the ultimate nature of physical reality. They contributed scientifically by offering *naturalistic* explanations. The Pre-Socratics' work in philosophy and science, however, was only half the story. As the Western rational mind began flexing its mental muscles for the very first time in the realm of physical science, it was only a matter of time before the hunger for knowledge would extend beyond probing the physical and move into other areas of human experience.

For the Pre-Socratics, philosophy and science were virtually inseparable. To them, the search for truth meant trying to answer questions about the natural universe using the tools of reason—namely, logic, mathematics, and rational speculation. But they fell short of our modern definitions of science in that they also invoked nonscientific principles—such as reincarnation and a nonphysical mind that organizes the universe—to try to give a meaningful context to their scientific ideas. Mysticism, in other words, still influenced their thinking. Even more importantly, the Pre-Socratics also did not develop a satisfactory "scientific method" in their approach to the natural world. Carefully controlled, measurable, and repeatable empirical experimentation guided by theory was beyond their grasp; it was not until the Renaissance that scientists like Leonardo, Bacon, Kepler, and—particularly—Galileo formulated the modern scientific method. In this sense, the science of the Pre-Socratics resembled modern philosophy in that rational speculation and logical consistency was their primary guide.

6.5

Philosophy and science began going their separate ways when Socrates (469–399 BCE) and Plato (427–347 BCE) changed the direction and scope of philosophy. Rather than being preoccupied with the natural world of science, this new brand of philosopher began investigating the nonphysical worlds of ethics, politics, knowledge, human experience, and human nature itself. They also investigated metaphysics, which, for Socrates and Plato, did not mean the Pre-Socratic idea of investigating the essence of the physical world but instead included the investigation of the alleged invisible one supporting it. Additionally, Plato's student Aristotle, while absorbing the contributions of his two great predecessors, also returned to the Pre-Socratic interest in science and welded together with his own original thoughts what he considered to be the proper balance between science and the natural, everyday world of human experience. With Socrates, Plato, and Aristotle, the West's two main cultural orientations were born: one focusing reason in the nonphysical world of ideas, concepts, and ideals (Socrates and Plato), and the other focusing reason on the natural world and the world of everyday experience (Aristotle).

Socrates is usually viewed as the patron saint of philosophy. Legend has it that the Oracle of Delphi told him that he was the wisest man in all of Athens; Socrates was purportedly stunned at this revelation, because, as far as he was concerned, he "knew nothing." He then went on a mission to discover why he was so wise. But that's not all. Socrates believed that his mission was divinely commanded, and, in practice, it amounted to trying to discover *truth*, no matter what the cost. This meant a lifestyle in which his sole concern was to engage noted citizens of Athens in relentless question-and-answer discussions regarding a variety of topics that his interlocutors claimed to have expert knowledge in. This form of dialogue has since come to be known as the "Socratic method."

His goal was simply to try to discover if, in fact, the positions that his opponents supported could stand up to reasoned arguments. His strategy was to question the meaning of the terms that his opponents used in their arguments and then to show, logically, that the propositions associated with these meanings conflicted with his opponents' own positions. Socrates was aggressively uncompromising in his often expertly reasoned logical attacks and would not relent until his opponents conceded his points or simply gave up. To make matters even more difficult for his opponents, Socrates never seemed to be able to commit to one, unchanging point of view; rather, he was more than willing to take both sides of an argument—at times even patching up his opponent's weak arguments against him—only to expose real the logical flaws in his opponent's position more forcefully. It's easy to see why those who engaged Socrates in this form of dialogue grew weary, frustrated, and angry with him.

Ultimately, he was put on trial for "corrupting the minds of the youth," questioning belief in the gods, and probably for his undemocratic political leanings (although this issue was not addressed in the trial). During his trial, Socrates defiantly dismissed all the charges that were leveled against him as being unjustified, thoughtless, and nothing more than slanderous gossip. He also chastised the Athenians for priding themselves on their freedom of thought while, at the same time, prosecuting a man for thinking freely. Socrates irritated the jury further by proclaiming that he was, in fact, heroic—both in the battlefield as well an in his mission to save the souls of his fellow Athenians by pointing them in the direction of truth and virtue. Socrates went on to tell the jury that he would never, under any circumstances, forsake his divine mission to philosophize. As a punishment for his so-called crimes, Socrates recommended that he be rewarded instead with a free meal in the public dining hall; and if this didn't antagonize the jury enough, when it was clear that he was facing the death penalty and was asked for his opinion for an alternative punishment, he suggested that he should pay a ridiculously low fine. It's clear that he was taunting the jury and giving them to choice but to order his death. But Socrates didn't seem to mind: he spoke inspiringly to the court of being fearless in the faith of death and how dying for truth is much better than living by forsaking it. He also warned the court that there will be many others who would come after him who will push them even harder for their lack of philosophical virtue. The result was inevitable: Socrates was ordered to be put in prison and to die by drinking poison hemlock. When his students and friends arranged for him to escape, he refused. He told them that if he were to escape form prison, he would be breaking the law, which would be an affront to rationality; after all, the rule of law is rationality as applied to the city-state. The principle of state-based rationality does not change just because the state may act unwisely. Socrates argued that was duty-bound to live in accordance to with reason—to act differently would be to make what he had lived and struggled for meaningless. Instead of escaping, Socrates cheerfully imbibed the poison hemlock, even as his horrified students and friends gathered around him and succumbed to grief and despair.

In Socrates, Western history had its first "great" philosopher, and in his death, philosophy had its greatest martyr. For many, Socrates was the greatest of all philosophers because of his ultimate belief in the power of reason to investigate reality without an appeal to authority or religious considerations, and because his commitment to pursuing truth was total and uncompromising. Socrates was philosophy incarnate, the greatest lover of truth that philosophy has ever known. To him, true spirituality was equivalent to a life devoted to the relentless pursuit of truth by means of human reason, a pursuit that became for Socrates literally a matter of life and death.

Socrates lived a hand-to-mouth existence and wrote nothing down. He simply walked, talked, and argued, and his students—mostly well-to-do young Athenians—listened and learned. One student, in particular, was a passionate devotee of Socrates and was present at his trial. Plato was traumatized when his hero and mentor was sentenced to death. But now Plato found his own mission: he would ensure that his master and his ideas would never be forgotten, and he would build on what Socrates had accomplished. Fortunately for Socrates and Western culture, Plato was a philosophical and literary genius, and through his "Platonic dialogues" not only do we know what Socrates taught, but we also have Plato's decisive answers and responses to Socrates. Using Socrates as his mouthpiece in a series of often combative dialogues, Plato created a body of philosophical work that was to penetrate and inform all areas of Western culture through the centuries—from its philosophical and scientific traditions to its political, religious, artistic, and literary ones. When one considers the extent of Plato's influence, it is not difficult to agree with American philosopher Alfred North Whitehead's assessment that the history of Western philosophical tradition "is a series of footnotes to Plato." And what was the essence of Plato's philosophy? First we must consider what Socrates had to say about the pursuit of wisdom and the philosophical method that he developed to help him in this pursuit.

As we noted, the Pre-Socratics were concerned primarily with questions about the physical universe, its fundamental makeup, and how it functioned. They were, in fact, "natural philosophers" because they attempted to rationally answer fundamental questions about physical nature. Socrates' revolution consisted in inventing a new conception of philosophy: he directed the philosophical mind away from trying to understand physical nature and argued that real wisdom is gained only in the *process* of understanding how one is to live. The quality of one's life, in other words, is what really matters, and this should be the ultimate concern for the "lover of wisdom." Socrates drove the point home when he famously said, "The unexamined life is not worth living." It is only in rationally examining one's life critically that the philosopher becomes noble and wise. But Socrates had another reason for promoting his version of philosophy.

There arrived in Athens teachers of rhetoric (composition) and oratory (speaking) who, for a fee, would pass on their skills. They were called Sophists. It was their view that these skills were the basis for mastering the "art of persuasion." Sophists like Protagoras (485–411 BCE), who is famous for saying, "Man is the measure of all things," and Gorgias of Leontini (485–380 BCE) focused on teaching the art of persuasion, because they believed that in the real world of thinking and behaving, this was all that really mattered. For these thinkers, *absolute truth* as a guide and goal for thinking, or even as the basis for moral action, was a fiction; it simply does not exist. In other words, all truth is relative. Different cultures and even different circumstances demand different standards of truth. This being so, the Sophists argued that the intelligent person should turn away from seeking absolute truth and should instead learn how to manipulate reason to achieve his goals, whatever they might be. The Sophists' idea that truth is a hollow convention, and that the point of reasoning should be only to persuade using clever twists of logic, had dire consequences for philosophical and political thinking. Socrates and his student Plato knew this.

It was against this cultural climate of intellectual and moral relativism that Socrates asserted his philosophy. Since Socrates didn't write down his teachings, our knowledge about his philosophy comes mostly from Plato's dialogues (also from another of Socrates' students, Xenophon (427–355 BCE), who wrote works that discussed Socrates' teachings). Scholars agree that it is not always clear whether Socrates or Plato is speaking in the dialogues. Nonetheless, it is obvious that Socrates' philosophical innovations included pursuing philosophical truth through rigorously cross-examining his opponents in individual debates; asking nuanced questions about the definitions of a wide variety of ethical topics; insisting that the true meanings of these topics are permanent and not relative; and, finally, arguing that, though scientific issues are not irrelevant, the moral quality of life is the most important issue for the true philosopher. Ethics, in other words, must take precedence over metaphysics or science. Plato added to Socrates' work by providing a coherent theory about what unchanging truth *is* and its source, how it's expressed in the world around us, and how it should be incorporated into all areas of life.

We noted above that the Pre-Socratic philosopher Heraclites held that reality is in a constant state of flux and that Parmenides opposed this view and tried to show that change is impossible—that reality is one and unchanging. It seemed clear to Socrates and Plato that both philosophers had points in their favor, and that some sort of middle ground was likely to be closer to the truth. Socrates argued that despite the change we see around us, there are "universal" truths that nonetheless exist within this change, and that these unchanging truths can be teased out by the focused application of philosophical reasoning—in fact by determining the clear *meaning* of words and concepts. By arriving at their exact definitions, the philosopher would know how to live a virtuous and noble life. Here we come upon another of Socrates' innovations: he believed that knowledge was the highest virtue and ignorance the greatest vice.

Socrates asked, for example, "What is good?" "What is holy?" "What is ugly?" "What is justice?" "What is a statesman?" "What is love?" Socrates believed that the answers to these questions exist in the world around us and can be discovered through philosophical dialogue with committed thinkers. It is here, however, where Plato took partial exception to his master's ideas and began to blaze a new path in philosophy, a path that represented one of the profound turning points of Western history.

6.6

Plato believed that philosophy was born out of the "wonder" of existence. By this, Plato didn't simply mean the existence of the physical universe, but *existence* as such—the startling fact that *something*, anything, "is." Even more stunning was the fact that "I am"—that within the vast expanse of this infinite universe, "I" emerged "to be"—not only as one who is immersed in existence, but as one who *beholds* this mystery, and tries, however imperfectly, to understand it. If Plato was right, then Socrates must be seen as the firstborn of this wondrous awakening in the West. Unlike the Pre-Socratics before him, he directed his philosophical gaze inward, to the mystifying fact of his own existence and his passion to know, and he realized that before all else, one must strive to understand the meaning and purpose of one's existence, however important other issues, such as scientific ones, might be. For Plato, no one had wondered at existence with such intensity, intelligence, integrity, and wisdom as Socrates had, and no one deserves the title of "Philosopher" more than Socrates

Nonetheless, mentors, however great they may be, are never beyond reproach. In fact, a good student does well only when he finds his own way, taking from the teacher what he thinks is valuable and then modifying, even parting altogether from, ideas or strategies that he deems problematic or simply dead wrong. While adopting Socrates' methodology for arriving at truth, Plato came to understand the philosophical enterprise itself in a totally different light.

Plato was in love with mathematics and realized, at least partly because of his acquaintance with the work of Pythagoras, that mathematics is a way of knowing that is precise, consistent, and reliable. At the same time, as Heraclites convincingly pointed out, the universe is always in motion. But could there be a connection between these two worlds that is not at first clear to the observing eye or the reflective mind? Well, Plato got another hint from the Pythagorean discovery that there is a precise mathematical relationship between notes and intervals in a musical scale. For Plato, the idea that *abstract* numbers applied to the *down-to-earth* world of music indicated that there is a connection between change and permanence. It was through pondering the undeniable fact that change and permanence have a relationship that Plato was led to his decisive innovation.

Although Plato accepted the Socratic program of pursuing knowledge to enhance the quality of one's life, he nonetheless concluded that Socrates' acute philosophical mind was looking in the wrong place. Socrates thought that truth—"universals"—could be found in the "particular." That is, they could be found in what is "here and now" in the various stuff of the real world—the thoughts, actions, and lives of normal human beings. Plato disagreed with this sort of "inductive" reasoning. His insights with respect to mathematics led him to the bizarre idea that truth exists apart from this world, in a realm of ideal forms, ideas, concepts, laws, and principles. By "ideal," Plato meant unchanging, precise, distinct, and timeless—in a word: *perfect*. In his theory of forms, Plato argued that the world around us—the world of never-ending movement, change, decay, and death—is the *imperfect reflection* of this ideal world of unchanging perfection. Moreover, the relation between the imperfect, inconstant world of our senses and the one of perfect, eternal truth is one of "participation," in which all the things that we see, hear, taste, touch, and smell are imperfect imprints or copies of this world of perfection—mere shadows.

Philosophy teachers enjoy using Plato's example of a *circle* to try to demonstrate what he is arguing for. If one tries to circumscribe the best circle possible, even using the most precise methods and tools, one will always find upon close inspection that the circle is far from perfect; that there are always slight deviations from a perfectly smooth circular line. Any circle that we can possibly circumscribe, in other words, is rough, at best. Yet when we *think* about a circle, we think in terms of a perfectly round circle, one without imperfections—precisely 360 degrees.

If we can never draw or even see in the real world a perfect circle, then where do we get the "idea" of perfect *circle-ness?* Plato would argue that we derive this idea from the invisible world of ideal forms with which we are unconsciously in contact. And what's more, everything that we think about and experience in the world has its ideal counterpart in this perfect world. All our ideas, concepts, and principles, whatever they may be—including all our moral ideas—have their perfect corollaries in another world. "Goodness," "beauty," and "justice," for example, however imperfectly they are realized in this world, are perfectly realized in the ideal world from which they are derived.

Plato went so far as to rate the importance of the forms and, for instance, rates the form of "the Good" as supreme among the forms. Plato used the sun as a metaphor for the Good because of the luminescent, revealing quality of the sun's light, not to mention because of how important the sun is to life on earth. The sun, as metaphor, makes its most exotic appearance in Plato's *Republic*, a dialogue that is often considered his greatest.

In his *Allegory of The Cave*, Plato situated a number of prisoners in a subterranean cave, where they are constrained in such a way that they can see only one of the cave's walls. On the wall the individuals observe shadow puppets of figures acting in various ways and being manipulated to perform different functions; they even hear voices coming from the shadows. There is a fire ablaze behind the prisoners and also behind the figures that are being reflected on the wall. Since the prisoners can't see the fire or the real people manipulating the figures behind them, they naïvely believe that what they are seeing on the wall in front of them are not shadows but *real* things; the voices echoing from the wall further confirm their belief that the shadows are what is real. Finally, one of the people breaks free of the constraints, turns toward the fire, and is momentarily blinded by the visual assault of the light. He begins to understand the defect in his prior belief that the shadows were reality. Then the prisoner is dragged from the cave into the light of day, only to be blinded even more intensely by the sun's effulgent light and is unable to behold the sun directly.

This prisoner's eyes gradually adjust to the outside world and see the world as it really is, and he is finally able to peer directly into the sun, the source of all light, all truth. Presented with the choice of either going on his merry way, having arrived at true knowledge, or returning to the cave to help free the others from the darkness of deception and ignorance, he chooses to return to the cave. But his fellow prisoners believe that his venture outside the cave has impaired his judgment, and they are violently resistant to his suggestion that they leave their home in the cave, even threatening their would-be liberator with death.

This allegory captures Plato's philosophy beautifully. The sun represents the transcendent truth of the forms. The departure from the cave represents the difficult intellectual movement from earthbound ignorance and illusion, to otherworldly enlightenment, where we overcome the deception of everyday perceptual reality; the deep-seeded, false cultural views and perspectives that we are born into; and the fictitious beliefs, opinions, and ideas that naturally populate and pollute our thinking. Discovering the truth is not only an arduous *spiritual* task, however; one must be willing to suffer the slings and arrows of those who choose to reside in untruth and who may resent, and even want to harm, the real truth seeker. The journey out of the cave and into the sunlight is, in effect, the dynamic philosophical process in action. Undoubtedly, Plato had Socrates in mind when he composed his allegory. The Cave allegory can be misleading, though, because for Plato, the Truth—the Light—is not *out there* somewhere but instead is locked inconspicuously inside the dark cave of one's own body.

For Plato, the fact that we can draw circles and approximate goodness in the world, for instance, was proof that we have at the very core of our being, however difficult it may be to access in its pure, unsullied form, a *repository* of perfect knowledge. This knowing component of our being is what he called the "soul"—the nonmaterial, immortal, and timeless source of absolute truth. Plato has been vilified at times throughout the ages for inventing this "dualistic" doctrine of a perfect soul caught in the grips of dumb, decaying matter that we call the body. As we noted earlier, Plato's idea of the immortal soul was ultimately absorbed into Christianity with the notable difference that Plato believed in a version of reincarnation, whereas the Christians terminated the soul's travel after only one lifetime. Plato had many profound and highly influential notions about the soul. Most provocatively, he divided the soul into three parts: reason, appetite, and passion. Plato believed that reason must be the organizing power of the soul and should keep the appetites and passions in control and in their proper balance. This idea has had many manifestations throughout Western history, with its most popular adaptation in the twentieth century with Freud's psychoanalytical theory of the unconscious.

One of the fascinating implications of Plato's doctrine of the knowing soul is that real knowledge involves revealing what already exists in the soul of each person. He argued that this could only mean that learning or gaining knowledge of any kind is *remembering* what the soul already knows. With this doctrine, one never learns anything new or foreign; one merely recalls or recollects it. To illustrate this point, Plato, in his dialogue the *Phaedo*, had a slave boy recognize the truth of a geometry problem without his ever learning anything about geometry beforehand. This is supposed to show that the truth of geometry already existed in the uneducated boy and emerged out of him, from his soul, when he was properly provoked. As further proof of his doctrine of recollection, Plato added that if truth did not preexist inside the truth seeker, how then would he know it when he saw it? We know truth only after comparing and matching it with what we already know is true, or else we would never know the difference between truth and falsehood.

Plato's thirty-six dialogues represent the systematic application of his theory of forms to virtually all areas of human life and experience.

They represent the first work of comprehensive and systematic philosophizing and provided the general intellectual framework in which the Western mind was to grow through the ages.

Plato argued that the genuine philosopher is always on the path to true knowledge of the ideal forms in their perfect, undistorted essence. The essence of the path is as follows: unlike other traditions such as Christianity and Buddhism—in which isolation, prayer, or meditation are understood as important ways of arriving at truth—the Socratic path to knowledge *always* involves engaging other thinkers in rigorously rational debates. Philosophical truth, in other words, is not obtained or reached in isolation, on one's own, but is a joint effort among like spirits. The actual process—first outlined by Socrates—follows this simple format: a philosophical conversation commences with respect to a particular topic, in which each person in the "dialogue" advances ideas and perspectives. The logical conflicts and disagreements that inevitably arise are addressed head on and analyzed by all parties in a fair and objective fashion until the initial conflicts are resolved to the satisfaction of all parties. This resolution takes all philosophical combatants one step closer to the truth of the topic under discussion. Each dialogue continues along these lines—philosophers grappling with difficult and confusing issues, confronting and overcoming logical impasses, unraveling logical knots, parties disagreeing when the arguments advanced are not convincing but at other times conceding logical victories to opponents when an honest assessment indicates that they put forth the stronger view. Even helping your opponent to understand or clarify his argument against your own is a part of the philosophical endeavor.

The ongoing process of ideas being presented, conflicts emerging, and conflict resolution is Platonic philosophy in action—always moving forward, always climbing upward and getting closer to philosophical victory. But total victory doesn't simply mean coming to know the truth of the topic that initiated the discussion. As truth emerges, the philosophical discussions naturally broaden and become more *inclusive*, where other important issues naturally arise and are in need of debating, understanding, and integrating into what is known so far. And so the onward advance toward total truth continues.

Not only will the movement toward the ideal forms reveal that all important philosophical questions and issues are fundamentally interconnected, it will also lead to the understanding of how and why the ideal forms themselves are interconnected. Seeing and understanding the philosophical harmony of the ideal forms in their pure state is the final goal of Platonic philosophy: this is absolute truth. And what actually happens at the moment of victory, when philosophers finally know the forms in their harmonious unity? Plato suggests a sort of mystical beholding of the forms, wherein words and logic fail and the philosophers' restless minds are finally stilled, without question, without issue. The truth seekers are literally speechless as they bask in the pure, transcendent experience of knowing the seamless perfection of the forms.

The Socratic path to knowledge puts enormous responsibility on the thinkers who desire to forge ahead. For Plato, the pursuit of philosophical truth is the noblest of human aspirations, one that requires a pure heart and a love of truth so deep that one must put aside all other considerations, such as ego and self-aggrandizement. Debates of all kinds often devolve into a desire for personal victory at all costs, even at the cost of truth. The real path to knowledge, on the other hand, is fueled not by ego needs or by the yearning for personal power and advantage but, rather, by the love of the truth. In this sense, those with whom you are grappling philosophically are more like close brethren working together to arrive at a common good: the Truth. But being a Platonic philosopher may seem unnatural, for one must learn to negate much of what one has naturally relied on and even loved.

Plato is arguing that the true philosopher is one who, one might say, practices death, one who lives with one foot in the casket. This is both a crushing indictment of the physical body as well as the apotheosis of pure thinking. Plato's condemnation of the body carries with it a dismal interpretation of everyday life, the arena where human beings live and act, and the world where our senses and commonsense thinking are our primary ways of knowing and navigating through the world. The implications of Plato's thinking, both in its promise of gaining truth through proper philosophical living and reasoning as well as its decidedly negative slant on earthly life, were to infiltrate and color many sectors of Western culture.

We spend a large portion of our days (and nights) thinking, wondering, figuring, and using "mental energy" to work out problems and discover more intelligent ways to reach our goals. And we typically don't use our minds thoughtlessly; we try to think logically and consistently. We also know to be careful not to let our emotions interfere in important decision-making. Modern humans spend a great deal of time using their minds; we are frequently "in our heads," and we are conscious that there are right and wrong ways of thinking. What we take to be a natural part of everyday living and working—rational thinking—is Plato's (and Socrates') greatest legacy to Western civilization.

Plato's ideas can lend themselves to entertaining, if not fascinating, speculation. As an example, when we are confronted with the need to find a solution to a problem, or to make an important decision, it's not uncommon for us to *look up*, as if by looking up we are able to find the answer we are seeking. But why up? Why not down, for example? Or why not simply focus inward, since thinking occurs in our minds—inside? Plato would say that we look up because *up* is away from the earth; after all, the earth is where the spirit of truth is mired and fettered in the quicksand of worldly ignorance, intellectual vice, and sensual illusion. By looking up, we feel as though we are transcending the *heaviness* of the earth and that our ideas can now flow forth effortlessly and spontaneously. When we are caught up in thought, our minds seem free and virtually limitless.

Or, to take another example, all of us have had feelings of intense joy, even a sort of ecstasy, when learning new information or gaining insight into an area of great interest. These sorts of feelings are quite mysterious and often seem disproportional to the knowledge that is gained. I recall experiencing overflowing delight and indescribable pleasure when I first realized that "time" was not a *thing* like an apple or house; that time is known in a way that is completely different from the way we know material things in experience. In pondering this startling idea, I was literally light-headed for an hour or so. How would we explain the depth and illumination of these sorts of emotions? Plato would say that such feelings are our bodies literally *remembering* aspects of truth that have been residing inconspicuously in our souls ever since our incarnation here on Earth, that these sorts of feelings represent the soul oozing out genuine knowledge as we move closer to even greater understanding of the forms.

Good ideas organize, harmonize, and balance—they are, in fact, reasonable. For Plato, this simply means that good ideas are closer to the truth than bad ideas, which create confusion, disharmony, and imbalance.

Whether or not we believe completely in Plato's theory as he articulated it, no one can deny that logical thinking is a requirement for successful living, that rational thinking is a way to knowledge. The "rule of law," for example, is Platonic; this principle implies imposing rational order on the chaos of political life. Creating order was a cardinal virtue for Plato and for him clearly points the way to the truth of the forms. And, of course, there are science and technology, the very embodiments of rational thinking. It is impossible to exhaust the ways in which Platonic thinking has influenced every area of Western culture.

Whenever we are interested in knowing the reason or meaning behind or inside a thought, feeling, statement, expression, artwork, or book, we are paying homage to the Socratic/Platonic tradition. This does not mean that before Socrates and Plato there was no thinking along these lines; there surely was. But it was only with Plato in particular that thinking began coming into its own and established clear guidelines about what thinking is and what it is not: arguing logically and consistently from premises to conclusions, requiring logical proof for positions, thinking in terms of strict "cause and effect," understanding complex arguments and issues by simplifying them, thinking "systematically," making rational generalizations based on a wide range of experiences, arguing with honesty and integrity, and neither employing rational argument to bolster one's ego nor using emotional outbursts to distract, persuade, or intimidate. Plato's work began a solid tradition of rational thinking, one that has informed Western culture for nearly two-and-a-half millennia.

When I was studying art history in Florence, Italy, I learned that the great artist Michelangelo was a Christian in his everyday life but as a sculptor he was a Platonist, because he believed that within the block of marble that he was about to sculpt, there was contained, already fully formed in perfect condition, the finished object. He believed that his work as a sculptor required only releasing this ideally formed object from the excess, unformed marble surrounding and constraining it. According to this idea, Michelangelo's genius lay, in part, in his preternatural ability to see the perfect object inside the gross slab of marble. It's not only in understanding genius, however, that Plato is an illuminating guide; whenever we try to reveal, clarify, tease out, or visualize something, we are acting as good Platonists. As pervasive and influential as Plato's ideas have been in Western culture, however, his was not the final word from ancient Greece. Another philosophic voice arose in Athens that rivaled, and many have argued clearly surpassed, Plato's—that of his student Aristotle.

The history of philosophy has often been described as "one long argument." It's certainly the case that philosophers—beginning with the Pre-Socratics and continuing until the present time—have debated endlessly and rigorously the great philosophical problems. Some modern philosophers have been convinced that this very long argument was misconceived from the outset, that philosophy has been misguided because of its failure to understand that the primary vehicle for philosophical ideas—*language*—is always "self referential" and can never get beyond itself and make contact with objective reality. In essence, they believe that philosophy speaks gibberish when it poses, and tries to answer, truth questions about the world.

The goal of philosophy, in this view, is not to understand reality but to investigate the structure and meaning of language to see how language functions as it does and to "clarify" language in the many contexts in which it is used. The irony here is that the question of the relationship between philosophy, language, and reality is itself an important philosophical question, one that has so far not admitted a compelling answer, and as such, is clearly a part of the very same millennia-long argument that some modern philosophers have tried to refute. Another irony is that the modern philosophers who argue that language is merely a convention are making a *reality claim* and, as such, are guilty of the same alleged philosophical naiveté as those whom they criticize. Clearly, the long argument continues unabated.

7

From Aristotle to
Renaissance Humanism,
and the Arts

7.1

Although the Pre-Socratics initiated the great philosophical argument with questions about the fundamental makeup of the universe—with natural philosophers, such as Heraclites and Parmenides, offering diametrically opposing answers—it was not until Plato that the great debate took off in earnest. And the reasons are clear: Plato's work represented the first great synthesis in philosophical history by integrating systematically into his own philosophy not only Socrates' views but also those of the Pre-Socratics, particularly Thales, Heraclites, Parmenides, and Pythagoras. Just as importantly, Plato gave further coherence, concreteness, and credibility to his ideas by writing them down, and doing so in a masterful way. It was with Plato's ingenious dialogues, in fact, that Western philosophy first took form, as he presented for the first time many of the great philosophical problems and issues in a clear, concise, comprehensive, and memorable (even entertaining) fashion. One could say that Plato's philosophy, taken as a whole, was the first serious argument in the history of philosophy. And who better to pose the first great challenge to the incomparable Plato than his formidable understudy Aristotle? Whereas Plato understood philosophy as the study of the transcendent world of ideal forms, Aristotle, by stark contrast, understood philosophy as the study of the essence of what has come to be actualized in the world of everyday experience.

That Aristotle's father was the court physician for the King of Macedonia probably accounts for Aristotle's early interest and schooling in science. When his father died in 367 BCE, the seventeen-year-old Aristotle moved to Athens and entered Plato's Academy, where he remained under Plato's tutelage for twenty years until Plato's death in 347 BCE. Notably, Aristotle then spent three years in Della, capital of Macedonia, teaching philosophy (to no avail) to the young and future world conqueror Alexander (later "The Great") before returning to Athens and opening his own rival school to Plato's Academy—the Lyceum. He taught and lectured at his school for twelve years. Aristotle's philosophy has survived mostly thanks to his extensive lecture notes.

Aristotle and Plato both viewed thinking as the "highest" of all human activities, but they differed radically as to *how* thinking should be used, *what* thinking is able to discover about reality, and *where* in human life thinking finds its proper place. Despite their differences, it is difficult to exaggerate the extent to which Plato influenced Aristotle. It was as though Plato was a great master of highly abstract painting and passed on to his precocious protégé Aristotle his many technical skills, the new colors that he had invented, and even his prize paintbrush. Aristotle, in turn, created new colors from Plato's original recipes, honed his technical skills to exceed even those of his teacher's, and applied Plato's paintbrush in new and bold ways. The results were nothing short of revolutionary.

In well-defined, naturalistic designs and colors, Aristotle painted real men, women, children, human faces, plants, animals, and natural phenomena, and he even rendered on canvas the visible details of human behavior of various kinds in many diverse situations. Further, Aristotle's paintings were not *static*, as were his teacher's, but were bustling with dynamic movement—with everything, everybody, and every form of behavior, doing something, or going somewhere, with a purpose—as they actually do in day-to-day life. Plato and Aristotle were indeed like painters who created two very different pictures of reality. Now let's see in which ways their two opposing worldviews clashed.

Aristotle charged that Plato's exclusive concern with the so-called "world of forms" led his profound intellect astray. By this criticism, Aristotle meant something quite simple, namely that Plato's ideas cannot explain much of what we know to be true about reality. For example, one of most salient characteristics of the world is that everything changes; Plato's theory, which focuses only on the unchanging, unseen world of the forms, is at a loss to explain how this change is possible or what change itself really is. Aristotle also wanted to know how *knowledge* of particular things would even be possible, if real knowledge exists only in the realm of ideal forms. To call worldly knowledge mere *belief* or *opinion*, as Plato did, is just playing a word game. Despite what Plato said, Aristotle argued that particular things are the only legitimate source of knowledge. And to account for knowledge of particular things, as Plato did, by saying that the ideal world of forms "participates" in the corrupt, imperfect items of the world, only begs the question: how does participation make knowledge of things possible? Perhaps more damaging is Aristotle's criticism that by focusing on perfect "universals," Plato was unable to explain the existence of particular items in the world. Why, in fact, do the items in the world exist at all? And moreover, what can existence mean if the particular things that do exist are only insubstantial shadows? How could something that *is not*, "be"? These logical difficulties were, for Aristotle, insurmountable and raised questions that are logically unanswerable. It became clear to Aristotle that Plato had used reason in ingenious ways to arrive at completely wrong conclusions. Aristotle believed that philosophy could do better!

One of the great paintings of the Italian Renaissance is *The School of Athens*, by Raphael. This painting is a celebration of humanistic values; it shows noted ancient Greek, Arabic, and Persian artists, philosophers, writers, and mathematicians sharing center stage with their Italian Renaissance counterparts. Some characters simply appear to be posing, others are in engaging dialogue with fellow cultural icons, and a number are busy measuring, designing, and reading. Personages like the Greek scientist Archimedes, the Arabic philosopher Averroes, natural philosophers Heraclites and Parmenides, the female mathematician Hypatia, the immortal Socrates, the artist Michelangelo, the poet Dante, and even Raphael himself are among the many luminaries depicted in the painting. In the very center of the painting are the imposing figures of Plato (with Leonardo da Vinci's head and face) and Aristotle in conversation with each other. What is most interesting about their exchange are their contrasting hand gestures. Plato is pointing up to the heavens with his right forefinger as if making an important point, and Aristotle, while looking at Plato, is gesturing toward the earth with his right hand, palm facing downward and his fingers expressively spread apart; he appears to be describing why he takes exception to what Plato is saying. Raphael's symbolism summarizes perfectly their divergent philosophical orientations: Plato is arguing passionately that truth exists only in the transcendent world of ideal forms above and beyond the world of everyday experience, and Aristotle is asserting confidently that the earth is the only realm where truth can be found.

Aristotle believed that knowledge could only be found in this world—specifically, through astute observation, analysis, and practical experience. Aristotle, in this way, was the first great "empiricist" (although Socrates was on the right path by looking to the *particulars* of human affairs and making general observations). He set himself the daunting task of making detailed observations of much of the natural and human world around him, dissecting and cataloguing almost everything that came before his penetrating eye. His investigations included physics, meteorology, zoology (which he invented), embryology, physiology, anatomy, biology, and mathematics. He studied five hundred species of life. Aristotle's contributions extended well beyond scientific interests and included all areas of philosophy, logic, politics, rhetoric, memory, and dreams. He also analyzed 158 constitutions of various Greek states. Below, I want to highlight what I consider to be his most significant contributions.

Plato tried to understand the whole of reality through his theory of forms. A theory in philosophy (and science) is a sort of pre-judgment about something that gives meaning and order to the thing or phenomena under investigation. The problem is that the meaning and order that a theory provides may have little or nothing to do with reality. Plato's theory, for example, argued that truth does not exist in the world. This means that the philosopher who believes the theory would, *in advance*, have to disregard statements about items of the world as having any truth-value, as all of our sensual experiences are illusions. But what if Plato's theory is wrong? What if truth does, after all, inhere in the world of our senses? Believing Plato's theory, then, would necessarily lead to a false interpretation of reality. This is Aristotle's point in a nutshell. Rather than directly investigating the world to see what is being presented, Plato mistakenly chose to look away. Aristotle, on the other hand, had a different vision, one that was forever focused on what he could see, touch, hear, smell, and taste—he saw the love of wisdom, in other words, as inextricably bound up with the natural world and humanity's experience within it.

Aristotle's counterpoint to Plato's notion that true being exists only in an ideal world was his position that truth is found only in the *substance* ("ousia") of something, and substance is the blending of *matter* ("hule") and *form* ("morphe" or "eidos"), just as we see it in direct experience. Real being, in other words, is in the *concrete* thing, and is not in some transcendent realm. Plato's theory of forms effectively separates form from matter and elevates forms to perfection, but Aristotle sees this dichotomy as a perversion of reality. Form and substance *together* constitute the true reality of something. There is no higher realm where only forms exist. However, because Aristotle was to argue that truth exists in the world, he had to account for what is most distinctive about it—*change*. What was Aristotle's solution to this long-standing problem?

In Aristotle's estimation, what is beyond question is that wherever you look in the world, you observe everything moving toward some end or "goal"; without a doubt, all nature is "teleological"—goal oriented. This means that all change has a purpose, a reason for moving from one moment in time to another. For instance, physical objects that are active appear to move to their natural place in the general scheme of things. When an object falls to the earth, it ends at its most natural place—on the ground; it never goes up, because it would be "unnatural" for it to do so.

With biological life—plants, animals, and human beings—it's more complicated, but no less understandable. And the key to unraveling the source of change in living reality is to focus on what is really occurring in each life-form. For Aristotle, observation clearly shows us that *within* life itself there is always a change from "potentiality" to "actuality." Within a tomato seed, for example, there is the potential for a fully ripened tomato, and in time the tomato does become—is actualized into—a mature tomato. When the human egg is fertilized, there exists at that moment the potential for a complete human being to be fully actualized. In Aristotle's view, the movement from potential to actual is the essential change in living things. This movement to actualization also clarifies the connection between matter and form: the form of something becomes more exact and concrete as matter actualizes its potential and becomes what it is. Now that we have an idea of where change is heading, we have to ask: what actually *causes* something to actualize, to become what it is?

Aristotle's answer is an historic one. He posited four causes as the grounds for something to be what it is:

1. *Material cause:* the elements out of which something is made
2. *Formal cause:* the shape or form something assumes
3. *Efficient cause:* the manner in which something is created
4. *Final cause:* the purpose for which something is made

So what are the four causes of an *ice cube*, for instance?

5. *Material cause:* H20
6. *Formal cause:* square
7. *Efficient cause:* frozen by very low temperatures—thirty-two degrees Fahrenheit
8. *Final cause:* to cool water and beverages for consumption, or to reduce swelling because of physical trauma to the body

Another of Aristotle's great contributions was his invention of *syllogistic* (deductive) logic, which was to become the foundation for Western thinking up into modern times. Basic to this form of reasoning is what is usually termed "the law of noncontradiction," which states simply that something can't be both "X" and "not X" at the same time.

1. All lawyers have a law degree.
2. John is a lawyer.
3. Therefore John has a law degree.

This is an example of how the law of noncontradiction works in Aristotelian deductive logic. Once premises are firmly established, and identities and definitions are clearly fixed, conclusions can be logically deduced—that is, shown to follow from the premises by *necessity*. This was a primary goal of Aristotle's syllogistic logic. True premises expressed using fixed identities and definitions imply conclusions with *necessity*—an essential goal of logical reasoning. Aristotle's innovations in logical thinking included rules and principles of correct reasoning, scientific methodology, and even rules of effective argument in social discourse. Aristotle's work in logic had an unparalleled influence in Western thinking, and its limitations started becoming evident only in recent times, when new forms of logic were invented to address the complexities that arose in philosophical and scientific thinking.

In contrast to Plato, Aristotle was a worldly philosopher, one whose total focus was to investigate, analyze, define, and categorize what was necessarily true about nature, the human world, and human experience. Rather than looking at the world through the prism of abstract theories such as Plato's theory of forms, Aristotle chose to look *directly* to the areas of his concern. He was confident in this empirical approach to philosophy because of his strong belief that the five bodily senses, guided by reason, could determine what was true about all areas of reality. When Aristotle did indulge in abstract reasoning, such as in his work in logic, it was almost always as a means to investigate and clarify some aspect of natural reality. The logical extension of this idea was that thinking is not simply a theoretical process for discovering abstract truths about ultimate reality or for investigating the physical world; rational thinking is also an indispensable, practical tool for *living well.*

In his *Nicomachean Ethics*, Aristotle outlined what he thought was the purpose of human life: *eudaimonia*—living well, *happiness.* Aristotle argued that happiness is the "good" toward which all human beings should aim. He did not, however, understand happiness to be a passive state of contentment, satisfaction, or inner serenity; instead, he thought that happiness followed naturally from proper thinking and decisive action over the course of an entire lifetime. In other words, happiness is the dynamic state of being that naturally follows from thinking and acting well as a habitual activity. Aristotle tried to be as *un-theoretical* as possible about happiness and argued that human beings need specific "goods" to live a happy life. These goods include friends, power, good habits, pleasure, good looks, health, wealth, and good fortune. Learning good habits in childhood, he said, goes a long way toward supporting one's lifelong efforts to be happy. Aristotle also understood the importance of pleasure and good friendship. His idea of friendship was that of mutual good will.

Aristotle believed that happiness and ethics were necessarily interconnected—essentially two sides of the same coin. By extension, because humans are necessarily social beings, he believed that politics should also be included in ethics. Aristotelian ethics was not an intellectual matter; one need not, as with Plato, understand mathematics or study metaphysics to gain insights as to the "form" of ethics. On the contrary, ethics is a thoroughly practical program in which reason is used in mundane ways, including fashioning together indispensable "goods" such as social skills, friendship, pleasure, honor, health, and wealth.

Aristotle followed Plato in assigning reason the moral function of controlling the appetites and passions, and likewise saw moral education (beginning in childhood) as critical. But how, for Aristotle, does one live morally? By using reason with excellence—*arête*—and doing so as a matter of habit. "Be the best that you can be in all situations" would be a concise statement of Aristotle's idea of virtuous moral behavior. As an added benefit, virtuous actions produce *proper moral feelings* that are themselves further inducements to act morally. But what exactly does arête mean to Aristotle? How does one act in the world to ensure that one is doing one's best? Aristotle, remaining consistent with his practical approach to morality, believed that he had the answer within his doctrine of the "mean." Simply put, moral virtue is the middle, or proper balance, between excess and deficiency. Aristotle believed that this simple principle is a valuable guide for proper moral action. For example, courage is a reasonable mean between cowardice on the one hand and rashness on the other. But Aristotle was quick to add that his doctrine is *situation-bound*; each circumstance in which one has to act has its own extreme limits and mean as the proper balance between the two. Living a happy life is to live a virtuous life, and virtue is grounded in using reason with excellence in all situations.

Aristotle's notion of God was to have an enormous impact on Western culture, especially on a number of Enlightenment thinkers. Aristotle believed fervently in the law of "cause and effect." In his view, any rigorous investigation of the physical world must conclude that everything is *moved* by something else and that something must also be moved by something else; movement, in short, is the life of the universe. Additionally, a movement that causes another movement had to exist *prior* to the thing that was moved; Aristotle argued that the fact that causal movements occur in temporal sequence is the basis for the future-oriented arrow of time. But it seemed to Aristotle that movement had to start somewhere, or else causal movements would stretch back to infinity, which did not seem reasonable to the great philosopher. To remedy this logical problem Aristotle posited the existence of an original "Unmoved Mover." With the Unmoved Mover, essentially, *moving itself,* an outside movement becomes unnecessary, and so the problem of an *infinite regress* is resolved, at least for Aristotle. Enlightenment thinkers in the eighteenth century were to embrace this purely logical, impersonal, and distant, unmoved God, and they used him in their doctrine of "Deism"—the belief that God created the universe and its natural laws and then retired from any further activity in the physical world. With Deism, it followed that God is not available under any conditions for consultation; he also does not provide revelation or solace; nor is he receptive to prayer; and, in fact, God not actively involved in the affairs of humankind at all.

In sum, Plato and Aristotle are the twin cultural pillars upon which much of what is most distinctive about Western civilization is based. Plato's early philosophy was a creative elaboration upon and culmination of the thinking of the Pre-Socratics and Socrates. In his mature thinking, Plato set out to redefine what philosophy was and to offer his own imaginative responses to the questions and issues first addressed by Socrates. His highly abstract theory of forms created the general framework for the substance of Plato's philosophizing, and for much subsequent thought in Western civilization.

Aristotle's philosophy also developed the ideas of the Pre-Socratics and those of Socrates and Plato, but his great revolution consisted in inverting Plato's thinking in fundamental ways, opening up and systematically exploring the multifaceted reality of the natural universe and the world of human beings. In the final analysis, Plato taught the West what thinking means, and Aristotle showed us what to think about and how to go about using thinking to understand nature and the many areas of human existence.

Taken together, these two intellectual giants have divided the Western world between them, and each one has been elaborated upon, in countless ways, to create the body of what is Western culture. But wait a moment. What about the Judeo-Christian tradition? Isn't it true, as many have argued, that we live in a Judeo-Christian civilization? Or is this designation grossly misleading and a profound overstatement? One merely needs to think of the domineering roles of democracy science, and technology—all three children of Greek thinking—to realize the ignorance of such proclamations. I should point out, again, that Greek thought has in numerous ways significantly influenced both Judaism and Christianity. The Jewish tradition of rationality, the Christian idea of an immortal soul imprisoned in a corrupt body, as well the dominance of Aristotle's thought in Medieval Christianity (and modern Catholicism) are just a few examples of the considerable impact of Greek thought on Western religion.

The area of Western culture that has been most influenced by Christian thought is ethics, particularly with respect to beliefs in the "sanctity" of human life and in individual human rights. How these notions have played themselves out over the troubled course of Western religious history is quite another story, and a tragically sad one at that. Additionally, one could easily and convincingly argue that much of what we accept as Christian, such as tolerance toward other views, particularly religious ones, is more pagan or humanistic based than Christian based. As integral as certain interpretations of Christianity are to Western culture, what is most distinctive are its many traditions that had their beginnings in ancient Greece.

But there is irony to the magnificent contributions of Plato and Aristotle. As much as their ideas have fertilized the soil from which the Western flower grew, they also had a retarding effect on the burgeoning potential of the West. Plato's obsession with ideal realities had the result of degrading the concrete here and now. It's difficult to embrace life with gusto, or to see one's life as singularly meaningful, if it is nothing more than an unfortunate illusion or simply a pale reflection of a higher, more important reality. And why should human beings waste their time pursuing scientific knowledge, if its object— the natural world—has no truth to be discovered? Plato dampened the scientific spirit considerably, even though he promoted mathematics as a superior form of knowledge. Plato's worldview also casts a negative view of art. What value could art possibly possess if it simply rearranges or reshapes various illusions in paint or marble? The result could only be new illusions in different configurations. In this view there can be no real truth-value to art, because it's mired in the falsehoods of perception and physical existence.

Another great irony of Plato's legacy was that, despite his belief that reason represents the highest aspect of a human being's nature, there was also what could be understood as a mystical dimension to his philosophy. Neo-Platonic philosophers like Plotinus (204–270CE) and Proclus (410–485CE) initiated and completed, respectively, this mystical, Neo-Platonic tradition. Neo-Platonisn was the last great Greek school of philosophy and integrated into a general worldview all of ancient Greek thought, along with Judeo-Christian ideas. It included the skepticism of the Skeptics, the austere ethical code of the Stoics, the logical ideas of Aristotle, but, most prominently, the otherworldliness of Plato. In his great dialogue *The Republic*, Plato argued that among all the ideal forms that constitute ultimate reality, one stands out as not only the highest, but also as dominant over all others: *the Good*. Neo-Platonist philosophers like Plotinus and Proclus seized on the form of the Good and attributed to it a divine, deity-like nature. Plotinus, in his *Enneads*, spoke of spiritual hierarchies, which began gloriously at the top with the Good and extended down with levels representing greater falsehood the closer they are to the earth; Proclus saw all of reality *emanating* from the all-divine Good.

The implications of, and elaborations on, Platonic thinking was a mixed bag of profound philosophical insights on one side and curious, if fascinating, otherworldly speculations on the other. Although one might say that Plato served both philosophy and mysticism with equal talent, it's clear that the mystical traditions received the greater historical benefit, at least up until the time of the Renaissance. In this sense, the supreme irony with respect to Plato was that for a thousand years or so, his legacy stood firmly against the very rationalistic tradition that he himself was instrumental in establishing. In Plato secular thought had its most profound progenitor, as well as one of its most formidable enemies. But how about the arch-realist Aristotle? Was he the antidote to a misguided Platonism?

Well, yes and no. Modern philosophers of science hail Aristotle as the legitimate founder of the scientific worldview, because not only did he see the natural world as the proper place where a rational mind should spend its precious time, he also carried out real scientific activities like categorizing and analyzing much of the natural world. As we have seen, he also invented logic and created the rational framework in which empiricist thinking was to flourish for over two thousand years. Humanists of all persuasions likewise see Aristotle as the groundbreaking genius who rescued philosophy from the destructive grip of Platonic otherworldly speculation; by seeing everyday life as both real and significant, Aristotle refocused the philosophical gaze back to the visceral, pulsating world of human beings.

Aristotle's legacy, like Plato's, served both secular and religious causes. As we noted earlier, Aristotle's works entered the European cultural bloodstream thanks to Arab and Jewish scholar-translators in the ninth and tenth centuries. Theologians like Aquinas devoted their careers to integrating Aristotle into Catholicism, which gave birth to Scholasticism—the theological basis for the church of the Middle Ages. But Aristotle's work in science was to have a wholly separate history.

His work in physics (for Aristotle, physics was the entirety of the natural world) was, in particular, to serve as the guide for naturalistic scholars and put a stranglehold on the pursuit of scientific knowledge for many centuries. If Aristotle had been correct about what he thought about the natural universe, then his ideas would have been a great boon to scientific progress. Unfortunately, despite his seminal work in laying the foundation for empirical investigation, many of his notions and principles were simply wrong and served to impede rather than advance real scientific understanding. For example, he believed in the *geocentric* view of the universe—that is, he saw the earth as the immobile center with all celestial objects revolving around it.

Some of Aristotle's most influential work was in the biological sciences. His organization of living things into general categories like genus and species was a great advance for modern science. But his "ladder of life"—his *scala natura*, with each life form stuck forever where it is without the possibility of changing—was static and served to obstruct the true understanding of all life as evolving dynamically over time. Aristotle actually made many erroneous observations regarding the natural world—in some cases, inexplicably so. For instance, the great philosopher of observation claimed that women had fewer teeth than men. Aristotle became such an obstacle to progress because, for many, including the great Aquinas himself, Aristotle's was the supreme authoritative voice of all advanced learning. To make intellectual matters even worse, it was considered almost blasphemy to challenge his viewpoints.

Aristotle arranged his ladder of life according to degree of complexity and function of life forms—the less complex were at the bottom of his ladder, with the more complex forms emerging as the ladder ascended. Aristotle's static conception of hierarchal life was eventually absorbed into what became known as the "Great Chain of Being"—the dominant religious, philosophical, and scientific paradigm of the Middle Ages. The Great Chain of Being went beyond Aristotle, however, for in this grander ladder, both natural and supernatural entities exist in a meticulously graded hierarchy—from inert matter all the way up to God himself, with humanity placed above animals but below the angels. This was accomplished with the addition of Plato's ideas, which transformed Aristotle's physical/biological conception into an enthralling metaphysical worldview.

In his dialogue *Timaeus*, Plato discussed how God created the universe and the relationships all entities have to one another. His view can be summed up in what has been called the *principle of plentitude*: God is all-good, therefore all things that he creates must necessarily be all good. God created a universe that is consistent with his perfect nature; all of creation, therefore, is totally complete and in need of nothing, with all created entities in perfect balance with each other and each one in its proper place within the general scheme of things.

With Plato's principle of plentitude integrated into Aristotle's hierarchal ladder of life, the Great Chain of Being gave the Middle Ages a powerful vision of reality, at once immediately accessible and grandiose. This worldview insinuated itself into all areas of medieval culture, particularly in literature (Dante), religion (Aquinas), and science (with the geocentric (earth-centered) view of the solar system). The general theme of the Great Chain of Being accorded well with the Bible: the perfect God creating and ordering a perfect universe with everything in it just as it should be. Astronomy was seen as the most direct evidence of God's inerrant plan: planets revolving around the stationary earth in perfect circles. In this view, the universe must be static, because what is perfect must be unchanging, like God himself. The Great Chain of Being framed Plato and Aristotle in a cohesive context, but as the High Middle Ages approached the fourteenth century, this cohesion began to loosen, and within a short time, the medieval worldview began unraveling all together.

7.2

As we noted earlier, the Renaissance was a turbulent time in which contending views, in different areas of cultural life, vied for dominance. The reemergence of pagan values within a medieval Christian civilization resulted in a dramatic clash of cultures, with the pagan glorifying the worldly, the human, the passions, and natural reason, and the Christian negating such things as worldly existence and humanistic values, focusing instead on faith and on life after death. A battle for the heart and mind of Western culture ensued. Indeed, the rediscovery of the literature and philosophy of ancient Greece and Rome ignited a cultural revolution that transformed Western civilization and ushered in the beginning of modern times.

As far as the works of Plato and Aristotle are concerned, Renaissance humanists had a field day squeezing their views into various contexts. Hence, Michelangelo's sculpture can be seen as "Platonic," because he was extracting ideal figures from gross blocks of marble with the aid of an exquisitely nuanced chisel, while Raphael, with his tenderly applied brushstrokes, was seen as Aristotelian, because his paintings depicted the simple beauty and mathematical order of *this* world. Of course, since both artists often used Christian subject matter, the church claimed their art was purely Christian, despite the fact that their work was paganism through and through. But even more complex conflicts emerged, ones with reverberations that can still be felt today. One of the great points of conflict during the Renaissance dealt with the issue of science—how it was to be pursued, its philosophical guidelines, its methods, and, particularly, its limits. By and large, initial scientific study followed along the course delineated by Aristotle.

However, as the pagan rebirth unfolded, Renaissance humanists began challenging important views of the ancients; the most dramatic result was the birth of modern science in the seventeenth century. Interestingly enough, it was the Renaissance artists who paved the way to the modern idea of science by first reclaiming the aesthetic vision of the ancient pagans and then reinterpreting their artistic realism along mathematical lines. The mathematization of experience through art, in fact, instigated the revolution that led directly to modern science.

Renaissance humanism was a peculiar mix of Christian otherworldliness and pagan worldliness, and the tension between these mutually antagonistic worldviews could not be sustained forever; something had to give, and it was paganism that eventually began gaining the upper hand. Inspired by the ancient pagans, artists like Giotto (1267–1337), Donatello (1386–1466), Masaccio (1401–1428), Brunelleschi (1377–1446), Leonardo (1452–1519), Raphael (1483–1520), and Michelangelo (1496–1564) rebuked the negative Christian view of nature and humanity (excepting Michelangelo, who was truly pessimistic about the nature of man) and devoted their genius to observing the real world, representing it in their art. But there is a caveat. Despite their new love for realism, however, these revolutionary artists did not strive to represent reality *exactly* as they saw it. Rather, Renaissance artists typically "idealized" their work—that is, they preferred to beautify what they perceived to be less than aesthetically acceptable. Beauty, in other words, trumped reality for these artists (Michelangelo, again, is the exception since, in some instances, he choice to distort natural harmony and balance in order to deliver an artistic message). Nature in idealized form is one of the most distinguishing qualities of Italian art, especially in comparison to the art of Northern countries, which typically produced art without idealization. It is interesting to note in passing that the Italian love affair with beauty has continued unabated until today. Many contemporary Italian products and creations are noted for their matchless beauty and exquisite design—from clothing and automobiles, to architecture and furniture.

Giotto was the first truly great painter to break with the medieval tradition of representing reality as an insignificant, dull, and dismal vale of tears. The art during this time was consumed with showing only religious truths and had no interest in realistic interpretations of the world. Medieval painters depicted personages in their works who were lifeless, stiff, anatomically distorted, unnaturally diminutive, and devoid of real feelings and personalities. These works offer a clear idea of the low status to which Christianity assigned the human race. Giotto's paintings, by contrast, showed a significant movement toward more realism and a greater appreciation for earthly existence and humanity, with more accurate representations of nature and people restored to their natural size, anatomy, and dimensions—with normal human feelings and distinct personalities. This realism is especially evident in one of his fresco (paint applied to fresh, wet plaster) in Padua, *The Mourning of the Christ*. In it, all the characters show real emotions, demonstrate natural body movements, are anatomically more realistic than previous medieval renderings, and are seen in believable perspective. Speaking of perspective, Giotto's treatment of space was equally revolutionary.

Objects in natural experience are typically seen in three dimensions: height, width, and depth. With respect to depth, if your mother, for example, were standing in front of you and pointing her finger at you, you would see that her finger would be *closer* to you than, say, her shoulder. In other words, her finger and her shoulder would be on two different *spatial planes*, with her finger on the one nearer you. This relationship between items on different spatial planes is called "perspective," or, in art parlance, "foreshortening." Foreshortening, then, is perspective applied to a particular visual viewpoint.

In the paintings of the Middle Ages, objects, people, and religious figures were depicted without realistic foreshortening; that is, they were painted *flat*, without natural depth, height, or width. As a result, they were singularly devoid of concreteness. Additionally, the foreshortening between the objects themselves was typically distorted and nonsensical. The effect frequently was bizarre-looking renderings. Modifying my earlier example of foreshortening for a moment, if a medieval painter were to depict your mother pointing her finger at you, the viewer, her finger would appear to be on the *same* spatial plane as her shoulder— in other words, her finger would appear to be *in* her shoulder, and not moving out from the shoulder and closer to you, as it would appear in reality. There would be no realistic perspective. But medieval painters tried to remedy the perspective problem.

Medieval artists differentiated spatial planes by positioning the figures or items in either higher or lower areas or "registers" in their paintings; figures in the upper registers signified that the characters were to be viewed as *farther* back from the viewer—on a *deeper* spatial plane in the painting than figures placed below them, which were intended to be seen as *closer* to the viewer. Needless to say, this makeshift solution to perspective was a poor one from the point of view of realism and drives home the point that the only goal of the medieval artists was depicting religious symbolism and relating what they believed to be otherworldly truth. Their disdain for, or indifference to, realism was the reason why medieval artists never addressed in any serious way the challenges of naturalistic foreshortening.

Giotto broke with this medieval tradition of perspective, rendering images with a technique of foreshortening that was much more naturalistic, and he did so purely *intuitively*—in a way that was not guided by precise principles of measured perspective, something left to his countrymen of the next generation. Giotto's reputation as being the first Renaissance painter is also based on his movement toward giving more accurate anatomical representations to his subjects as well as infusing them with real emotions. In his earliest frescoes of the *Life of Saint Francis* (1290s), found in the Church of Assisi outside Rome, we see the individuality and emotions of his subjects as well as a glimpse of the gentle nature of Saint Francis himself—all embodied within a more realistic sense of perspective. Other great examples of Giotto's departure from medievalism are his frescoes of 1306 in the Arena Chapel in Padua, whose subject was the lives of Jesus and the Virgin Mary. In these frescoes, the emotions emanating from the subjects are even more expressive and individualistic.

What we see in Giotto is the Renaissance spirit of humanism taking its first steps in realizing itself—individualistic and this-worldly. It is fascinating to consider once again the odd blend of Christian and secular orientations. The tension between the two became more apparent as the Renaissance unfolded. Using biblical stories and themes to interject secular concerns would eventually become a very popular Western tradition, even though the differences between both traditions are at bottom irreconcilable. That a Renaissance artist would sign, even take credit for, his creations was a tremendous advance on the Middle Ages, during which time such prideful actions were looked upon with holy scorn; the church saw individual pride as the worst of all sins. Giotto was, then, unbeknownst to him, the firstborn among the earliest spirits for humanism and secularism—despite the fact that he was a devout Catholic.

Three artists in particular—Donatello, Brunelleschi, and Masaccio—were among the first to build on Giotto's breakthroughs, and they established technical and aesthetic principles that guided the work of all the greatest artists of the Italian Renaissance. Donatello reinvented sculpture and worked admirably in marble, bronze, and wood. He also sculpted flat reliefs, one of his own innovations, in which figures are inscribed on a flat surface, with the surface area itself serving as the landscape and backdrop for his figures. In all his work, he brought together the technical skill and aesthetic sensibility of the ancient Greeks and Romans and the humanistic spirit of the Italian Renaissance. In his realistic marble statues, such as Saint. Mark and Saint George for the Church of San Michele, we see the first statues since antiquity that emanated self-confidence and personal worth, and his free-standing bronze *David* was the first nude statue since ancient Roman times.

One of the pivotal innovators of the Italian Renaissance was the architect, mathematician, sculptor, and goldsmith Fillipo Brunelleschi. It was in architecture that his greatest influence was felt. An argument could be made that Brunelleschi's contribution to Italian art was the decisive one, not only with respect to the rebirth of pagan artistic values, but also for its role in unleashing the Italian imagination, which would create the cultural framework of the modern world. How could a mere architect have accomplished such a momentous feat? The answer is that he was no mere architect. His discoveries not only directed the Renaissance mind to observe the outside world with meticulous attention, but they also brilliantly embodied the humanistic ideas that the world is truly worthy of human concern; that the world contains real beauty and truth; that the human mind is good and has the power to discover, analyze, and measure worldly truth; and that humankind itself is worthy of admiration and reverence because of its godlike capacity for thought, analysis, and creative expression. In this way, Brunelleschi's art had the effect of elevating to new heights the value of both the world and humankind and convincing a whole generation of geniuses to follow in his footsteps. Let's see how he did this.

Brunelleschi, like so many Italian humanists, was enamored of the ancient pagan cultures. Being primarily an architect and mathematician, he was fascinated with the amazing achievements of Roman engineering and studied in detail many famous buildings, like the Pantheon in Rome. His particular brilliance consisted in his ability to bring together in a focused unity extraordinary artistic talent and understanding, expert mathematical knowledge, and engineering mastery. His primary contribution, in which he employed all of these talents, was his discovery (some would argue rediscovery) of "linear perspective." He understood that in constructing a building, for instance, there is a single "vanishing point" to which all parallel lines in a plane converge following precise measurements. Put another way, he solved the problem of how the length of an object fits mathematically within the spatial planes of a designated area. This was truly a watershed in the history of Western art, for what the great Giotto intuited before him with admirable naturalness became an exact science in the hands of the mathematically minded Brunelleschi.

The results of Brunelleschi's application of exact mathematical principles to buildings and space were elegantly rendered architectural masterpieces that stunningly highlighted the beauty of detail. Among his many remarkable architectural achievements, the one for which he is most celebrated and revered was his design and construction of the cupola for Santa Maria del Fiore, the main cathedral in Florence. The size of the space above this octagonal baptistery was enormous; additionally, the dome had to be built in such a way that the support systems were not visible. The gargantuan size of the cupola (forty-six meters at the base and ninety-one meters high) also made virtually impossible the usual technique of using fixed scaffolding from the ground. The cupola's size, coupled with seemingly impossible engineering demands and aesthetic requirements, presented what appeared to be an intractable design, the solutions to which escaped everyone—everyone, that is, except Brunelleschi. This became clear when his amazing design won the contest for the commission, in which a number of Florentine artists competed, including his great rival Lorenzo Ghiberti (1378–1455), who had beat him out earlier for a different commission.

Bringing together his vast understanding of Roman engineering, his expert knowledge in mathematics, his resourcefulness as an architect, his unerring eye for beauty, and his abundant confidence in his own powers, Brunelleschi decided on the bold plan of a double-reinforced shell and rib structure using bricks in herringbone patterns. To aid in the construction of the cupola, Brunelleschi invented hydraulic machines to do labor too difficult for human muscles. Brunelleschi worked on the cupola from 1420 until his death in 1434—the masterpiece was finished, absent the lantern that was placed on top, later, when he was on his deathbed. Brunelleschi's achievement stands today as one of the great wonders of the architectural world.

During his fourteen years of working on the cupola, Brunelleschi also designed other breathtaking buildings in Florence, such as the Pazzi Chapel. His other contributions included the motif of constructing a series of arches supported on columns, as well as inventing the technique of using mirrors to determine how to represent three-dimensional objects on two-dimensional canvas—he was an innovator in the technique of painting as well as a revolutionary figure in architecture.

Brunelleschi's designs and constructions made a bold statement for the new spirit of the Italian Renaissance. And it wasn't long before many of his most gifted contemporaries also became infatuated with the pagan revival and charted new courses of their own. Most notably, painter Sandro Botticelli (1445–1510) became caught up in the humanistic love for antiquity and focused on mythical topics such as in his mystical *Birth of Venus*. Another, Titian Vecellio (1487–1576), the greatest Venetian painter and one of the most influential painters of all time, was noted for his masterful use of thickly applied, brilliant colors and for his dramatic brushstrokes. His *Bacchus and Ariande*— still exploring the Renaissance love for all themes pagan—is one of his most famous masterpieces.

In his notable book *De Pictura*, the prodigious polymath Leon Battista Alberti (1404–1472) gave the first scholarly exposition on the mathematical approach to architecture. Although he was a lawyer, philosopher, architect, painter, musician, poet, linguist, and cryptographer, it is his book on architecture upon which his fame rests. Besides giving scientific coherence to the techniques employed in art and architecture, he argued that an artist is not simply a common craftsman but instead announced the emergence of the "artist" as a noble servant to truth. The Renaissance idea of the creative genius had its roots in Alberti's work.

One artist in particular who immediately rushed to incorporate Brunelleschi's breakthrough in perspective into his own work was the immensely precocious painter Masaccio (1401–1428). Although underestimated in his tragically short lifetime, he is now regarded as the founder of modern painting, and the reason is clear: in Masaccio's work came together a wonderful synthesis of Giotto's humanistic sensibilities, Brunelleschi's linear perspective, and Donatello's full-bodied, classically rendered, and sensuously infused figures. In his painting *La Trinita* (1415) in Florence, we see the very first painting in Western history in which exact mathematical perspective is used consistently. In his frescoes in the Bernacci Chapel (1427), we find what is usually understood as his masterpiece: *The Expulsion from Paradise*. Real human anguish is seen on the faces of Adam and Eve as they are being driven from paradise by an angel, and the anatomy of the subjects is both naturalistic and classical in treatment. Masaccio's high estimation is also based on his innovative treatment of light. In a series of frescoes, for example, Masaccio did something new in the history of art. Rather than illuminating his paintings by dispersing light evenly throughout, Masaccio treated light as a technique for defining the contours of the bodies and also uses light as a way for creating different moods.

If Brunelleschi, Donatello, and Masaccio gave mathematical precision, realistic form, and humanistic richness to the intuitions of Giotto, then it was in the matchless genius of Leonardo da Vinci that Italian art reached an astonishing climax, one that exploded the very boundaries of art itself and opened the way to the modern world. For Leonardo, artistic expression was not simply a way to pay homage to the external beauty and wonder of nature but was also a creative way *into* nature, into the realm where nature's secrets could be to revealed, described, and understood.

Thinking orders, simplifies, and integrates human experience. However indispensable these functions are on a practical, day-to-day level, they can also be real obstacles to true understanding. Simplifying, ordering, and integrating experience means categorizing human reality into manageable units. Unfortunately, reality does not often fit into neat categories. Judging someone as being unintelligent, for instance, is often to miss the truth that perhaps the individual is genuinely intelligent and gifted in certain areas. The modern school of thinking called "fuzzy logic" is based on the premise that even the simplest slice of reality is often a combination of many diverse, even contradictory, elements. Fuzzy logicians argue, therefore, that blanket statements are usually misguided, and that reality is better served by assigning numerical values to the different qualities or characteristics that make up the item or issue in question. In other words, they hold that nuanced descriptions are more accurate reflections of reality. As an example, human sexual orientation may not be an either/or proposition; instead, it may exist on a *continuum* in which, on one extreme end, someone may be gay, and on the opposite end, someone may be straight. In between these extremes there are numerical gradations of sexuality that combine both orientations to varying degrees. The problem of understanding and judgment becomes very complicated indeed when the item in question is a human being—the rich variations that define human nature is resistant both to general or narrow categories.

7.3

The challenge of trying to understand Leonardo da Vinci seems desperately hopeless. He appeared to be many different extraordinary individuals wrapped up in one person—all with different talents and aptitudes. And the scope of his interests was incredible: art, physics, biology, natural history, aerodynamics, philosophy, botany, optics, acoustics, hydraulics, engineering, architecture, music, archaeology, geology, mathematics, and sculpture. His contributions to art alone—the technique of painting as well as the creation of art itself—were revolutionary: from applying double glazes to give his paintings their misty appearance, to his handling of perspective, to his infusion of his subjects with unprecedented richness and subtlety of personality and expression. In his painting *The Last Supper*, the rich diversity of extreme human emotions, the explosive balance of hand gestures and body movements, the perfect foreshortening and overall integration of subjects with one another and into the surrounding space combine to make this work one of the greatest and most influential masterpieces in the history of Western art.

Many people also credit Leonardo with having laid the foundations for the modern idea of the scientific method; he conducted measured experimentation to test his ideas. Also, found in the thousands of scattered leafs that comprised his notebooks are sketches of parachutes, helicopters, tanks, repeating rifles, motor cars, war machines, submarines, scuba suits, flying machines, even a bicycle, not to mention all his dazzling anatomical renderings. The quality of many of his mere *sketches* rank them among the world's greatest works of art, and a number of his anatomical drawings are so accurate that they have been used for scientific and medical education. The list of Leonardo's interests and investigations goes on and on—there seems to be no end to his natural curiosity and creative expression.

In addition to possessing an expansive, agile mind and multiple gifts, Leonardo was also strikingly beautiful (so much so that many artists wanted him to pose for their work), and he was endowed with remarkable physical strength (apparently, he could bend a horseshoe with his bare hands). His sexual preference seemed to be for the male gender (he often had a coterie of young boys who accompanied him about town). He typically walked through the streets of Florence wearing colorful, silk clothing and sported long hair that reached down to the middle of his back—both personal choices that were not in keeping with the Florentine style of the time. He was a vegetarian and an ardent lover of animals, especially horses, and he was known to purchase caged pigeons only to set them free immediately.

Just when you might think that he couldn't be any stranger, you discover that not only was Leonardo left handed, but that he also wrote backwards (from right to left) in many of his notebooks. His interest in Christianity was unclear—some of his friends and associates believed that he had no interest at all; whatever he believed, it likely would have shocked his contemporaries. And did I fail to mention that he played (and invented) musical instruments, as well, and apparently had a beautiful singing voice? When he wasn't creating some of the world's greatest masterpieces; arguing philosophy; inventing art and science in his notebooks; sketching futuristic machines; analyzing plants; describing and showing birds in flight; revealing in sketches the dynamic movement of natural catastrophes; laying out in exquisite detail an unborn baby in the womb; reproducing in brutal figures physically deformed faces; and even fabricating a fantastic dragon; you might find his perfectly manicured fingers plunging deeply into the steaming bowels of a recently deceased human body for the sake of gaining understanding of its structures and their functions. Is it any wonder that he has frustrated even the most heroic attempts—by some of our most exceptional scholars—to put him in the typical boxes of our understanding? One might say he was fuzzy logic incarnate.

I hope I whetted your appetite to explore further the great man's fascinating life in the many excellent books that have been written on the topic. And, of course, one could spend an entire lifetime (and some have) dissecting and analyzing the many facets of his multidimensional personality and creative output. My interest here, however, is with his revolutionary thinking process and how it set the stage for the continued development of secular thought.

A basic aspect of Leonardo's genius was his preternatural ability to consider one idea from multiple, often divergent, points of view. We can observe this amazing mental dexterity in all of his art and thought. In the *Mona Lisa*, for instance, the attention to detail is astonishing, but so is the general layout of the painting—it actually offers two contrasting points of view: the left side of the painting presents a birds-eye view, and the right side offers the usual, horizontal viewpoint. Leonardo also created irresistible images that were both naturalistic and highly idealized; the overall mathematical structure of the work is perfectly balanced, yet it does not appear in any sense to be rigidly harmonious or sterile. On the contrary, its organic unity is one of its glories. Leonardo also strove deliberately and tirelessly to realize the *inner intention* of Mona Lisa, while at the same time mystifying the viewer as to what her intention might be. One could review each of his paintings and discover the same mindset continuously at work. His capacity for integrating multiple, contrasting perspectives seamlessly into a captivating artistic whole was one of the hallmarks of his art, and his artistic breakthroughs not only revolutionized Italian art but, more dramatically, signified the onset of a wholly new European cultural orientation. But Leonardo's mode of thinking had other dimensions that were equally important to his status as the first truly modern thinker.

In his work, he was—unlike his contemporaries—interested not only in the outward appearance of things, but also in their internal natures, structures, and functions. His approach to designing a machine such as a repeating rifle involved first understanding what the rifle was required to do, then designing its individual parts to carry out the various functions, and, finally, if necessary, rearranging or modifying the parts. This concern for the internal structures and functions of things was another innovation, and is basic not only to his technological creations but also to his investigations into all areas of the natural world.

His studies of the human body moved boldly into the modern world with accurate cross-sectional representations of the body's parts. Leonardo was also on the brink of modern physics with his concern for the forces of nature—apparently, he conducted experiments with respect to gravity, anticipating Galileo. But Leonardo's ultimate ambition was even greater than trying to understand and describe the human body and the laws of physics: he set himself the gargantuan task of investigating the *entire* natural world. He wanted to describe the totality of its structures and functions and represent them through precise sketches, drawings, and pictures exactly as they really are. As time passed, the pure scientist in Leonardo began exercising greater authority over the artist, and he started filling his notebooks more and more with his scientific studies at the expense of applying paint to canvas or pursuing other artistic projects. Nonetheless, he considered art a part of science and believed that the artist possesses powers of perception and observation that non-artists lack, and that, therefore, the artist/scientist is best equipped to pursue and discover the truth about the natural world.

Leonardo did not publish his scientific studies. If he had, the birth of modern science would have occurred sooner. Nonetheless, the world that he revealed and the thinking process that made this unveiling possible made their way, albeit indirectly, into the growing secular culture of the Italian Renaissance, and it wasn't long before other geniuses began carrying out Leonardo's great ambition in the sciences. His employment of mathematics as a tool for understanding nature, the priority he placed on objective observation, his descriptive approach to exposing the truth of the natural world, his focus on the inner structures of physical reality and their functions, his interest in the natural forces of nature, and his interest in testing his ideas by carrying out experiments—these in essence represent the elements of the modern approach to science. But before his legacy bore significant scientific fruit, it first galvanized the artistic spirit in Italy—and, most spectacularly, two other artistic giants.

Leonardo's reputation as one of the greatest painters in history (some would even argue *the* greatest) is based on only a handful of paintings—a testimony to the quality of his output. Yet despite his peerless technical skill, boundless creativity, and groundbreaking advances in art, Leonardo was still not the greatest artist of the Italian Renaissance. One could argue that had he managed to focus his multifaceted genius only on art, perhaps he would have outstripped his competition. But this hypothetical is farfetched. Basic to Leonardo's genius was not only his profound love for art but also his unquenchable curiosity and passion for understanding all aspects of the natural world. Artistic expression—to a great extent—became a tool that Leonardo employed to that end.

Leonardo was unable to complete many projects because he had so many interests, was a slow, fastidious worker, and could easily grow weary of a project right in the middle of it and quit; he even admitted sadly at end of his life that his lack of focus had dissipated his creative energy. But there is another credible reason why even a reconstituted Leonardo, one with a dogged interest solely in creating great art, would still have been only the second-best artist in the Italian Renaissance: his Olympian rival—*Il Divino*—the divine Michelangelo Buonarroti.

Michelangelo is an important figure in the history of secular thought because he is a rare example of a man of supreme genius in whom both Christianity and paganism laid strong claims to his allegiances. He was, in fact, racked with religious doubt all through his life, professing absolute devotion to Catholicism while at the same time being passionately caught up, body and soul, in the world of pagan values and aesthetic sensibilities. Some thinkers (including Nietzsche) have argued that it was precisely the tension produced by the conflicting belief systems and worldviews that made Michelangelo's art possible. This is a view of art based on the idea of *sublimation*, wherein feelings and passions (often uncomfortable or conflicting ones) are transformed and then redirected into artistic expression.

Michelangelo is a terrific example of what one typically finds in the Renaissance: a person paying lip service (and some life service) to Christianity while at the same time executing his artistic gifts like a true-blue pagan. That Michelangelo's greatest masterpieces—such as the *Pietà*, the *David*, and the Sistine Chapel—are Bible based should not mislead us. His love affair with the male nude alone fully discloses his pagan priorities. That he worshipped the religious (and quasi-humanist) poet Dante, and unlike Leonardo, lived an ascetic life, is also not evidence of a thoroughly Christian devotion. Again, with a genius like Michelangelo, one must always refer to his work as the final reference point for his deepest commitments.

Even though Michelangelo lived in a transitional time, when religion was loosening its grip on people's lives, the reigning worldview was still the biblical one. Italy may have been undergoing a pagan revival, but it was still a Catholic country.

It's difficult for us to realize today in the West that in earlier times, people were not psychologically and intellectually free to depart from Christianity at will, were not free to adopt just any philosophical or religious view. From a psychological standpoint, the rebirth of paganism occurred within a long-standing Christian, philosophical context, and it would not have occurred to people at that time to abandon Christianity altogether. For one, the implications of such a life shift would be so mind-boggling as to be literally beyond their comprehension. The church told people what to believe and how to live their personal and public lives; it defined how people should interact with each other at all times and in all situations—the church, in sum, provided beliefs and values that gave people's lives meaning, coherence, and purpose. It also quelled their fear of the final and most horrifying event of their lives: death. The people—even the geniuses—of the Renaissance were not psychologically free to leave, completely, the emotional comfort that Christianity provided. Let's explore the intellectual component of this mindset.

8

Atheism, Art, Galileo, and the Beginnings of the Age of Reason

8.1

Today, many people boast a confident disbelief in the moral creator-God of the Bible and Koran. If asked for the reasons for their vibrant atheism, a number might offer a long laundry list of reasons such as: there is no compelling, objective evidence that there is such a God; God is not logically necessary to account for the creation of the universe; the theory of evolution has shown conclusively that the belief in God is not necessary to account for life or the physical universe; developments in quantum physics have shown that "randomness" and "chance" are fundamental features of the universe, and that "cause" is not; the outrageous horrors and cruelty that make up Western religious history are not consistent with the idea that a good and perfectly moral God is alive and well in the world; belief in God is not necessary to live a moral, good, and happy life; belief in God is not necessary to account for goodness, beauty, and justice in the world; belief in God is not necessary for a society to maintain its moral, social, political, and economic order; the numerous contradictions in the Bible are not consistent with the alleged perfect "Word of God"; many biblical ideas are absurd or silly, such as Noah's ark, demon possession, the evil nature of nonbelievers, and heaven and hell; many sincerely devoted truth seekers have come up empty-handed in their search for God; God rarely, if ever, answers the prayers of the faithful and truth seekers alike, even though he is compelled to do so, without fail, by his own promise in the Christian scriptures; the overwhelming surplus of gratuitous pain, suffering, and cruelty in the world—at the hands of both humankind and nature—is not consistent with a caring, loving, moral God for whom every soul is precious and is addressed with justice and dignity.

It's important to note that none of the scientific positions for atheism were available to the pre-scientific West, and the philosophical attacks that have since demolished all arguments in favor of God had yet to be formulated. Additionally, the rational investigation into the authenticity and veracity of the scriptures—biblical scholarship—had not yet been invented. The full impact of the God-religions on the West was, at the time of the Renaissance, still a work in progress. Finally, there was not a free marketplace of different worldviews, religions, and lifestyles that the people of the Renaissance could explore and consider.

Even the exceptional people of the Italian Renaissance were unable to move beyond the Christian worldview and belief system of the time (with the possible exception of Leonardo)—there simply were no viable philosophical alternatives. It's important to note that the church was still the cultural powerhouse in the Italian Renaissance, and as far as the great artists were concerned, the church was their principal financial supporter. The church would obviously patronize only Christian art, so artists had to be careful not to displease the pope and his underlings. But Michelangelo, as was typical for him, was often at odds with Catholic authority figures. The problem was that the pagan in him was screaming out for expression.

8.2

Even though Michelangelo was still mired in an oppressive Christian culture and really had no choice but to think and live along Christian lines, his powerful art strained his Christian commitments to the maximum degree—and ultimately transcended them. He first began to feel the strain in the years between 1490–92, when, at the age of thirteen, he fell in love with the sculpture of the ancient Greeks and Romans. At the time, he was living at the house of Florence's leading independent art patron, Lorenzo de Medici. "Lorenzo the Magnificent" had a good collection of ancient Greek and Roman sculpture that the youthful Michelangelo studied and apparently copied so faithfully that his reproductions appeared identical to the originals. Gathered together in the great Medici household during this time were many of Florence's most noted scholars, artists, and poets—it was a humanistic feast for the eager Michelangelo, who became known among this elite gathering for his remarkable memory. Plato, Aristotle, Seneca, and Cicero were only some the ancient greats that the group recited, discussed, and hotly debated.

It was through this unique process of exceptional humanists interacting and learning from one another that Michelangelo grew as a cultured Florentine, came to his own ideas, and developed considerable literary skill. It's also likely that he completed his first original works in sculpture during this residency. The Medici experience offered Michelangelo an education fit for a king and had a profound effect on all areas of his art.

By the time he entered the Medici household, Michelangelo had already studied in the workshop of the popular artist Domenico Ghirlandaio, where he learned the proper techniques for drawing, sculpture, and painting (both *tempera*—painting using a mixture of water, egg yolk, and sometimes glue—and fresco). Before entering the Medici household, he also had studied anatomy and actually performed dissections on corpses. Like all Florentine artists of the time, his artistic training was grounded in *desegno*—the use of drawing, or "the line," to duplicate nature with precision. It was the perspective of all Florentine masters that learning desegno was an indispensable first step in creating great art, and Michelangelo applied himself whole-heartedly to this technique and became one of its great practitioners. With all this technical schooling behind him, and with his secure grounding in the highest humanist ideals of both the past and present, Michelangelo was now ready to make his own original mark and to take the future of Western art into his own hands.

In fact, he was now seen as the next Phidias (490–430 BCE), the greatest Greek sculptor, who designed the incomparable Parthenon and sculpted the wondrous *Statue of Zeus*. Although Michelangelo was greatly honored by such high praise, it put him in a very difficult situation. However enthusiastically he would strive to live up to the excellence of his ancient predecessor, the fact remained that he still considered himself a devout Christian and found himself having to serve several gods at same time: the Christian God and the various gods that inspired pagan art. This unsolvable conflict was to become a source of unbearable agony for the serious-minded artist. To make matters worse, not only did Michelangelo match his great pagan predecessor, he often exceeded him in technical skill, naturalistic beauty of form, and humanistic richness. It followed naturally that in growing into an authentic artist in his own right, he actually *deepened* his pagan commitments in his art.

In his drunken *Bacchus* (1496–98), an early marble statue that he created based on Greek models, the curves of the body are soft, and the form is more androgynous than masculine. This work is clearly a tribute to the great artistic traditions of ancient Greece and Rome. If Michelangelo did not conceal his love for the ancient pagans with his *Bacchus*, in his *Pietà* (1498–1500) at least the subject matter was Christian. This work, completed when the artist was about twenty-four, represented a creative breakthrough of the highest order. The life-sized marble statue shows a perfectly serene Virgin Mary holding across her lap the crucified Jesus. Its beautiful simplicity, accuracy of detail, and richness of human feeling distinguish the work. The contrasting images of a resigned Mary looking down lovingly at her broken son and her poor Jesus tragically wasted in the cold, unforgiving grip of death pull the viewer into the work. The attention to naturalistic detail is nothing short of breathtaking, and yet the work is lovingly idealized to give the overall sense of celestial grace. It was clear that with this artistic wonder, Michelangelo had transcended even the ancient Greeks. At a tender age, Michelangelo had produced the finest marble work the world had ever seen.

That Michelangelo produced such a marvel was for him only a beginning. In fact, despite the utter perfection of the work, it did not reflect what he was ultimately trying to accomplish. What he was after was not only realizing the pagan aesthetic ideals of earthbound beauty, elegance, balance, proportion, and grace; he strove toward something even more ambitious, something more pagan: the elevation of a man above the limits and constraints of nature altogether. But not just an ordinary man—man as supremely powerful, beautiful, and possessing great moral purpose. As we learned earlier, the idea of the philosopher breaking free of nature in order to dwell in the perfect (which also means perfectly Beautiful and perfectly Good) realm of the *forms* was the essential idea in Plato's philosophy. In fact, during the Italian Renaissance, Neo-Platonism—a blend of Greek thought, especially

Plato's, with Christianity—was very popular. Michelangelo absorbed Neo-Platonist ideas during his humanistic tutelage in the Medici household, particularly from the greatest Greek scholar and translator of the time, Marsilio Facino (1433–1499). Although the *Pietà* is a deeply religious work, the common humanity of its Virgin Mary and Jesus is what is most conspicuous; one never gets the sense that super-human or supernatural power is on display. Now, with Plato pressing ever so impatiently on Michelangelo's artistic soul, everything changed.

In his next period of work (1501–1504), the full range of Michelangelo's mature vision sprang stunningly into existence in the personage of the *David*—one of the heroes of the Old Testament. Donatello, Michelangelo's great predecessor, produced his own version of the David, which was a five-foot-tall, freestanding, bronze nude—the first nude sculpture since antiquity. Donatello's *David* caused a storm of controversy because of its distinctly androgynous appearance—he's presented as a naked warrior with a lovely, boyish face, sporting only a hat and boots; he also has long, beautiful hair, feminized breasts, a tummy, and a waistline, as well as a sensuously elongated, pre-pubescent body. Most shocking, however, was David's male genitalia, which were on full display.

When the twenty-six-year-old Michelangelo presented his own totally nude *David* to his fellow Florentines in 1504, the response was both shock and amazement. At fourteen feet, twenty-four inches high, the *David* clearly signaled the birth of a new kind of human being in the world of the Renaissance: beautiful, powerful, audacious, possessed of unshakable moral duty, and fiercely heroic. The androgynous nature of both Michelangelo's earlier *Bacchus* and Donatello's *David* gave way to a dazzling masculinity, where the awesome muscularity of physical detail was ideally balanced with an overall naturalistic beauty of form— resulting in a riveting presence that is both fearsome and breathtaking. Michelangelo even presented David's genitalia in a battle-ready, tensed, shrunken condition; clearly this *David* was prepared for combat—both physically and psychologically—against his formidable foe, Goliath.

The results of Michelangelo's study of anatomy are on full display here, not simply in the way he mastered the realistic presentation of a body's proportions, but also in the way he demonstrated the physical temperament of a body that is, at once, relaxed but also ready to spring into action without hesitation. The problem with many anatomical representations, in both sculpture and painting, is that artists often have little understanding that, at any given moment, a body's muscles are in different states of relaxation, tension, and readiness. Many artists make the mistake of tensing *all* the body's muscles at the same time, which gives the disconcerting impression that a body is in some kind of pathological physical or psychological condition. In the masterpiece of *David*, Michelangelo's aesthetic intelligence and technical expertise mastered not only precise anatomical proportions and the natural mechanics of body function but also captured the heart, mind, and spirit of the heroic man destined for physical and moral greatness.

In the spring of 2004, I was on holiday in Florence and went to see the *David*, as I always do whenever I visit Florence. One of the tour guides in the Galleria dell' Academia, where the statue is on display, related a story to me. He said that during one of his recent tours, a middle-aged American woman, resting her eyes upon the marble sculpture for the first time, fainted on the spot. When she finally regained consciousness, she admitted that when she gazed at the *David*, "feelings of love" filled her so quickly and so intensely that she began to feel very dizzy, and then before she knew it, she was on her back trying to regain consciousness. There is no question that experiencing the colossal hero up close and personal for the first time can be quite an emotional experience.

Michelangelo hit his artistic stride as a very young man with the *David*; it showcased a number of features that came to define much of his future work. Although the artist's relationship with women has never been clearly understood, we can safely say that the male gender—at least in his art—is what attracted him aesthetically. His love for the masculine physique was so pronounced, in fact, that when he depicted female forms, such as in the frescoes of the Sistine Chapel ceiling, he gave them highly muscular, virile bodies. That Michelangelo's males and females inhabit very similarly powerful physiques speaks to another of his artistic motifs: his love of extraordinary physical prowess and spiritual/psychological fortitude.

It is important to note that, in contrast to the *Pietà*, the *David* is structurally imperfect—anatomically unbalanced in one particular aspect: the size of David's hands. One oversized hand dangles threateningly down by one thigh, relaxed but clearly poised and ready for action, while the other enormous appendage is cocked and locked in attack mode, resting on a shoulder. Somewhat reminiscent of Leonardo's multiple perspective technique, the tension between David's exquisitely gorgeous body and his powerful hands creates conflicting emotions in the onlooker: one is captivated by his highly refined physical beauty but also taken aback by the raw, explosive strength that could be unleashed at any moment.

Michelangelo's art, taken together, is highly dramatic, with passions that ranged to extremes in all directions; this is true whether he was sculpting, painting, designing architecture, or even writing poetry. He was also capable of gracefully serene, elegant creations, such as his *Pietà* or the cupola for St. Peter's Basilica, but evenly tempered emotions and perfect compositional symmetry were not his usual modes of expression.

Typical are his frescoes on the ceiling of the Sistine Chapel. These frescoes—which depict stories from the Old Testament—are considered not only the greatest work of painting ever conceived and produced in the West but also the most heroic goal yet achieved in the arts. It took Michelangelo over four years to complete the ceiling, and he did it against his will and on his own, without help. The many figures, stories, and images are powerfully and provocatively depicted so as to produce mind-blowing awe in the viewer. The physical, technical, and artistic demands in painting the ceiling were so arduous—and would have been even for a group of extraordinary painters, let alone for one solitary artist—that Michelangelo's accomplishment borders on the miraculous. The knowledge that he was primarily a sculptor makes this work all the more outrageous. Unlike his more measured works, the Sistine Chapel ceiling was not the expression of a calm, serene, and harmonious vision of life; rather, it expressed what he understood to be the discordant nature of human existence, especially the tension between the lusts and imperfections of the flesh, as against the noble pursuits of the spirit. Michelangelo ultimately became a poster child for the temperamental, brooding, willful, and isolated genius, whose flights of dazzling creative expression appeared to arise from another world. The highly dramatic quality of his art can only be understood in this light. From this perspective, Michelangelo shares a great deal with that other lonely genius—Beethoven.

Michelangelo's Neo-Platonic education provided him with a philosophy of art that had a direct bearing on what he believed human being should do and become: overcome what you are (gross, unformed matter, so to speak) and realize your inborn human potential, your ideal self; that is, *become* powerful, beautiful, creative, and courageous—a virtual superman, a heroic being.

His final tribute to his pagan idols was his insistence on sculpting and painting nude figures—against the insistence of church authorities. He was known by some as the "inventor of obscenities" because of this preoccupation with nudity in his art. He even went so far as to depict Jesus Christ as one of the nude figures in his fresco *The Last Judgment*, a terrifying work that he painted on the rear wall of the Sistine Chapel. A subsequent pope was so offended by the nude renderings that he had other artists (who were mediocre at best) paint clothing over the sensitive parts.

Leonardo and Michelangelo were the most dominant figures of the Italian Renaissance, so it might seem surprising to discover that, for many at the time, the most *appealing* artist of all—and the one whose masterpieces were often considered the most beautiful—was their younger understudy Raffaello Sanzio, otherwise known as Raphael. The "prince of painters" lived only to his thirty-seventh year, but within his short life he managed to wrest technical and compositional secrets from his mentors and create a new artistic worldview. Both Leonardo and Michelangelo possessed complex personalities—they were highly eccentric, personally inaccessible, and irritably unpredictable—and, as we saw, both had conflicting psychological orientations that showed up unmistakably in their art. Raphael, by comparison, was relatively normal. By all accounts, he was a kind, warm, gentle, and even-tempered man with a happy disposition, who also had a keen interest in the opposite sex. His handsome appearance made him particularly attractive to women. As we will see, his art was a faithful reflection of the man.

Raphael absorbed the mathematical rules of perspective from Brunelleschi, Masaccio, Leonardo, and Michelangelo. From the latter two, he learned how to pictorially represent anatomical structures— how they should appear in various positions and in dynamic movement. From Masaccio, Leonardo, and Michelangelo, he learned how to infuse his subjects with feeling and individuality. From Michelangelo, he learned how to add realistic mass to his subjects. From Leonardo and Michelangelo, he learned how to organize his paintings in a coordinated and balanced fashion—for example, how to represent a *frozen* portrait naturalistically within a particular landscape or how to integrate many individuals, displaying different kinds of behavior, into a visually meaningful whole. He also mastered Leonardo's technical innovations, such as his procedure of subtly distorting colors as a way to soften the curves of objects. However, the greatness of his art didn't arise simply from his mastery of his mentors' critical principles and techniques; it was because of the way he used what he learned to create something refreshingly new and captivating.

Remember, the general theme of Italian Renaissance art was the representation of the real world accurately—as if one were looking out of a window and seeing clearly and accurately what was actually there. This movement began with Giotto and progressed dramatically when Brunelleschi and Masaccio introduced mathematical perspective into architecture and painting, respectively. This naturalistic trend finally culminated in Leonardo, who not only described precisely the surface of many areas of the natural and human world but who also revealed for the first time their underlying structures and functions. Although Michelangelo further developed the naturalistic trends in his work, he also broke with this tradition by producing art that appeared to transcend the natural limitations of the physical world. However, this trend toward increased naturalism was accompanied by a counter-tendency toward *idealizing* (refining) the natural world.

Raphael's masters idealized their works to varying degrees and employed different strategies to highlight these efforts. Leonardo, for example, often placed beautiful images and subjects within uninviting and even visually repellent surroundings, as in his *Virgins of the Rocks*, in which a cold, ominous, and lifeless cave is the landscape for the lovely Virgin Mary and her holy family. And however blissfully sublime Michelangelo's art could be, the perverse and dissonant were never far away. His Sistine Chapel ceiling and Last Judgment frescos embody this tendency famously, and, as we noted earlier, even in his exultant *David*, the artist veered from the ideal of harmonious beauty by exaggerating the size of David's hands.

151

Artists typically idealize their figures to express different feelings. Michelangelo often gave his figures, like *David* and the Christ in *The Last Judgment*, a heroic demeanor that unambiguously projects strength of body and character. Leonardo's idealizing, by contrast, was multilayered, nuanced, and much more difficult to decipher—the most famous examples of this are the *Mona Lisa*'s "enigmatic" eyes and her smile, but virtually every one of his paintings has an inexplicable quality of some sort. The paintings' beauty seems to derive not only from the refined physical characteristics of his characters but also from what appears to be a lovely, transcendent light delicately shining through the canvases. At other times, such as in his *Virgin of the Rocks*, Leonardo challenged our normal sense of what is aesthetically appealing by bringing together into one artistic whole extremely beautiful and extremely ugly images.

Although early Renaissance masters like Giotto revolutionized Italian art by introducing naturalism into their works, these early attempts were still fraught with anatomical mistakes and problems with perspective. In the hands of artists like Masaccio, Leonardo, and Michelangelo, such technical problems were solved, and a greater naturalism emerged. The same artists also advanced the humanistic cause by presenting not just simple subjects but *individuals*—living, breathing people with distinctive feelings, passions, and attitudes— true-to-life personalities. With Leonardo and Michelangelo, the psychology of the individual became a legitimate concern for the artist. Michelangelo, in particular, often highlighted personal and existential conflicts. Raphael looked upon the staggering artistic achievements of his mentors with deep veneration and concluded that the best way to honor them was to build upon their work and to find his own way. And the results changed the history of Western art.

Raphael used his natural genius and acquired skills to create art that was both exquisitely idealized and flawlessly harmonious *in every detail*. Unlike his mentors, he strove to eliminate all tension, conflict, and imbalance from his masterpieces. The trials and tribulations of the human condition, which characterized much of Michelangelo's work were not themes in Raphael's art, and Leonardo's keen interest in exploring deeper, more complex emotions had no purchase with Raphael—nor did Leonardo's fascination with multiple, even mystical, perspectives. Raphael's humanistic art was, in large part, unreservedly committed to the aesthetic ideals of classical beauty in which balance, proportion, and simple elegance are the guiding themes. But within this framework, Raphael found his own aesthetic voice—a voice that became most apparent in the way he idealized his subjects.

His *Madonna with the Goldfinch* (1506) strikes the viewer with the graceful symmetry of the painting, not to mention its superbly rendered foreshortening. But there is much more. The influence of Leonardo and Michelangelo is obvious: the face of the Madonna resembles Leonardo's own efforts, and Raphael's use of Leonardo's *chiaroscuro* technique (light and dark shading to form the shapes of figures) is in prominent display—with even more subtlety than in Leonardo's own work. Michelangelo's influence is equally apparent in the painting's fully rounded figures. But what is most inviting about the painting is the spirit of loving-kindness that imbues its characters.

The Christ Child's depiction as *playful* is nothing short of charming, but the tender affection shared between the Christ and an equally young John the Baptist is what is most surprising. The intimacy between subjects is pervasive throughout the work, as we see the Christ Child resting his cute, little foot delicately upon that of the Virgin Mary in an image that one can only describe as adorable. And the Madonna herself is filled with maternal pride as she looks down lovingly at the two delightful children.

You may have noted that I have consistently used words like playful, charming, et cetera to describe Raphael's characters and their relationships. This goes a long way toward illuminating a central aspect of Raphael's contribution to European art: *warm* feelings often colored the way he beautified his subjects and represented something new in the evolution of aesthetic expression in the West. Raphael's art was an honest expression of his kind and gentle nature. One would have to go back to the lovable Catholic ascetic Saint Francis of Assisi (1181–1226) to find a comparable spirit.

Saint Francis has to be given credit for being perhaps the first important historical person in the medieval era to transcend the dismal, life-negating worldview of the church of his time and to find nature beautiful and deserving of respect, even reverence. Saint Francis was very fond of all forms of life and had a special fondness for flowers and little animals. It was his idea that since God created nature and all the beauty in it, humankind has a moral duty to respect God's creation. Saint Francis' affirmation of personal experience was a great boon to the humanistic cause and had reverberations down through the centuries, most conspicuously in the work of Raphael.

When we consider Raphael's masterpiece in fresco *The Triumph of Galatea* (1511), another marvel of his art comes to light: his seemingly effortless ability to organize, coordinate, and balance freely moving characters without sacrificing the unity and focus of the entire work. His "easy" composition with respect to complex challenges is one of the hallmarks of his art. A great artist often approaches a particular work as a series of technical difficulties that need to be overcome. It is from this perspective that we can begin to appreciate the brilliant solutions that Raphael devised with respect to *The Triumph of Galatea*. His greatest technical challenge here was to decide how to situate, within the space of a fresco, the numerous figures—each one in dynamic movement—without the work, as a whole, becoming frenetic and agitating.

He solved all technical problems in one stroke by establishing the face and body of the sea-nymph Galatea as the main focal point. He harmonized the potential chaos by creating a beautiful symphony of action that directs all movements to Galatea. The result is a graceful painting that guides the eye and mind with perfect ease over its surface and into its meaning. Hence the boys with arrows floating above Galatea, equally balanced on her left and right side, take aim—Cupid style—at her heart. As Galatea's chariot is being drawn from left to right, her veil is seen blowing backward in the opposite direction; this sort of movement/counter-movement activity was Raphael's strategy for keeping all the different behaviors of his figures balanced and integrated. Raphael's most elegant solution to the flurry of activity in the painting was to show the activities as though they were all occurring on *invisible lines* leading directly to the face of Galatea.

Raphael redefined the meaning of beauty in the Renaissance. His art integrated the classical ideals of elegant simplicity and balanced proportion with new values of beauty—values that spoke the truths of the human heart. He is justly celebrated for his innovations in balancing and integrating figures in dynamic movement and the utter harmony of his compositions. His most important achievement, however, was to balance these advances with the artistic exploration of what he viewed to be the positive side of human character and, especially, the warm and soft emotions that color our interpersonal relationships. This is not to say that his art was excessively concerned with the tender side of human nature. As we see in his most famous painting, *The School of Athens*, his subjects were always portrayed as balanced, well-adjusted people, and for him this meant individuals who embodied intelligence, moral strength, and nobility of character *as well as* a capacity for highly intimate feelings and sensibilities. Raphael here, as always, remained devoted to the pagan ideal of symmetry.

Raphael's genius shone through in his peerless ability to beautify nature and humanity without leaving the real world behind. His art never appears artificial, stilted, or disconnected from everyday life, even though he always remained true to his elevated aesthetic ideals. The meaning of his art calls to mind an analogy: if Michelangelo had his spiritual counterpart in the unpredictably explosive Beethoven, then Raphael's counterpart was the beautifully nuanced, charming prince of musicians, Mozart, whose music could be described in much the same way that we talk about Raphael's painting. When the German philosopher Friedrich Nietzsche (1844–1900) was composing his wonderful book *Joyful Wisdom* (sometimes called *The Gay Science*), more than halfway through the process, he fell into a moment of critical self-reflection. Then he proclaimed, in a timeless aphorism, a new philosophy for his life: "May I proceed like Raphael and never paint another image of torture." The gentle artist's fate was to be much more than the originator of some of the most beautiful paintings in history; his art also announced to the modern world the emergence of a fresh vision of earthly existence—life-affirming, noble, and beautiful, and thus he gave considerable substance and momentum to the humanistic cause.

8.3

The reader might be wondering why, in a discussion on the evolution of secular thought, I have taken some time on the important artists and masterpieces of the Italian Renaissance. This question is a good one. Painters, sculptors, and architects—despite how crucial their works may be to art history and to the happiness of those who appreciate them—are typically not what the German philosopher Georg Friedrich Hegel (1770–1831) called "world-historical" individuals—

that is, people who influence, in important ways, the overall unfolding of history. If the immortal Rembrandt (1606–1669) had never existed, for example, it certainly would have been an incalculable loss to the world of art, to other artists whom he may have influenced, and to his admirers, but from an historical perspective, his absence would not have altered in any profound way the course of Western history. The same could *not* be said of people like Aristotle, Emperor Constantine, Thomas Jefferson, or Albert Einstein. When we think of the significant artists of the Italian Renaissance, as is the case with great philosophers, political leaders, or scientists, we are dealing with people who are remarkable precisely because their genius transcended their art, and, as a result, they became genuine world-historical individuals.

Leonardo, Michelangelo, and Raphael reintroduced cultural values, interests, and intellectual strategies that would ultimately reorient Western culture on many different levels. As we noted, what the Renaissance accomplished in all areas of culture was first seeded and cultivated to some extent in the late Middle Ages, but it was only with the Italian Renaissance that we recognize the first full blossoming of the real beginning of modern culture. But what, in fact, did the great Renaissance artists accomplish that meant so much to Western culture in general? And to what extent were these artists *indispensable* to the unfolding of Western history?

The advent of the Italian Renaissance was inevitable. Too much before it had prepared the way for its arrival. Giotto, Masaccio, and Brunelleschi are rightfully given the credit for reintroducing realism into the world of art and architecture. This was the foundational shift away from the medieval world and represented the real beginning of the Italian Renaissance. Nonetheless, it seems clear that if these three artists had not made the critical breakthroughs—such as the rediscovery of mathematical perspective—other artists at least equally as brilliant would have eventually emerged and carried out the mission. This is not to diminish the genius and accomplishments of Giotto, Masaccio, and, particularly, Brunelleschi, whose contributions to Renaissance art and humanism were astonishing; it is more to acknowledge that the spirit of realism was *in the air*, as it were. With genius in no short supply at this critical moment in Western history, the major advances in realism were always just around the corner.

When we discuss Leonardo, Michelangelo, and Raphael, it becomes very difficult to maintain this position. Even though much of Leonardo's work in science and technology was not formally published in his lifetime, his impact was nevertheless profound in both areas and served as a direct link to the birth of modern science and technology. So immense and prescient was his intellect and imagination that he represented a new kind of human being in modern times. He was indeed a "world-historical" personage, not only because of his contributions to science and technology, but also because he illustrated a new definition of what being an "individual" meant in the modern world: physically self-assured, psychologically self-sufficient, intellectually brilliant and multifaceted, artistically profound, creatively unbounded, boldly inquisitive and independent, and passionately committed to rational and empirical investigation. Leonardo was simply incomparable; no one was likely to have come along to take his place and have his level of cultural impact on the Renaissance and, by extension, Western history.

A similar argument could be made of Michelangelo. For many, he was the greatest artist in Western history, and, not unlike Shakespeare, he was a talent so beyond comparisons to anyone else that one must be careful not to underestimate his particular influence on Western culture. If Leonardo represented the power of the mind both to investigate and discover the truths of the natural world, as well as to imagine the most fantastic futuristic realities, then what Michelangelo represented was the power of the mind, imagination, and human will to *control*, *form*, and *recreate* nature from his own—very personal—point of view. Michelangelo's accomplishments with his chisel and paintbrush transcended his art and became a sort of modern archetype that served as a stimulus and guide to a young, energetic culture trying to find and reconstitute itself. Even in his lifetime, he was seen as the incarnation of almost supernatural powers. Yet his "human-all-too-human" qualities (including arrogance, vanity, capriciousness, argumentativeness) were a constant reminder that he was, after all, simply human. In other words, Michelangelo the person helped to humanize his incomprehensible talent and allowed other gifted individuals to see themselves as possible geniuses. The Michelangelo *archetype* entered the consciousness and subconscious of Western culture and has manifested itself in countless ways in the birthing and evolution of modern history. This is not to undervalue the rationalistic rigor that he brought to bear in his masterpieces. In all his work in sculpture, painting, and architecture, we see a powerfully rational mind at work.

What I have been hinting at with respect to Leonardo and Michelangelo is that they embodied, in conspicuous detail, the modern spirit of the rational pursuit of truth, creative self-expression, and the audacious confidence in the human ability to recreate nature in mankind's image. Michelangelo, unlike Leonardo, did not have purely scientific interests, despite his immaculate anatomical sketches, but his *defiant* mindset with respect to forcing recalcitrant physical nature to comply with his creative will and vision became enshrined in modern science and technology.

Could Western history have survived unchanged without the influence of Leonardo and Michelangelo? Would their absence have made all that much difference? I have already given my answer, but my response will become even clearer once we answer a more general question: how important was Italian Renaissance art to Western history as a whole? The answer is simple: the scientific and technological revolutions of the seventeenth, eighteenth, and nineteenth centuries began with Italian Renaissance artists studiously observing, measuring, and reproducing the natural world for their masterpieces. It follows, then, that they first envisaged the worldview that made the Age of Reason possible.

A critical step in the evolution of science was the reinvention and perfection of mathematical perspective in the hands of the great artists. The trend toward naturalistic and humanistic realism came to a culmination in the art of Leonardo and Michelangelo (and, as we shall see, Raphael), although with the caveat that they also idealized their subjects. Besides the sheer revolutionary brilliance that they brought to their art, these artists were modern spirits—individuals whose distinctive philosophical viewpoints were at least as influential in the developing modern world as their art. With the unparalleled sway that these two artists had over all aspects of the Italian Renaissance, how could one imagine that their absence would not have altered the course of Western history in countless ways?

At first glance, Raphael appears to be more difficult to position as world-historical. After all, a large part of his art was derived from his open adoption of the innovations of Leonardo and Michelangelo—an honest admission that what his mentors had discovered and created was of revolutionary importance. Nonetheless, learning their secrets was just a beginning for him. His own creative work focused, in part, on realizing fully the classical ideals of beauty. Although Leonardo and Michelangelo brought Renaissance art to unprecedented excellence, *disharmonies* of various kinds were often self-consciously integrated into their greatest masterpieces. Leonardo frequently introduced multiple (often conflicting) perspectives into his art, and Michelangelo (notwithstanding his exquisite work in architecture, design, and his perfect *Pietà*) projected spiritual tension and imbalance through his masterpieces and also used anatomical inaccuracies to drive home important humanistic themes. The incongruities in Leonardo and Michelangelo's art, relative to the classical ideals of balance and symmetry, were actually artistic choices that they made and were defining qualities of their work. And their masterpieces were not simply the natural consequence of the artistic trends of the Italian Renaissance; they represented and reflected the emergence of new philosophical trends for a new humanistic age.

Raphael, by contrast, moved along a different trail, developing artistic techniques and themes that were only partially explored by his great contemporaries and then integrating them with his own ideas. And what emerged from this artistic and humanistic mix was yet another vision of art and life. The ultimate value of a work of art exists in its ability to alter our experience of the world and even influence how we view ourselves. The greatest art does not simply affect us emotionally; it also rouses our imaginations and compels us to see reality with different eyes and to think thoughts that may be foreign to us. One of the most remarkable aspects of Raphael's art is the ease with which the viewer is seduced by its beatific vision. The world that Raphael presents to us is one where absolute harmony reigns, where what is ugly, unbalanced, and discordant has been corrected by the genius of human mind and heart to create order and express warmth and tender compassion. The power of his art consists in its ability to project one simple mood, one feeling, and one all-consuming emotional experience. This is in no small part due to the harmony of composition and the delicacy of feeling that integrates all his paintings.

Although Leonardo and Michelangelo transfigured, refined, and organized Italian art into a potent cultural force, it was only in Raphael that one clear, humanistic vision was attained, where the mind and the heart are placed in ideal balance with one other, and the creative power to think rationally and produce beauty are in seamless harmony. Raphael's ideal world of sweeping elegance, unerring symmetry, and heartfelt emotions is certainly not the typical world we see around us. It was a fantasy of his imagination—but it was a fantasy irresistible to the emerging culture still struggling to discover what it believed and valued. By allowing this fantasy to inform his art, he was the first artist to articulate—in lucid, unambiguous form—the most ambitious version of the humanist model. And as was the case with Leonardo and Michelangelo, his vision was absorbed into the European cultural bloodstream and has nourished, in countless ways, the blossoming of Western civilization. It is in this light that Raphael can easily be seen as a world-historical figure.

These Renaissance artists laid the foundation for the emergence of the modern worldview, which proclaimed that human existence is good, that human reason and creativity are good, that human beings themselves are good, and that the future will *necessarily* lead to greater prosperity and happiness for all humankind. Behind all this goodness and optimism for the future lay the ever-expanding confidence in the power of reason to understand reality—something quite new in the fourteenth and fifteenth centuries. Let's be clear about this. The Renaissance world was still mired in superstition and religious dogma. It still had one foot firmly stuck in the Middle Ages and the other in the modern world.

As we saw with medieval thinkers like Thomas Aquinas, the value of reason was finally affirmed after centuries of degradation at the hands of the church, but this endorsement of reason was limited to rigid, Catholic interpretations. Reason is useful for gaining partial knowledge about reality, but it needs help from faith-based understanding in order to be complete. Put another way, reason was at an underdeveloped stage. The Renaissance, by contrast, represents the first full blossoming of the humanist seed planted by Aquinas and other medieval thinkers; the Renaissance flower—under the watchful eye of the great artistic caretakers—finally pushed through the weeds of cultural thoughtlessness, and it was strong, healthy, and fragrant. But this was only a beginning—a thriving garden had yet to be cultivated.

Before Giotto committed a single brushstroke to the first *realistic* painting since ancient Greece and Rome, before Brunelleschi revolutionized Italian art with his ingenious architectural ideas and formulas, before Masaccio organized the first painting in the Renaissance in terms of exact mathematical proportions, before Leonardo pierced the surface of the natural world to observe and describe the structures and functions of things, before Michelangelo wrested from obdurate marble his beautifully heroic *David* and painted the Sistine Chapel ceiling in *his* own vision of power and spirituality, and before Raphael projected the world of nature and man as enchantingly graceful and harmonious—there was the *rational mind* affirming, challenging, probing, dissecting, calculating, rebuilding, and taking delight in its own powers to comprehend and refashion the world. Indeed, the rational mind was about to move to center stage in Western culture for the first time since the ancient Greeks.

History creates the conditions for significant individuals to emerge, who in turn create the conditions for history to unfold in very specific ways. Although this simplistic chicken-and-egg version of history ignores many significant, complex psychological and social/political factors, it's still the most convenient way for historians to isolate and plot the most obvious causal factors of historical change. We have discussed a number of the important Italian artists, and we observed in passing that their work has transcended the history of art—and has profoundly impacted the emergence of the modern world. But as remarkable as these artists were, from the general point of view of the unfolding of history, they were *preparatory* figures, setting the stage for the emergence of an even more remarkable world-historical person—one who would take their contributions and transform them into the cultural watershed of the late Italian Renaissance. This amazing person was the astronomer, scientist, inventor, mathematician, and writer Galileo Galilei (1564–1642).

8.4

Galileo is famous for many reasons:

- Writing his great scientific books not in Latin (the long-standing tradition) but in his native Italian.

- His invention of the astronomical telescope, military compass, the pendulum clock, the water clock, and the thermometer.
- His support for the Nicolaus Copernicus' "heliocentric theory" (the idea that the sun, and not the earth, is the center of the solar system).
- His falling-out with the church and his being forced to recant publicly his support for the heliocentric theory—under threat of torture.
- His astronomical discoveries of mountains and valleys on the moon, sunspots, satellites around Jupiter, and the phases of Venus.
- His mathematical formulations and demonstrations of the "Law of Falling Bodies," which states that all objects, regardless of their weight, fall at a constant rate of acceleration.
- His discovery of the "Law of Inertia," which states that an object in motion will continue moving in a straight line unless it is influenced by another force like gravity or air resistance.
- His formulation of his "relativity principle" that maintains that the laws of physics are the same for all observers moving at a constant speed in a straight line.
- His formulation of the modern scientific method, which focused on mathematical theory *in conjunction with* empirical observation, data collection, and testing hypotheses (intelligent conjecture) through precise experimentation.

Galileo's many accomplishments in astronomy, physics, and technology have rightly earned him several titles, including the "Father of Modern Astronomy," the "Father of Modern Physics," and the "Father of Modern Science." But there is another sense in which he was modern science's first real advocate. Galileo was radically antiauthoritarian at a time when Aristotle—in partnership with the church—was the unquestioned scientific authority. To the chagrin of his academic colleagues, he openly challenged, in lectures and various publications, Aristotle's physics and pointed to what he considered to be Aristotle's vague, unscientific pronouncements, such as his idea that all objects move to their *natural* place in the universe. To drive his point home forcefully, Galileo devised theories and experiments that gave precise mathematical descriptions and demonstrations of how objects really move through space. Galileo then pushed the envelope even further.

In an open letter to the church, in 1632, Galileo maintained that God inspired the writing of the Holy Bible for the purpose of showing humanity how to go to heaven, not to give an unambiguous account of the way the natural world behaves. He also argued that the reality disclosed through the five senses is the real one and that human reason is well equipped to understand this reality. Since our senses and capacity for reasoning are gifts from God, he said, it would make little sense to disregard what they so plainly show us. The language of the Bible is profoundly mysterious and is frequently veiled in allegory and metaphor. It's for this reason that its deepest wisdom often eludes our normal powers of understanding. We do well, then, to allow scientific truth—in particular, the truth that Galileo himself revealed—to provide the exact meaning of especially abstruse biblical passages about the relation between the earth and the sun and about the nature of the solar system in general.

On this score, Copernicus' sun-centered solar system—the heliocentric theory—is not really in conflict with the Bible. It's simply the case that the religious authorities in the past had not understood the real meaning of the scriptures that refer to the natural position of the earth in relation to the sun. If these authorities had, they would never have supported the earth-centered viewpoint. This is where Galileo's science came in to save the day. Scientific reasoning and observation clearly show that the sun, and not the earth, is the center of the solar system, and that the earth simply revolves around the sun. According to Galileo, this is what the Bible really meant to say. The "geocentric" or "Ptolemaic Theory"—the earth-centered view of the solar system—had been the official position of the church for over two thousand years, and Aristotle himself held it to be correct. Galileo had little respect for long-standing traditions or authority and argued that *his* scientific work—because of its grounding in reason and empirical demonstration—was not only the true interpretation of the natural universe but was also the correct interpretation of all biblical scriptures that refer to the relationship of the earth to the sun. Such was Galileo's audacious position as he took on both "The Philosopher" Aristotle and the church itself. If ever there was a case of hubris, this was it. It is important to note, however, that the church in Galileo's time was not the uncompromising, anti-intellectual monster that it is often depicted to be. It was still intolerant of ideas that threatened its position as the repository of ultimate truth and knowledge, but its grip on the European mind and imagination was beginning to loosen considerably. Its position on the Copernican theory is a good case in point.

Contrary to popular myth, the church was not, in principle, opposed to the heliocentric theory, but instead it insisted that Galileo present the theory only as a *hypothesis*—a mere possibility—unless he could provide hard evidence in its favor. Galileo was not a man who did well with following orders from authority figures, and he was still committed to spreading what he considered to be the truth about the Copernican theory. It was at this point that Galileo's desire for fame and status—he wanted the position of scientific leader of the church—got the better of his intellectual conscience. He wrote in his native Italian tongue a brilliant, Platonic-style dialogue, *Dialogue About Two Chief Systems* (1632), that in no uncertain terms presented Copernicus' theory as factual, and, even more incendiary, he offered a bogus scientific proof—his theory of tides—as justification for his position. The truth is that Galileo was never able to show conclusively that the earth revolved around the sun. The best he could do was to provide empirical evidence that lent indirect support to the theory, such as his observations of the phases of Venus and his discovery that there are four satellites that revolve around Jupiter.

After tolerating Galileo's boisterous arguments for Copernicus' uncomfortable theory—and even permitting him the freedom to publish his controversial ideas under mutually agreed-upon conditions—the church finally decreed that Galileo had gone too far; he had blatantly and arrogantly brushed aside his arrangement with religious authorities. He was forced to recant publicly his belief in the Copernican theory—under the threat of torture. And as punishment, he was put under house arrest (although a very comfortable version of it), during which time, again contrary to orders and despite going blind, he continued to write. During his incarceration, he produced his greatest, most influential work in pure physics, *Discourse on Two Sciences* (1638), and had it smuggled out of Italy and published in Holland.

Historically, Galileo had won the day. The church made the mistake of giving him too much freedom while he was under house arrest, and at the very last moment, the ever-determined blind, seventy-four-year-old scientist created the epochal book that sent modern science on its way. Christianity has been fighting a losing battle with science ever since. The church in Galileo's time was certainly in transition. It was beginning to recognize the value of scientific efforts, as long as the Bible was not blatantly contradicted. From this point of view, Galileo was an unwise advocate for the scientific cause. If he had been more diplomatic and had presented his ideas in less antagonistic forms—and had not foolishly adduced his phony "tides theory" as support for the heliocentric theory—he possibly could have had his cake and eaten it, too. Nonetheless, it is naïve to think that the church could have become a true bastion of scientific thought and inquiry under any circumstances. The fact is that the ideas in the Bible and the important discoveries of science are strongly incompatible, as their histories have shown. Even given a receptive church, it was only a matter of time before religion and science (especially biological science) went their separate ways.

As far as his work in astronomy is concerned, some have argued that Galileo's aiming his homemade telescope toward the heavens and describing accurately what he observed was one of the three most significant events in modern history—the other two being the invention of the movable type printing press by the German Johannes Gutenberg in 1450 and the discovery of America by Christopher Columbus in 1492. Galileo's contributions to pure science followed naturally from the work of mathematically orientated artists like Brunelleschi and Leonardo. In his book *The Assayer* (1623), Galileo declared, "Nature is written in the language of mathematics." These words could easily have emanated from the lips of a number of his fellow artistic countrymen. Like Leonardo, he also tied his science to everyday experience as it is disclosed through the senses and grounded his science in what can be verified through repeatable, empirical demonstration. But there was a caveat: Galileo, again like his artistic predecessors, *idealized* the physical world, but in a way that was specifically suited to his scientific investigations.

His idealizations took three forms: First, he recast nature in the ideal forms of geometry, so when he described, measured, and tested nature, it was a mathematically idealized nature that was the object of his study. Secondly, he famously divided nature into primary and secondary qualities, primary qualities being aspects of the physical things that are objectively measurable and quantifiable, such as weight, height, length, width, depth, and velocity. Secondary qualities, by contrast, are the characteristics of things that cannot be measured, such as color, taste, sound, smell, and feeling. Physical science, as a matter of principle, must focus exclusively on that aspect of reality that can be reduced to mathematical description and analysis—primary qualities. Galileo's elimination of secondary qualities from serious scientific study had a profound influence on all future thought in the Western world, both inside and outside of science. For example, subjective experience in general came to be viewed as an inferior source of knowledge and truth, a viewpoint that guided much of modern philosophy.

And thirdly, Galileo's invention of the "thought experiment" was another important aspect of his idealization of nature. Galileo reasoned that mathematical laws govern nature, and this is why a scientist can imagine any number of logically possible scenarios in which natural laws necessitate that nature behave in an absolutely predictable way. To name just one, his idea that objects of different weights and sizes accelerate at the same constant speed required him first to imagine objects falling through space without air resistance. Ultimately, he tested and confirmed this thought experiment by rolling balls of different weights down inclined planes (which had the effect of neutralizing the effects of air resistance) and observing their mutually constant acceleration. The thought experiment became one of the critical components of the modern scientific method and was an important tool for the continued progress of science. Later, the greatest physicist of modern times, Albert Einstein (1879–1955), used thought experiments extensively in the development of his two theories of relativity.

The most important guide to scientific, philosophical, and even commonsense thinking is the idea that there is an "objective" reality that exists independent of our awareness of it, and that our investigation of it does not change it objective nature. This foundational belief in objectivity comes straight out of Galileo's understanding of science and, more specifically, from his ideas about what makes up the physical universe.

Galileo realized that his focus on measurable, objective reality required another imaginative leap that challenged not only common sense, but also the physical senses themselves. As far as he was concerned, the heliocentric version of the solar system was a scientific truth. His discoveries of the laws of falling bodies were also truths, but in both cases, he arrived at these conclusions by suspending his typical ways of experiencing and understanding the world. In other words, Galileo's science was *counterintuitive*. Indeed, the earth *appears* to our eyes not to move, and the sun clearly seems to be revolving around it. But scientific observation and reasoning have shown this interpretation to be incorrect. The sun-centered solar system is also an affront to common sense. If the earth were whizzing through space at some fantastic speed, then throwing a ball up in the air should result in it returning to the earth at a different location in relation to where it was thrown. Likewise, Galileo's idea that objects accelerate at a constant rate independent of weight and size is also counterintuitive for the same sort of reasons. The interesting paradox in Galileo's procedures is that he based his science on the ability of the senses and mind to know reality, while at the same time he realized that both avenues of possible knowledge could be totally misleading. This is why mathematical reasoning together with experimentation is so critical to his enterprise: they are the necessary correctives that have the power to guide the senses and the mind through the labyrinth of false leads and impressions, in order to discover the principles that guide the physical universe.

Galileo's advocacy for a mathematically defined and structured, but empirically verifiable, science was the perfect blend of Plato's emphasis on the world of ideal forms—the world of mathematics—and Aristotle's contrasting emphasis on the physical world—the empirical realm of the five senses. After the many centuries of contentious exchange, Galileo found a way to modify and unite his two great predecessors' theories into one formidable system. The mathematical truths that Plato strove to reveal through philosophy and mathematics were not located in an ideal realm apart from the physical world; rather, they were intrinsic to it. Aristotle, for his part, was not a mathematician, and he believed too much in the truth of mere appearances, natural intuition, and common sense. As a result, his scientific reasoning went astray. Galileo's science corrected most of these mistakes, and thus science, for the first time, became a reliable way to describe and understand the natural world. One of the keys to Galileo's breakthrough was that he was the first to use mathematics as a strategy to describe *relationships* between items of physical reality and not simply as a way to weigh or measure physical things. As an example, his application of algebraic mathematics to the physical universe allowed him to discover and demonstrate natural laws, such as the law of falling bodies.

Besides taking Renaissance trends in naturalistic art to their logical conclusions, Galileo contributed to modern humanism in another way: reminiscent of Michelangelo's, Galileo's fiercely individualistic and defiant spirit with respect to what he believed to be true was a prophetic sign of the times. His muscular confidence in his own powers of reasoning, and his conviction that the rational approach to understanding the world is superior to all others, created the modern humanistic roadmap for all future science—indeed, for scholarship in general. What began in the thirteenth century with Thomas Aquinas and other churchmen's reintroduction of Aristotelian reason and logic as important tools for understanding, finally came to full term with Galileo's assault on Aristotle and the elevation of rigorous scientific reasoning as the ultimate arbiter of what is true about physical nature, even surpassing the authority of the Bible. In summary, one could easily argue that besides his many contributions to science and to the culture of humanistic scholarship, what Galileo represents more broadly is nothing less than the bold march of reason into the very heart of Western civilization.

Although Galileo represented the grand finale of certain strains of Italian humanism, he was still only a beginning. What started in Italy as a rebirth of pagan culture quickly turned into a cultural revolution that spread very quickly beyond the borders of the "Golden Boot" to fertilize the whole of European culture. The essence of this revolution was the meteoric rise in the belief that rational thinking would solve the world's ills, would unlock the philosophical and scientific mysteries of the universe, and finally would guide *all* of humanity to even greater well-being and prosperity. "Progress" became the watchword for this modern "cult of reason." The strong belief in progress is based on the well-evidenced fact that rational thinking is a reliable problem solver. Its most effective tool for solving problems is its power of criticism—a well-criticized situation or issue can lead to the solution of problems, which clearly is progress; it's that simple. Now, if critical thinking could be so enormously successful in at least some instances, then why could it not be as successful in *all* instances? The modern age, beginning after Galileo, was nothing less than a series of cultural experiments in which this thesis was tested. And to ask about the precise nature of this experiment is simply to ask what made the modern age different from all those that preceded it.

Great advances in science and technology are distinguishing aspects of the modern age. The scientific advances of Copernicus, Kepler (who discovered that planets revolve around the sun in ellipses), and Galileo, and the creation of new devices—such as Gutenberg's printing press and Galileo's astronomical telescope—are just a few of the countless examples of how individual rational thinking and innovation overcame the scientific and technological errors, limitations, and problems of the times.

9
Rationality, the Rise of Liberal Democracy, Ignorance, and Technology

9.1

As Europe began taking form, so did its economic life, and this process represented another crucial test for the power of rational thinking. As contrasted with the medieval practices of preventing individuals from freely determining their financial fate, the free market economy came into existence. The basic idea was that individuals, and groups of individuals, should be given the freedom and responsibility to make rational decisions about the production, consumption, and trading of goods. In extending this free market experiment further, other innovations such as the *division of labor* provided rational solutions to questions of production efficiency. Another novel aspect of the free market system was the emphasis on creating *new* goods and wealth, as contrasted with the medieval idea that all the goods and wealth that humanity would ever require had already been provided in abundance by God and that the long-term goal of any business-related activity was only the fair and just *redistribution* of these things.

In no uncertain terms, the emergence of the free market economy represented a swelling confidence in the power of individuals to create new goods and wealth and to make the right choices that benefited the economic well-being of society and even humanity as a whole. But the growth of science and technology, as well as the birth of the free market, reflected a new vision of society, one that was to contend for, and ultimately gain, political dominance in the Western world: *liberal democracy*.

The early developments of liberal democracy—first in Great Britain—were not only the most radical byproducts of the newly emerging belief in progress—they became the very basis of the modern world order and the embodiment of what the modern world means. And what is the meaning of liberal democracy? We could say that the foundation of liberal democracy is the principle of individual human rights; the "rule of law"; a government elected by the majority of the people, with protection and respect for minority groups; a society with a free press and the freedom to speak one's mind openly without fear of punishment; a political system where the government is prevented from unjust interference in the personal, economic, and religious lives of citizens; the freedom to own private property; the right of people to vote into office leaders and representatives who have the people's best interests at heart and who are protected from special interest groups, the power of citizens to vote out of office elected officials who have failed in their sworn duties; and finally, living in a society that promotes mutual self-respect, ethnic and religious tolerance, and happiness for all.

The real difficulty in liberal democracies comes in trying to balance liberalism—individual self-determination and the requirement of personal freedom—with the democratic principle of rule *by the people*. This natural antagonism is a constant challenge to liberal democracies, but the positive aspect of this sociopolitical tug-of-war is that it forces liberal democracies to confront their moral and philosophical weaknesses, find creative solutions and compromises, and, ultimately, to evolve to a more just and benevolent society for all citizens.

One needs to appreciate that the emergence of liberal democracy stands as an extreme contradiction to the Christian culture of the Middle Ages and even to much of the culture of the Italian Renaissance. At its core, this difference hinges on two different ideas of human nature, one medieval Christian and the other secular. The modern view of human nature was first conceived in ancient Greece and Rome; was obliterated by Christian notions of inborn human sin during the early Middle Ages; began to reappear in the late Middle Ages with thinkers like Aquinas; made a spectacular showing with poets, artists, writers, and thinkers of the Italian Renaissance and the Enlightenment; and, finally, became fully and permanently enshrined in the political framework of modern Western democracies beginning in the eighteenth century. So what was this definition of human nature, and how was it different from medieval versions?

From the moment the pre-Socratics began investigating the nature of the physical universe by using rational arguments and simple mathematical descriptions, a new conception of what it means to be human began forming. Using reason in this way individualizes and empowers a human being insofar as rational evaluations of any kind confer the power of judgment on the evaluating person. Judging is personal and individual: it automatically refers back to the thinking person as the source of the judgment and makes this person responsible for what is thought. Unlike irrational or thoughtless judgments, rational evaluations strive to *integrate experience* and make broad logical connections that make sense. But what does this mean regarding the Greek definition of human nature?

To question and find rational answers says that the seeker of knowledge is both capable of acquiring knowledge and worthy of doing so. For the Greeks, the capacity for rational thought represented not only what is best and *highest* in a human being, it actually defined what is unique about human nature. Although both Socrates and Plato recognized that passion and the life of the senses have their functions, they thought that they should be strictly controlled and restrained by the rational faculty. Even Aristotle, who gave the passions and the senses the dignity they deserved, ultimately viewed rationality as the apex of human accomplishment. The world is a storehouse of truth waiting to be discovered by a sufficiently devoted and acute mind. For Aristotle, the excellent use of the rational faculty to discover this knowledge brings the most pleasure in human life and in fact is what it means to be human.

Thinking rationally became a thriving humanistic tradition in ancient Greece and gave birth to Western science, new areas of mathematics, philosophy, symbolic logic, democracy, and human-ennobling art. It is important, however, not to see Greek humanism as sterile and stiff or bereft of life, feeling, and passion. As Nietzsche pointed out in his *Birth of Tragedy*, the Greek accomplishments in all areas of culture, and especially art, could only mean that reason and passion struck a spectacularly productive balance, in which the unruly forces of human nature were restrained, redirected, and brought to a higher aesthetic integration by the awesome controlling and directing power of human reason. In other words, the clash between instinct and reason produced explosive, creative tension that ultimately birthed the Greek accomplishment. But the Greek definition of human nature as rational, good, noble, creative, and even godlike was driven underground at the hands of the Roman Church during the first eleven hundred years of the Common Era.

The Romans, in general, were not smitten with the rational investigation of reality, as were the Greeks. The Romans were practical above all else. Their love of reason was primarily based on what it could *do*, what it could create to make the world ever-lasting, convenient, and predictable. Romans were obsessed with power, for they understood that visual reminders of Roman muscle fortified and inspired the Roman spirit—and intimidated Rome's enemies. The sheer size and sturdiness of their architecture, as evidenced by the Pantheon, is a prime example of Roman rationality put to great practical effect. Where Greek architecture was focused on creating perfect balance and proportion in the exteriors of their buildings, the Romans also used their rational know-how to create immense *inner space*. They felt that buildings need to be lived in—that is, felt and experienced—*from the inside*. The Pantheon is immense both externally and internally and reflects the Roman ideal of a world that will be seen *and* inhabited for an eternity. It naturally follows that human nature for the Romans was not abstract; it was not, as it was for the Greeks, a detached and invisible dimension that is present mostly in philosophy, literature, and mathematics. Instead, for the Romans, human nature was a creative force seen in the practical world of working, creating, and organizing earthly institutions, enjoying life, and, last but not least, conquering the world. Human nature for them was most authentically revealed in their passionate commitment to the various tasks that comprise typical daily life.

The Romans adopted Stoicism from the ancient Greeks and gave it their own cultural twist. The result was a worldview that focused on the Roman virtues of tough-minded devotion to work, duty, self-sacrifice, and the rule of law. This reflected their belief that not only were Rome and the universe in perfect harmony, but Rome was actually part and parcel of the law-driven cosmos—and fated to civilize all of humanity. Roman law, one of the great gifts from antiquity, was meant to be the mundane corollary of the cosmic law above, and, indeed, it organized and civilized the vast Roman world in countless ways.

For the Romans, human nature deserved the highest respect, admiration, and even celebration because of its awe-inspiring accomplishments in all areas of practical existence. And what's more, they believed that human nature would ultimately reach its highest expression when the Romans fulfilled their *cosmic destiny* of spreading their wondrous civilization across the entire face of the earth. Humanity would then be one, and it would remain eternally Roman.

However, the world did not have to wait an eternity to see that the grandiose world that Rome had originally conceived was only an imagined ideal. The many flaws and vices in its government, economy, and policy decisions ultimately led to its collapse in the fifth century CE, when the empire fell to Germanic invaders. As a result, the Roman goal of universal domination was only partially realized. The Western empire came to a formal end at this time, but its decline had actually begun centuries earlier at the time of the rise of Christianity. It was during the time of a burgeoning Christianity that a new idea of human nature began vying for dominance and eventually suppressed the Greco-Roman one almost without a trace.

How does Christianity define human nature? Again, it depends on the historical Christian installment we are considering. If we are trying to remain true to what the New Testament says, then human nature can only be seen as incorrigibly corrupt because of its sinful essence, varying interpretations notwithstanding. I can't think of a single passage where a contrary interpretation is even possible. The depravity of human nature is clearly the main presupposition of the Gospel's "good news," as it is the sine qua non of Christ's life, death, and resurrection. Mankind, as represented in the original people of Adam and Eve, was created good by God and placed in paradise to live in absolute happiness forever. But because Eve, and then Adam, disobeyed God's direct orders (the meaning of sin), they were cast out of paradise and cursed with mortality, pain, suffering, childbirth, work, and general spiritual darkness. Their "fall from grace" is automatically extended to all subsequent humanity. According to biblical scriptures, "the penalty of sin is death," and death is the fate of all humankind, unless God provides a way out. As far as the most popular interpretation of the New Testament is concerned, it was the infinite love of Jesus Christ—"God in the flesh"—that offered humankind the only way to escape its hell-bound destiny. Jesus was, in effect, the sacrificial lamb for a sin-ridden humanity. By living a perfect life, "dying for our sins" on the cross, and being resurrected by God to new life, Jesus was, in a way, the antidote to human nature. By believing sincerely, on faith, in this promise, one is guaranteed a fresh spiritual slate and a place close to God in heaven after death. Of course, this simple recipe for salvation based on faith hides a number of philosophical and interpretive difficulties that have produced wide divisions, if not open warfare, between the various sects of Christianity.

By focusing the Christian mind so exclusively on the evils of human nature and the world in general, in favor of the perfect world to come, it was only natural for early Christians to believe that anything associated with human nature and life in this world must necessarily be corrupt, sinful, and thus best avoided or even annihilated. On this score, sexual desire or the love for material possessions are, by extension, also evil and must be expunged at all costs. The use of rational thinking to gain worldly or philosophical knowledge was also seen as ungodly and as another shameful aspect of human nature. One of the gravest sins of human nature is its tendency for self-love or excessive pride. Given the fallen state of humankind, to be prideful is a serious affront to God and is a further indication of how foolish and corrupt human nature is. That is, human nature is so blinded by its own self-absorbing pride that it can't even see its own morally depraved state. But the larger issue in satisfying sensual desires and selfish cravings, in using thinking as a tool for gaining knowledge, and in being prideful is the clear suggestion that pleasure, knowledge, and pride are good and valuable in themselves and are worth pursuing. For conservative Christians, this value system is pure evil simply because it contradicts the Gospel of Jesus Christ and is more in alignment with the values of Satan himself.

A new installment of Christianity slowly emerged as a consequence of the philosophical clash between paganism and medieval Christianity. This transformation began in the late Middle Ages when Aristotle and other pagan thinkers were reintroduced into European thinking. Slowly, the value of rational thinking began rising, and, with it, the world of everyday experience also started increasing in significance. With the full emergence of pagan values and sensibilities during the

Renaissance, human nature was, for all intents and purposes, completely rehabilitated: thinking, sensual experience, pride, individuality, and personal power were now seen by many as good and deserving of being enthusiastically encouraged and even cultivated. The great artists, writers, and thinkers of the Renaissance became human testaments to this transfigured vision of human nature. But there was a serious cultural problem. How could these two mutually exclusive viewpoints of human nature coexist within the Christian culture of the Italian Renaissance? The answer is that they couldn't for long, and eventually pagan ideas of human nature reconfigured medieval ones. This new version was to play a dominant role in the ideological foundation of Western liberal democracy.

A good example of this is the famous dictum in the Declaration of Independence that all men are given certain natural rights by their Creator, including "Life, Liberty, and the Pursuit of Happiness" ("Pursuit of Happiness" originally meant the right to own property). This clearly represents an optimistic idea about human nature and its great prospects for a good life for all human beings in this world. This notion of human rights and its implications for the quality of life on Earth is a far cry from the medieval evaluation that human nature is corrupt and that life on Earth is a dismal, demon-laden "vale of tears." Where in the New Testament, one might ask, are the natural rights that Thomas Jefferson argued for in his Declaration and the values that the document presupposes? Is a free, happy life on Earth, where natural reason is respectfully embraced as humanity's most valuable earthly guide, anywhere supported in the New Testament? And where in the New Testament are the personal pursuits of worldly goods and private properly described as natural rights? Where in the New Testament, in fact, is this world presented as good and filled with wonderful possibilities for the sufficiently optimistic human being? And where in the New Testament is the secular-based, liberal government (with church/state separation) championed as the best possible government, one best suited to the nature of human nature? These positions are so far beyond the intentions and meanings in the biblical worldview that one cannot find New Testament scriptures that offer even possible interpretations that would lend support to these views.

In fact, the Jeffersonian values are not Bible-based values at all, but instead are Enlightenment values rooted in eighteenth-century critiques of traditional Christianity. Jefferson was not speaking as a traditional Christian when he wrote the Declaration, but as a *deist*, which was a very popular quasi-religious movement at that time in Europe, particularly in France. As we noted earlier, deism, as a religious perspective, exists somewhere between theism and atheism and maintains that God created the universe and the rational laws that govern it but is not personally involved with his creation in any way, did not send himself in Jesus Christ for the sins of humanity, is not available to hear and respond to prayers, and does not reveal himself in revelations to devoted disciples. Furthermore, truth, for the deist, is to be found by optimistically investigating nature (nature is good and contains the promise of truth) by utilizing the God-given power of reasoning, particularly reasoning guided by the principles of science. Reminiscent of Aristotle's Unmoved Mover, the deist God is a cold and aloof, absentee deity who placed human beings in the midst of this God-made universe to employ their imperfect intellectual and ethical powers to do what is rational and moral. Jefferson borrowed this religious worldview from the French Enlightenment philosophers, such as the skeptical deist Voltaire, who also inspired Jefferson's thoughts with respect to the founding of America. Jefferson believed, nonetheless, in the Religion of Jesus, which he maintained was the greatest moral code ever devised by humankind, but he did not believe in the divinity of Jesus, the Trinity, or the supernatural content of Christianity. Although he was fervently anticlerical, that is, was against what priests and ministers had made of Christianity, Jefferson did believe that the traditional Christian religion was healthy for the moral fiber of America. He attended church and even endorsed Christian practices. However, in echoing English liberal ideas of the eighteenth century, he believed that the government itself must remain neutral with respect to specific religious doctrines. If the American population had been largely Buddhist rather than Christian, Jefferson would not have altered his political or moral worldview in any way. His only concern would have been that Buddhism promoted good moral behavior and encouraged citizens to be good Americans.

9.2

When rational thinking began gaining renewed esteem in the late Middle Ages, its full return to prominence was only a matter of time. Its first impressive showing in the Italian Renaissance met with great resistance, as Italy was still caught between two radically different worlds: the archaic Christianity of the Middle Ages and the pagan rebirth of Greece and Rome. As a result, Italy was unable to carry the cause of secular modernism to its natural conclusion. After the Galileo affair, Italian science was close to its end, and the torch of rational inquiry was passed to other countries. In England, the great Francis Bacon (1561–1626), Isaac Newton (1641–1727), John Locke (1632–1704), and Adam Smith (1732–1790) set the philosophical stage for the European Enlightenment—or the Age of Reason—which championed the causes of unbridled critical thinking, scientific progress, free rational inquiry, free market economy, modern technology, and the experiment of liberal democracy. France and Germany soon followed with their own critiques of Western religious, political, and philosophical traditions as well as their own significant scientific and philosophical contributions to the new world order.

Interestingly enough, Enlightenment thinkers were not all in agreement that rational thinking could provide all the answers that the philosophical and scientific mind demanded. Philosophers like Scotsman David Hume (1711–1776) and the German Immanuel Kant (1724–1804), for example, put firm restrictions on what human beings could comprehend rationally and argued that reason, because of its finite nature, is ill-equipped to know much of reality. In sum, the Enlightenment represented two distinct traditions: one in which rationality was promoted as the faculty that could provide all the answers to human existence and the other a profound skepticism about the power of reason to grasp essential truth—and the two traditions have been doing battle ever since.

9.3

Another essential component of the emergence of Western liberalism was the philosophy of utilitarianism. When English philosopher and political thinker Jeremy Bentham (1742–1832) wrote his *Fragment on Government* and *Principles of Morals and Legislation*, he didn't realize to what extent his ideas would reconfigure much of modern Western culture. In fact, the influence of his ideas in his own lifetime was meager; it was really through his students, like John Stuart Mill (1806–1873), that utilitarianism took its most potent and influential form. The foundation of utilitarianism is Bentham's principle of utility, which says that the desire for happiness motivates all human behavior. For him, it followed naturally that the basis for moral action is the desire for the "greatest happiness for the greatest number of people." Happiness, in this sense, simply means the absence of pain and the presence of pleasure. Thus, the ideal world for a believer in utilitarianism is one in which individual hedonism is perfectly balanced by social hedonism—that is, where one's own pleasure and everyone else's pleasure are maximized, and where one's own pain and every one else's are minimized. For Bentham, this should be the goal of our civilization: *happiness for all!*

If ever a view of proper moral behavior—and of correct social, political, economic, and even legal policies—followed directly from historical developments, it was utilitarianism. An important aspect of utilitarianism, and one that more than any other feature influenced all areas of modern culture, was its emphasis on effects or *consequences* of actions. What matters most in a moral act, utilitarianism holds, are not its motivations or guiding principles but, rather, the consequences. Did the act achieve a good that we value or not? If it did, then it has fulfilled its requirement of moral decency. The emphasis on consequences could be seen as one of the most characteristic aspects of eighteenth- and nineteenth-century Europe, whether in politics, economics, or in the social arena. Although this view has a natural appeal to it, its ends-justify-the-means orientation has obvious ethical faults and logical incompatibilities with other moral intuitions. For one, it could easily promote deception and dishonesty as essential tools for happiness. If I steal my friend's money without his knowledge, this could result in an overall greater sum of happiness, since my personal pleasure has been increased and my friend's remains unchanged—assuming, of course, that the amount I stole does not financially handicap my friend and assuming that he never discovers the theft.

The most difficult aspect of the grand experiment of utilitarianism is the philosophical and existential tension that quickly develops in a culture that is, on the one hand, guided by the rule-of-law and, on the other hand, guided by the promotion of the idea that consequences are the only test of what is good. With the rule of law, universal moral principles and general and unchanging codes of conduct *predetermine* what is good and bad; we don't wait to see the consequences of specific acts to conclude, for instance, that murder, political oppression, and public sexuality are unacceptable behavior, because we have laws and moral principles that provide these judgments in advance. But the problem is that universal, general principles of any kind are often ill suited to particular situations. For instance, stealing top secrets from a potentially lethal enemy could easily result in a greater good as compared to not stealing them and jeopardizing the lives and liberties of many people. Because the bottom line for utilitarianism is the greatest happiness for as many as people as possible, laws are critical; laws, at least in principle, should promote the *common good* and militate against special-interest groups.

On a larger scale, it is conceivable that a whole civilization could, in utilitarian terms, be achieving immediate happiness while ultimately destroying itself—for example, by overpopulating the earth through excessive sexual reproduction and *consequently* using up the earth's limited natural resources. The immediate result might be pleasurable for everyone concerned, but, in the long run, it could result in ecological and human catastrophes. Another fascinating distinction in utilitarianism is one between "act utilitarianism" and "rule utilitarianism." Act utilitarianism focuses exclusively on the consequences of actions, while rule utilitarianism focuses on the consequences of actions as they apply to *general* rules. Here's an example of the former: is it morally good to lie to your business partner about a major deal that that you foolishly but secretly lost, if there is no chance of recovering the deal, and if telling your partner the truth would definitely destroy your business relationship with him and seriously destabilize both of your lives personally and financially? In act-based utilitarianism, this question could be answered by arguing that the lie should be kept a secret, since it would minimize the pain and terrible inconvenience that would most certainly follow from telling the truth. On the other hand, rule-based utilitarianism would want to know if telling a lie in this situation could be used as a general rule for doing business. What would happen if lying to your business partner became a *typical* business practice? It's likely that lying to your partner would backfire in the long run, since successful businesses require honesty between partners, and, besides, there is an excellent chance that the *practice of lying* would eventually be discovered and could end in an ugly lawsuit or even criminal actions like, perhaps, murder.

There are countless examples that point to a limited legitimacy of utilitarianism as a moral philosophy. The same sort of hedonistic calculus could prove to be equally deleterious to a country's economic and political well-being. The lesson to be learned is that emphasizing consequences alone is no guarantee that the consequences will necessarily be good for one's self or for society as a whole, either in the short or long term. Nonetheless, it's hard to argue against the great success of utilitarian thinking and policies from a political and economic point of view. The emphasis on financial gain is the foundation of capitalism and is a wholly consequence-based way of operating. And didn't dropping two atomic bombs on the Japanese result in the rapid end of World War II and save many lives, despite the unspeakable horrors that the bombs perpetrated on many innocent victims? Most experts would say yes.

Once the Renaissance resurrected the power and dignity of human reason and creativity; once becoming a sovereign individual became a primary purpose of life; once European societies grew weary of tyrannical monarchies and oppressive religious intolerance; once the Enlightenment birthed the Age of Reason, in which natural rationality was seen as the panacea for all of humanity's ills; once the American Revolution showed that democratic self-rule is a viable alternative to oppressive higher authorities; and once the Industrial Age began creating "wealth" and gaining enormous momentum—utilitarianism was really inevitable as a political, economical, and social policy. Striking a workable balance between personal hedonism and social hedonism, on the other hand, has proved to be an extremely challenging process, but one that is the very foundation of Western liberal democracy.

9.4

Along with being biological animals, human beings are also cultural beings whose lives are guided by and reflect the various traditions in which they are born. Even reasoning—the celebrated hallmark of human nature—is thoroughly absent from human newborns.

Additionally, human babies are born with only the minimum of instinctual behavioral patterns, such as sucking and crying, as well as more basic biological processes like breathing and elimination.

Human beings are born prematurely, and for good reasons. The mechanics of childbirth, especially the requirement for a baby's head to pass through the birth canal, necessitated its early arrival into the world. A larger head would make the delivery process impossible if a child were to remain in the womb until it was sufficiently mentally and physically mature. Nature instead opted for premature human beings coming into the world, putting the onus of responsibility on human parents to care for their offspring until their bodies and brains have grown enough to gain a sufficient measure of self-reliance.

According to fossil records and geological studies, countless life forms came into existence only to flicker out soon after. The story of life on Earth is largely a story of one failure after another, with only a few fortunate success stories—successes that have led to the proliferation of life throughout the planet. As I mentioned previously, the disappearance of species on the earth has been so pervasive that scientists estimate that 99 percent of all life that has come into existence has subsequently gone extinct. Insurmountable challenges to biological existence led to mass extinctions at least five times—where, in some cases, almost all of life on Earth went extinct. The life forms that did manage to survive to ensure the continued survival of their kind were fortunate enough either to inherit naturally adaptive qualities that prevented their destruction, or else they *learned* to survive.

One of the most truly mind-boggling "extinction events" occurred about forty-five million years ago, when a gigantic asteroid crashed into the earth and wiped out most of its life, including our beloved dinosaurs after their 150-million-year reign. The asteroid's impact apparently disrupted the prevailing ecosystems to the extent that many life forms could not adapt sufficiently well to survive. Massive amounts of debris exploded into the sky, blocking the sun's light, and lethal gas likely poisoned the earth's atmosphere—these were two likely ecological consequences that made life on the earth very difficult and even, in most instances, impossible. The loss of the dinosaurs, however, created a safe ecological space for rodent-sized mammals to survive and flourish. It stretches credibility to imagine that a vagabond celestial rock destroyed the dinosaurs and gave small mammals the opportunity to survive, increase in number, and ultimately evolve into human beings. But beyond the benefit to humanity, this mass extinction led directly to an astounding proliferation of all life on the earth. Three cheers for that asteroid! Unfortunately, it's inevitable that someday we will be visited by another crazy mass of ice and rock, and there is no telling how it will all turn out. Might we go the way of the dinosaurs? Very likely, unless we use science and technology to figure out workable methods of deflecting asteroid trajectories.

9.5

How much does a newborn baby know? Is it possible that nature has abandoned the human baby and left it helpless in a strange and dangerous world without inborn mechanisms or instincts that would promote its survival? The question automatically implies the nature/nurture issue that has been raging for centuries. In the past century, we discovered that genes, hormones, and enzymes are passed on from one generation to the next and determine many characteristics of a human's physical, emotional, and mental makeup. Nonetheless, the importance of the influence of the *biological environments* in which life grows and develops (and in which genes *express* themselves) can never be doubted or underestimated. The old nature/nurture distinction may have been too simplistic a dichotomy, but, nonetheless, the question is still a real one. How much knowledge and understanding does a human bring into the world, and how much is learned or acquired? To what is extent is human nature and human knowledge a function of genes and other inborn biological mechanisms, and to what extent are external, accidental factors—including environment, experience, upbringing, and learning—responsible? Is a child's biological being nothing more than a repository of pre-programmed mental, psychological, and physical patterns and behaviors poised to be activated at a predetermined time or when the appropriate external cues or stimuli are present? Is a human being a tabula rasa requiring external factors to provide it with the information and knowledge needed to survive in a human way? Scientists have shed some light on this controversy, and most would now agree that human nature could take many forms, with each one comprising a unique blend of genetic, environmental, and social factors. Human genetic makeup—the "human genome"—was assembled over the course of million of years of life on Earth "in the wild," in pure nature, but sheer survival meant more than inheriting the right genes; it also meant possessing enough creative intelligence to learn to cope resourcefully with the challenging twists and turns of everyday life.

The gradual emergence of human culture drastically retarded, and ultimately ended, human, biological evolution to any significant degree. On the other hand, "sexual selection"—a mild form of natural selection in which mates are chosen based on their *appealing* qualities—continued to be a causal factor in evolution. Typical natural selection, by contrast, was a brutal natural force that destroyed countless life forms, including several primitive, human species. The human species that survived did so by creating an ingenious, protective barrier between them and nature. This protective barrier was *human culture*. The effectiveness of cultural protection, however, was initially very slight, as early humankind had to learn—through trial and error—how to use their creative intelligence in the practical affairs of daily survival. As humans reasoned, learned, and experimented with survival strategies, human culture quickly developed to the point that humans were no longer forced to adapt physically—in any substantial way—to the pressures of natural selection. Eventually, biological evolution was largely supplanted by *cultural* evolution, and human history was off and running.

9.6

The physical development of a baby is fast and dramatic—literally, every moment, its physical existence is constructed before our very eyes. Genes, hormones, enzymes, and a dizzying array of biochemical processes underlie a whole host of programmed patterns of behavior that guide this "coming-to-life" of the baby's body.

As we know, when a baby is born, its head is underdeveloped and undersized. The immature head houses an immature brain. As the newborn grows, her brain develops along with her head. During this process, brain cells and their connections increase in complexity and specificity. Stimulation from the outside world (early sensory and cognitive experiences) and proper nutrition both play a significant role in how the brain gets "wired." The construction of the brain's ultimate biochemical, electrophysiological, and functional anatomy, then, reflects the dynamic interaction between an internal environment and the outside world stimulating it.

Newly birthed human beings also must adapt to a foreign, external presence and force: *objective reality.* Lights, sounds, smells, voices, external sensations, erratic movements, and unexpected interruptions all serve as shocks to, and intrusions into, a newborn's biological existence. The growing baby is interconnected with the outside world—after all, a substantial part of its nature is derived from it, but that world is beyond the baby's control. Care providers like parents and relatives typically are in charge of the newborn, but this is always a risky undertaking, because errors, poor judgment, misunderstanding, and ignorance often invade and compromise a child's support and care system.

So ever-present is the power of the outer world that its influences are part of a human's normal existence from the very outset, making the influences an ineradicable part of human nature. Indeed, the extent to which there is a human nature at all is largely a question of which ways, and to what degree, the outside forces influence, incline, or shape a human being to think, emote, and act in particular ways. For purposes of discussion and analysis, we can separate a human being's biological nature from his environment and gain some understanding and insight. However, this "reductionism" is an extreme abstraction and ultimately cannot settle to a satisfactory degree any issue regarding human biological or cultural existence.

9.7

Education—teaching ignorant animals how to live and for which reasons—is the primary task of culture. This function has been a daunting one, and the results have not been good. The problem begins because each generation of babies, born as blank slates, must begin anew the process of becoming cultural beings. A baby newly birthed in 300 BCE was as culturally ignorant as a baby born in 2000 CE, or at any other time in history. The accumulative wealth of knowledge, information, and wisdom that has been gathered and transmitted down through thousands of centuries is actually lost on each newly born baby. Unlike physical or psychological characteristics, this cultural treasure is not transmitted by biological mechanisms such as genes, hormones, or enzymes. And this is why the chief function of culture is *to teach.* Humans absorb, refashion, and build on whatever traditions have passed down. The cultural responsibility of the proper and effective education of each generation of children is humanity's greatest challenge and its most significant goal. And humankind must be vigilant with each newborn—much more so than it has been thus far.

9.8

Ignorance is a basic condition of human existence. Human beings are finite and can only possess partial knowledge. Mythology, religion, philosophy, science, and thinking of any kind are all attempts to remedy this primordial ignorance. Knowledge is the basic issue—knowledge about how to survive, live life, work, play, believe, create and find pleasure, make love, behave, think, get along in society, gain power, attain happiness, prepare for death, and so on. Knowledge has been, and will always be, humanity's "Holy Grail."

The story of humanity is the epic drama of the pursuit of knowledge and its countless failures, successes, and applications. Although the various forms of knowledge—whether common sense, intuitive, artistic, religious, scientific, or philosophical—have all claimed to possess the whole truth, every solution to the problem of knowledge has always been flawed and incomplete, at best. That is to say, the solutions, depictions, and descriptions offered up have never lived up to the lofty ideals of truthfulness that humans have erected. The question—What is true about *what is?*—still remains as important and relevant as ever, and for good reason: it's the rock-solid foundation upon which all other questioning—in fact, all thinking—rests.

9.9

How does science address the problem of humanity's natural state of ignorance? Science has built up an astounding body of knowledge that not only has altered the way we experience the world and the universe, but its child, technology, has also radically changed the way we think and act in every sphere of our lives. The scientific model for knowledge is, without a doubt, the best model for knowledge ever devised. Its appeal lies specifically in the fact that its knowledge is powerful, reliable, awe-inspiring, and often practical.

Western religions promise to pass on to the true believer spiritual truth and to show them how to understand and resolve many of the difficult issues of life. Prayer and revelation, the two principal paths through which spiritual truth is suppose to reach the true believer, have not proved to be reliable methods for achieving this end. It's common for believers to be profoundly perplexed about many spiritual and mundane issues even after considerable praying and waiting for God's words to be revealed. Of course, God's failure to give clear and distinct answers to the prayers of the devotee is attributable, or so true believers claim, to the belief that God's ways are "mysterious," or that we could never know the will of God, or that he will reveal his answers at the perfect time, which is unknown to the true believer. It doesn't seem to matter to believers that the New Testament promises that God will *always* answer the faithful prayers of the true believers, without qualification, and to their satisfaction. Regardless of the reasons *why* prayer fails so miserably, it's undeniable that prayer is a deeply flawed mechanism for gaining sound, predictable knowledge or finding satisfactory solutions to life's problems in a timely manner. Compare this unreliable system of gaining knowledge to the reliable, concrete information that one discovers from studying, say, an instruction manual for an appliance. Of course, life's problems are complex and profound and, as a result, require more complex answers. But the fact remains that relying on prayer and revelation for truth or knowledge is a risky business, which brings up the question: why do prayer and revelation perform so badly? We cannot neglect the idea that their poor showing may be based on the possibility that both are fraudulent practices, that prayer squanders words or thoughts, and that waiting for God to reveal truth is a waste of time.

Philosophical knowledge, like religion, also has not made good on its promise to deliver the long-sought-after solutions to life's major problems and issues. The great Western philosophies, beginning in Greece and continuing in Europe through the centuries, all provided what they considered to be complete answers to some, if not all, of the major philosophical issues. Even though many of the famous philosophers are among humanity's greatest geniuses, their ideas, systems, and solutions have simply not met the standard of logical consistency, and they frequently do not hold up to the facts gained through reflective and lived experience.

Religion and philosophy live in two very different epistemological worlds to the extent that philosophical knowledge, like science, must meet the standards of rational analysis and logical consistency, whereas the religious treatment of truth is framed mostly in dogmatic assertions. This term refers to statements of alleged truth that are true simply because they are the truths of God. Rational analysis or logical consistency is actually inappropriate in the religious context, because God's truth transcends the limitations of rationality and logic. Therefore, the Bible is not a philosophy book, rooted in logical analysis and rational argumentation, but is the alleged "inspired Word of God," rooted in simple faith. In this sense, religion and philosophy could not be more estranged ways of approaching truth and reality.

Nonetheless, the history of religion and philosophy respectively show religion time and time again trying to use philosophy to prove religious principles. Consider Thomas Aquinas employing Aristotle's ideas and logic in his writings to "prove" that God exists. Consider philosophy incorporating religious principles, and even God himself, in rational arguments, like Descartes using God's supposed perfection and goodness as a step in his logical/deductive proof of the existence of the outside world. Both approaches paid the price for their inconsistencies. Once the knife of reason was applied to religious dogma, it was only a matter of time until each and every aspect of religion was cut to shreds. Philosophies that incorporated religious ideas likewise suffered the indignity of being pummeled into smithereens by critics like Friedrich Nietzsche, who wanted to know how God could be used in a rational argument, since there was nothing rational about God or the belief in God.

In the end, God failed religion miserably as the indubitable source of spiritual truth, and reason failed philosophy as the royal road to the ultimate truth about reality. The failures of religion are much more serious, however, because what is at stake there is the very meaning of human existence—of life and death. There is nothing gained for Christianity, for instance, from its adherents failing to find "the truth" in the Bible. Religious pioneers such as Jesus may have shed light on certain aspects of human existence, such as the importance of showing compassion, but even this valuable insight does little for the religion if its ultimate spiritual claims, such as the "good news" of salvation and eternal life, are found to be fictions. Furthermore, if Jesus is *not* God in the flesh, it is a disaster for Christianity—in fact, the whole of religion would be rendered ultimately useless, even though it may have conferred some benefits on humankind.

Philosophy, by contrast, has gained a great deal from its failures to discover ultimate truth through reason, such as the wisdom that truth, in any form, could never be contained in one system, however profound. In fact, failure in philosophy, as in science, has always represented the chance for growth and deeper understanding. Philosophy has also produced countless insights into the nature of human experience and into what is real and worthy of consideration and what is not. And let's not forget that science is not only the child of philosophy, but philosophical thinking itself—including science's analytical skills and the skeptical mindset—is an essential component of the scientific method.

9.10

Technology has become the *new nature*—that toward which much of human endeavor aims. In pre-modern times, technological items, such as tools for constructing shelters or weapons for hunting and protection, were ways of dealing with and adapting to the demands of living in the natural world. That is to say, technology was a means to an end, that end being living in nature with greater comfort and safety. Today, by contrast, the reverse is true: we typically use our natural minds and bodies to make contact with, and relate to, the universe of technology. In other words, civilized humans now serve technology. A good example is modern business, which is thoroughly dependent on computers; employees and businessmen of all stripes typically do much of their work on computers and then use the computers to make contact with other computers. And the computer craze has led to the creation of the Internet—the latest and, next to television, the greatest technological object of human passion.

Virtually every area of modern life is dominated by technology, and its omnipresence has invaded modern consciousness itself to the extent that we typically think, reflect, choose, will, intend, and even emote through the prism of technology. Technology, in fact, has become a veritable worldview. To wit: the moon is no longer an exotic object of poetic loveliness and timeless mystery but instead is known to be made of such-and-such elements and compounds and, more importantly, is seen as an inevitable destination for future inhabitation and even exploitation as our technology advances. It is no surprise that, with technological filters firmly in place, modern humans are gradually losing their ability to be lost in the stars, as it were, and to know the wonder of seeing what is beautiful, whether it's the beautiful moon or a beautiful idea.

9.11

That technology has assumed control of the human mind and imagination raises the question of the nature of human nature. Is human nature so malleable that it could assume any form whatsoever without harm to its own well-being? And how would we recognize that human nature has lost its own preferred state of well-being? We must address these questions by inquiring into the relationship between human happiness and human nature. They are interconnected, because either notion cannot be considered in any depth without reference to the other. The major stumbling block in trying to capture a sustaining meaning of happiness is that happiness has many dimensions to it, as does human nature.

The experience of the psycho-emotional state that we call happiness is an emergent property of human consciousness that has become objectified as a sort of timeless archetype toward which thinking and acting typically move. Happiness, as a *reason-for-being,* emerged with the conscious and unconscious awareness of the essential uncertainty of existence. Pursuing happiness, most of us would say, *is* the meaning of life. But happiness, as a psycho-emotional state or goal of living, has no relevance to other life forms. And why? Because happiness has validity only if it is *pursued,* and only human beings have the capacity and interest to pursue it. Various Buddhist traditions would undoubtedly take exception to the idea that pursuing happiness is basic to the meaning of happiness itself. In this view, pursuing happiness is a profound illusion that becomes clear once one understands that happiness is an *effortless* state of conscious being that reflects, and is undifferentiated from, the oneness of *what is*: pure being. Put simply, effort is a movement away from happiness. But this idea is wrong, even from a Buddhist perspective. We need only to think about the life of the Buddha himself to understand why. Didn't the Buddha *pursue* nirvana—blissful, spiritual happiness—and actually experiment with different devotional lifestyles before finding nirvana by meditating under the Bodhi tree? The point is aptly summed up in this Eastern aphorism: "The best way to moderation is through excess." It may be true that real happiness will never be attained by anxiously pursuing it; nonetheless, one will never come to this spiritual insight unless, like the Buddha, one tries and discovers, through realistic experience and experiment, this truth for oneself.

9.12

The typical black-and-white division—*nature* as distinct from *nurture*—is not an accurate description of the relationship between nature and human culture, however convenient it might be for general discussion. The connection between nature and culture is best understood as being on a *continuum*, where at one extreme thoughtless, instinctive programming is dominant, and at the other, culture is clearly the principal guide. In between these two extremes, a sort of biological and cultural tug-of-war takes place, where in some instances nature clearly has the advantage, and in others, culture gains sway. But in all cases, *both* orientations are always in play to varying degrees. And right in the middle of this disharmonious, often antagonistic tug-of-war relationship is the human capacity to influence its final balance through the power of thought and reflective choice. The study of human nature largely involves trying to gain an accurate understanding of the relative strengths of each aspect of human nature by discovering the general biological and cultural principles that mold it.

10

Pleasure, Real Experience, and the Happiness Pill

10.1

Nature is not happy, only nurture can be. Both have two different orientations with respect to pleasure and happiness: one toward physical and sensual gratification, and the other toward stable, emotional connections, meaning-filled answers, and active purpose. Although happiness without some form of pleasure is inconceivable, happiness cannot be reduced to physical gratification alone. Experiencing pleasure does not necessarily make one happy; it simply gives one pleasure. Satisfying a powerful craving or addiction is certainly pleasurable, but it can, as in the case of overeating or abusive drug use, leave a person miserable and distraught. On the other hand, a happy person's sense of well-being is always increased when he is experiencing physical pleasure. Happiness, compared to pleasure, is not simply a physical sensation or a series of them but is a feeling of emotional and mental health rooted in what I call the "philo/moral sentiment." One never experiences happiness in a vacuum but always within a framework of tightly integrated philosophical and moral sensibilities and reasoning that give substance and purpose to happiness. The philo/moral sentiment is experienced as a sort of *background feeling* to our everyday decisions and actions and provides a stable and gratifying mental state in which happiness is nourished and sustained over time.

Natural pleasure is gratification that normally begins receding right after an urge, need, or hunger is satisfied. One could think of the immense pleasure, however short, that we derive from sneezing, scratching an itch, having a fulfilling sexual experience, or finishing a particularly delicious meal. These forms of pleasure I call "reflexive hedonism," because the needs and urges are purely biology based and largely unlearned, and human beings typically satisfy them in a rather straightforward fashion: they are reflexive actions of physical satisfaction. Of course, not all natural needs and urges are of equal importance and intensity; one could live without sexual gratification, for example, but not without food and water. But reflexive hedonism is not equivalent to happiness.

In addition to the physical satisfaction derived from reflexive hedonism, there is also the gratification and joy that human beings experience when they fulfill their needs for the following:

1. *Stable emotional connections*—finding and sustaining personal, social, and spiritual relationships that connect a person emotionally and psychologically to the universe at large.

2. *Meaningful philosophical answers to life-questions*—often resulting in a "philosophy of life."

3. *Engaging actively in purposeful actions*—having something "to do" on a daily basis that gives one's life passion, direction, and focus.

I call this form of satisfaction and joy "dynamic hedonism." Humans don't possess inborn guides that lead them directly to stable emotional/psychological connections, meaningful answers to philosophical questions, and active purpose. We can only experience dynamic hedonism by actively and consciously participating in life through individual thought, choice, and action. An important goal of education is—and should be—to develop the aptitudes and skills that are basic to this process.

Dynamic hedonism is the realm in which human happiness grows and ultimately flourishes, although dynamic hedonism is also not exactly equivalent to human happiness. Let's consider the interrelationship between reflexive and dynamic hedonism for a moment. Part of the problem is that it is easy to understand them as one and the same experience. In fact, reflexive hedonism derives exclusively from our biological nature, and dynamic hedonism derives, to a great, from the existential/cultural conditions of human existence. With dynamic hedonism, we must acknowledge the influence of biological/genetic factors in all areas of human nature and experience. The nature of romantic love, the human capacity for selfless behavior toward others, and the dynamics of interpersonal relationships all have roots in genetic programming, at least to some degree. What this means is that all human orientations are a mix of many tendencies and influences. Nonetheless, it's still clear that reflexive hedonistic pleasure is derived from physical gratification alone, whereas dynamic hedonism follows from personal choices and actions.

Another issue is one of balance: at one extreme, an obsessive submission to reflexive hedonism could lead to a destabilizing and debilitating hedonism in which one does not meet the all-important requirements of dynamic hedonism. At the other extreme, excessive preoccupation with dynamic hedonism, at the expense of reflexive hedonism, could lead to harmful, life-negating tendencies and practices, such as abstinence from sensual gratification, destructive repression of one's instinctive feelings and urges, and a deprecating attitude toward the simple joy of living passionately on a daily basis. The two forms of pleasure are interrelated in important ways. For example, pursuing dynamic hedonism frequently requires suppressing or minimizing the pursuit of reflexive hedonism. This is essentially the meaning of "being disciplined" in trying to achieve difficult but meaningful goals, such as writing books, exercising, or raising a family. On the other hand, "having fun"—by indulging in amorous pastimes, consuming your favorite meal, or being thrilled by viscerally stimulating experiences like viewing great films—are expressions of reflexive hedonism and are more fully enjoyed when one temporarily suspends one's interest in dynamic hedonism. The inter-relationship, then, is one of *dominant tendencies*, where, in some instances, reflexive hedonism is primary, and in other instances dynamic hedonism is in greater command. Balancing the two orientations so that they mutually support and promote each other is nothing less than the meaning of "the art of living well."

The essential principle of human happiness is finally becoming clear: both reflexive and dynamic hedonism are essential to human happiness, providing that the two are in proper balance. And what is the correct proportion between the two forms of hedonism? This balance is particular to each person and can only be discovered by individual experimentation throughout a lifetime. The cardinal principle is the following: Each person is a unique being with particular strengths and weaknesses with respect to the capacity of experiencing pleasure and achieving happiness. When an individual discovers his or her particular balance between reflexive and dynamic hedonism, the person has achieved what I call "holistic hedonism." But there are still other considerations about the nature of happiness.

Certain biology-based conditions in human physiology and psychology, such as chemical imbalances and mental disorders, can determine or radically alter personality and mental/emotional states independent of one's choices and decisions. How do we understand happiness within the context of the mental states over which the individual has little or no control? One could argue that these conditions are not typical of human beings and could easily be judged as abnormal and anomalous, and that, therefore, they have no true bearing on the true nature of human happiness. But isn't this simply begging the following question: if crazy people feel pleasure and believe that they are happy, aren't they? And are the rest of us justified in saying that they are not? What about drug-induced mental states that produce feelings of euphoria? Cocaine and ecstasy are drugs that have this effect; are bliss-chasing drug users happy? And, finally, there is the question of inherited dispositions that affect, if not determine, individuals' various states of mind. All of us know people who appear "good-natured"—are *naturally* drawn toward other people and to enjoying life in general. These sorts of people with sunny personalities tend to "see the cup as half full rather than half empty." And all of us know others who see the world the other way around. The issue of natural disposition is so typically believed to be self-evident that whole ethnic groups are commonly categorized according to national dispositions.

The Spanish, Italian, South American, and Mexican people, for instance, are known worldwide for their personal warmth and spontaneous friendliness, even toward perfect strangers; these national characteristics are well documented by cultural observers and simple travelers, and have been throughout the centuries. The Southern people appear to be gifted with an inborn happiness that they are eager to share with others. The opposite seems to be the case with Northern Europeans. The citizens of France (especially Paris), Germany, Austria, and the Scandinavian countries generally have reputations for being reserved, if not downright distant and cold, toward strangers and even toward one another. And speaking of sour dispositions, cases of severe depression and even suicide also appear to afflict Northern Europeans, particularly Scandinavians, more so than the people in southern Europe and other Latin countries. Some commentators attribute Northern personality traits to unfavorable weather conditions, most notably the absence of sunshine for much of the year. Off course, there are always exceptions to these generalizations. I have known in my own experiences very cold, unfriendly, and distant Italians, as well as passionate, happy-go-lucky Swedes. And the dark side of human nature is part of all people, regardless of their ethnicity. Nonetheless, these stereotypes, as *general* descriptions, are accurate. But then are we saying that Spaniards are really happier than Finns?

What an exuberant but chemically and mentally unbalanced person has in common with an ecstatic drug user is that both individuals are not reflexively or dynamically causing their pleasurable experiences. Pleasure simply *happens* to them. The same is true for what we see as the naturally warm and cheerful personality. In these instances, the pleasure that the individuals experience is effortless, as if it had been imposed upon the individual from the outside, independent of his or her choices and actions. I call this form of gratification "passive pleasure," the third and final happiness category that we will consider. I use the descriptive term "pleasure" rather than "hedonism" here, because hedonism as I understand it is pursued by personal choice and action, whereas pleasure is not—pleasure just happens.

Passive pleasure is a sort of virtual happiness that is effortlessly acquired. But let's be clear. Chemically or mentally unbalanced people are victimized by their mental states. Although they may be experiencing passive pleasure, they have little or no control over their emotions or states of mind, and so there is no guarantee that the pleasurable experience will not suddenly become a nightmarish one. Therefore, emotionally and mentally unstable people typically are prescribed medications of various sorts to control undesirable emotional and mental states. The result of medicating patients is usually an overall reduction of their quality of life, in which both "lows" and "highs" are neutralized, leaving the patients living in a kind of emotional temperate zone where nothing goes terribly wrong, but nothing goes terribly right, either. Many drug users, by contrast, have a greater control over their state of mind than the emotionally and mentally challenged do, because, except for the desperately addicted, they can choose not to indulge in the drug habit. But persistent use of drugs, especially cocaine and cocaine derivatives, is extremely damaging to the body and mind; it is not uncommon for this form of instant gratification to end in tragedy.

After dismissing mental instability and the use of narcotics as unacceptable versions of passive pleasure, we continue with what appears to be a rather hopeful form of passive pleasure: the good-natured person who, for no apparent reason, seems to be naturally happy and well-disposed toward himself, others, and life in general. Now, it's clear that the good-natured person, as well as the mentally unstable person and the pill-deluded person, experience their version of happiness as something that is *happening* to them, independent of their choices, and not something they have earned, accomplished, or pursued. What distinguishes the good-natured person, however, is that her pleasant state of mind is *natural* and not artificially created. Nor is this apparent form of happiness the result of abnormal psycho/physical causes like mental or emotional instability. Is this agreeable temperament *learned* in childhood? It's difficult to say what the causal dynamics are, but whatever its causes, it's experienced by the person as a perfectly natural and spontaneous *way to be*, and, in fact, good-natured people are typically "normal" people—that is, aside from their unusually good natures, they are just like the rest of us.

We are left with the naturally good-natured person who is not only disposed kindly toward him or herself, other people, and life in general, but is also resilient enough to cope well with adversity and recover rather quickly from tragic events. These people are typically not subject to fluctuating emotions. Outside of their seemingly perpetual cheerfulness, they are perfectly normal human beings. So is there a downside to this disposition-based pleasure? Not necessarily, but possibly. If one realizes holistic hedonism to a high degree, and happens to enjoy a naturally cheery disposition as well, then one is very fortunate indeed. Happiness abounds when we are with such people, and we are all the better for having them in our lives. On the other hand, a person who is cheery without seriously pursuing and knowing both reflexive and dynamic pleasure does not, in my view, experience real happiness. Such a person is left instead with a passive, happiness—not with the same consequences that befall the emotionally and mentally challenged person or the drug user, but a virtual happiness nevertheless. Let's explore this idea a little further and see how the ideas of reflexive hedonism, dynamic hedonism, and passive pleasure first occurred to me.

10.2

One of my favorite challenges to friends and acquaintances over the years has been is to ask them to consider the following scenario and question: Imagine that I asked you to lie on a comfortable couch in the secure privacy of your own home and to take a pill, one that you absolutely trust is perfectly safe and one that will, *without question*, do the following: give you the illusion of living a thoroughly fulfilled life with the normal ups and downs, except that, in this illusory life, you will always come out "on top"—that is, you will feel, believe, and think that you are happy. Your will effectively meet and overcome your most difficult obstacles, and you will ultimately realize your most far-fetched fantasies: you may, for example, win at a very young age a highly prestigious professional position that pays you an enormous salary, enabling you to retire at the age of twenty-eight to travel with your beautiful spouse and children to fantastic destinations. If a professional life and marriage are not what you had in mind, then perhaps you would have an unbelievably thrilling, jet-set lifestyle—maybe as a famous rock or film star—with all the material and romantic perks that go along with being rich, famous, and beautiful. In short, your happiness-of-choice would be yours by virtue of a lifelong mind-trip, and, what's more, you would *never be aware that your happy life was an illusion*. So, from your point of view, this fantasy would be as real as the book you are now holding in your hands. All the typical struggles and accidental twists and turns that are a part of normal living would be flawlessly duplicated in your fantasy and would seem to be concretely real. The inevitable victories that you will celebrate in your dream world will be as thrilling and rewarding as if you had truly succeeded by real talent and by committed, honest effort. In short, you would emote, think, and act as you do in your everyday life, except, of course, it would all be in your imagination. Another interesting perk of taking the happiness pill is that you would not be committed to the kind of happiness that you began with; you could, if you desired, alter your fantasy quickly, easily, and painlessly according to your new happiness interest, without missing a pleasurable stroke, and continue unimpeded down your exciting path of personal bliss.

Now, presuming that you believe that finding happiness is the meaning of your life, would you then opt for an illusion that promises, *without fail*, to deliver on this happiness?

Before answering this question, however, please understand that should you take the pill, you would never awaken from this dream, but would live the rest of your natural life on your back, engulfed in a perpetual illusion. Now what would be your decision? A fantasy life of fulfilling happiness, or your real, everyday life that has no guarantee of happiness at all, with the very real prospect, in fact, of more sadness, loss, and heartache than you care to endure? And don't forget that at your life's end, you might have to face up to the reality that small, ephemeral episodes of pleasure and fragmented moments of partial happiness are all that you have to show for your life.

When I first conceived this little thought experiment in 1990, I didn't realize the philosophical and psychological gems that lay buried behind and beneath the responses and reactions of the people who offered their points of view. Initially, it was fascinating simply to observe people wrestle with a hypothetical situation that brought their cherished beliefs and convictions to the fore, many of which were hidden from their conscious awareness or only partially thought through. But I quickly realized that important issues and insights were emerging, and so I made it a point to document, in a very casual way, the responses of a number of people and their positions.

Of the 116 people whom I have queried over the past fifteen years, five of them answered immediately that they would take the pill. Once I went into more detail regarding the unreality of the world in which they would live for the rest of their natural lives, three of the five changed their minds and wanted to think about it longer. The two who remained committed to their initial response were not doing well in either their personal or professional lives; at the time of our discussions, they were what one might call "lost souls," looking for love and something meaningful to do with their lives. And even in these cases, they clearly seemed to be close to changing their minds when I challenged them. The ones who wanted to think a little longer claimed that they had felt "uncomfortable" and uneasy about taking the pill;

one said that he would feel too "vulnerable" just lying on his back and was now leaning toward not taking the "risk." The other one just didn't know what to say and finally admitted that he couldn't commit fully because he "felt funny" about it, though he didn't know why. All five said that they were mildly religious and "spiritual," and they believed that all religions were good.

Thirty-one of the people I queried were self-proclaimed Christians and Jews (about half were Christian and half were Jewish). Virtually all of them said that they would not take the pill, because, in their view, the meaning of life was not necessarily happiness but service to Jesus and/or God. When I asked them if they would change their minds if they had a de-conversion experience, in which they lost their belief in Jesus or God, or had a radical philosophical insight that led them either to agnosticism or atheism, all of them remained steadfast in their position. I told them that I didn't understand their stubbornness—after all, without the reality of Jesus and/or God, finding happiness in *this world* should be their new philosophy. All were emotionally uncomfortable with this new possibility, and some actually became irritated with me; a number of them said something like this: "But the happiness you're talking about would not be real; it would not be in this world; it would be all in my head." In response, I said something like, "What would it matter? After all, you would definitely think that you were in the real world and happy, and since happiness is the bottom line, what would be the difference? There is no hell, no Judgment Day after death that one has to fear, and no heaven in which to float about blissfully for an eternity. This time on Earth is it! Why not make it a fantastic experience?" Still, they all remained closed to the possibility, and many of them wanted to move on to other topics.

Nineteen of the people with whom I spoke had Buddhist leanings with a belief in reincarnation and said that they would not take the pill because it would sabotage their road to enlightenment; it is in the "real world," according to their Buddhist views, that one has to make spiritual progress. Choosing a fantasy-based happiness was "bad karma"—moral/spiritual cause and effect that's based on our free choices. It's that simple! But when I told them that the happiness pill experience would necessarily provide them with valuable spiritual lessons and, as a result, would ultimately accelerate their movement toward enlightenment, many of them genuinely hesitated.

I made them admit that, based on their own belief system, any experience presented to them potentially holds valuable, and perhaps decisive, insights that could enrich and possibly transform their spiritual lives now and in future incarnations. Additionally, according to Buddhism, this world is *maya*, anyway—a great illusion. It's likely that their extended rest on their couches would teach them profound verities about the nature of untruth and sharpen their spiritual vision to see the truth more clearly in future lifetimes. Taking the happiness pill, in other words, would be the right thing to do—it would be "good karma!" After all this logical maneuvering, a few of the holdouts finally said that they might consider taking the pill. But when I insisted on a firm commitment one way or the other right then, all but one said they couldn't give an answer at the time, and the one who did make a decision finally declined the offer. The one man who fully committed believed that whatever happens in life has a reason and a "deeper purpose," and so he had no fear about the experience as long as he knew that it was safe. I told him that it was, in principle, safe, but I reminded him that even if something went wrong, it would make little difference, because from his Buddhist point of view, he would still have learned valuable lessons that would push him farther along the path toward enlightenment. After hearing this, he said, "Where do I sign up?"

Sixty-one of the people considering the happiness pill stood outside the traditional religious mainstream. Twenty-two were science-minded skeptics, most of whom were self-congratulatory atheists; nineteen defined themselves as agnostics; and twenty held a mixed bag of quasi-traditional religious views thoughtlessly thrown together with secular viewpoints, such as a confident belief in a Darwinian-type evolution. As you might imagine, the skeptics were skeptical about the whole program and wanted to know how they could be sure that the happiness pill would match perfectly their ideal of happiness. A few of the agnostics weren't sure that my proposal wasn't some kind of April Fools' joke, but generally they were in the same camp as the atheists. Some of the people in both groups were concerned about possible toxic side-effects. I had to explain to these people that their concerns were not relevant, since the whole scenario was only an imaginary *thought experiment*, in which all parties assume, without reservation, its absolute veracity, accuracy, and safety, as well as the happy outcome of the situation precisely as I had described it. In other words, all participants must put all extraneous concerns aside and focus only on whether they would take the pill that would, *without fail*, guarantee them the fantasy of amazing happiness—an illusion that would be, for those experiencing it, indistinguishable from reality.

A number of the people couldn't accept the situation as I explained it. Some argued that, unlike an Einsteinian thought experiment in which the descriptions are clear and the conclusions logically irrefutable, my thought experiment seemed vague and logically unsound. Happiness is too complicated and multifaceted an experience, they argued, to reduce to a simple, logical formula that included a silly pill. While I conceded that my fictitious scenario was not a true thought experiment in the strictly scientific sense, it nonetheless allowed for meaningful, logical deductions that pertained to human reality. The larger point I made, however, was that their objection to my alleged thought experiment was merely a diversion, an obvious attempt to try to avoid answering the question. By making my scenario more complicated than it is, and focusing on irrelevant points, they became absorbed in the details and never addressed the simple bottom line. Still, the vast majority said that they would not take the pill because they could not, under any circumstances, imagine that it could work; they just couldn't take the proposal seriously. Others said that they would not take the pill because the *pre-knowledge* that their happiness would be a fantasy created a daunting psychological gulf over which they could not travel philosophically. For them, the illusion of happiness was impossible to accept. Either you are *really* happy, or you're fooling yourself, and they are not the same thing. A few said that they might take the pill but would have to think about it further.

What I found most illuminating about the hypothetical pill scenario was not only that almost all of the candidates for the happiness pill found the idea of having illusory happiness unacceptable, but also, as we saw, that the reasons for their refusal were mostly unclear, often irrational, and sometimes difficult, if not impossible, to decipher. Let's pursue this a little further. The religious group offered reasons that were, in themselves, beyond reason, because their belief system itself had little to do with rationality in the first place. There is not much room for rational debate with someone who claims that God, the creator of the universe, would not allow for such imaginative excursions into fantasy for a lifetime. Something I heard frequently from both Jews and Christians was, "God created us to serve him and not to serve ourselves." One educated Christian said, "It would be contrary to God's values to have his children indulging in a life of pleasure, real or imagined." When I finally pulled the religious rug out from under them and asked how they would answer if they had lost their secure belief or faith in God, no one would even entertain the idea seriously. And when I insisted on, at least, their trying to imagine this possibility, just for purposes of discussion, most of the people said that the idea was "stupid" or "silly" and not worth thinking about any further.

The Buddhist candidates were, at first, more reasonable than the God-based religionists, and the reason is clear: to Buddhists, *illusion* has a great deal of meaning. Buddhism is a psychological/spiritual practice that has two ultimate goals: cleansing one's spiritual vision to allow one to see the truth that is ever-present in everyday experience—enlightenment (awakening)—and overcoming the unending suffering of incarnated, fractured existence by finally becoming reabsorbed back into the blissful oneness of ultimate reality—"nirvana."

The real truth seeker does not discover truth "out there" in the world or "up there" in a transcendent, supernatural realm but, instead, modifies the erroneous ways that she naturally sees (experiences) the everyday world so that the truth *in it* and *in herself* becomes visible, tangible, and understood as inseparable—as identical. Buddhism holds that our normal ways of perceiving and thinking about the world falsify reality and make it into what it is not—fragmented. And how do we typically respond to being caught-up in this fragmented world? By allowing our "desires" to control how we feel, think, and act—for example, we become obsessed with obtaining material possessions as well as fulfilling emotional and physical gratification of various kinds.

But worldly desire is a trap, a spiritual dead-end and vicious circle: we inevitably become blinded by this illusion and spend our precious lives (many of them) trying to satisfy false needs—which only gives birth to other desires that are equally impossible to satisfy. The inevitable result of trying to satisfy our desires is the benighted spiritual condition of "suffering"—the existential plight of all living things. There is no way out of this spiritual/psychological/intellectual quagmire as long as we are the willing, believing, and active participants in this false reality. For Buddhists, gaining enlightenment involves realizing, over the course of many lifetimes, the actual fact of this illusion and the folly of desperately pursuing the objects of our desires, which, in reality, could never be truly fulfilling. It's not surprising, then, that the allure of physical pleasure and our desire for material possessions, personal and worldly power, and ego fulfillment only serve to block our way to enlightenment; they force us to continue the futile circle of false consciousness, suffering, and rebirth.

But breaking the chain of illusion is not easy. We normally understand the world in terms of black-and-white categories such as *subject* and *object, inside* and *outside,* and *you* and *me.* For Buddhists, these are false dichotomies; behind these artificial divisions there is simply one reality—eternal and unchanging, in which all differences and disjunctions are dissolved. All separateness, in other words, is illusory. Reality is one. The literal moment of truth has real power, however, only when the Buddhist learns to realize his or her insights into practical, day-to-day living. The Buddha outlined in some detail what he believed to be the right life path for spiritual beings to take in order to overcome separateness and to become reabsorbed back into ultimate reality—*Being.* At the source of Buddhist spirituality is the mindset of compassion.

Compassion—literally, "to suffer with"—is the profound awareness that all beings, both animate and inanimate, suffer physically and spiritually by virtue of existing in this disunited, disharmonious, and fractured universe. Inanimate things suffer from the very physical-ness of their being, which is devoid of the sufficient awareness necessary to move them ahead steadily to enlightenment. This form of suffering is based in the spiritually poor condition of inanimate matter slowly moving toward animate existence, only afterward to have to continue to endure the long suffering of animate existence, incarnation after incarnation, until enlightenment. Sentient beings—both nonhuman human—suffer because their biological constitutions are fragile and susceptible to painful illnesses, diseases, and the ravages of old age and death; human beings also suffer emotionally, psychologically, and spiritually from never completely satisfying their endless need for desire-fulfillment regardless of their most passionate and sincere efforts.

The real basis for suffering for all existent things, whether inanimate or animate, is that to exist at all in the universe means, from a Buddhist point of view, to be necessarily *separated and isolated* from the one true, seamless reality—the very same reality that is perverted by our illusory ways of seeing the world. One of the most intriguing ideas in Buddhism is that even though all beings appear to be so many different things and individuals, in reality they are all individualized forms of the infinite one, however incomplete and finite. In this sense, seeking reunion with ultimate reality also means *becoming one* with one another. When a Buddhist gains full spiritual understanding of this reality, and expresses this understanding faithfully in his or her everyday life, then the pain-filled cycle of rebirth will come to an end, and the individual will become reabsorbed back into the one—that is, the suffering, ego-driven flame of isolated, detached personhood will be extinguished forever. This blissful state of returning back to the undifferentiated one is what the Buddhists call "nirvana." Spiritual practices, such as meditation and yoga, are important disciplines that Buddhists practice dutifully to help them to move closer toward this ultimate good.

That the happiness pill promotes illusion as a *good* is what captured the attention and imagination of the Buddhists, but ultimately, not their enthusiasm. At first, they thought that the illusion of happiness, by way of a pill, would make a mockery of their spirituality by substituting reality for a fantasy and giving fantasy equal spiritual status. After all, what the pill promises is what Buddhism maintains is impossible: absolute happiness through illusion. What was surprising was their inflexibility once they realized that this illusionary experience, from the perspective of gaining transforming insights from many lifetimes, would ultimately serve their spiritual values and goals. What better way to understand the nature of illusion, with the ultimate goal of transcending it, than to indulge in it fully? That one would choose to take the pill with the pure karmic intention of gaining greater understanding of illusion could only be seen as a proper spiritual decision and could only result in gaining mountains of "good karma."

The one person who finally agreed to take the happiness pill grasped this point clearly. Initially, many of the Buddhists appeared to think seriously about taking the pill, but again, like the religious group, they finally declined—and actually became both irrational and angry with me when I asked the reasons for their refusal to join their Buddhist brother. In some instances, they accused me of trying to undermine their spiritual commitments, and no less than five thought that I was a fundamentalist Christian masquerading as a philosopher with the intention of converting them. Most of them could not give cogent reasons why they would not take the pill and resorted to gut-level-feeling arguments, and a number of them asked me not to pursue the matter any further. A few stated that, in principle, the pill could not produce the experience of happiness, because Buddhism says explicitly that happiness requires overcoming illusion. To indulge in this experience, then, would be bad karma.

At first, I thought that, in comparison to the other groups, the scientific-minded people, atheists, and agnostics would be more responsive to rational discussion. But this did not turn out to be the case. The science enthusiasts and atheists, in large measure, thought that the whole idea was below their philosophical dignity. They consistently questioned my credibility, and they addressed me as though I were a philosophical novice—too naïve intellectually to understand that my scenario could not be taken seriously. I heard many times that we know far too little about the dynamics and content of happiness to reduce it to a simple formula, and that, as a result, any intelligent person could not in good intellectual conscience make the leap of faith into the world of illusionary happiness. When I tried to repeat to them what I had told many others, that it is important to assume that what I am saying is true for the sake of argument, they would not grant me that liberty. They held that my scenario had too many hidden assumptions that needed to be exposed and clarified. For example, my scenario assumes that each individual's idea of happiness is what the person really wants. What if the person is wrong about what happiness should be or changes his or her mind as to what happiness is, during the fantasy? Then the wonderful dream could easily turn into a lifelong nightmare. They concluded that, without a sound scientific and philosophical understanding about the nature of happiness and a deeper knowledge of human nature, my scenario could not be taken seriously.

The agnostics were more open minded but less interesting than their fellow skeptics. Less committed to an ideology, they had less at stake emotionally and philosophically, and, as a result, their rationalizations were more relaxed and less sensational. Logic can be spun in countless ways to justify many often contradictory positions. The history of philosophy is replete with arguments for or against particular points of view, all claiming superior logical power over the other. But a fair assessment of this tradition clearly shows that logic has been made to serve many masters, including falsehoods. We now know that logical argumentation typically requires the aid of personal and/or observable experience to settle satisfactorily any philosophical issue of real human importance. And this point has relevance to the meaning of agnosticism.

Agnosticism, in essence, maintains that human beings don't know, and could never know, nearly enough to make a definitive statement about the existence or nonexistence of God. Finite minds, in short, have finite capacities and can know only finite items. The question of an infinite God, then, is, in principle, not a topic that human beings could know anything about. There are various forms of agnosticism, from the superficial dismissal of the whole issue as being unworthy of serious thought—I call this "soft agnosticism," to a more committed version where the agnostic appears to be interested in discussing the topic seriously. This is the version that interests me and is the version that I documented in my little thought experiment. I call this version "hard agnosticism."

The hard agnostic's claims of uncertainty give the impression that a thoughtful and careful thinker is at work. But in fact, the agnostic position reflects quite the opposite: it is thinking that is fruitlessly self-referential to the point of becoming detached from, and indifferent to, the real object of thinking—understanding reality. Agnosticism is nothing less than a retreat from the facts of reality, insofar as measuring, balancing, and arguing logical nuances become an endless point/counter-point *theoretical* dance.

Logical reasoning *left unchecked* has no natural termination, because the scenario of finite minds confronted with infinite possibilities guarantees the endless process of trying to realize infinite possibilities. This is the problem with hard agnosticism as a general mindset: without reality serving as a guide and corrective to theoretical thinking, there is no way for agnostics to know if they are moving toward intensifying light or blinding darkness. Put differently, thinking that hangs continually in theoretical space is condemned to perpetual uncertainty, while thinking that is constrained, ordered, and guided by the curvatures of earthly reality has the real hope of gaining true understanding of *what is*. And what are the facts of reality with which anyone interested in the existence or nonexistence of God should be concerned?

10.3

The Christian God is not available for direct observation like a tree or a person, but unlike the gods and spirits in the pagan and mystical traditions, we have a book that he allegedly authored—the Bible. The Bible, being the supposed world of God, should not fail to provide the necessary information, knowledge, or insights to show conclusively that God—the God of the New Testament—should be believed to exist. Examining the New Testament, in other world, should be sufficient for a truth seeker to come to a confident conclusion about the existence of the Christian God. The crucial Christian idea in the New Testament is that it contains spiritual truth and wisdom that has ultimate importance to all of humanity; this tenet clearly represents the basic premise of the religion. Let's see if this basic premise is sufficient to make the New Testament, and the belief in its God, credible.

Let's start with the conclusion of my argument and then work backward to see how I supported my conclusion: the New Testament has failed time and time again to convince sincere truth seekers of its truthfulness and, more particularly, to compel them to believe that a transcendent, creator God is its author. There have been countless highly moral truth seekers who have read the New Testament in earnest and who have—following its directives—"given themselves over" to God, but without ever becoming convinced of his existence experientially, logically, or by means of revelation. Are we prepared to disregard their personal experiences entirely and conclude, as the New Testament suggests, that they are all liars, morally corrupt, and perhaps even devil worshippers?

The New Testament places a special emphasis on faith as the only method through which devoted truth seekers can achieve salvation—i.e., become spiritually reunited with God—and, as a result, know with abiding confidence that God exists. Faith in Christianity means believing, in advance—without proof—that Jesus of Nazareth was God in the flesh; that he lived a perfect—sinless—life as a man; that he died on the cross for the sins of humanity; was buried; was resurrected three days later; and finally made supernatural appearances to some of his followers before ascending to heaven to be with God the Father. The life, death, and resurrection of Jesus were the steps that God decided to take in order to rescue humankind from its sinfulness and from its being eternally damned—from spending an eternity in hell; after all, as the Bible says, "the penalty of sin is death." And why did God feel compelled to send himself in the mortal person of Jesus to save humankind? Because of his perfect love for all his children. This is the Gospel story in its most simple form. Let's clarify the main points of the story.

According to the New Testament, sinful mortals are unable, on their own, to believe the Gospel story, so God, in his infinite grace, wisdom, and love, imputed to the human race the priceless gift of faith. Faith, in Christianity, is the divine power that enables human beings to transcend their intellectual and spiritual limitations in order to believe, without proof, in the miracle of God's salvation through Jesus. Faith is the spiritual force that ensures that *anyone* who wants to find the truth—the ultimate meaning of life—will be able to do so. An important consequence of faith is that no one has an excuse for not discovering God's plan and not accepting his gift of salvation. No matter how difficult it is to believe in the Gospel story, faith exists in all human beings to overcome all the obstacles to belief and to guide the *willing heart* to salvation through Jesus. Once faith does its work then God will grant the truth believer knowledge of his presence.

My conclusion that the Christian God cannot exist is very simple and can be reduced to single statement: in no uncertain terms, the failure of the New Testament to convince sincere truth seekers of God's existence spells disaster for the credibility of his existence; even the failure of one committed truth seeker to discover the New Testament God is sufficient to show beyond any reasonable doubt that no such being exists. But how could the existence of an infinite God be legitimately negated by the judgments of morally, intellectually, and spiritually flawed humans? Isn't this arrogance in its most outrageous and perverted form?

This argument follows quite naturally from the premises in the New Testament Gospel story. Regardless of how unbelievable and irrational the Gospel story may be to an objective observer, there is, nevertheless, a logical structure to the tale that remains consistent. The whole Christian narrative is integrated by cause and effect relationships: God created humankind; humanity sinned; since the "penalty of sin is death," God sent himself to live, die, and to be resurrected—to wash away the sins of all people; "seek and ye shall find"—by seeking out God and accepting on faith the Gospel story, one will necessarily achieve salvation; once one finds salvation, God's presence in one's life will become clear. We see here a whole series of causal relations without which there would not be a comprehensible story. By *A* happening, then *B* necessarily follows—this is the logic that is repeated over and over again in the New Testament (and in the Bible as a whole).

One of the most important causal relations in the Gospels amount to an unambiguous guarantee: by the truth seeker honestly seeking spiritual truth, God will unconditionally reveal himself and the person will begin to see God's work in his or her life. God's revealing himself in the truth seeker's life, in this way, is God's gift to his faith-oriented believers. Without this guarantee, the Gospel makes no sense at all. On the other hand, if this guarantee proves to be fraudulent even once, then the Gospel in its totality is equally fraudulent. God—by his own declaration in the Bible—is the origin of all that is good, just, and righteous; he is, therefore, morally bound to live-up to all his promises. God literally has no choice in the matter. For him to be inconsistent in this regard would make him into a liar, deceiver, hypocrite, and quire frankly, sinister—adjectives that we certainly would not employ to describe a perfect God. If a truth seeker, after absorbing the information in the Gospels and following its directives, comes up empty-handed with respect to having confidence in God's existence, then there is only one possibility: the Christian God does not exist. I call this argument against the existence of God "The Truth Seeker's Proof of God's Non-existence." The short form of this proof is as follows: "as a truth seeker, I know that God does not exist, because if he did, I'd believe in him!"

As we noted, the New Testament states that *anyone* who sincerely wants to know the truth will without fail be led to God through Jesus Christ. This position clearly implies that even truth seekers who are born within non-theistic or polytheistic traditions such as the Buddhist, Hindu, and atheistic traditions, will find that Christian God is alive and well. In actuality, people from these traditions rarely convert to Christianity, a situation that has frustrated Christian proselytizers and missionaries. And what about the truth seekers who have never read the Bible, who have never heard of the Gospel of Jesus Christ, or who, because of radical cultural differences, are unable to make sense of the logic of the Gospels' salvation story? The Truth Seeker's Proof of God's Nonexistence is equally valid in all of these cases and demonstrates, once again, that God cannot exist.

I cannot refrain from laying out briefly another argument against the belief in God, one that I call "The Broken Child's Proof of God's Nonexistence." Zoologists—biologists who specialize in the study of animals and animal life—generally agree that the most characteristic distinction among different species of life is that members of one species cannot naturally breed with members of another. Dogs cannot breed with cats, and horses can't breed with chimpanzees. The same restriction on breeding is also true for plant species. Physical limitations aside, breeding *within* the same species, however, is almost unlimited, and human beings are no exception: indeed, the history of the human species is the literal documentation of this complex interbreeding between many breeds of humans for as long as two-hundred-thousand years.

That human beings can interbreed freely introduces important issues from a Christian viewpoint, such as how and to what extent an alleged all-knowing, all-powerful, and perfectly moral God is involved in, or even concerned with, the procreative process. According to the New Testament, God has an abiding love and concern for each and every one of his human creations. This can only mean that, from God's perspective, all children who come into this world are equally deserving of God's love. At the very least, this suggests that they should be raised in a caring and nurturing family and social environment that would afford them the opportunity for salvation through Jesus Christ. A perfectly just God could not have it any other way. The question of children is a critical one, because the circumstances into which children are born, the state of their biological well-being at birth, and the general care that they receive, or do not receive, have a profound effect on the children's physical, emotional, and psychological health. Indeed, these circumstances create the conditions for the children's future successes or failures in all areas of life, including in the area of spirituality.

Consider the idea that any reproductively healthy female can become pregnant and give birth to a child. This includes the physically, mentally, and emotionally challenged; criminals; drug users; and women who live in abject poverty. Who would deny that the children born to such mothers are beginning their lives with enormous disadvantages? Countless numbers of children are routinely born to parents who lack the ability to care for them adequately. It's also not uncommon for psychologically and emotionally unbalanced, drug-addicted parents to give birth to babies with severely debilitating physical and mental defects and diseases, or for the children to be brought to these conditions soon after birth through physical abuse and poor nutrition. Some babies are even born as drug addicts and remain that way for the rest of their tragically short lives, which are often filled with violence and crime.

From a religious perspective, it's difficult, if not impossible, to explain how the "miracle of birth" could be so arbitrary. How could God allow the precious souls of innocent children to be subject to physically, emotionally, and psychologically challenged caretakers in the worst possible environments to raise children? How could just *anyone* be given the supremely important tasks of bringing young souls into the world, developing their characters, and preparing them for the many challenges of living? The answer is that this should never be the case—that is, if the New Testament God really existed. And the tragic consequences for many of these children are often so horrendous that it sounds ludicrous to raise the question of their sins and their need of salvation through Jesus Christ, especially when one considers the hell on Earth that they are forced to endure on a daily basis, through no fault of their own. The believability of God's existence is, once again, damaged beyond repair by the question of how he could permit countless innocent children (actually, as with my former proof, it only takes one) to suffer.

Without a compelling answer to the "broken-child" problem, God's nonexistence is beyond dispute! And the truth is that there is no acceptable answer. To suggest that the ways of God are *mysterious* and that we have to accept, on faith, that there are hidden reasons why unspeakable tragedies befall innocent children is simply asking too much—our intellectual and moral sensibilities should scream out in protest at such a suggestion.

The problem is further highlighted if we compare children who are born in a poverty stricken world—where crime, drugs, malnutrition, and physical and emotional abuse have a significant impact on a child's development—to children born in a typical, middle-class world to healthy, caring, and responsible parents. Where the former have every misfortune that guarantees, at best, a very difficult life, the latter have every opportunity to live a healthy, happy, and productive life in a good community where the future is filled with promise. How are we to accept the New Testament doctrine that God loves and cares *equally* for the children from both worlds? In good conscience we cannot, and we are forced to conclude, once again, that God does not exist.

The hard agnostics whom I interviewed about the happiness pill quickly took flight into the free and open space of theoretical thinking, with little concern for the concrete issues that could lead them to a firm conclusion about the pill proposition. The scenario was, for them, surrounded by too many uncertainties and logical ambiguities. Unlike the scientists, atheists, and skeptics, they were not interested in the real-life implications of taking the pill. What is happiness, after all? How could we presume to guarantee it without answering this question? We don't know what happiness really is; we only know what some people *think* happiness is, which may not be happiness at all. In other words, we don't know what we must know about happiness in order to say anything absolutely true about it—so how could one take a pill that promises what we don't know?

10.4

This kind of extreme skepticism was typical of many of the hard agnostics. They were unable to get past definitions and clarifications to make contact with the concrete issues. In short, they were not facing the real facts of the experiment: that we don't need a mutually agreed upon definition of happiness to take the pill. Again, as far as this experiment is concerned, happiness is what each person imagines that it might be, and she could even, at any time, change her current happiness for a new happiness du jour. And the test to determine if a person is happy is a rather simple one: if she could say to herself in complete sincerity, "I am really happy," then the person is happy, at least in that moment. This is not impossibly abstract or complex thinking, but follows easily and naturally from the real conditions and practical consequences of taking the happiness pill. Nonetheless, the hard agnostics would have nothing to do with the experiment, and they would not consider coming down to Earth to go on the fantasy trip of a lifetime for a lifetime.

Why was it that the overwhelming majority of people found reasons, mostly flimsy ones, for not taking the happiness pill? The question became even more interesting when I realized that, given the opportunity, I would not take the happiness pill, either. It was clear that there had to be something wrong with my experiment. Perhaps my premise was incorrect; maybe it's not true that happiness is the meaning of human life after all! Or if it is, maybe happiness is not what we think it is, as some of the people I interviewed argued. The logic that I employed in the experiment was simple enough: if you really feel, think, and believe that you are happy, then you are happy. This particular notion of effortless, self-styled, improvisational happiness was actually what the experiment tested. I realized that this version of happiness is nothing out of the ordinary; it has a great deal in common with what many people today in Western culture desire. If the form of happiness that my experiment endorsed was similar to what modern, Western humans seem to crave, then why did most of the people I interviewed decline the opportunity to experience it on a continuous basis? Something is obviously missing from my experiment's equation of happiness.

My notions of passive pleasure and reflexive, dynamic, and holistic hedonism give us a sturdy framework in which we can answer this question. The answer can be summarized in the following way: happiness consists of pleasurable thoughts, sensations, emotions, moods, and actions that naturally arise out of, and accompany, realizing personal values, ideals, and goals. A few points need to be stressed: "pleasurable" in this context does not necessarily mean "without what is unpleasant"; quite the contrary. Confronting and overcoming mental, emotional, and physical limitations, although not pleasurable experiences, is often a key ingredient in the experiential mix of what is pleasurable. A good analogy is that of sports and exercise. Running, swimming, or playing tennis, for example, always involves discomfort of varying degrees— from sheer physical stress to the psychological exhaustion that often accompanies disciplined performances.

That playing sports can be exhilarating and gratifying is due, in no small part, to the unpleasant elements of physical and emotional exertion serving as intense stimulants and provocations to excel or to win. Moreover, the thrill of overcoming obstacles—both physical and psychological—is perhaps the main reason why people derive such satisfaction from sports and exercise: meeting great resistance is often a harsh reminder of our human limitations, but to break free of the mortal chains that bind us—even for just a few moments—can promote a tremendous sense of expanding personal power and even ecstatic release. This is the real psychology behind the love of sports and exercising.

Finally, anyone who exercises understands the common experience of being able to endure physical discomfort and fatigue because of the psychological pleasure derived from knowing in advance the health benefits that will result from "toughing it out." And, of course, once one has completed a grueling sport or exercise routine, the sheer physical pleasure from resting is always exceptional, and the knowledge that the athletic ordeal was "worth it" bestows a deep sense of satisfaction, as well. The interesting relation between pleasure and pain in sports is not dissimilar to the inner dynamics of happiness. In both cases, pleasure and pain are twin existential companions that define each other, and, in the case of happiness, the inner tension between pleasure and pain shapes the quantity and quality of its expression.

Another important idea in my notion of happiness is the verb "realizing." In this context, realizing means "bringing into being or achieving an ultimate end." This is clearly a process that calls for *action*—a conscious assertion of will, intelligence, and physical labor to reach particular goals. We've come to an important moment: if realizing personal values, ideals, and goals is the way to achieve a happy life, then concrete action is the only possible strategy that one can employ to achieve this end. Action is the great engine of human happiness, because it unleashes the mental, emotional, and physical energies that give a human life order, focus, and purpose. We are now in the position to give a simple structure to the happy life.

Based on this model, we will also be able to uncover the problem with my happiness experiment: happiness—holistic hedonism—results when the satisfaction of biological needs, sensual urges, and enjoyable desires—reflexive hedonism—is in proper balance with the sense of fulfillment that comes from successfully maintaining meaningful connections, finding meaningful answers to basic philosophical questions, and engaging habitually in purposeful action—dynamic hedonism. Presupposed in dynamic hedonism is the active realization of personal values, ideals, and goals. As far as passive pleasure is concerned—the optimistic worldview of a person who enjoys himself, other people, and life in general by virtue of a natural disposition— we can only conclude that there is no necessary connection between passive pleasure and the happiness model that I have just outlined. Some individuals are fortunate enough to experience both holistic hedonism and passive pleasure, while others are not inclined toward passive pleasure and must rely exclusively on holistic hedonism. On the other hand, it is not uncommon for one who possesses holistic hedonism also to develop over time a version of passive pleasure, where an optimistic view of life becomes a sort of psycho-emotional reflex. Finally, each individual is a unique, pleasure-seeking being who pursues and sustains the different forms of pleasure with varying degrees of intensity and success.

What the happiness model presupposes, but does not address directly, is the all-important requirement of physical health for happiness. It often is the case that thinkers reduce happiness to simple states of mind, or to an "outlook on life," without considering that all minds are housed within the confines of our physical bodies. The biological health of the body—its vitality—both directly and indirectly influences all dimensions of pleasure and happiness. Excellent physical health is the foundation upon which holistic hedonism rests.

A great advance in modern science and philosophy has been in overcoming, in many areas of thought, the antiquated division of human beings into *body* and *mind* (actually, more like body *versus* mind). Here, the components were viewed as disconnected from each other, with the body having a life (an inferior one, at that) of its own and the mind existing on a wholly different plane (a higher, superior one). Today, we know that in many instances such a radical disjunction, along with the traditional value judgments attached, has hindered our understanding of human nature. This fact is nowhere more evident than in human health, where it has been shown conclusively that ideas, beliefs, and emotions can *interconnect* with the body, influencing its biochemical functioning. It should come as no surprise that likewise, the activities of the body have been shown to be absorbed in emotional and psychological dimensions. We all know from firsthand experience the effects that a particularly good or bad idea can have on our physical well-being. Stressful thoughts or ideas can have physical consequences, including headaches, general nervousness, or ulcers. And great news—like a significant financial gain or a new love affair—can have the opposite effect and might produce, for example, great bursts of exhilarating energy. We are also familiar with the negative effects that poor health can have on our emotional and psychological states.

In much of modern psychology and philosophy, experience has come to be understood from the perspective of mind *and* body union, and we now know that the life of the body is often reflected in the life of the mind, and vice versa. It is for this reason that happiness requires good health for its full expression. Does this mean that individuals with physical disabilities or poor health cannot know holistic hedonism? Happiness will always be configured uniquely for each person, with each person having to adjust to the conditions and limitations of his or her reality. No life is perfect, and no one is perfectly happy. The answer is that health problems certainly make living a complete life more difficult, but they do not necessarily preclude someone from experiencing happiness. Everything being equal, however, *very* poor health inhibits holistic hedonism. Handicapped people who are in good health, on the other hand, can—and often do—live lives of exuberant holistic hedonism.

What, then, did my happiness experiment fail to take into account that made it unacceptable to almost everyone I consulted? One could argue, for instance, that I failed to consider the requirements of reflexive and dynamic hedonism for happiness. The form of happiness that my experiment promised actually appears to be a version of passive pleasure, because like the pleasure of the schizophrenic, the drug-deluded addict, and the good-natured optimist, the pleasure granted in my experiment is also unearned—in other words, it's not achieved through real thought and concrete action in the pursuit of realizing personal values, ideals, and goals. Reflexive hedonism in the fantasy world is also unreal; it's just an illusion. But wait a moment—didn't I dispose of these objections earlier by explaining that the person in the fantasy would believe *without question* that he or she is engaging in *real* thought, is having *honest* emotions, and is exerting *concrete* effort in overcoming the many challenges that inevitably arise in the quest for happiness? And wouldn't the person think that the people, places, things and events that present themselves are *real* and *solid*, accurate reflections of reality? It becomes even more interesting when we realize that it's only we, the outside observers, who are justified in judging the pill-induced happiness as a total self-delusion. The person *in* the happiness dream could never know and would never even suspect as much.

We are finally zooming in on the problem with my experiment, and, as a bonus, unexpected surprises are bubbling to the surface. The theoretical person in the fantasy world, and the people considering entering that world, abide in two different dimensions of human experience. As far as the person in the fantasy is concerned, he or she is living an authentic, happy life, and as long as the pill continues to work (and it always will), this dimension will remain stable. The *pre-knowledge* that the happiness pill grants only a fictitious happiness, on the other hand, is intolerable to the outside observer and possible participant. But why is this so? This pre-knowledge, in itself, could never guarantee happiness of any kind, and certainly the state of mind that it creates—from the viewpoint of simple pleasure—is no match for the form of happiness promised by the pill, however illusory. So what is the outside observer gaining by not taking the happiness trip? I soon realized that this was the wrong question and that I was moving in the wrong direction. Rather, the crucial question needed to address what a person would be *losing* by experiencing a lifetime of illusory happiness.

I noted frequently in the people I interviewed their passionate responses to my proposition. By and large, they became irritated with my probing into the reasons why they found my experiment unacceptable, and their irritation often escalated into anger the more I requested additional support for their positions. It became clear in most cases that the vast majority had made up their minds at the outset not to take the happiness pill, and no rational argument, regardless of its merit, was about to change their minds. To me this meant that something deeper than reason was resisting my invitation to happiness. What was the *something* that caused such visceral responses?

This is my idea: the potential participants knew that the pill-induced happiness was not real and were repulsed by this knowledge. I use the word *repulsed* in this context to point to the peculiar nature of their responses, which were often pre-rational and negatively visceral. The reactions were pre-rational insofar as they were not based on reasoned perspectives grounded in good logic and analysis, nor were they based on "common sense"—that is, an intuitive reasonableness that makes sense of a given situation. Rather, a *defensive* posture typically accompanied their positions and, on many occasions, quickly turned into anger. The arguments that sprang from their negative emotional state were characterized by varying degrees of rationality and irrationality, often carelessly blended together. Clearly this meant that their excuses for not taking the happiness pill were mostly superficial rationalizations and not thoughtful responses. What was the source of their repulsion and bad reasoning?

10.5

What is real serves as a human being's biological, psychological, and philosophical support systems. First and foremost, human life is about survival—staying alive from day to day. From a biological perspective, this means adapting to the real demands of physical existence by eating and sleeping, finding warmth when it's cold and remaining sufficiently cool when it's hot, being cared for at birth by parents and possibly the community, being able to fend off environmental dangers with or without the help of others, and so on. Then, for the species as a whole to survive, there is the additional requirement of successful reproduction.

Humans are also psychological beings. This means that *how* a person experiences himself, other people, and the world in general has a direct bearing on his or her survival. This requires having accurate sensory interpretations of the outside world, so one can detect what is really there. Without this knowledge, adapting to the real challenges and satisfying our essential biological needs are impossible. "Experiencing" in this context also means that humans must *think* in order to survive. Defective or misguided thinking, which misinterprets the real demands and requirements of living, can easily spell disaster for survival. Reflecting, analyzing, measuring, deciding, weighing, integrating, simplifying, and negotiating are some of the critical psychological processes basic to human survival.

Humans are also *meaning-based*, *meaning-orientated*, and *meaning-seeking* beings. Because we have lost most of the guiding influence of thoughtless, pre-programmed, biological determinism (often termed "instincts"), we have to rely on the guidance of meaning. But what is meaning? It is first of all the substance of thought—what I call *thought-meaning*. Ideas, beliefs, concepts, choices, and judgments are some examples of the many forms that thought-meaning can assume in the world of the mind. Conversations, dreams, fantasies, and "thinking out loud" are examples of thought-meanings in action in their role of activating our mental existence. And what is thinking itself but the process by which humans organize, integrate, simplify, and prioritize all the forms of thought-meaning for their varied uses in the practical world? What is common to all the forms of thought-meaning is that they are nonphysical—that is, they are not tactile, measurable, material objects like trees, running shoes, and planets that exist in the outside world. Their existence is in the nonphysical, subjective realm of pure thought.

Be that as it may, one must not suppose that the *origin* of thought-meaning is the mind itself. Proper mental function, in fact, lies in the ability of our mental and sense faculties to take in the meaning attached to all that we see in the outside world and to reconstruct it in our minds, so that our thought-meanings accurately represent what exists in the outside world. The word "see" is used here as the metaphor for all that we experience with our five senses and with the organizational aid of our mental capacities. Every item that we experience has a meaning—has identifiable characteristics that make sense to us: particular shapes, sizes, and tactile sensations, for example, are typical *definable* qualities of some items of experience that *call to mind* particular meanings; other objects have distinctive smells or sounds, such as a rose or the wind, that have meaning for us; still other items have specific meanings because of their use for personal or public functions and purposes, such as razor blades and cars. That we can *define* an item in experience as having certain characteristics and functions allows us to assign a name to it and put it in its proper place within the context of other defined and named items. *Naming*, in fact, is the *ultimate act of recognizing and assigning meaning to something*. All items that we can possibly name in the outside world are defined by what I call their "object-meaning."

A name is verbalized shorthand for an object-meaning. The most difficult concept to grasp about object-meanings is that, like thought-meanings, they are also nonphysical. The easiest way to comprehend the nonphysicality of object-meanings is to imagine, for example, a person from an extremely primitive culture—one who has been isolated from the cultural events and developments in the rest of the world—seeing an automobile for the first time. What would this primitive person really see? What meaning would the automobile have for him? Clearly, he would see a physical object with a certain shape, size, smell, taste (yuck!), color, and tactile sensation. But these qualities would *mean* very little, and they certainly would not add up to what we have named a car. In other words, the meaning of "car" would be literally beyond the person's comprehension. It's likely that he would believe that what we call a car was some kind of bizarre animal or perhaps a metaphysical incarnation of an unfriendly spirit, conclusions that would reflect the primitive person's own cultural judgments about reality. If this individual began to assimilate into the modern world, though, he would soon learn the meaning of "car" and the distinctive qualities that make up *car-ness*.

The point is that the meaning, "car," is not a physical characteristic; it is a general identity—a name that Western culture has assigned to a particular material object. In other words, unlike the measurable, physical structures that make up the object before us, the object-meaning—"car"—is not a *necessary* attribute of the material object, but a *contingent* meaning that our culture gave to it. We seem to be suggesting that the meaning of something has purchase and stability only within the culture that has created and/or defined and named it. This is only partially true. There are two other species of meaning that are *not* culturally derived, but instead are rooted in nature itself and in the biological constitution of human beings. What this signifies is that the meaning that we see, and the physical items to which they

221

are attached, are more closely interconnected than those of object-meaning.

I've labeled this first form of meaning "nature-meaning," because the items to which it is attached are products of nature. The source of the universal meaning of these items is that they are directly connected to the biological imperative to survive and reproduce. Hence, natural survival items, like food and water and protective natural shelters, are universally understood as having the same meaning: critical to physical survival. Also universally meaningful are visually provocative colors and body shapes because of their capacity to evoke sexual responses for purposes of reproduction. Closely related to nature-meaning is another form of meaning that I call "subject-meaning." I use the word "subject" to indicate the meaning that derives from the human subject as a member of the human species, all of whom possess a common nature because of a common genetic constitution.

However incorrect our primitive person's ideas might be about the meaning of a Western object that we have named "car," what would happen if we were to show him Westernized sexual images—e.g., the pop star Madonna trying to provoke sexual reactions in music videos and employing popular Western versions of sexiness, such as erotic cowgirl dancing? He would undoubtedly understand that what he is experiencing has sexual content and would feel the sexual meaning of what was being shown. He would be equally expert at correctly interpreting a whole host of Western facial expressions that denote, for instance, happiness, tenderness, and anger, as well as hand and body movements that indicate emotions such as aggression, pride, and friendliness. It is significant that the meanings expressed in these instances are embodied in typical *behaviors and images of human subjects* and not in physical objects (except when they appear in pictorial or artistic renderings). What is of particular interest is that, unlike thought-meaning and object-meaning, the meanings that are expressed in subject-meaning are not cultural creations, but an authentic *creation of human, biological nature*. How do we make sense of this suggestion?

10.6

Biological life has existed on Earth for approximately four billion years, which is a testament to life's ability to survive the most difficult environmental challenges. From a purely biological view, life, including human life, has continued to exist because it was able to survive and reproduce; it stands to reason that strategies had to evolve in order for human beings to accomplish these two tasks. The emergence a few million years ago of subject-meaning—out of nature—was this strategy. This is the reason why, for example, sexual meanings (such as seduction rituals and erotic kissing) became "hardwired" in humans: they increased the likelihood that sexual intercourse would be carried out. Likewise all subject-meanings are *universal* experiences in all humans and not dependent on cultural orientations and influences. Subject-meanings go a long way in revealing essential aspects of human nature and how it formed in relation to survival strategies.

Emotionalized physical behaviors, such as threatening facial expressions and intimidating body posturing, were often instrumental in neutralizing the threats of enemies and competitors and became universalized in subject-meanings. Other physical signs like smiling and physical gestures of friendship promoted cooperation among potential adversaries and likely contributed decisively to the continued survival of humankind. And, of course, there is the rich universe of sexually unambiguous facial, body, and verbal invitations. It's no wonder that all these behaviors have the same meaning to all people in all cultures; they were basic ingredients in the original human recipe for survival and reproduction. Although subject-meanings exist objectively and have the same meaning universally, they are also, like the other forms of meaning, nonphysical. They are general concepts—ideas about specific forms of behaviors and images that we observe in the outside world of human affairs.

The four forms of meaning that we have discussed so far—thought-meaning, object-meaning, nature-meaning, and subject-meaning—dealt specifically with our mind-based and sense-based experience of physical and human reality. But meaning has yet another critical role to fulfill: to give definition, organization, and purpose to each human life and to cultural life in general. The unfolding of the bio-ontological shift a few million years ago signaled the decline of the pre-human, instinct-based existence and the birth of meaning-based existence—human culture. Human culture became a sort of "new nature," in which the question of how to survive in order to reproduce became inextricably connected to new but equally pressing questions, such as:

How to live? For what reason? To what end? Human life, then, became more than a matter of survival and reproduction; it became an arena for self-motivated action fueled by *searches for meaning and purpose.*

Although the meanings that we isolated in thought (thought-meaning), in objects (object-meaning), in nature (nature-meaning), and in universally understandable human presences and behavior (subject-meaning) are not physical items, they are nonetheless *there* in our minds, or attached to the natural and cultural items in the world, or projected from observable behavior of human beings. The new form of meaning, by contrast, is not, in any sense, simply an idea or complex of ideas upon which to reflect, nor is it *present* before us like a usual entity in the outside world. Instead, it is an emergent *aspect* of thinking, emoting, and acting—in sum, of living in our cultural world. I call this form of meaning "life-meaning," because it arises not as a result of thinking alone or pure emotionalism, or out of thoughtless, emotionless action, but as an all-inclusive, *holistic process of daily living.* And what does "aspect" mean in my definition of life-meaning?

Here is where we meet both logical and linguistic limitations. Let's begin by making a difficult statement: life-meaning is notable for being both present and fleeting at the same time. We must, for the moment, refrain from saying precisely what life-meaning *is*, and instead focus on how it is manifested and what it does. Life-meaning is present in three ways: as a general organizing principle of day-to-day thinking; as an emotional filter through which one gains a very personal, visceral sense of being alive; and as an instigator to action, that is, as a philosophical/psychological imperative to pursue actively and with purpose both short- and long-term goals. Life-meaning, then, appears to show itself as a sort of comprehensive *life philosophy* that first arises from, and then orientates, the mental, emotional, and active dimensions of human nature. Despite the difficulty we may have in clearly defining life-meaning, its presence in our lives can be powerful and unmistakable. Part of the problem is that life-meaning resists fitting neatly into our normal categories of understanding—it is nonphysical, has no specific location in space, and has no typical concrete attachments to particular objects, as does, for instance, object-meaning. It is simply an aspect of our meaning-based existence, without itself being a tangible item that can be isolated from the process of living and investigated. But there is another complication.

We mentioned earlier that life-meaning is also defined by its fleeting nature. How could life-meaning be both present and fleeting at the same time? Simply stated: since life-meaning is necessarily tied to our mental, emotional, and active lives, it is only as present, stable, and enduring as are our thoughts, feelings, and actions. Life-meaning is produced by an individual being caught up in the process of living and is not an independent entity that stands fixed and unmoved before us. This means that life-meaning could instantly vanish with the cessation of real thought, deeply felt emotions, and purposeless, robotic action. And, in fact, the fluctuating presence of life-meaning is a natural part of human experience. The absolute dependence of life-meaning on the individual, however, does not mean that's simply a mental reality, like thought-meaning. On the contrary, the source of life-meaning is the dynamic *fusion* of the mental, emotional, and active energies of human experience in real, concrete living.

It's also true that it is unreasonable to expect life-meaning to persist during moments when genuine thought, feeling, and action have receded or have disappeared altogether. Part of the psychological challenge of life-meaning is the following: the sense of personal fulfillment that is experienced during truly meaningful moments is such that it *feels* as though it will endure unabated for an entire lifetime. But this delusion is shattered countless times as the vacillating nature of thought, feeling, and action makes itself felt during the course of normal living.

So what can we conclude about the nature of life-meaning? We can conclude that it is a nonphysical, nonspecific, emergent meaning complex of mental, emotional, and active living that organizes, orientates, and vitalizes an individual life, and that its presence ebbs and flows with the quality of the thinking, feeling, and actions that produce and support it. The theory of life-meaning resonates within certain strands of existentialist thinking. For instance, the absolute dependence of the *experience of meaning* on the thoughts, feelings, and actions of a person is roughly analogous to the existentialist idea that human beings, freely making choices on a daily basis, create the meaning that makes living worthwhile. Also, the fluctuating presence and intensity of life-meaning is related to the existentialist notion that human life is inherently ambiguous, unstable, and riddled with existential uncertainty.

The importance of life-meaning is not limited to the single individual, but is also essential to the life of a society in general. Social scientists have noted many times that a societies develop typical character traits, behavior patterns, and even value systems that are somewhat similar to those of individual persons. It's not uncommon, for example, to hear a historian refer to certain societies as "decadent" (ancient Rome in its final years of decline) or "humanitarian" (America for its generosity to other countries in times of disaster). Societies—like human beings—also are born, develop, eventually decline, and ultimately die. They, too, have common goals and purposes as well as strategies for how to achieve them. Here's an example: a democratic society embodies a specific value system, focusing on the rule of law, human rights, and personal freedoms of various kinds, including the freedom of speech, freedom of religion, free debate, and free elections. These cultural features are, as it were, *personality characteristics* of a democratic society. Indeed, all societies have their own personally characteristics, that generate social movement. And as life meaning for individuals requires the constant support of thought, feeling, and action, so too does a culture's life remain meaningful only to the extent that collective thoughts, passions, and actions remain vital.

It would be easy for some people to attribute metaphysical or supernatural qualities to life-meaning: life-meaning is physically invisible, yet powerfully present; it has no specific location in space; it feels as though it is somehow *around us* and even *in us*; and it appears to have a sort of moral dimension insofar as the intensity of its presence and impact on our lives is contingent upon the quality of the thoughts, feelings, and actions of individuals and societies. All of these facts are remarkable indeed. Some important questions about life-meaning are very difficult to answer, such as—how could such an abstract meaning complex possess the power to order and guide an individual human life and society as a whole? Why does life-meaning appear to have intelligence and purpose, almost independent of our awareness?

Despite the difficulty we may have in explaining the nature of life meaning, it's important that we refrain from seeing it in supernatural terms. To do so would be equivalent to a philosophical rush to judgment. How could we be sure that what we think is a supernatural process is not, in reality, an as of yet-undiscovered, *natural* part of the human world? Only further philosophical and scientific investigation could answer this question. There is one fact, however, of which we can be sure: life-meaning, like the other forms of meaning, emerged in the natural evolutionary history of humankind as a replacement for the dramatic weakening of pre-programmed, biological determinism. It was, at least initially, humanity's strategy for survival. That life-meaning turned out to be much more than a pure survival tactic is as fascinating as it is difficult to explain. Finally, it is important to keep in mind that both philosophy and science are not only on the road of discovery, but are also on the road of *self-discovery*. There is no way of knowing what future breakthroughs in both areas will tell us about the limits and capabilities of philosophy and science themselves and what new light these breakthroughs might shed on our understanding of life-meaning.

10.7

In addressing the question of why most of the people whom I interviewed refused to take my hypothetical happiness pill, we considered the idea that what is real supports a human being's biological and psychological support systems. In our discussions of the various forms of meaning, we must bring into focus our final support system—the *philosophical*. What is the connection between meaning and philosophy?

Philosophy is often understood as a subject matter that is unrelated to our normal ways of thinking and disconnected from the issues and problems that are of real, practical concern. Students at the university level sometimes take a philosophy class as a requirement or "elective" for some other "major" or decide to take philosophy as a primary area of study. And qualified students can go to graduate school after their initial four-year degree to earn either a master's degree or Ph.D. in philosophy. There are different areas of philosophy that a student could study, although most universities focus on particular areas, sometimes to the exclusion of others. One can study, for example, the great ancient Greek philosophers like Socrates, Plato, and Aristotle, as well as the most famous European philosophers like Descartes, Hume, Kant, and Nietzsche. In courses on these thinkers, students learn what these philosophers thought about a wide range of philosophical topics such as metaphysics, ethics, political thought, religion and epistemology. Students are also required to offer their own well-thought-out critiques and solutions to the various "philosophical problems" that the classic philosophers attempted to resolve.

In many universities today, however, the great philosophers and their long-argued "philosophical problems" have been brushed aside for what is often called "language philosophy." Philosophers such as Scotsman David Hume, the Austrian Ludwig Wittgenstein, and a whole host of European and American language philosophers are common points of departure for many students as they grapple with the complexities of language structure, linguistic components, and the meaning of language in general. Many language philosophers consider the traditional interests in metaphysics and epistemology a senseless and silly waste of time, because, in their view, such thinking is nothing more than airy-fairy, groundless speculation. For language philosophers, the result of 2,500 years of useless philosophizing carries a clear message: philosophy must change directions and begin doing what it does best—defining concepts and clarifying language. This form of philosophy has been shown to be very useful as a practical tool in, for example, science, where concept and language clarification are key. But many traditionalists look dishearteningly at this redefinition and redirection of philosophy, seeing it as one of the more absurd and tragic developments in modern thought. The great and noble enterprise of philosophy that began two-and-a-half millennia ago, and one of the Western world's most profound contributions to humanity, has been nothing more than *talking about talk*! But there is much more to the story.

Whether one subscribes to the traditional or the linguistic school of thinking, philosophy is not simply a world of fascinating topics, abstract arguments, and linguistic complexities to discuss, debate, and clarify in college classrooms and in written exams. The original inspiration for philosophy in ancient Greece, according to the words of the first Western thinkers, was the *experience of wonder* at the mystery of existence. And what set the Greek philosophical tradition apart from any other before, or from those contemporaneous with it, was that it moved to respond to this experience by *thinking*—that is, by asking rational questions—about the universe and the human world and then trying to answer the questions by giving logical explanations, and in some cases verifying their explanations through actually observing the natural and human world. By asking questions, the Greeks entered fully into a different universe of meaning.

Rather than appealing to a divine authority for guidance, relying on supernatural revelation, or seeking answers in mythological interpretations, the ancient Greeks began asking questions like: What is the world made of? How does the world function? What's the difference between plants, animals, and human beings? What's the shape of the earth? What does living the "good life" mean? What is noble? What is justice? What is the best society in which to live? The Greeks, in believing that the universe and humankind could be *known* by employing the sheer power of the human mind—again, by thinking—created a new vision of reality, one that was the literal, spiritual foundation of Western culture. Although the ancient Greeks made startling advances in all areas of knowledge and in culture in general, they were also frequently incorrect in their scientific understanding (e.g., their conclusions about the workings and makeup of the universe and their understanding of human biology). Although the Greeks showed that thinking rationally was the correct way to understand physical reality, they did not formulate the correct scientific method, in which what is thought to be true is *tested* methodically and repeatedly by mathematically meticulous experimentation. As we saw, this final breakthrough was left to the founder of modern physics, Galileo in the seventeenth century. Nonetheless, the great Greek thinker Aristotle set the stage for all future scientific progress by understanding the universe, in principle, as *knowable* through rational investigation and by careful and rigorous categorization.

As far as their philosophical contributions are concerned, much of the thought of Socrates, Plato, and Aristotle is still highly revered by those modern philosophers who continue to believe in the traditional goals of philosophy. It is important to understand that the Greek conquest of reality through reason was a new enterprise so making logical, strategic, and factual errors was only to be expected. After all, pursuing knowledge is a human affair that is fraught with all the natural limitations of human nature; human beings always have only limited knowledge. Moreover, the Greeks had no prior or contemporary rationalistic tradition from which to draw that served as a guide and corrective to their investigations. Nonetheless, the ancient Greeks' reason-based approach to interpreting the universe and humankind represented one of the profound cultural breakthroughs in the history of the human species.

In speaking of a philosophical support system as a source of what is real, the Greek experience of philosophy comes to mind as the best starting point, and the reason is clear: what the Greeks brought to light was not only a new way to live, think, and understand existence, but a *human dimension* that had lain hidden in the bosom of humanity since its emergence. With the arrival of the human species, uncertainty and purposelessness made their first appearance in nature. In this sense, the human species has the unique distinction of being the first truly *ignorant* species. And of what were they ignorant? Virtually everything. What is more helpless and pathetically ignorant than a newly born baby? From this viewpoint, the meaning of cultural life is the process of educating human beings with the purpose of replacing their primal ignorance.

10.8

The emergence of elementary culture and meaning occurred at this same historical time, perhaps as much as two million years ago. Initially, thought-meaning, object-meaning, subject-meaning, nature-meaning, and life-meaning were concretized and harmonized within humanity's *mythic* understanding of nature and human life. It was here that reality for the first time became *full of meaning* and, particularly, full of mythic meaning. The objects of experience—both inanimate and animate nature—were *alive*, were *spirits*, and were thought to be directly responsible for giving the gift of life, and they worked to protect the individual from enemies. The mythical meaning in the outside world of nature, however, was not sufficient for the primitive mind to satisfy its need for meaning and purpose; it also required the support of *unseen powers* to guarantee the stability and permanence of meaning that was seen on the earthly plane. Primitive peoples thought that invisible gods and spirits populated transcendent realms and were ultimately responsible for all the events and activities on the earthly plane, including all human affairs. The powers and forces in the outside world—the sky, the sun, the mountains—and the invisible powers and spirits that supported them essentially assumed the responsibilities previously held by our all-determining, natural instincts. This remarkable accomplishment in thought was the result of the primitive individual *assimilating this outside world of meaning* within him or herself; this internalization of meaning became the essence of thought-meaning and served to guide the individual through the twists and turns of a normal life. Here we find meaning coming to the rescue of an instinct-challenged humanity.

The mythic interpretation of the outside world of nature and human life and their internalization into the individual represent the very first installment of a meaningful, purposeful existence for the human species. The newly emerging worlds of meaning became more narrowly defined and structured as human beings began seeing and experiencing the world in more precise and complicated ways. For example, humans began living more and more in communities, because doing so conferred added advantages, such as the potential for joining forces to combat common enemies or to overcome ecological disasters. But community life also presented unprecedented complications on virtually every level of existence, from learning how to share food and other necessities of life, to determining how and when to circumscribe personal versus public boundaries, to learning how to live and work together productively and peacefully with many different people, to establishing laws and customs. Additionally, the social quality of community existence contributed immensely to further defining the different forms of meaning. "Self-consciousness," for example, became more crystallized as individual humans began confronting and interacting with others. Seeing and reflecting on oneself, *in relation to other self-conscious beings*, highlighted one's sense of selfhood and intensified the personal experience of thought-meaning. And with this further clarification, all the other forms of meaning naturally became more defined and stabilized. Life-meaning, in particular, began infiltrating each human life with greater force as human beings began thinking and acting collectively. Experiencing the world in terms of short and long-term goals *with one's people* created a sort of communal spirit that gave cultural nourishment and purpose to each person.

Closely related to the mythic world of meaning was the *religious mentality*. In this context, meaning became subject to the moral judgments of spiritual authorities. Religious leaders were believed to possess supernatural powers (powers derived from transcendent realms and spirits) and, as a result, were granted the freedom to create new meanings and to give more exact definition to all the varieties of human experience. In particular, they proclaimed that meaning of every kind has *moral value* (what is good or virtuous as against what is bad or sinful behavior) and that some expressions of meaning have greater moral value than others.

Let's use my scheme of differentiating among the forms of meaning in order to understand what the ancient religious leaders believed. We could say that thought-meaning could be judged as base, or it could reflect higher ideals. Object-meaning could be seen as holy or profane, subject-meaning could be interpreted as virtuous or sinful, and natural-meaning could represent what is beautiful or repulsive. Finally, life-meaning could be understood as leading one down the path either to spiritual purity or moral bankruptcy. In essence, the mythic/religious mind experienced reality through the *moral prism of religious meaning* as determined by religious authorities. Thinking, in this context, meant accepting—without question—the standardized religious meaning presented by religious leaders, as well as using one's power of thought to be fiercely *self-critical* in order to make sure that one's intentions, thoughts, and actions were consistent with one's moral principles.

During the high Greek civilization (seventh century BCE to fourth century BCE), however, human culture underwent a drastic transformation, one that broke radically from both past and contemporaneous mythic/religious traditions. The most revolutionary result was the emergence of new kind of thinking—rational thinking—along with new kinds of meanings. How and why this fabulous metamorphosis occurred in ancient Greece has vexed the minds of historians and philosophers for centuries. What cannot be doubted is that, for ancient Greeks, thinking rationally came to define all their cultural activities, at least long enough to change the course of Western history. The result was the creation of much that we associate with Western culture: democracy, rule of law, scientific and mathematical thinking, reason-based philosophy, the beginning of all the basic sciences, drama and many literary forms, and the humanistic tradition in which living with purpose and passion *in this world* and not in some imaginary one became the guiding cultural theme.

The traditional mythic/religious understanding of everyday life was replaced by a progressive rational orderliness of human life in all of its departments and groupings: you and I; us and they; private and public; thought and action; master and slave; government and governed; sacred and profane; virtue and sin; good and evil; and civilized and barbarian. These are just a few examples of the ways that humans began organizing the meanings in their worlds. Many of these categories were important to previous mythic/religious traditions, but in earlier times these distinctions were not clearly defined and taken to their logical conclusions. With the Greeks, there were reasons for such distinctions, and they explained them. That their reasoning was often naïve, ill informed, or simply wrong is beside the point. Their *intention* was to use the power of rational thought to arrive at a deeper understanding of the human world, and in many cases they made many significant advances.

Critical thinking is a qualitatively different form of thinking from mythical or religious thinking because of its demand for logical justification for any point of view. Reason-based thinking rejects following the commandments of mythical or religious authority figures without good reasons, or simply believing propositions or alleged statements of truth without proof or justification. By thinking critically, the ancient Greeks were empowered to challenge, create, and interpret meaning from a highly personal perspective, independent of external authorities of any kind. This is the essence of individuality, and it represents the greatest and most profound discovery of the ancient Greek civilization.

The ascent of rational meaning in Greek culture signaled a spectacular moment in the history of humanity, one in which the most distinctive dimension of human nature blossomed fully for the first time. And this is the crux of the matter: the Greek experience of wonder at the presence of *what is*, and the rational response it evoked, created the conditions for the *questioning attitude* to arise in dramatic fashion. The questioning attitude is not simply what one does with one's thinking ability but is the very *ground of meaning* that makes thinking—and individuality—possible. In this sense, thinking is the questioning attitude in action. And which areas of human experience largely escape the reach of the questioning attitude? Only those areas in which true thinking is forfeited, such as in religious or political obedience to dogmatic authorities and the meanings they promote. But even in these cases, a form of pseudo-thinking occurs, in which the believer uses critical thinking to negate thinking itself for the sake of one belief system or another.

Thinking, questioning, and creativity—these are the multiple aspects of genuine individuality and constitute the true essence of human nature. But these characteristics exist in both potential and actual form. For countless millennia, genuine thinking was held captive and remained unexpressed because of the dominance of mythic and religious worldviews. In other words, mythic/religious meanings imposed a sort of mind-control on the true believer, in which thinking was rigorously and systematically suppressed. From this perspective, the Greek experience and discovery of rational meaning represented the grand liberation of human nature from the shackles of thoughtless, dogmatic traditions.

Human freedom is located—and flourishes—in the precise point in philosophical space where the questioning attitude and *what is* meet. Without this direct, head-on contact with *what is*, one remains forever trapped in a pure, psychological universe, in which nothing exists but the contents of one's mind—in philosophy, this doctrine is called "solipsism." A solipsistic universe can never allow for freedom, because freedom requires that an individual be aware of that which threatens to constrain it, and this can only be *what is*. In this sense, free acts, free choices, and free expression can exist only when there is a possibility that they may be squashed by the hard facts of reality. This is precisely why the experience of freedom, in any form, creates a powerful feeling of liberation: one can only know freedom when one is liberated from that which tries to constrict or extinguish it altogether.

In the end, freedom of thought is nothing more than an individual's ability to engage *what is* and to respond freely to this experience—to ask rational questions about it. But this ability presupposes openness to *what is*. The simple attempt to try to answer the questions that emerge in this openness is one of the profound expressions of human freedom. Free acts of creativity represent human freedom at its most expressive. Creativity means going beyond what is already realized in order to produce new items and meanings that the individual had not previously found in the natural or human world. Going beyond what is already realized first requires intuiting or surveying *what is*, questioning it, and then, in an act of philosophical or artistic defiance, transcending or transfiguring it by genuine actions that produce change and novelty. Producing something that is seen as original is actually the most powerful act of freedom, and it follows naturally that it also grants the creative individual the deepest sense of liberation. This is the primary reason why the arts have such a visceral and imaginative grip on us, both as viewers and performers: these creative mediums enable us break free of the constraints and banality of what is predictable, typical, repetitive, limited, and controlling—the existential gravity of everyday life.

But don't allow this abstract talk about questioning *what is*, rational meaning, freedom, and creativity mislead you. The simple lesson to learn is that the questioning attitude is not merely a skill that one cultivates to answer difficult philosophical questions; instead, it is a natural dimension of human nature that is an indispensable aspect of all human affairs. As such, it is as important as oxygen to the pure survival and day-today life of vital human beings. Every situation presents a cluster of crucial questions or meanings that require focused attention. Whether or not you have to decide if you should go to work today, if you should consume this or that food, or how to tell your love interest that your passions have run dry, asking questions and finding answers is how human beings order and orient their affairs.

We are now in a position to address the connection between meaning and philosophy and, in so doing, answer our primary question of how *what is* sustains an individual's philosophical support system. First and foremost, philosophy is the art and science of questioning meaning. And where must any potential answer reside? Only in the universe of meaning, since questioning and meaning were born of the same bio-ontological shift away from determinate nature, and they necessarily imply each other. And where does meaning derive? At its base, meaning derives from both the common nature of all human beings (subject-meaning) and the dynamic interface between the human mind and the infinity of *what is*. Meaning, in this latter sense, is *what happens* in this exchange—that is, it is an emergent property of the primal human interaction between the finite mind and infinity. It seems unlikely that this exact form of meaning exists for nonhuman animals, since they are naturally oblivious to the infinity of *what is* and therefore have no interest in it. Based on our earlier discussion about the nature of meaning, animals don't separate a physical item from its meaning in their actual experience and have little imaginative ability to do so. This means that animal meaning is to a great extent, not culturally dependent. Instead, animals are largely fixed in the moment, to their immediate, limited interests of survival and reproduction. Simply stated, animals do not possess a philosophical dimension— animals don't ask questions.

But there is another source of meaning: the cultural traditions into which all humans are born. With the newborn, developing baby, cultural meaning is slowly reconstructed to the point that the person's subjective meanings are directly reflective of the objective meanings that exist in the outside world. This building process occurs on two levels that continuously interpenetrate each other: *organically*, as the physical brain grows in its ability to interpret, synthesize, and simplify meaning, as well as *educationally*, as the individual learns how to connect meanings to the objects of experience. Additionally, subjective meanings can interact with each other, and they may unite, alter, or give birth to new variations or even completely novel meanings. Occasionally, an extraordinary individual relives and re-experiences a sort of primal confrontation with infinity—with *what is*—and discovers powerfully new meanings that reconfigure prevailing meanings and ultimately have a profound impact on some area of human understanding or endeavor. We commonly call this sort of individual a "genius." The contributions of geniuses, in fact, represent the highest expression of philosophy.

However, as I have been struggling to express, the work of philosophy is not restricted to professional philosophers or geniuses, but is a natural part of human nature. From this perspective, not only is philosophy *not* an abstract and detached way of thinking, but it is practical through and through and has concrete applications in all situations in life. So the real question, then, is not whether or not one chooses to indulge in philosophical thought, it's only how well or poorly one philosophizes. Now back to happiness pill story.

10.9

Once we comprehend the importance of possessing healthy biological, psychological, and philosophical support systems, then the decisions and emotional responses of my candidates for the happiness pill can begin to make sense. What I am proposing is actually quite extraordinary—namely that the candidates not only *unconsciously intuited* the requirements of happy living, but that this intuition also guided their decision not to take the happiness pill and caused them to have negative responses at the thought of doing so. I am further suggesting that most of the stated reasons for declining my invitation were at best only partly thought through excuses or, at worst, thinly disguised rationalizations. It was in considering the general responses to the happiness experiment that I realized conclusively that I had misconceived my proposal.

My arguments for taking the happiness pill were riddled with no fewer than twenty fallacies:

1. That physical or sensuous pleasure (reflexive hedonism) is equivalent to happiness (holistic hedonism). **Correction:** Pleasure is an important ingredient of happiness, but happiness cannot be reduced to it.

2. That happiness is best served by the avoidance of pain and struggle. **Correction:** The experience of happiness is relative—that is, one can know happiness (and pleasure, for that matter) only if one has experienced, and continues to experience, what is unpleasant and difficult.

3. That doing what one wants at every moment is the essence of happiness. **Correction:** What we want at any given time does not (and often does not) necessarily lead to pleasure, much less happiness.

4. That fulfilling our fantasies is the path to happiness. **Correction:** Fantasy is mostly preoccupied with *public values*—such as pursuing wealth, power, and status—that can never replace the vital role of *personal values*—such as experiencing love, cultivating friendships, and building integrity—which are some of the crucial building blocks of happiness.

5. That happiness is a "state of mind" or natural disposition (passive pleasure). **Correction:** Happiness always includes the

influence of the biological facts of the body, the physical facts of the world, relations with other people, and social reality.

6. That there are no objective principles and standards of happiness. **Correction:** The indispensable requirements of a vital human life—including physical health, a nurturing childhood, good friendships, public respect, intellectual stimulation, and psychological/emotional balance—are the principal sources of objective standards of happiness.

7. That happiness is the grand "goal" toward which one's life should be aimed. **Correction:** Although happiness must be pursued, this ideal is not a distant item, quantity, or experience; instead, it is a gradually unfolding existential process that presupposes achieving numerous, daily, short-term goals (dynamic hedonism); making good choices; initiating effective action; practicing creative thinking; knowing sensual delight; achieving gratifying victories; and even experiencing painful failures.

8. That happiness is different for each individual. **Correction:** All the rich differences in psychological types, lifestyles, and belief systems can easily hide the common, inherited cluster of universal happiness requirements and experiences.

9. That one's happiness has no necessary connection to other people. **Correction:** Human beings need each other to survive physically and are naturally social beings that require personal communication and intimate emotional and physical contact with other people.

10. That desiring happiness is the most dominant aspect of human nature. **Correction:** The experience and value of happiness are among the extravagant cultural "luxuries" made possible by advancing civilization. (For thousands of millennia previously, pure survival for purposes of reproduction was the early humankind's *only* value).

11. That people naturally know the meaning of happiness. **Correction:** Humans are famously ignorant of the requirements of happiness and frequently decide on ways of living that systematically annihilate their chances for happiness (like pursuing reflexive pleasure as a means to happiness).

12. That happiness is a movement toward pure, pleasurable feeling and away from dispassionate, analytical thinking. **Correction:** One of the casualties of modern, anti-intellectual pop culture is critical thinking, which is indispensable to the ongoing experience of making decisions and value judgments that promote happiness.

13. That the goal of happiness is to experience pleasure and joy at all times. **Correction:** Perpetual feelings of pleasure and joy would eventually dull, and ultimately undermine, the experience of happiness, because true happiness also requires knowing personally what is unpleasant and sorrowful.

14. That action in the real world is not necessary to happiness. **Correction:** Human nature is inherently "worldly," that is, action-prone.

15. That happiness is the spiritual birthright of all human beings. **Correction:** Happiness is an evolved cultural strategy that emerged in relatively recent human history.

16. That the mind, independent of the outside world, can orchestrate all the dynamics of happiness. **Correction:** Ideas, judgments, and strategies need to be expressed in the real world for one to understand their relevance to happiness.

17. That a life without happiness has no value. **Correction:** For some people, a life of extreme self-sacrifice (for a higher cause, for example) has its own reward for the individual (e.g., benefiting society or humanity) that frequently precludes what we would normally understand as a happy life.

18. That there is a simple recipe for happiness. **Correction:** Although there are universal principles to happiness, one must "experiment" daily to discover how these principles play themselves out in one's life.

19. That the mind can be separated from the outside world. **Correction:** The mind is forever "in and of the body," the body being a natural part of the physical and cultural world.

20. That the body is inferior to the mind. **Correction:** The body houses the mind, gives it nourishment, and is what "acts" in the outside world. Further, the body's requirements for health are essential to the emergence and growth of happiness.

This line of thinking suggests that happiness is not what many people believe it to be, and, further, that many people simply don't know what happiness is. Detractors might ask, but how do we measure happiness, anyway? Isn't it clear that the question of one's happiness is best understood by the person who knows intimately his or her own feelings, thoughts, and experiences? How could I be so presumptuous as to judge the value of other people's experiences? These objections are excellent examples of a form of false reasoning that is called in philosophy "begging the question." Put simply, "begging the question" means including in your argument the very points that you need to defend and justify. This argument simply says that I know what happiness is because I experience it and I know what I experience. This sort of circular reasoning brings all rational dialogue to a virtual standstill. This is a *dogmatic* claim, in other words—a groundless assertion without rational integrity. It is noteworthy that people are always free to be dogmatic, but doing so keeps them solidly in the realm of religion or fantasy and are no longer thinking philosophical or scientifically.

My point is that happiness is not a matter of personal opinion or judgment or personal taste—it is a very specific kind of personal experience that is shared by all genuinely happy people. This is true despite that fact that, for example, one person might understand happiness to be enjoying as many pleasurable experiences as possible, pursuing numerous sexual partners, and accumulating vast sums of money, while another person might require simply good health, a steady love interest, and a modest income. All people have their own ideas of what makes them happy. But why should we allow happiness be defined in any way that people like? Why do we have this absurd notion that one's personal ideas and judgments—as long as they don't offend our sensibilities and values—are accurate reflections of reality? Human beings are famously ignorant of what is best for them, and human history tells many sad tales of sincere human stupidities and their tragic consequences. Allowing happiness to mean virtually anything strips it of all meaning and reduces it to an empty idea. In fact, the meaning of happiness must be saved from extinction by saying clearly what it is and, equally importantly, what it isn't.

I have already given my answer as to what happiness is: happiness—holistic hedonism—is the harmonious balance between reflexive hedonism and dynamic hedonism. This notion gathers in itself the bi-directionality of human nature: one orientation steeped in its animal past, in which fulfilling instinctive desires is paramount; and another moving toward the future, where human culture provides the opportunities for stable emotional connections, having satisfying philosophical answers, and living purposeful, active lives. It's clear from this definition that happiness exists in the middle of a continuum where, at one extreme, reflexive hedonism is pursued aggressively, and at the other extreme, dynamic hedonism is of primary concern. Either extreme represents a significant imbalance, and in the case of reflexive hedonism, the excessive preoccupation with immediate gratification could easily result in personal destruction.

As we noted earlier, passive pleasure is similar to the pleasure theoretically granted by my happiness pill, insofar as, in both cases, no effort is required. We also saw that passive happiness resembles the altered states of mind that result from emotional/psychological disorders and personality-altering narcotics. We concluded that among all the installments of passive pleasure, the only version that can grant real, lasting benefit is the pleasure provided by possessing a naturally positive, sunny, and optimistic disposition. The great danger of passive pleasure, however, is that, taken to an extreme, it can substantially diminish the intensity of unpleasant experiences, which are vital guides to understanding human life and navigating successfully through it. In effect, it could produce unhealthy and imbalanced delusions about oneself and reality. Like pleasure in general, passive pleasure also exists on a broad continuum, in which different people affected by passive pleasure see the world in varying degrees of optimism, cheerfulness, and buoyancy.

Reserving a special category for happiness suggests that the majority of humans are not living happy lives. This is true. The essential problem for most people is that happiness—as I understand it—is not a gift of nature, but emerges in one's life in the course of successfully meeting the requirements for happiness. And the requirements for happiness (e.g., good thinking, disciplined lifestyle, proper balance between reflexive, dynamic hedonism) must be absorbed both from informal (family life) and formal education and also from the culture in which one lives. Paying homage to Aristotle's notion of learning "good habits" as foundational to happiness, the values and virtues of happiness must be *practiced* in the course of daily living. Unfortunately, human nature is not intrinsically designed for happiness. It is naturally inclined to excessive reflexive hedonism, irrationality, thoughtless behaviors, laziness, and groupthink—making it appear ill suited to what I call happiness. On the other hand, human nature is also a part of the cultural fiber in which it thrives. Culture is, in no uncertain terms, the *womb of meaning* in which human nature is nourished and from which it receives guidance. The overall result of human nature being largely culture-bound is that it is always *caught up in meaning*. Human nature's absolute reliance on meaning, however, is the key to achieving human happiness, because with the proper education and creative environmental guidance, human nature can be reconfigured to pursue happiness—holistic hedonism. Unfortunately, because of poor cultural and educational guidance, most human beings live, at best, only partially satisfactory lives. Not happy ones.

The theoretical happiness pill experiment died stillborn. Most of the potential takers would not, in principle, take the fast track to bliss, even though their own ideas about what they thought would make them happy would be realized without fail. The problem was that they knew—*in advance*—that their happiness would be an illusion, a mind-blowing fraud, and this knowledge was repulsive to their natural, ethical sensibilities. It became clear to me that my experiment was founded on many misconceptions about human nature, pleasure, and happiness. The most fascinating insight that this little thought experiment manifested was that it seemed to suggest that people— often contrary to their stated views—have a general, intuitive sense of a fundamental requirement of happiness: that it must occur within the context of *real*, day-to-day living with all its stressful uncertainties and unfortunate occurrences.

11

Purpose, Einstein, the Material Universe, and a Tapestry of Ideas

11.1

Cultural activities differ radically from culture to culture, from one epoch to another, but purposeful behavior is common to them all. When we consider highly controlled and oppressive societies, such as fascistic dictatorships, in which free thinking is discouraged, where one's actions are rigidly controlled, and where even simple freedoms, such as freedom of speech, are outlawed, we still find human beings living highly purposeful, active lives. But in these cases, their purposes are not of their own choosing or making but are imposed on them. This is why we must be careful in affirming this or that way of life simply because the participants are living purposeful lives. A "quality life" is not only a purposeful life; it's one in which purpose serves the individual's richer unfolding.

11.2

Thinking and acting with a purpose is culture's answer to humanity's loss of instinctive ways of behaving.

11.3

With the decline of religious belief, humans are forced to discover new ways of thinking and behaving purposefully or risk slipping into the abyss.

11.4

Christian philosophy must argue for a *static* view of knowledge and human life—that is, *what* a Christian should think, believe, feel, and strive for; and *how* a Christian should behave now and in the future must never change. And why? Because all this information is already contained in the self-proclaimed, unchanging, all-encompassing, eternal truth of God as presented in the New Testament. That many modern Christians have revised the teaching of the New Testament—or more often have ignored many inconvenient scriptural teachings—does not alter this principle one bit. The Bible may be vague and contradictory in regard to important topics, but, in many instances, the meanings and messages are unambiguous. For example, Jesus is clear about the need for his followers to live an ascetic life, one disinterested in accumulating material possessions or wining worldly position, and one devoted only to otherworldly, spiritual values like humility, charity, care for the poor and sick, and total reliance on God for daily guidance. This is the Jesus that is has been lost in the modern, capitalistic translations of the New Testament. There are many examples along these lines. The general point is that the validity of the Bible, as a repository of spiritual truth, rests completely on the idea that its truths are eternal and not subject to alteration given historical or cultural developments. From this perspective and for better or worse, the world of Christian spirituality is a *closed* one—eternal truth is eternal truth—once it's revealed, there is nothing that can be added or subtracted.

Liberal democratic philosophy, in sharp contrast, is a dynamic, *open-ended* worldview that reflects the rapid, spectacular, and often unexpected developments in secular thought, science, and technology. Its strives to reconfigure, expand, or discard old, worn out, or simply wrong ideas or plans of action, and replace them with improved, novel, and even revolutionary ones. This program of discovery and change is an unending process, and it defines the very essence of liberal democratic thinking. That Christianity and liberal democratic philosophy are promoted, through various media, educational systems, and publications, as mutually harmonious is only possible in a culture of ignorance and misinformation, where the capacity for critical thinking and thoughtful reading have not been cultivated or have been suppressed in the general population. This cultural trend has caused not a little trouble.

11.5

To what extent has modern culture met the basic human need for purposeful behavior? The answer is that modern culture has provided the means for purposeful behavior, but, ultimately, the results have been mixed. Science and technology have provided jobs, professions, and pastimes that had never existed before—from working as rocket scientists to "flipping burgers" at the local fast food restaurant, to playing computer games. Computer technology itself has created a universe of virtually unlimited occupational opportunities. But there is a fatal flaw in all culturally derived activities: because cultural purposes are human fabrications, they are fraught with numerous liabilities, limitations, and uncertainties. The problem is simple but resolutely impossible to resolve: *human purposes are inherently contingent.* For example, economic, political, and social factors make purposeful activities vulnerable to disruption and even annihilation. One could lose one's employment if economic conditions change for the worse; one could experience a radical life change if political realities, such as a war, intrude upon and alter what one does on a daily basis; and cultural shifts, such as new a technology, could force occupations literally out of existence—many skilled professions have been lost to advances in computer capability, for instance. And then there is the frailty of human health, which is subject to violence both from within the human body and from without. Indeed, poor health or a serious accident could ambush the most profoundly purposeful existence and render it pathetically irrelevant. In a word, human purpose, unlike the biological, predetermined programming of nonhuman life, is forever under assault by the possibility, and frequent actuality, of *purposelessness*

11.6

Materialistic humanism is the worldview that adamantly rejects all forms of supernaturalism. It sees the methods used in the physical, and to a lesser degree the biological sciences, as the only legitimate way to gain an understanding of reality. Materialistic humanism received its greatest inspiration from the science of Sir Isaac Newton (1642–1727), whose laws of physics not only gave modern humankind unprecedented belief in the power of the human mind to understand all aspects of the physical universe, but also gave birth to modern technological revolution. With the "classical" model so successful in both gaining understanding of the physical universe and providing a scientific framework for the wonder of technology, it was only natural to think that it was *the* key to unlocking all the secrets of reality. The idea that mathematics was the way to ultimate truth got immense support a bit earlier with the philosopher/mathematician/physicist René Descartes (1596–1650). He argued, picking up where physicist Galileo Galilei (1564–1642) had left off, that mathematically based thinking was the only way to gain knowledge of reality. Descartes not only was the principal inventor of analytic geometry, but he also maintained that mathematics provides the sole acceptable model for acquiring any kind of knowledge, including philosophical truth. In other words, the "deductive method" of geometry must be followed precisely if there was any hope of gaining certain knowledge. Descartes is normally considered the "Father of Modern Philosophy," because he introduced ideas into the philosophy mainstream that dramatically altered the course of modern philosophy and—both directly and indirectly—modern science as well as generally influencing aspects of modern culture. He is notorious for his method of doubting any form of alleged knowledge that does not meet rigorous mathematical standards: for knowledge to be beyond doubt, it must be *deduced*—geometry-like—from premises that, in themselves, cannot be doubted, and this newly deduced knowledge could then serve as the premises from which further truths could be deduced. We can see that deduction is a form of logical thinking that derives knowledge that already exists in earlier premises but has not been brought to light. The "syllogism"—invented first by Aristotle—is an example of deductive reasoning. As an example:

All brides are female. ("first premise")

Janet is a bride.

Therefore, Janet is female.

In this syllogism, the conclusion "Janet is female" follows necessarily from the two premises—or, to put it differently, the conclusion follows *deductively* from the premises. The virtue of proper deductive reasoning is that the conclusions must be true if the premises are true. The problem is, of course, that the premises might not be true in the first place, which means that the conclusion may not be true. Deductive reasoning is successful because we can derive *universal* truths from *particular* truths. On the other hand, assuming that a first premise is true is a long way from showing that it is true. Descartes believed that he found an indisputable first premise from which general truth could be deduced: the existence of the individual.

Descartes' most famous and controversial example of his deductive method regards his idea that *all* knowledge must begin with an absolutely unquestionable foundation or "first premise." This first premise, for Descartes, is based in the logically undeniable fact of one's actual existence. For him, in the simple *act of thinking* (which he defined as the essence of what is means to be human), one's existence is being posited without question. One cannot even legitimately *doubt* that one exists, for in doubting, one is, in principle, confirming the doubter's existence. It was for this reason that he believed that his "cogito ergo sum"—I think therefore I am—is the *indubitable* first premise, from which all other forms of genuine knowledge could be deduced, whether in mathematics, science, or philosophy. Descartes' idea of building up the whole edifice of knowledge by using deductive reasoning, however, was more convincing in the abstract than in his highly questionable applications.

Descartes thought, for example, that he could prove the existence of the outside world by deducing it from the reality, goodness, and perfection of God, whose existence he claimed could be shown to be deductively true. How did he do this? One of his approaches was his doctrine of "innate ideas": my idea of God as being perfect could not have originated from me, a mere imperfect mortal, because I have no experience or understanding of perfection, and therefore I could never have caused the idea of perfection to arise in my thinking to begin with; it stands to reason, then, that the idea of perfection must have been caused by a being who is perfect—God. Therefore, God must exist—this is simple deduction! And if God necessarily exists, then he could not be a "deceiver," because a deceptive God could not be perfect and would be a contradiction in terms. Therefore, the outside world must necessarily exist, because God, being perfectly moral and not a deceiver, would never allow his human creations to believe it to be true. This is a prime example of how Descartes believed that the deductive process leads to real knowledge.

Although Descartes' mathematical approach to reality was immensely influential in Western thinking, his most famous example is feeble at best and has not sustained many supporters over the centuries. Nonetheless, Descartes' obsession with philosophical certainty altered the course of Western thinking. With him was born the area of philosophy called "epistemology," which raises the basic question: how do you know that you know? This issue rose directly out of his interest in grounding all knowledge in mathematical methods for arriving at knowledge. Although many thinkers strongly disagreed with this approach, no genuine philosopher since Descartes could proceed without addressing the issues of epistemology. The great philosophers before Descartes—including Plato and Aristotle—largely ignored epistemology (actually, they were largely unaware of epistemological concerns) and naturally assumed that thinking correctly, in the effort to arrive at truth, simply meant reasoning properly. Bad thinking would lead one astray, just as good thinking would lead one to real knowledge. With epistemology, the very question of being able to think correctly was thrown into question. So problematic became the question of epistemology that even the greatest modern philosophers were unable to escape it, and all of them spent a great deal of time not discussing what reality is, but how to be sure that we have the capacity to arrive at this knowledge. As such, many thoughtful critics look at Descartes' introduction of epistemology as a veritable disaster and the tragic beginning of the end of legitimate philosophy. Others argue that unless epistemology is successfully addressed, no real philosophy is possible. The epistemological concerns that Descartes brought to light have been called collectively in philosophy the "transcendental realm," which means philosophizing that is focused on justifying or debunking the *possibility* of knowledge.

Another aspect of Descartes' thinking that has been extraordinarily powerful in Western culture is his idea that reality exists in two dimensions: thinking things—"res cogitans"—and extended things— "res extensa." By "thinking things" he meant consciousness or that part of a human being that thinks and contains thought. By "extended things" he meant all things that have physical extension in space. Not only has this dualistic conception of reality influenced many philosophers, it has also helped produce a worldview that is definitive of Western culture as a whole. Descartes' belief in the high value of extended things took on various forms as it circulated through the lifeblood of Western culture. One striking development was that it fostered the idea that a human being is nothing more than a sort a *mechanical* item—a human machine that functions by various physical pushes, pulls, and tensions. This highly materialistic interpretation of a human being has had an unfortunate history over the centuries and has contributed significantly to highly damaging misconceptions about how the human body functions and how humans think, emote, and act. For example, science and technology hold that not only is the material world of primary importance, but that what cannot be defined in physical terms—namely consciousness and all that is related to it (e.g., emotions)—is of lesser value. Although Descartes may not have argued that physical reality is all that matters, how his thoughts played themselves out often led to extreme conclusions. The hard materialism of science and technology is the most significant case in point.

So how do thinking things fit into the philosophical scheme of things? How are we to understand their relation to extended things? In Descartes' philosophy, this question took the form trying to account for the undeniable interaction between nonphysical thinking/thought and the physical brain. This conundrum has come to be known famously as the "mind/body problem." The mind/body problem is relatively simple: how could something physical—like the apple on the table in front of me—become a nonphysical *representation* in my mind? Where precisely in the sensory sequence of physically perceiving the physical apple is it changed into a nonphysical, conscious *idea* of the apple that will remain, clearly and distinctly, in my mind even when I turn from the actual apple and walk into the next room? Put slightly differently, how could something physical like an apple have a *causal* effect on something nonphysical—my consciousness? Descartes' answer, which has no scientific basis whatsoever, was that the transition from the physical action of perception to the nonphysical world of thought or representation occurs by virtue of the pineal gland, which is an actual gland in the brain.

The mind/body problem challenged and exasperated some of the finest minds, then and ever since, and the solutions that have been proposed have never been satisfactory. One solution, called "pre-established harmony" and originated by the German philosopher/mathematician/logician Gottfried Leibniz (1632–1677), argued that mind and body never really interact to begin with but instead have been arranged by God to be in perfect synchronicity, with only the appearance of interacting. The Dutch philosopher Baruch Spinoza (1632–1677) proposed that reality is one (usually termed "monism"), and all apparent differences are just aspects or "modes" of nature, which in his view is *God*, the one basic reality. Descartes' dualism began a long, combative tradition, and the modern bias toward strict *monistic materialism* has been the latest victor in this philosophical battle and has come to color our understanding of what is real and of highest value. Despite all the confusion and ambiguity that Descartes generated with his mind/body duality, it is perfectly clear that he believed that physical reality is primary, that it is measurable and quantifiable, and, finally, that it must be approached with the methodological precision of mathematics. It is for this reason that, along with Galileo and Newton, he stands as one of the significant architects of materialistic humanism.

11.7

With the developments of relativity and quantum theory in the twentieth century, the existence of energy was firmly established. One of the profound breakthroughs—led by German physicist Albert Einstein (1879–1955)—was the discovery that mass (matter) and energy are the *same* physical reality in two different states, as represented in his famous equation, $E=mc^2$. Einstein also established that mass and energy could move from one state to the other given the correct conditions, such as when an object is increasing or decreasing in speed—in other words, as an object increases speed, its mass *necessarily* increases as well, and the opposite is also true. Just as radical was Einstein's idea that time and space are not absolute, unchanging frames of references, but rather change relative to different observers—for instance, the time it takes for an object to travel from one point to another is different for different frames of reference. The accepted view at the time was there was invisible "ether" that served as the medium through which all items of nature travel—the ether was seen logically as the unchanging frame of reference with respect to which time and space were constant. The scientific belief in ether was passionate even though its existence was never experimentally proved. Einstein showed that the belief in ether was unnecessary to account for the behavior of physical reality. But the implications of this Einstein's revolutionary idea meant nothing less than the complete restructuring of our understanding of the physical world. Rather than describing physical reality from the perspective of unchanging frames of references—which was the practice for over two-hundred years—Einstein showed that physical reality is always *relative* to different frames of reference.

Einstein also showed that time and space should never be considered apart from each other, but must be treated as one, inseparable "time-space continuum." As a logical extension of his theory, he further held that the length of objects must *shorten* in the direction of their movements, as their speed increases. Einstein's bizarre ideas about mass, energy, space, and time were aspects of his "Special theory of Relativity," the foundation of which was his belief that the laws of nature are the same in all uniformly moving reference frames and that speed of light is "constant" and could never be exceeded.

If you are traveling in a train that is moving at a constant—that is, uniform—velocity, for instance, there is no way for you to tell by simple observation that the train is moving and the people waving goodbye to you from the station are not moving—based on how it looks and feels either could be the case for it. Additionally, if your passport falls to the floor of your uniformly moving train, it would do so as if you were not moving at all; these are examples of how the laws of nature are the same for all uniformly moving reference frames. The speed of light—186,000 miles per second—was, for Einstein, the fastest speed in the universe; the speed of light has the additional property of remaining constant independent of the motion of its source (see below).

These two ideas became for Einstein, the *postulates* for his new science and led him to his mind-boggling discoveries about the changeable nature of time, space, length, energy, mass, and energy-mass equivalence. The constant and unsurpassable speed of light means that instantaneous communication is a fiction, because the speed of all signals is always finite. For instance, the light from a flashlight that is flashed to different people at what appears to be exactly the same time would not reach each person at the same time if they all were in various distances (different reference frames) from the flashlight, even though it might *seem* to be the case. The person who was the closest to flashlight at the moment of the flash would, in fact, see the signal first. The finite, but constant speed of light has other fascinating implications.

The stars that you see populating the dark sky at night actually may not be there at all! What you are really seeing are not the stars themselves but only their *light*. Because starlight travels many light-years (a "light-year" is the distance that light travels in one year) to reach you, it's possible that the stars that originally produced the light now striking your retina have long since died and disappeared altogether from the actual universe, perhaps centuries ago or even longer. Remember: even light, like every movement in the universe, takes time to travel.

And then there is the dynamic nature of time. As an object increases in speed, special relativity has shown that the speed at which the object moves *slows down*. This is because, as we noted, an increase in speed causes an object to increase in mass, which makes time "drag"—that is, slow down. Theoretically, if an object were to reach the speed of light, time would stop altogether—time would literally stand still. But according to Einstein, this could never happen, because the mass increase of an object at the speed of light would be *infinite*—which is a nonsensical possibility. And experiments with objects that travel at nearly the speed of light—subatomic particles—have confirmed mass increases in accordance with Einstein's predictions. For the moment, it appears that we are stuck in the here and now with only meager wiggle room to play within the space-time continuum.

Nonetheless, it is interesting to note that time travel is not only a possibility, but it actually occurs whenever anything moves at any speed. The simple rule is this: the faster the speed, the slower time moves. If we ever were able to travel significantly close to the speed of light, from an *earthly perspective*, we would live to be many thousands of years old. But, according to relativity theory, from your personal frame of reference, you would age normally. The reason why the effects of relativity have remained hidden from common sense—why we don't, for example, experience time changing whenever we move—is because relativity modifications are very small in everyday life and only become conspicuous in objects approaching 186,000 miles per second—the speed of light.

The key idea in all the surprising effects of special relativity is the mystery of the constant and unsurpassable speed of light. There is no explanation as to why the universe has this absolute speed limit. It simply does, and the laws of the universe adjust to it unfailingly. One of the more difficult ideas to grasp is that in order for the speed of light to remain constant, all other speeds must be modified precisely in accordance with this speed. Let's do a simple thought experiment that will elucidate this bazaar notion.

Imagine that you are standing on the dock near your beach house and watching a cruise ship moving past you at ten miles per hour. On the deck of the ship there are two people throwing a baseball to each other, and the ball is traveling at ten miles per hour. From the perspective of the people on the ship, the ball is traveling at ten miles per hour, but from your perspective standing on the dock, what is the speed of the ball? That's easy: ten plus ten, so the speed is twenty miles per hour.

Now imagine that one of the ball throwers, still traveling at ten miles per hour on the ship, decides to send a flash of light, from a handheld flashlight, to his friend, who remains the same distance from him as they were when they were playing catch. What would be the speed of the light when it arrives at his friend's location? Well, we know that light travels at 186,000 miles per second, so that's our answer. But from your *perspective*, standing on the dock, how fast would the light be moving? If common sense prevails, we would simply do what we did before with the two people throwing the ball to each other—add together the respective speeds. But this is where the mystery begins. In fact, the speed of the light from your perspective standing on the dock is *exactly the same* as the speed of light traveling on the ship! Adding the two velocities together simply doesn't work. Physicists wrestled with this mystery but were unable to come up with a good explanation until Einstein's audacious solution: using my example, Einstein would say that the ship that is passing you at ten miles an hour is not really traveling at that speed any longer, but has *slowed down* just enough so that the speed of the light would remain constant at 186,000 miles per second! The ship's slowing down is not perceivable to the naked eye, because our sense perceptions are not fine-tuned enough to observe such minute changes. This is true no less with mass increases, and time and length modifications. On the other hand, with objects that travel close to the speed of light, such as subatomic particles, scientists see relativity modifications occur all the time, and quite clearly—because the closer to the speed of light something travels, the greater the changes. Whether we find these results unsatisfactory or not is irrelevant, because this is the way nature operates, and there is simply no arguing with nature. The speed of light rules!

But Einstein's master-stroke, and where his genius shone through even more brilliantly, was in his "General theory of Relativity," in which he demonstrated that gravity was not a distant force, as Newton had thought, but rather a particular *curvature* of space-time that is dependent upon the *mass* of the objects that populate it. The critical idea is: the greater the mass, the more extreme the "warping" of space-time. Put another way, objects move through space by following the *geometric structure* of the space-time that is being configured—warped—by the nearby mass of objects. Unlike Newton's theory of gravity that argued for some gravitational force acting "at a distance," Einstein discovered that objects simply follow the shortest paths ("geodesics") that have been grooved-out in space-time, like tennis balls rolling to the center of a trampoline that has a heavy weight sitting in its middle. The fabric of the trampoline is informed by the mass of the heavy weight and objects in its vicinity behave accordingly. It's that simple.

Actually, it wasn't that simple. Einstein realized that his knowledge in advanced mathematics was inadequate to the task at hand, so he underwent mathematical instruction in order to be able to brave the turbulent waters of general relativity. For ten years (after he published his special relativity theory), Einstein struggled desperately to find a way to generalize his ideas to make them apply to the universe as a whole—that is, to objects that move not only at uniform speeds (which is what his special relativity theory focused on) but also to objects that speed up or slow down. Finally, after a number of failed attempts, he found his spectacular solution: ten stunningly elegant equations that accurately described the movement of objects through space-time at any velocity. So rich in explanatory power were his equations that they provided profound clues as to the age, structure, movement, and even origin of the universe, and they opened the eyes of unbelieving scientists and laymen alike to undreamed realities, such as "black holes" (dead stars that are no longer visible, but whose masses have become so concentrated and powerful that they suck in everything in their vicinity, inescapably, including light and space-time) and "dark matter" (invisible mass that makes up most of the universe, and which is the invisible hand behind the scenes manipulating much of what we can observe). Einstein's general relativity theory was put to the test during a total eclipse in 1919, which showed that light from stars passing close to the sun was pulled from its normal course at a rate approximately matching Einstein's mathematical predictions.

The darkened sun made it possible to observe the starlight's "shift" ever so slightly toward the sun, confirming the warping of the starlight through space-time. With this astonishing confirmation of Einstein's outrageous theory, the world was soon at his feet. He was heralded as the greatest scientific mind since Newton, and he quickly became an international celebrity and icon. In the popular imagination, he is still seen as the epitome of genius.

It's amazing to realize that Einstein's insights directly contradicted the received wisdom of Newtonian physics, the very wisdom that up to the 20th century provided the scientific understanding of the nature, gave birth to modern technology, and informed the optimistic spirit of the modern world. The victory of Einsteinian science was one of humanity's greatest achievements, even though its ascendance over Newtonian science has raised disturbing questions about the status of accepted truth of any kind and has contributed the general philosophical vertigo of modern culture.

Interestingly and regrettably, Einstein did not always have the courage to believe in what his general relativity equations suggested, and in one instance, he actually modified them to support his skepticism. Most famously, he believed that the universe had to be *static*, even though his equation clearly indicated that it was *expanding*, and so he inserted his infamous "cosmological constant"—a mathematical alteration to his equations—to recast the universe as purely static. When it was later discovered experimentally by astrophysicist/cosmologist Edwin Hubble (1889–1953) that Einstein's initial equations were correct—that the universe was, indeed, expanding, and at an ever-increasing speed— Einstein openly admitted that his lack of trust in his own work was the "biggest blunder of his life." Thus, it was left to others to draw out from Einstein's equations additional aspects about the universe that most scientists have since accepted as correct. Most notable among these are the big bang theory and the existence of black holes.

One of the final contributions that Einstein gleaned about physical reality was that the universe is *finite, yet boundless*. The universe has no boundaries, no termination, and space-time ultimately turns in on itself; for instance if a beam of light were directed straight out into space, it would, given enough time, eventually return to itself. Other important contributions of Einstein include the papers he wrote that showed the existence and size of atoms and molecules and how they silently underlay and disturb some observable phenomena. Later in his career Einstein also helped to develop the new and important field of statistical mechanics and also helped explain how the quantum particles of gas condense into a form of liquid without the benefit of mutual attraction—now called Bose-Einstein condensation. If you think that relativity theories were mind-twisting then quantum physics may very well blow your mind.

Quantum physics—as embodied in the famous "Copenhagen Interpretation"—revealed a strange world where "cause and effect" doesn't exist; where solid, tactile, and geometric objects don't exist (only vague *energy configurations*); where subatomic particles have *both* particle and wave characteristics; where precise and simultaneous knowledge about the location and velocity of subatomic particles is not possible ("Uncertainly Principle"); where the observer, and even measuring equipment, influence what is being observed and measured in experiments—where, in short, "objective" investigation is not possible; where "probability waves" determine how subatomic particles will *probably* behave; where subatomic particles come into being *only when they are observed*; where local events are *instantaneously* connected to very distant ones (even those millions of miles apart); and where randomness is a real, fundamental attribute of the fundamental reality.

These strange ideas are based on the discoveries by: Max Planck (1858–1947); Niels Bohr (1885–1962); Werner Heisenberg (1901–1976); Max Born (1882–1970); Louis de Broglie (1892–1987); Erwin Schrodinger (1887–1961); John Von Neumann; and by Einstein himself, who, near the beginning of the quantum revolution, introduced the revolutionary notion that light is not a continuous stream or wave of energy but is composed of energy units that were later called "photons." (He won the Nobel Prize when he used the idea of photons to explain the "Photoelectric Effect"—the discharge of electrons from materials such as metal, as a result of their being bombarded by photons).

Before too long, the bazaar world of quantum physics was more fully exposed and described by other ingenious quantum scientists, and physical science has not been the same since. In fact, quantum physics represents a radical break with traditional science, of which the two relativity theories were still a part. Even though both theories were very different from Newtonian physics, they were still "classical theories," insofar as they were grounded in common-sense ideas and principles, such as local cause and effect, determinism, predictability, and clear observer-observed separation in experimentation (in which the observer of an experiment was seen as totally unrelated to what was being observed).

The world of quantum physics—the subatomic world—does not operate by classical rules as defined by Newton or even Einstein, but leaves them far behind. It has been the bane of modern physics that the universe at large and the subatomic world seem to operate with different laws and principles. It would be difficult to argue convincingly against the truth of quantum mechanic after considering that its many applications in technology such as lasers, cell phones, CD players, television, and the universe of medical technology. The list of quantum applications is endless and shows clearly that quantum physics is a concrete reality, not some abstract mathematical entity. Nevertheless, how could relativity and quantum theories—based on totally different premises—both be right? How could physical reality be so radically divided?

Beginning most prominently with ancient Greeks, a guiding vision has illuminated the heart, soul, and mind of Western culture: that truth is one; that, in the final analysis, all differences, conflicts, and tensions will be resolved, and that *one seamless truth* will emerge—unchanging and eternal. This faith is as much a part of our great intellectual and artistic traditions as our religious ones. Moving toward oneness figured, and still figures, prominently in the sciences; unifying different areas and aspects of physical reality, with one set of mathematical equations, has been the most revered accomplishment in all of science. This was true for Newton and was no less true for Einstein. With his one "Law of Gravitation," Newton unified vastly different areas of physical reality, from the movement of objects on Earth to the movement of objects throughout the entire universe. And what mystifies scientists about Einstein's general relativity theory in particular is how comprehensive it is—even exceeding Newton's work by accounting for more complex areas of physical reality with ever-greater precision, and doing so with a single set of beautiful equations. This accomplishment is extraordinarily pleasing to the rational mind that is forever trying to reduce complexity to simplicity and difference to unity. Einstein's general relativity theory is like one of Mozart's gorgeous symphonies: exquisitely balanced, seamlessly integrated, and perfectly harmonious.

We can see why the great Einstein—always guided by the vision of the harmonious oneness of nature—was perplexed by the emotionally and philosophically troublesome findings of quantum physics and was unable to accept them as representing the final truth. For him, those who argue for the ultimate truthfulness of quantum physics must address some critical questions: How could chance, randomness, nonlocal affects, and probability rule fundamental physical reality? How could we dispatch with strict cause and effect in accounting for the laws of the universe? How could we do away with the idea that there is a reality that can be known "objectively"—that is, independently of the influence of investigating scientists? And finally, how could relativity and quantum physics *both* be true? Reality cannot be defined by two conflicting truths, Einstein believed; reality must be rationally balanced and integrated, it must have only one set of explanatory principles. Because he had utter faith in a objective, rationally integrated universe, where all that occurs could be understood with absolute, law-bound precision, he concluded that there must be a deeper set of mathematical equations ("hidden variables") that would account objectively for all the quantum confusion and messiness. And so he courageously embarked on a lonely and frustrating journey, spending the last thirty years of his life trying to develop a "unified field theory" that would bring together the classical and quantum theories under one set of classical equations. His great antagonist during this time was the brilliant Danish physicist Niels Bohr (1885–1962), who was himself an important contributor to quantum physics. Bohr also was a staunch supporter of the idea that the insights and descriptions of quantum physics are not only accurate, but they are also final. In Bohr's view, Einstein was simply wrong in his skepticism about quantum science, and was clinging to outdated philosophical biases that didn't reflect what the universe is showing us. Ironically, according to Bohr, Einstein was guilty of the very same unscientific blindness that plagued the prominent thinkers who were unwilling to embrace Einstein's own relativity theories years earlier.

The two giants of physics battled over the years in a series of, one might say, scientific prize fights. In front of the whole community of outstanding physicists at various conferences, Einstein would offer for Bohr's consideration various thought-experiments that he believed would show clearly that quantum physics was incomplete and in need of being reformulated. But in each case, Bohr was able to answer Einstein's objections convincingly and to the satisfaction of all the other scientists present, which sent Einstein back to the drawing board time and time again. Although Einstein would not give up the fight and worked on various, creative solutions to his dying day, ultimately Bohr prevailed and emerged as the new Heavyweight Champion of the world of physics; Outside of helping his opponents gain more logical security in their positions, Einstein was shown to have wasted a great deal of time and mental energy for very little. Sadly, it became clear that the old man of physics lost his erstwhile miraculous instinct for uncovering the hidden truths of nature. The unfortunate reality was that Einstein was on the wrong path to begin with. He did not realize that not only did electromagnetic and gravitational forces need to be unified, but there were two other forces in nature—quantum forces— that any unified theory must incorporate. These were the "strong nuclear force" (the force that holds atomic nucleus together) and the "weak nuclear force" (the force that keeps important subatomic particles functioning properly). In the end, Einstein showed himself to be a mere mortal after all.

Einstein's most important contributions to science—his discovery of the photon, his energy/mass equivalence equation, his explanation for the photoelectric effect, his papers that gave compelling support for the existence and sizes of atoms and molecules, his special and general relativity theories, his work in quantum statistical mathematics, and his notions about the structure and size of the universe—will always remain among the most astonishingly creative feats in all of human history, on the level of those of Aristotle, Michelangelo, Leonardo, Shakespeare, Newton, and Mozart. And more than any one of them, he opened the universe to infinite possibilities that countless brilliant minds in the future will spend many lifetimes trying to realize.

Einstein's dream of discovering the Holy Grail of physics—the one rational framework that will account for all the laws and forces of nature—has not died. Far from it. Modern physics is in hot pursuit of a quantum-based unified theory, one that will absorb relativity into it. At present, the most promising contenders for the mantle are a variety of theories called "superstring" theories, which work on the premise that fundamental reality is composed of tightly coiled energy strings that coordinate with breathtaking dexterity and completeness all the different levels and laws of physical reality.

The flaw with this approach is that, at present, physicists cannot think of any feasible way of testing string theories, which was not the case with Einstein's theories, for instance. It's not uncommon for solutions to scientific problems to be found in the abstract world of mathematics but then fall apart when they are tested in the real world. The impractical nature of superstring theories is their major stumbling block. For these theories to work, we must assume that there are at least ten or eleven dimensions to physical reality, many more dimensions that our puny human brains could possibly observe, even theoretically. How do we test imaginary solutions for their faithfulness to reality? Mathematics can only go so far. Nonetheless, the search continues unabated for un-thought-of ideas, principles, and laws that may lead to major breakthroughs. And, of course, if a future Einstein should come along and unlock the final secret to a completely satisfactory, test-proven quantum theory, you can be sure that scientists would not rest until they devised even more elaborate theories that incorporated ever-greater chunks of the natural and human world. This process will continue until finally humanity has before it one set of unchanging laws that could account for every area, level, and dimension of human experience. Only then will Western humanity fully realize its majestic vision of oneness. It's a wild fantasy that may not be realizable.

Even though the worlds of relativity and quantum science appear, at first thought, to be thoroughly unnatural, we must never forget that they have uncovered genuine facts about the natural universe. Physical reality cannot be expected to bend to the biases and prejudices of our typical, commonsense worldviews. As Galileo demonstrated centuries ago, the truths about the physical universe are often counterintuitive, and we must be very creative in wresting from the universe its well-hidden secrets. Even though relativity and quantum physics have given new eyes to physicists, their approach to nature is basically the same as before: scientists still describe, quantify, and use mathematical reasoning, and they still do not appeal to any power or intelligence outside the physical universe to account for their discoveries and successes. We must not forget that energy is a wholly natural and materialistic phenomenon, however invisible it has been for most of the history of science.

11.8

The other main supporting structure of materialistic humanism is in the biological sciences, beginning with the discoveries of naturalist Charles Darwin (1809–1882). When the full meaning of Darwin's theory of evolution by natural selection became known, the implications sent shock waves through Western scientific and religious culture, and continue to do so even today. Life emerged on Earth accidentally some four billion years ago, and beginning as simple bacteria, evolved gradually into all the divergent life forms that exist on Earth today. It follows that *all* species of plants and animals are biologically (genetically) related and have evolved from common ancestors. Moreover, Darwinian evolution suggests that there is no force, no overarching intelligence, no plan—cosmic or otherwise— that *guides* the process of evolution.

Evolution has neither a goal nor an inherent mechanism that guarantees the progress of life to greater complexity or intelligence. Evolution is simply a biochemical, naturalistic process that billions of years ago accidentally created simple life forms, which, in turn, produced countless other life forms. Those life forms that survived the wrath of a murderous, natural environment—through natural selection—are responsible for the varieties of life that we see around us today. Chance plays an important (but not exclusive) role in the movement of evolution, in that chance mutations and the *randomness* of "recombination"—the mixing of genetic materials of parent life forms—are largely responsible for genetic variety, on which natural selection—which is *not* chance-based—operates. With Darwinian evolution, then, there is no directing power inside or outside of life that is required to account for the evolution and diversity of life. All that was needed is natural selection: the ruthless and purposeless tendency of nature to destroy all life forms that are unable to adapt to an ever-changing, ever-threatening environment. It became immediately clear that not only was Darwinism consonant with an atheistic worldview, it actually lent support to it. For example, it's difficult to argue, as some religious apologists try to do, for a God-directed form of evolution (so-called "theistic evolution") when one considers the kind of God that would permit the horrific savagery that defines evolution's history. Remember, 99 percent of all species that ever came in to existence are now extinct! Equally damaging to the likelihood of any atheistic form of evolution is that the evolution of life has occurred in such a wasteful and even careless fashion—hardly what we would expect from a wise and intelligent caretaker, much less from a perfect designer. Furthermore, the history of evolution does not in any way indicate the purposeful hand of a God. On the contrary, evolution reflects non-purposeful movements.

People often don't fully understand that the methods of acquiring knowledge in the biological sciences are very different from those of the physical sciences, in that the mathematical, quantitative model is mostly inadequate in biology. Life is much too complex and dynamic to remain within a rigid mathematical framework. Additionally, biology interconnects with many other disciplines, like genetics, geography, chemistry, and history, and requires different forms of investigation, like deciphering genetic codes, determining chemical compositions, giving visual descriptions of species, and detecting the physical changes that occur over great lengths of time. It even poses critical questions such as, why do different species that are geographically close to each other have more in common anatomically than other species that are geographically distant from one another? Despite these differences, both the physical and biological sciences are closely related in that they seek answers within the natural world, and they have become interdependent in important ways—as an example, the chemical makeup of an area of the earth says a great deal about the life forms that once thrived there, since all life is chemical based. Even though traditional materialistic humanism often ignores the life sciences, it naturally includes them.

Here are the main ideas of materialistic humanism:

1. The universe began some thirteen billion years ago by accident—the big bang theory—and has been cooling down ever since.

2. Earth is approximately four-and-a-half-billion years old.

3. Life on Earth began approximately four billion years ago and has existed during most of this time as bacteria.

4. Darwinian evolution is the key to understanding biological life and its diversity—life began as an accident and evolved to all its present forms over the course of billions of years primarily through the deterministic force of natural selection, which is the tendency of nature to kill off all life that is maladaptive.

5. All reality is essentially energy in motion; matter is congealed energy.

6. Physical reality can be described mathematically and quantified.

7. The study of biology often requires a variety of nonmathematical, scientific approaches, like descriptive, historical, and language-based analysis.

8. Life, at its base, is nothing more than a special recipe of biochemical ingredients.

9. The universe is self-creating and emerged by accident.

10. Mind/consciousness is not a distinct dimension unto itself but is an expression of quantifiable brain activity.

11. Consciousness will one day be explained exclusively by physics, biology, and chemistry.

12. There is no need to include God or any other "nonphysical force" or "intelligence" external to the natural universe to explain the laws of nature, the cultural world, or any aspect of human reality.

13. Human beings are not special or privileged within the cosmic scheme of things but are simply highly evolved apes.

14. There is no higher or transcendent reality that exists outside natural space and time.

15. There are no nonphysical realities, but only various configurations and forms of quantifiable energy.

16. To achieve scientific legitimacy, all alleged entities, powers, and dimensions must meet the highest standard of scientific scrutiny. In other words, they must be quantifiable and verifiable by other scientists, and they must withstand multiple testing and "falsifiability"—that is, whatever is proposed as real

or true must, in principle, be able to be proved wrong through experimentation or rigorous scientific reasoning.

17. Technology is concrete proof that science is correct in its theories and ambitions.

18. Science has the potential to explain every aspect of physical, biological, cultural, and human reality, and to contain this understanding within one comprehensive theory.

19. Humanity's ultimate survival and the resolution of its social, ecological, and political problems are solely in the hands of proper reasoning, including scientific reasoning.

20. Our solar system will be destroyed in approximately four billion years when the sun runs out of energy.

11.9

On one side there isn't, and on the other side there is. No compromise or negotiation is warranted or even justified—only the exploration of one into the other.

11.10

Exploratory humanism is the art and science of using what we think we know about *what is,* to discover and bring to light what we don't.

11.11

With exploratory humanism, all preconceptions, theories, traditions, and intuitions may only offer general orientations to the pursuit and understanding of *what is*, but they must never become ends in themselves and close off other possible avenues of exploration.

11.12

Discovery is a lively dance with infinity—not a sluggish crawl to an imagined end.

11.13

Knowledge is an orientation, more than goal, the goal of which is an orientation.

11.14

Creativity, observation, and logic are the indispensable guides to explore the unknown, but they must also explore and redefine themselves along the way.

11.15

There is truth, for there is much that we know to be true, like this statement.

11.16

The "Truth" is knowledge that reflects the way that *it is* from any cultural point of view—it is universal, objective truth. The essential requirements for physical survival—for example, food, shelter, and protection—can be said to represent aspects of the Truth, because all people, regardless of culture, need food, shelter, and protection in order to survive. There are countless other examples of the Truth: *philosophical*—humans are meaning-seeking and meaning-creating beings; *social*—children absorb the norms of the culture into which they are born; *scientific*—energy is real; *historical*—myth has been a part of all cultural traditions. But what about moral truth? Are there moral truths that are universal?

There are three sorts of morality: *cultural morality*—the code of right and wrong behaviors that each culture creates and codifies; *philosophical morality*—an understanding of what is right and wrong that naturally emerges in the experience of the wonder and awe of being alive and in the presence of *what is*; and *pragmatic morality*— ideas of right and wrong that are based on the requirements for survival. Because moral codes typically change from culture to culture, cultural morality could not be said to be universally true. It's common, for example, for culture-based moral behavior to be an expression of a particular pop culture—such as sexual mores and lifestyle choices— which can be as specific to a culture as its language.

On the other hand, philosophical morality could make claims of universal validity, because the experience of wonder and awe in the face of sheer existence is a universal experience with typical insights and calls to action. Religions and spiritual traditions can have their origins, at least in part, from this experience. And the birth of philosophy in ancient Greece was, according to the words of the ancient philosophers themselves, a response to the wondrous presence of *what is*. Philosophical morality is an essential part of the traditions of all societies.

And what are some examples of philosophical morality? Thinking, questioning, naming, and defining—these activities are moral activities because lead a person to behave in good and bad ways. Good philosophical, moral acts promote the well being of all those in society, and conversely, bad philosophical work against the wellbeing of a society and are injurious to one's self and to other people.

Pragmatic morality also has a claim to universality, because the challenges to survival, both from nature and from human beings themselves, are the same universally. Humanity has always been vulnerable to the unexpected thrusts of nature that often had lethal results on human populations. Floods, earthquakes, storms, meteors, diseases, and plagues have decimated human populations countless times. Human beings have also been the source of endless woes—wars, murder, and genocide have defined much of human history. Questions of right and wrong in relation to natural and human threats to survival are intimately related to the general question: which behaviors will tend to promote the survival of people in society, as well as in the global society? If humans were solitary beings, living in absolute isolation from other human beings, then being concerned with moral actions would make little sense. You could simply and thoughtlessly do what you wanted, and there would be no one who would be affected by your actions. But human beings live in a populated world, which means that what they decide to do individually has a direct impact on other people.

The behaviors that tend to promote individual survival are those that can be carried out *together*, in order to maximize everyone's chances for success. Joining together to fight a common enemy or to rebuild a flood-damaged community, for example, are collective actions that benefit each individual involved. But the *togetherness* of society automatically requires considering the needs, interests, and actions of not only yourself, but also of others, because other people will have a significant impact on your survival (and happiness).

From an evolutionary perspective, many scientists believe that genetic factors are responsible for at least some forms of moral behavior, such as "altruism"—selfless giving, sometimes even at personal risk. Natural selection works to eliminate maladaptive life forms, which mean that those life forms that do survive and pass on their genes to subsequent generations. But what benefit would there be for these individuals to demonstrate selfless behavior, if this behavior could cost them their lives? Would this not defeat the whole purpose of survival, which is to pass on genes to future generations? A form of altruistic behavior is often seen in the animal kingdom, such as in certain species of squirrels that give off warning calls to relatives who might be in danger, but in so doing, reveal their own location, which could, and sometimes does, result in the squirrel being killed by predators. The generally agreed upon explanation for this form of altruism comes from biologist H. W. Hamilton who, in 1964, introduced the notion of "kin selection." This theory argues that relatives carry many of the same genes and that one member of a family may sacrifice its own life for the sake of its relatives, because, as a result, a *greater number of genes* will be passed to subsequent generations through the relatives' survival than through the survival of only one individual.

In this light, altruism in this context is a strategy of trying to maximize the number of genes passed on. There are two ways, then, that genes are moved to future generations: one is through an individual surviving and reproducing; the other is for the individual to sacrifice its own its own life for its relatives, which ensures that more of its genes will be passed on. Together, these two approaches are called "inclusive fitness." Moral behavior is a much more complicated process for humans, however, and cannot be reduced to only genetic factors, any more than it can be reduced to only existential/cultural conditions; clearly, the dynamic of human morality includes both.

In today's global world, all societies are interconnected and, in a sense, represent one society: the society of humanity. This is where a universal morality has its ultimate validity. On a practical level, we should commit compassionate, kind, and generous acts, because we ourselves will benefit from them, either in the short or long term. These acts are not just good for one person, but they are good for all—they are universally good. Following a moral system that benefits everyone is the best way to ensure that all members of all societies receive all the support and protection they need. So in this respect, pragmatic morality, as compared to philosophical morality, is a question of mutual self-interest and survival.

11.17

What blazes most intensely in the human heart is not the passion for absolute knowledge but the passion for absolute ignorance.

11.18

The strange findings of quantum physics have given new life to modern-day mysticism and metaphysical belief systems, such as New Age thinking—the growing belief among eager, metaphysical thrill-seekers in the existence of a mystical reality. Notions that have contributed to

New Age thinking include the well-documented, quantum world of energy flickering randomly in and out of existence inexplicably; the fact that subatomic objects are nothing more than *probable* energy states; human observation unavoidably affecting the outcome of quantum experiments; and the evidence that even very distant events are *instantly* connected to local ones. Some people believe that the fact that Western science has uncovered these quantum effects gives the mystical world, and by extension even Eastern spirituality, that much more credibility. One area where quantum reality is clearly present, New Age mystics argue, is in the nature of *thought*: thought is a form of energy that can move faster than the speed of light, is able see into the future, can read other minds, can move physical objects, and even can heal physical and psycho-emotional infirmities. And why? Because all reality—nature, bodies, minds, and even time—is just *energy in motion*. This means that by proper thinking, all energies can *communicate* with each other, so to speak, and the mystical experiences will result.

As promising as these metaphysical claims may seem, however, scientists have never found convincing evidence that they are valid. In fact, none of the leading voices in "quantum mysticism" are well-respected scientists in quantum physics. Indeed, most do not work in science-related fields at all. And all the experiments that have tried to show the reality of quantum mysticism have always come up short when they were properly conducted.

It is not surprising that quantum discoveries would invite such metaphysical interpretations—the founders of quantum theory themselves were baffled by what they found and initially were at a loss to account for the results of quantum experiments. Nobel Laureate and physicist Richard Feynman (1918–1888) once said something to the effect that if you *think* that you comprehend quantum physics, then you don't. Einstein was so outraged by the idea of "chance" being at the foundation of physical reality that he fought against it with a vengeance for the last thirty years of his life. Other physicists like Werner Heisenberg (1901–1976) were "mystified" by quantum physics.

Nonetheless, leading physicists today, who have been able to digest more thoroughly the findings in quantum physics, are emphatic in stating that recasting quantum physics in mystical terms has no legitimate scientific basis. Unfortunately, there are great financial rewards to be gained from convincing a naïve, unscientific, meaning-hungry people that, although Moses, Jesus, and Allah may have let them down, not to worry; quantum mysticism—often dressed in the garb of cultish, spiritual belief systems like the Kabala (Jewish mysticism)—will come to their rescue, and lift them from their meaningless existence and lead them to the land of Oz.

11.19

When I look into the sweet, tender faces of my little Italian Greyhounds, I wonder what it is that brings tears to my eyes time and time again. Is it that they seem to be so much like me? That they, too, feel lost and homeless? It couldn't simply be that, like me, they go through the day much as they did the day before: they come to consciousness every morning and lapse into unconsciousness every night; they embrace pleasure when it arrives, tolerate pain and sorrow until it leaves, and endure the boredom that sometimes emerges in between. And like me, they also play senselessly and excessively and find comfort in both isolation and companionship. But there must be more to it than that. Why do I sense that Sophie, Mia, Primo, and I are joined together fatefully? What is it that I recognize in their blameless eyes that affects me so?—My mother? My father? My brother?—All mothers? All fathers? All brothers? That all of us share a common journey must mean that we also share a common destiny. Thus it will be that at the end of their short lives—I will, with a broken heart, bid farewell once again to those whom I have loved the most. And I, too, will depart one day to a chorus of sad good-byes.

11.20

The bio-ontological shift—the weakening of instinct-driven life concurrent with the movement toward meaning/culture-based life—made it necessary to find, discover, and create purposeful activity. Enter: myth, art, family life, religion, politics, philosophy, science, technology, work, pleasure, fun, and entertainment!

11.21

The primary meaning of human culture is to provide people with ways to busy themselves purposefully. The vast universe that science and technology has opened up has meant a great deal for a confused and uncertain species in need of things to know and things to do. During the Middle Ages, the church assumed a similar responsibility, in which what one thought and did on a daily basis was clearly defined and sometimes even enforced by religious authorities. Although most of us today in the West look back with horror on that era of physical, psychological, and existential oppression, many of us still long to be told what to think and do. And what are science and technology but our new authority figures that insist that we think scientifically and act with the purpose, efficiency, and effectiveness of our technological creations? That some of us appear to resist this godlike pressure from above is disingenuous at best. Despite our prayers, meditations, organic foods, hikes, and road trips, we are the good servants of science and technology and busy ourselves doing exactly what they tell us to do.

11.22

Whatever can be said against medieval life, at least everyone knew his or her place in the private, public, political, and cosmic scheme of things. They also knew what precisely *to do* on a daily basis—whether it was fulfilling their clearly defined, religious duties to their family, meeting the strict religious responsibilities as a member of their local community, or fulfilling their obligations to God and the church. It's a general principle that religions keep people very busy, and the more severe the religious doctrine, the busier are its adherents.

11.23

Although the medieval church was successful in both destroying many of the contributions of ancient Greece and Rome, in some cases, and concealing them in others, the effort was not exhaustive. Nor was the church vigilant enough in insisting that people submit—body and soul—to church authority. For in the very womb of the medieval, Christian hearth, the first stirrings of the modern, pagan spirit began to be heard and felt by modern individuals such as Aquinas, Dante, Saint Francis, and Duns Scotus.

11.24

Even the most radical individual always expresses herself within the context of a cultural tradition. She may criticize his world and all that it stands for, assume different social identities, and even devise contrarian political and social philosophies, but she can never shed her cultural skin. By the very activity of moving away from a tradition, the individual affirms her inextricable connection to it.

11.25

Even the simplest meaning is perpetually pregnant with the infinity of all meanings.

11.26

Technology and capitalism are the twin engines of material progress. They mutually promote and reinforce each other. This symbiotic relationship lives by its own logic, so to speak, where financial support is rewarded in technological success that promises to produce increased profits.

Success in technology means making a profit by providing culture with desired products or the means of doing something at a cost that people can afford. Success in capitalism is simply making a profit, a percentage of which is used for continuing technological support.

11.27

It's not uncommon for an accusatory finger to be pointed at science, the mother of technology, to blame it for the sins of its precocious child. The promise of technology was to increase the quality of human life, but an objective eye could only conclude that what we have gained in comfort, convenience, health enhancement, and entertainment, we have lost in the way of such things as the emission of lethal poisons, actual and potential ecological disasters, and weapons of mass destruction. Many have argued that human nature itself has also been damaged by the power of technology, that technology has alienated humans both from nature and each other, with destructive psychological/spiritual results. But scientists maintain that science was not conceived to promote moral values or to promote any particular cause, philosophy, or worldview. Rather, science is simply devoted to discovering, describing, and quantifying (when possible) the basic laws and principles that underlie physical, biological, and human reality.

The problem is that both perspectives are legitimate. Without scientific progress, technology would never pose threats to our lives, but without a free and unconstrained search for objective knowledge, the spirit of inquiry would soon suffocate. Western science and technology were the logical consequences of a society breaking free of the moral, intellectual, and psychological restrictions of medieval Europe. They were, in fact, among the first fruits of a new world order—*liberal democracy*. But freedom carries with it immense responsibilities.

The principal problem with the philosophy of liberal democracy is that in order for it to flourish, *the people* have to be wise enough to make intelligent and informed decisions. It's absolutely imperative, therefore, that citizens in a liberal democracy not only be in possession of sufficient information and knowledge to make the right choices, but that they also learn how to think logically and clearly. For this reason, the importance of education is paramount. Science and technology have tapped into the seemingly endless powers of the universe, and now they structure every aspect of our lives. To have such awesome powers in our hands is a frightening responsibility, even though most of us are not conscious of it. But individual choices and actions are not isolated behaviors that occur in a vacuum; instead, they are part of the vast human world, and collectively, they determine what society or even civilization does as a whole.

The dangers of technology are even greater when we realize that there is no turning back. Few of us would willingly return our cellular phones for the good of the human race and resume the use of pay phones. Technology is now an integral part of our cultural nature, and it could never be otherwise. Our only option is to do what we do with care and consideration for our fellow humans and our home, planet Earth.

Where the free and open quest for scientific knowledge is fueled by the passion to know, the quest for technological progress is fueled by the passion to make profits. The "profit motive" is morally neutral; making money by marketing health foods, for instance, and making money by marketing cigarettes are morally equivalent activities, even though the former promotes life and the latter often takes it away and always reduces its quality. As long as there is a profit, almost anything goes—at least this is what many free-market capitalists believe. And this is the problem. The "market system" is the life of the capitalistic system of which technology is the major player. Left to its own amoral logic, the market system would ultimately destroy all life, both natural and cultural, because the natural and human worlds represent nothing more than inexhaustible shopping markets, in which every aspect, item, and portion has a price tag attached to it. So what is the answer? The only feasible answer is a technology guided by absolute principles of human health, the preservation and promotion of the natural environment, and the humanistic advancement of all humanity. Ironically, the precocious child of science has to attain to a moral maturity that its mother could never be bothered with. To this end, technology must serve as the moral balance to science's amoral passion to explore and to know at all costs.

11.28

Pure science, as a fact-seeking enterprise, is, by this logic, free of ethical responsibility, although, as critics are quick to point out, that scientists are moral beings and as such are morally tied to science— even in its purest, theoretical form.

Scientists often retort that science must be free to pursue, unfettered, its goal of physical discovery—without this purity of purpose, science will lose its spiritual energy. Science must remain dispassionate in its search for physical laws and principles. Being the good children of Galileo, scientists must be diligent in excluding from their work personal, subjective qualities—including biases and moral positions. We forget, however, that even the greatest scientists are still human, which means that personal biases, prejudices, and agendas tend to creep into their work. And even on a purely scientific level, experimental procedures are biased to the extent that they offer perspectives that always contain unexamined, unjustified, or unclear assumptions—all of which play a part in scientific work.

11.29

For many centuries, humans did poorly in science, because the essential rules of science lay undiscovered, distorted, or misinterpreted. In its adolescence, human understanding was not even able to comprehend the need for rules. For instance, the ancient Greeks placed their hopes for discovering the truth of reality in the abstract world of mathematics and rarely considered how truth could be observed in the real world. In other words, they missed the crucial rule that mathematical ideas are relevant to earthly existence, and need to be validated by testing them through actual empirical experimentation. Even the modern spirit Aristotle missed the critical need. One of the great modern scientific innovators, Francis Bacon, made the opposite mistake by looking only to observation to find scientific truth without proper guidance in the world of theory and mathematics. Finally, with Galileo, the Golden Rule of physical science came into focus, as he struck the proper balance between precise mathematical description and theory on the one hand,

and methodical, empirical observation and meticulous experimentation on the other. Newton, Darwin, Einstein, Plank, Heisenberg, Bohr, and others discovered many more rules.

11.30

Good biologists, physicists, and chemists are those who are fully cognizant of the current rules of their respective fields and follow them with disciplined devotion. The better the scientist, the better she is at allowing the rules of her scientific domain to guide her efforts. In this sense, the rules of scientific exploration, and not the scientists themselves, are guiding the future and success of science.

11.31

We must approach the purpose of a culture by considering it within the context of its vast reservoir of unrealized thoughts, actions, intentions, and achievements. In this way, *purpose* stands at the beginning of a culture as an infinite universe of potential goals, some of which are realizable, and some of which are only guiding ideals toward which culture moves but could never reach—such as the philosophical/scientific goal of comprehending all of reality.

11.32

Each human being is suckled, nurtured, and carried along by a culture's purpose. A cultural purpose is the "invisible hand" that predisposes people to possible ways of living and interpreting the world. A cultural purpose is not the "spirit" of an age, its *zeitgeist*; instead, it is what invokes and provokes general cultural attitudes and sensibilities. It is the ideal object toward which culture moves. In the West, transforming the world, the cosmos, and humanity itself into rational terms has always stood as its purpose. This is true despite the many irrational episodes that define much of Western history. In fact, the collapse and rehabilitation of reason, as well as the rise and fall of superstition, are indispensable plot points in the rich story of Western humanity's purpose.

11.33

A finite history, in itself, has no ideal goal or grand aim toward which it inexorably moves; instead, it has only vaguely understood purposes toward which imperfect human beings—thinking and acting alone or in unison—stumble, ever so carelessly, ever so accidentally.

11.34

The genius, whose intuition of purpose is awesomely preternatural, is something altogether different and quite extraordinary. Genius is nature's brilliance at it most incisive, concrete, *and* mysterious—and with the emergence of true genius, history itself seems to stand still for a moment, almost as if to admire its own handiwork.

11.35

What does purpose do? Purpose energizes, compels, calls forth, elevates, empowers, and enforces; purpose holds us in place—while moving us from here to there; purpose is a series of "from-here-to-there" movements; purpose confirms, establishes, points to, and propels; purpose is a moving present that gathers up the past, impregnates the present, and gives birth to the future and to *future* futures; purpose captures the imagination, releases its powers, and focuses its intensity; purpose is the "ruling idea" and "guiding light"; purpose reconnects a human being to the world of humanity and opens new ways to thought, action, and passion; purpose is what *making sense* of it all is all about.

11.36

Meaning is an element of purpose, but it is stagnant and a-historical by comparison. Meaning can keep us frozen in the past, but only purpose thrusts us into the future at blazing velocities. Meaning describes a state of being, a *resting in*, where purpose describes modes of future activities.

11.37

Purpose is human action that has meaning.

11.38

The bio-ontological shift has resulted in an "existential fluctuation" in the very core of a human being—a sort of "in-and-out" of being/nonbeing. And how is this oscillation manifested in human life? In the various "negatives" that define human experience such as the natural condition of human ignorance and the occasional feelings of being lost and alone in a vastness of what is.

11.39

A "call to action" has its source in the absence of an instinctive drive that determines human behavior in particular ways. The result is that the various answers to the call always remain elusive and ambiguous, even when they are fully embraced. And why? Because every call to action must *mean something* in order for it to have significance; meaning in this context is frequently unclear and always subject to personal interpretation, which is incorrigibly limited and particular to the unstable interpretative powers of the interpreter. Basic needs such as food and water, by contrast, predate the call to action—they don't call, as it were: they *command*. Biological needs cannot be met in a variety of ways, but only in *particular*, singular ways—by eating and drinking, for example. The call to action, by contrast, can be met in many ways—by the endless miscellany of human actions that define all cultures now, in the past, and in the future. And the call to action requires a particular human capability: creative responsiveness—the ability to think, decide, self-reflect, analyze, and enact behavior—at times *independent* of basic biological needs. This responsibility is carried out by the latest evolutionary addition—the *cerebral cortex*. Animals don't require a call to action—they act! And although learning and role-playing have an essential role in some animal life, they live mostly at the level of biological determinism—they are necessarily primary-needs orientated. With animals there is no call to action, because there is no highly evolved *self-conscious self* to answer the call, and therefore there is no need for a purposeful call to begin with.

11.40

The success of the materialist model through technology has precipitated a crisis that is profound in its depth and scope. The crisis, however, has remained largely undetected, because it is hidden behind and within the distracting presence of *busy-ness*. If modern culture is anything, it's busy. Technology has provided the materials and mechanisms to keep humans occupied and "on the go"—but to where and for what reason? And wait—isn't busy-ness a response to the call to action? Not necessarily. Although there is much to do with purpose in the modern (or as some would say, postmodern) world, our doing is more often a *redundancy ad absurdum*—mindless repetitions of past actions without final goals or deeply felt purpose. And what of the fruits of our actions? Efficiency and convenience—yes—but otherwise, there is typically no excellently produced finished product (much less beautifully crafted product) or accomplishment that faithfully reflects our individual efforts and pride, but only identical items, anonymous tasks of merely sufficient quality at best. In these instances, we are caught in a sort of contradiction: we are forever on the go with nowhere definite to end up, and with little of real personal, fulfilling value to show for all our going. Sadly, the extent of our busyness is all too often a sign of our futility of purpose.

11.41

As we have seen, both science and technology are governed by rules and procedures, which have a commanding life of their own. Good scientists and technologists have a deep understanding of the rules of their respective disciplines and devote themselves to discovery and refinement. The result has been the stupendous flowering of our scientific/technological culture, which has come to define modern Western culture as a whole. How this new version of culture may inform and recreate human nature, which is in part culture-based, is one of the intriguing questions for the future.

11.42

Purpose has an intended goal—the completion of an initial aim. Purpose is not only seen in the behavior of humans and in the natural universe; items of technology are also created and designed with specific purposes in mind. Cars, sunglasses, computers, and umbrellas—all technological items—are purpose-orientated. The purposes for which technology is created, however, have a very specific meaning. They are what I call "purposes of function"—they achieve or realize predetermined, finite goals. The hammer was designed for hammering nails; cars were built for transporting people; a coffee maker was produced for making coffee—in all three cases, the purposes of these actions are set *in advance* and are fully exhausted with the attainment of their respective goals. This is always the case in technology.

Purposes of function are also necessarily bidirectional: they move forward in time, and they achieve their goals in the ever-changing world of the future, but this forward movement in time is really a mere repetition of the past as far as purposes of function are concerned. The toaster toasts many times, and every slice of bread ever placed in it is toasted in the same way. The same is true for all technological devices. Part of the psychological grip that technology has on humans, in fact, is that, in a sense, purposes of function never age—they are timeless. Machines, parts, and material processes may break down, wear out, erode, or malfunction, but their purposes of function remain untouched by the ravages of time. All that is required is that we repair, replace, or adjust whatever is failing, and then everything will be as good as new. Purposes of function are like immortal spirits that inhabit our material creations only to be reincarnated, usually in more sophisticated ways, into new, more advanced technological products.

11.42

Culture has picked up and led, where nature has lost its grip and has fallen away.

11.43

Biological and cultural forces are fierce competitors for the command of human reality—and both must win, or humanity loses.

11.44

Before the emergence of the human culture, life on Earth was dominated by "purposes-of-function," such as reproduction behaviors, finding food, and securing shelter. With the rise of humanity, however, a radically different kind of purpose emerged: even as Homo sapiens were busy meeting their biological and survival needs, they also had to create a cultural life to replace the loss of their strict, instinct-based existence. It is here in this realm of meaning—in this *worldscape*— where "purposes-of-meaning" made their first appearance.

Biological purposes-of-function are purely genetic-based, *teleological*—goal oriented—actions that fulfill only survival needs and strategies; they are largely repetitive, and once purposes-of-function are fulfilled, their actions are terminated, at least until it's necessary to repeat these sorts of actions again. Although it is always risky to speculate as to whether or not nonhuman life *thinks*, at least we could safely say that for the most part, purposes-of-function are largely thoughtless, gene-based actions.

Purposes-of-meaning, by contrast, are *thoughtful* actions that have wide variety of possible goals that extend far beyond those of pure survival and reproduction. Humans routinely make decisions and pursue goals that also do *not* aim at fulfilling genetic-based survival strategies— pursuing musical or sports interests, receiving a higher education, going the gym, reading philosophy books, meeting up with a friend at a café, vacationing in Venice, attending birthday parties, watching television— these are typical purposes-of-meaning actions that are goal based but, nonetheless, have nothing to do with meeting basic biological needs or fulfilling survival strategies. Moreover, other forms of purposes-of-meaning—such as walking aimlessly through the streets of Manhattan or talking to a friend about nothing in particular—are not necessarily carried out to realize specific aims or strategies.

Purposes-of-meaning constitute what is most particular about human reality. Whenever we ask what human life means, or how we should live, or what we should do, or what we should believe, we are seeking purposes-of-meaning answers. But there is a problem: modern culture has a glaring and ever-expanding contradiction right in its midst—*technology*. Technology is no less than an obsession with purposes-of-function. But even more interesting is that technology represents, to a large extent, a well-disguised movement back to our primitive, instinct-based existence in nature. So what does this mean? What defines the life of technology? Goal-based, repetitive actions. And which values does technology strive ceaselessly to realize? Reliability, resourcefulness, and predictability. Now let's ask two additional questions: what defines biological life? Goal-based, repetitive actions. And which values does biological life strive ceaselessly to realize? Reliability, resourcefulness, and predictability. Technology and biology, as radically different as they are, serve a common master: nature.

Technology, as the dominant cultural force in modern civilization, signaled the great reemergence of biological imperatives into human existence. The most fascinating result has been the gradual reshuffling of human nature to the point where technological values—like reliability, resourcefulness, and predictability—have also come to represent the highest ideals toward which human thought and actions aim. By contrast, mundane human qualities like playfulness and impulsiveness are often seen as weaknesses that don't lead to success in the "real world."

Technology strives to imitate the actions of nature, so, in this way, technology is a sort of "second nature." But technology also succeeds in transcending—some would even say perfecting—nature to the extent that the very engine of technology is *change through innovation*. Unlike the natural world, where repetitions of old patterns may last for a considerable time, technology is perpetually moving forward with new and ingenious developments and newly formed, repeatable patterns, which will themselves be replaced sooner rather than later by even more novel, repeatable patterns. But the amazing dominance of technology has caused considerable fallout.

Purposes-of-function, within the context of an ever-growing technological culture, naturally suppress purposes-of-meaning, because the latter, as opposed to the former, do not lead to greater technological productivity. This suppression could never be complete, however, because human beings, *by nature*, are, and forever will be, grounded into existence through purposes-of-meaning. In no uncertain terms, humanity seeks answers to questions that bear no relation to purposes-of-function. Put simply, human beings are not like espresso machines—each exists in a radically different ontological world, and the values that organize and guide one could never successfully be reduced to that of the other. This means that the conflict between the two kinds of purposes is both natural and inevitable. It's also true that the human species could never return to its former intimacy with nature; nor would humanity live without technology.

The extent to which purposes-of-meaning are squashed by the requirements of purposes-of-function is also the extent to which we are in jeopardy of losing our humanity. We have no choice but to allow the Aristotelian principle of balance to assert itself through proper education and enlightened legislation to ensure that human nature and life-affirming human values remain intact, even as technology continues to challenge the very meaning of human existence.

11.46

Within each of us there exists what we call a "mind." What is a mind? It is the sum total of the ideas, feelings, intentions, attitudes, and moods that abide in both the conscious and subconscious dimensions of an individual's experience, and the various ways—meaning integration, reformulation, recreation, and intentionality—in which these meanings take form and relate to each other, one's self, and the outside world.

11.47

Although the presence of meaning requires the functioning of a physical brain as a necessary condition for its emergence, brain activity itself is not the same as the presence or showing of meaning. Meaning is an *experiential* reality and not a biophysical, material one. For example, a work of art could be analyzed scientifically and dissected through verbal, written, or even mathematical language, but the true *meaning* of the artwork can only come to life through directly experiencing it; only then does a presence of meaning emerge that says something genuine to the viewer. Meaning, and the neurological functioning that helped to produce it, are also analogous to the relationship between one's image as it is directly seen in a mirror, and the physical mirror that produces the image. No analysis of the structure or makeup of the mirror, however sophisticated and exhaustive, could ever show—bring to light—your image as well as your simple reflection in the mirror.

11.48

Moreover, if I am watching myself in the mirror and then decide to move my head to the right, for instance, the movement causes the mirror to reflect precisely that exact movement (also causing chemical changes in the mirror). In the same sense that the mirror creates the *physical conditions* for the image to be reflected, but is not the image itself, so too does the image *determine* what the mirror reflects and is not the physical item itself. And so it is with meaning: meaning is intimately related to, and interconnected with, the physical and biological world but occupies a different dimension altogether. In carrying the mirror analogy a little further, we may have noticed that neither the mirror nor the reflection is the source of the image. *You* are the genuine source of the image, and you occupy another dimension altogether. We could easily conclude that human reality is a multidimensional world of matter fused with meaning, with its source being the dynamic interplay between subject and object, as they continually create each other. I call the process of mutual self-creating "bipolar dimensionalizing."

11.49

Most scientists agree that the critical moment in human evolution was the emergence of the *cerebral cortex* of the brain—with its new capacity for symbolic language, social intelligence, and rational thought. In their view, this development was an "adaptive" response to new environmental and social challenges. For example, when humans began living together in communities, a more agile and creative intelligence became necessary.

The movement from the pre-human to the human brain, scientists agree, may have been a profound change in terms of what the human brain was able to accomplish, but from a strictly biological perspective, the transition was no more dramatic than the change from one-celled life to multi-celled: both transitions were nothing more than *quantitative* developments that consisted of increased biological complexity and efficiency. The new human brain, in other words, was just as physical as the pre-human one.

11.50

The transition from the pre-human, mammalian brain to the human one, however continuous it might appear to a biologist's eye, belies a development so momentous that one could easily say that it represented the greatest single event in the four-billion-year residency of life on Earth. Life forms, at their most basic level, have two purposes: survival and reproductive. These purposes are pursued by virtue of *genetic hardwiring*. With animals, strong genetic controls are still in place, but to a lesser degree in comparison to more primitive life forms like plants and insects. For many animals, learning, for example, through role-playing, became an additional means to achieve nature's end of survival and reproduction. But with Homo sapiens, something new appeared on planet earth. The evolution of the human brain signaled the birth of humanity, and with this new species, *meaning* made its most profound appearance. But meaning did not remain connected to the particular items, actions, and happenings in the outside world, but became detached from them, and took up residency in the human mind, in the abstract, nonphysical world of sensations, ideas, and meanings. The world now became a different place altogether: wondrous and frightening, inviting and mysterious. And with the ongoing creation of human culture, even more meanings began in inhabit the human mind and filling the human world with new realities.

11.51

Meaning is difficult to define, because not only is the idea of meaning used in different ways, but, in many instances, its various uses also appear to be unrelated. Let's cite a few examples:

"What did you mean by that?" Here the intention of the questioner is to discover the *definition* of a statement, idea, or action.

An individual with a sore throat may ask his doctor, "What does this mean?" In this instance, the person wants to know the *cause* of the sore throat.

After being told in detail that the transmission of his car is worn out, the owner may ask the mechanic, "What does all this mean?" Here the owner wants to know what has to be *done* to the car and what the *cost* will be to repair it.

After witnessing a magnificent sunset, one might ask, "What does it mean?" invoking a cosmic sense of *wonderment*, reflecting a desire for a metaphysical answer to the experience of such awesome beauty.

Someone might ask about the meaning of life, in which case one wants to know the *purpose* of being alive.

What unites all these versions of meaning is that they arise out of the interrogative mood—that is, they take form as questions. Questioning, in fact, is the *meaning* of human meaning in all its variations.

11.51

The close attachment of animals to their environment, and to their genetic and hormone-based actions, can pose real dangers. If there are significant changes, disruptions, or catastrophes in the natural environment—such as extreme climate changes, sudden disappearance of food sources, or massive earthquakes—life forms in the affected area could be completely annihilated. Biological determinism is not naturally flexible and adaptive, but requires relatively stable environmental variables for it to continue to aid in an animal's survival. This is especially true in environments where life forms are always on the verge of perishing, such as in the desert, where even slight temperature changes above or below the mean temperature could devastate plants and animals.

Human behavior, by contrast, is not under the strict guidance of biological/genetic factors. This discontinuous relationship with nature has put humanity out of context with the natural world, and it would not have been a feasible evolutionary strategy if it were not for the concurrent rise of human culture. The emergence of human culture, at least 150,000 years ago, became humanity's new guide and caretaker—its "second nature," so to speak. The movement away from nature, however, was not a complete one, but was more of a veering away from biological/genetic determinism. It was, in my words, a "bio-ontological shift." This concept is so important that it's worth revisiting.

Ontology is the study of being—an investigation into how *what is*, is. The best approach to understanding ontology is by example. A stone is larger than, say, a pebble. In describing stones and pebbles along these lines, we have used a quantitative measure: size. Now let's consider the question: does a stone *exist more* than a pebble? Or, put differently: does a stone *have more existence* than a pebble? Clearly not. But why? Why doesn't bigger mean more existence? The answer is that existence is not a *quantitative* attribute of something—existence simply means that something *is*. The *is-ness* of something, in other words, is an empty concept—it has no measurable attributes or physical qualities. Eyebrows, mosquitoes, and solar systems all exist—this is the underlying fact that unites them, and it is *equally* true for all three categories of existing items; from this perspective all three items are identical—that is, one cannot have any more or less existence than any other.

This talk about ontology and existence is very abstract, and the question must be asked as to the ultimate value of such thought. Is it possible that this kind of thinking is nothing more than a logical game enjoyed primarily by armchair philosophers, and has little significance to the rest of us living and working in the real world? We can respond to this important question by considering additional ontological issues. Even though existence is an empty concept, does it necessarily follow that all items that exist, exist in the same way? Or are there radical differences between the *ways* in which items exist?

For example, although a stone and a human being both exist, is there an *ontological distinction* between the two? How does a stone exist? A stone—any stone—is a lifeless thing that simply rests on or in the earth. On an atomic and subatomic scale, there is much energetic movement in the stone, but the stone as it exists on the earth *does* absolutely nothing. It has no inherent capacity for movement through space, and it can change locations only when outside forces like bulldozers push it or scoop it up. Furthermore, the stone was not born, it does not grow and develop, and it does not die. A stone does not know time or *know* anything. A stone has no typically unfolding history—no self-generated future, or a past that impelled it to its present state, and it has no personal interaction with other stones, other existing items, or with its general surroundings. It's affected only accidentally by environmental conditions that can, for instance, change its physical structure; for example, very extreme temperatures can cause a stone to melt. What about human beings? In which ways does a human being exist?

Humans—all humans—exist exclusively by thinking, emoting, and desiring and by acting in, through, and in relation to the long-standing traditions—worlds of meaning that were themselves created by humans. Existing in a world of meaning requires that humans must constantly deploy thinking to interpret, decipher, analyze, simplify, and integrate the endless barrage of meanings with which each human being is confronted every moment beginning at birth. Existing in a world of meaning also offers the possibility of creating new meanings when there is a need to define something new. The fact that all human beings are born into, and will forever remain within, a long-standing world of meaning, as well as the unconditional requirement for all human beings to think—are really two sides of the same ontological coin. They both equally define the ontological status of human beings—a way of being, moreover, that is unique to human beings. So the paradox of being is that although it is an empty concept, the way items *are*, are different.

11.52

The emergence of human culture does not mean that nature has been extirpated from human existence. Far from it. Human passions, such as our sexual and survival drives and the various natural urges that intrude upon our daily human lives, are our constant reminders that nature's ways are still integral to our human ways. And, of course, we are forever shackled with our flesh-and-bone companion that we call the body. Along with its pleasures and delights, we also experience the daily aches and pains of its natural, fragile existence. We watch our body age and grow old before our very eyes, while knowing with regret that these natural processes will one day lead to our complete enfeeblement and ultimately will terminate our existence. Indeed, human existence is a complex blend of nature and culture—instinct and meaning—one incorrigibly mortal and the other virtually immortal. Meanings may be temporally forgotten, but they never die. *This existential couplet and contradiction is the essence of humanity's ontological existence.* The experience of human freedom; the need for stable connections; the search for meaning, purpose, and action; the fear of death; the feelings of aloneness in the vast infinity that is the universe; the clinging to the hope of finding true love; the pursuit of personal and worldly success; the creation of art; the quest for philosophical, scientific, and religious truth; and the desire for union with *what is* through moments of ecstasy—all follow from the ontological distinction of human beings, which is better understood as the bio-ontological shift.

11.53

From one perspective, nature could never be transcended, since all things that occur, regardless of their distinctions, are just variations of the same natural world. Nonetheless, the ways of existing are so vastly different—between inert matter and the living world, for instance, or between the various forms that life has taken within the living world itself—that we can justifiably speak of animals living in nature as distinct from humans living in culture. Of course, human nature also participates abundantly in the natural world, and some animals have a form of primitive culture. The bio-ontological shift can now be brought into focus. The movement of humanity away from its animal past represents a fundamental movement away from living instinctively in nature, to living meaningfully in human culture. We can maintain this distinction while recognizing that humanity still has one foot firmly planted in nature. For all the enthusiastic arguments that emphasize humanity's animal past and the many close connections to it, we still must resist the temptation to understand the human race in purely biological terms. Humanity is not one with nature, but two with nature *and* culture. To be human is to live a *dualistic* existence, however distasteful this may be to modern philosophical and scientific sensibilities. How to negotiate successfully this instinct/meaning tug-of-war, is the ultimate purpose of culture and education—and its distinguished ambassadors of diplomacy: myth, art, religion, politics, philosophy, and science.

11.54

The knowledge that human beings have a different ontological status than simple inanimate things or our animal relatives helps us to understand more deeply what is distinctive about human life and forces us to use different categories in trying to understand it. Human beings don't just exist on the earth like a lifeless twig lying motionlessly on the frigid ground—they abide *thoughtfully* in an ever-changing universe of meaning that itself is the product of human creativity. And their movements through their world are not defined by thoughtless modes of redundant survival strategies in order to reproduce. Rather, they are self-generated projections that move through avenues of meaning of their *choosing*—in some extraordinary cases, avenues of meaning that they have created—all in the effort to *make sense* out of their existence. This attempt at sense making is not for the exclusive purpose of reproduction, but for the purpose of having a meaningful life, although reproduction is often an aspect of it. It is the very essence of the ontological status of human beings that it is continually a work in progress—for each person; and the nature of this work is always a matter of what they decide to do or not do as individuals forever subject to the tensions of the bio-ontological shift. The ontological status of humanity is not simply a conflict between two ways of being: *it is also nature caught in the very act of transcending itself.* The outcome of this movement toward transcendence, however, is far from certain and the reason is clear: the bio-ontological shift is still shifting as human culture, and human nature along with it, are continuously takes on new forms and moving in new directions; and it's beyond dispute that this unfolding will never arrive at solid ground.

11.55

But what is really happening in the imaginary world of young children? Their boundless creativity exists in part because their immature minds are unable to *connect up*—in a fixed and consistent way—the meanings that are ceaselessly wafting through their minds, with the physical items, actions and happenings in the outside world. The *disconnect* between meanings, and outside items, actions, and happenings, produces a frenzied world of experiential flux and even chaos. In this world, meanings flash randomly, and without restraint, across their horizon of consciousness, producing a dizzying array of imaginary realities—where dogs are monsters, rabbits fly, and dolls are real people. This is the actual meaning of children "living in a world of their own." It also offers us a little glimpse into the strange world of the schizophrenic.

11.56

Creativity is the play of meaning—meaning-forms in constant and fluid interactivity, and the mind itself is the nonphysical playground where this playing takes place.

11.57

The metaphor that a newborn child is like a "sponge" is appropriate, as far as meaning is concerned. From a cultural perspective, the newborn is an incomplete being, designed by nature not only to fulfill biological strategies, but also to absorb meanings and to do so at an astonishing rate.

11.58

If the life of the child is dominated by fantasy—the free-flowing action of an imagination disconnected from the outside world—then maturity must be the slow but inexorable "connecting up" of the various meanings that sift through the youthful mind to the bare objects, actions, and happenings in the outside world. A crucial goal of education is precisely this: to guide the process of *linking* meanings to their correlates.

11.59

The conspicuous lack of creativity in adult humans is largely due to the decline of meaning-forms flowing freely and effortlessly through their minds, in conjunction their mind's increasingly secure connections to the items, actions, and happenings in the outside world.

11.60

Although human beings are not strictly controlled by nature, this does not mean we have moved beyond nature, but instead represent a new form of nature: biological beings supercharged with meaning.

11.61

We experience our own bodies and selves as an intricate system of meaning-forms, and not as naked biological/material *things and functions*. Hence it's how we "feel" or how "we are doing" that is our concern and not how we are "functioning." That we don't see ourselves as things and functions means that we should be careful not to reduce other people to mechanical categories as well, as we tend to do. Seeing and embracing people as beings of meaning and not as things and functions to be manipulated, controlled, and rearranged will go a long way in improving our relationships with them.

11.62

Creative thinking first began to emerge during the bio-ontological shift when *what is* opened the human mind to *what could be.*

11.63

Ideas are meanings that have clear and distinct identities that retain their individuality, despite their interaction with other meanings.

11.64

Important ideas are *historical events pregnant with the future*—they are created, modified, or transformed, as they live through different cultures, and naturally produce other important ideas that likewise are projected into the future.

11.65

Much of the life of meaning is embodied in language—the "caretaker of ideas."

11.66

To think is simply to be a human, but to think well is to be in the company of exceptional beings upon whose shoulders rests nothing less than the fate of humankind.

11.67

The general awareness of time is produced by meaning-forms entering consciousness—flowing freely through awareness—one after the other.

11.68

Animals don't possess time awareness, because their senses are totally absorbed in, and fixed on, the objects, actions and happenings of their *immediate* interest, exclusively for the sake of survival and reproduction. That animals may act in a "timely fashion" is not due to the awareness of the passage of time or the awareness of the need to act at a particular time. Rather, it is due to evolutionary-based, *need-sensitive intuitions*. An example of this is the sensation of hunger, which instantly activates the animal's awareness of its physical need and mobilizes the animal's actions to meet it *now*, independently of any sort of time consciousness.

11.69

So often has my ire been aroused when I hear a bright, well-educated individual critique a particular position, supply this analysis with impressive insights, and then provide a very compelling counterargument buffeted with considerable rational muscle; and then hear the very same person, sometime later, espouse religious convictions and support them with the most ludicrous, irrational, and disingenuous reasons one could imagine. Indeed, it can be very painful to observe normally intelligent, critical and honest people suffer the collapse of their thinking skills and intellectual conscience when speaking on religious matters. How might we account for this bizarre occurrence?

Each year in America, well over a hundred thousand people fall asleep while they are driving; many are seriously injured or killed. How could this happen? We all know when we are tired and are in immediate need of sleep, so why don't overly fatigued drivers? When it finally happened to me one late night, the reason became obvious. With the drowsy driver, fatigue effectively switches off the focused attentiveness that he normally deploys to survey the driving landscape; the result is that the driver's decision-making capacity is effectively neutralized. In other words, falling asleep at the wheel *shuts down* the awareness that one is driving in the first place. This is why it is so dangerous. Fatigued drivers don't even know that it is happening. It's really that simple. But what does falling sleeping at the wheel have to do with the person of faith?

It's not uncommon for believers of the type I have described to ask nonbelievers what they fear about religion, and to do so with sincerity. Do we fear the reemergence of religious attacks on secular thought and institutions, for example, or intensified intolerance toward nonbelievers? No. The real danger with religion is not what it attempts to accomplish in the clear light of day. In these instances, the various challenges to a free and open way of life can be met head-on and dealt with by all the democratic means that are at our disposal. What is truly frightening about religion is the way it can *quietly*, and one could even say *secretly*, rearrange the thinking of the unwitting believer to the point where clear logical reasoning has only selective and safe applications. One of my friends—a normally very intelligent and sane man—has argued with great conviction that Noah was able to squeeze two of each the kind of bird and animal in the world in his ark, including all the dinosaurs ("baby dinosaurs," he argued), because "God can do anything." I suggest that this kind of logical blindness is similar to the person falling asleep at the wheel of a car: my religious friend is wholly *unaware* of the literal breakdown of his rational faculty, and therefore is oblivious to the logical fiasco that is occurring right before his mind's eye. With the religious mindset, the very psycho/emotional/intellectual mechanisms that should be (and normally are) alert to irrationality are rendered incapacitated. This extreme form of rational myopia appears almost sinister, because from a psychological perspective, the "person of faith" is actually not responsible for what he says or even does, and a person who thinks and acts *in the dark* is a very dangerous person indeed. Where a driver is asleep at the wheel and has no awareness that he is about to crash into oncoming traffic, the religious person is philosophically asleep and unable to see or recognize the logical absurdities that are sending the person's thinking on a collision course with reality—at minimum, logical reality—and the possibilities for unfortunate consequences are many. The well-chronicled and well-bloodied history of religion demonstrates this point well.

So what is the payoff for such philosophical blindness? Pleasurable *psycho-emotional feelings*. Pleasure, at least as a temporary measure, is an effective buffer against the painful facts of reality. The awareness of the inevitability of death, physical and emotional suffering, the loss of loved ones, feelings of profound separation and loneliness, moments of despair and fear, and philosophical/existential uncertainty—these are some of the natural sorrows of life. The desire to replace these unpleasantries with pleasurable alternatives is among the most powerful forces in the human psyche. Since feeling is deeper than logic and is often its master, it makes sense that, left unchecked, the desire for pleasure will dominate, and that logical reasoning will be destroyed when it interferes with the continued experience of pleasure. Intelligence, logic, rationality, and the facts of reality, in other words, are typically no match for fantasy, illusion, and self-deception, if the latter prove to be more pleasurable. So what could be done? The solution to ridding society of the religious mindset is really very simple: train the youthful mind to appreciate the many pleasures of thinking with intelligence, honesty, and courage. Learning to face reality gladly with philosophical toughness is the antidote to all the perils of religious thinking. The desire for pleasure is here to stay, so why not use it to our advantage?

11.70

The insidious takeover of the logical faculty by religious illogic is by no means always as conspicuous as the example I cited regarding the belief that somehow God arranged to fit two of each kind of bird and animal, including dinosaurs, into Noah's ark. In most cases, the breakdown of intellectual integrity among religionists is well hidden inside reasonable positions and can be fleshed out only by incisive questioning and analysis. This dressing up of irrational arguments with reasonable ones is a practice that I label "stealth-thought." This common tactic can be seen, for example, in the position that gay couples should not be allowed to adopt babies because all the scientific studies have shown conclusively that children grow up more balanced and psychologically healthier with opposite-sex parents. In reality, the studies are inconclusive at best and lean toward the opposite conclusion, but the larger point is that the honest reason why religionists are opposed to gay adoptions is that the Bible clearly states, in both the Old and New Testaments, that homosexuality is a horrible sin. In the Old Testament, it's actually punishable by death.

The position for the sinfulness of homosexuality in the Bible is based on the idea that one's sexual orientation is a *moral choice* over which one has control. The scientific evidence that sexual orientation has a biological basis, however, is growing, and it may ultimately establish conclusively that personal choice has little to do with sexual desire or orientation. If pressed about this possibility, religionists will often change the argument and insist that it's only if people *act* on their homosexual desires that they commit a sin. In other words, by shifting the sinfulness to actions instead of desires, they want you to believe that the logical and ethical problems are avoided. However, there is a larger difficulty with this. It's hard to imagine that a loving and just God would create a person whose overpowering sexual desire is only for his or her own sex and then require the person *never* to act on it. This would be nothing short of cruel and heartless—actually, a rather sinister form of torture.

In fact, sinfulness based purely in desire, independent of actions, is well substantiated in the Bible. Let's not forget Jesus' statement to the effect that if a man simply "looks upon" a woman and lusts, he has already committed the sin. What this means is that, from a Christian perspective, the *desire* for homosexual gratification is a sin. The New Testament states that God curses certain people with the disgusting and unclean desire for those of the same sex because they have turned the truth of God into a lie—that is, they prefer to live in spiritual darkness rather than embrace the truth of the Gospels. Needless to say, this strong position against homosexuality opens up a philosophical, psychological, and ethical can of worms that religionists would like to avoid at all costs. They prefer to hide the genuine source of their belief against gay adoption, because they know that it cannot be morally or scientifically justified. It's much safer to retreat into stealth-thought and hope that nobody notices.

The same sort of dishonest reasoning—reasoning that, as we noted, is typically carried out largely independently of the person's awareness—can also be heard in religionists' positions regarding the theory of evolution. The factual basis for biological evolution is so overwhelming that only the most ill-informed or unbalanced person would deny it. Many religious people recognize this, and now support a sort of God-based evolution that incorporates the evolutionary model. In fact, this is the official position of the Catholic Church.

And how precisely does God fit into the evolutionary scheme? We are told that he created all life and then guided the whole process of evolution throughout the history of life on Earth with immaculate attention to detail. One glaring problem with this extraordinary exercise in stealth-thought is one that we talked about earlier in this book: namely, it presupposes that Darwin, and not Moses, the Old Testament prophets, or even Jesus Christ, laid bare the Truth about the development of life on Earth. It's worth posing the question a second time: how is it possible that the most truthful book the world has ever seen—the Bible, a book inspired by the Almighty himself—did not provide this essential truth about life on Earth? This is not unimportant information! It seems to me that a great case could be made to include Darwin as one of the great prophets, since he was the *only* one to reveal the ultimate truth about the nature of life on Earth! But let's not be facetious.

The Bible does not allow for any theory of evolution under any circumstances. The Old Testament clearly says that God created each distinct life-form to remain the same over time, and he did so only a few thousand years ago. The creation of humanity is of special significance in the Bible: the human race was brought into existence exclusively for the purpose of having a personal relationship with God. Because of this unique spiritual relationship, there is an *unbridgeable gap* between nonhuman and human life.

The well-documented facts of biological evolution are devastating to the status of religion: the evolution of life on Earth was careless, wasteful, and even murderous, with the accidental occurrence of genetic mutations playing the key role. Moreover, the physical evidence clearly shows that there is no discernable direction or goal to evolution and no necessary movement to higher complexity. There is, in short, no inevitable progress in evolution—just life forms adapting to their environment and reproducing or life forms failing to adapt and dying out. The startling implication is abundantly clear: humanity itself did not have to be, but was just another accidental variation that managed to survive and successfully reproduce. As far as the origin of life is concerned, there is mounting evidence that it, too, was accidental, although precisely how it happened is still unclear and is the subject of intense scientific research.

A God-based theory of evolution does not fit with what we know scientifically about the development of life on Earth. Religionists really are very short on detail and logical persuasion in trying to deal with this dilemma. They question, for example, the validity of natural selection and the evolutionary timetable, and they argue that life is too complex and well designed for it to have resulted from random forces. They also misunderstand the influence of chance in evolution and suggest that evolution is ruled by chance alone and is therefore highly improbable, when in fact natural selection is highly deterministic. Ironically, the religionists' questioning of the validity of natural selection is particularly counterproductive and is actually quite embarrassing. Without the theory of natural selection, one should note, scientists would never have been able to devise vaccines and pesticides, and the science of biology itself would lose all coherence.

But the validity of biological ideas and principles is irrelevant to stealth-thought. When a religious position attaches itself to any science, it is only for the purpose of stealing its credibility, so it can surreptitiously advance its own dogmatic agenda. But stealth-thought cannot always escape the court of simple common sense. To maintain a God-basis for evolution, for instance, one would have to accept that God was the kind of being who would allow, or somehow guide, the chaotic, wholesale slaughter and unimaginable suffering of countless life forms that have gone extinct (and continue to do so) in the history of life on Earth. Stealth-thought in this context also undermines the very theory that theistic evolution supporters feel compelled to embrace. What makes the theory of evolution so irresistible is the mountain of evidence that supports it. If we were to change or eliminate its essential component—natural selection—it would no longer be a feasible and compelling scientific theory. Stealth-thought therefore has the highly absurd task of trying to keep God in the evolutionary picture by eliminating or distorting those features of biological evolution that made it so compelling to begin with.

Examples of stealth-thought are many, and they point to an unavoidable truth: religious thinking is implicitly designed to move *away* from what is truthful. It is deceitful through and through, and those who indulge in it are typically victimized by their own misguided psychology, over which they have little awareness or control. Could this natural, human illness ever be eradicated? Yes, but never permanently: each generation of young human beings needs to be newly inoculated against it with proper education, beginning first at home and then with formal schooling. This is our only hope against this human-all-too-human vice that has wrought so much havoc in human affairs at every level and continues to do so today.

The Enlightenment: Cause, Morality, and Reality 12

12.1

For over two thousand years philosophy has defined itself as the rational pursuit of reality. In the 20th century, this venture took an unexpected turn with the birth of a new school of thought called phenomenology. Phenomenology, as it was originally defined and practiced, claimed to be able to get to the raw, unadorned "structures" of things in experience, by reducing them to their bare "essences"; once these essences are exposed, phenomenologists argued, they can be rationally analyzed to determine how they organize and define the meanings that we see in experience: by getting to the basic structures of things, *what is* could then be objectively, described, explained, and understood. "Objectively," in this context, means without subjective or cultural influences. But modern critics argue, however, that even at this alleged sub-cultural level, subjective and/or cultural meanings still intrude because of the necessary employment of *language*—including quantitative language such as mathematics—as a tool for description, analysis, and comprehension. In this view, language is never devoid of unconfirmed premises, and subjective or cultural biases. If this is true, does it mean that philosophy—and by extension much of science—could never get to the truth of reality? It's fascinating to observe that this problematic situation is analogous to issues relating to the famous Heisenberg uncertainty principle in quantum physics. According to this principle, there is a necessary limit to what we can know about physical reality, because our normal categories of understanding and powers of perception break down at the atomic and subatomic level.

For instance, we take it for granted that we can know, with mathematical precision, the velocity (directional speed) and location of any moving object, such as a car moving along a highway. But this viewpoint is legitimate only in cases where the object under consideration retains its well-defined structure. A car keeps its physical structure whether it is moving or not, so it is easy to make precise statements about it. On the other hand, if a car began losing its shape as it moved, to the point that it became *spread out* over an extremely broad area, then it would be impossible to attribute a precise location to it. This sort of development occurs with elementary particles at the atomic and subatomic levels under certain conditions. Electrons, for instance, possess wavelike qualities that become increasingly pronounced when scientists try to determine the particle's velocity. Since waves are spread out through space, scientists can only speak of a general or probable location of the electron. The opposite is true, as well: electrons also have *particle-like* qualities that become pronounced when scientists focus in on only the electron's *location*—that is, when the velocity of the electron is not being measured.

But never is it logically or physically possible to measure *both* aspects of the electron simultaneously—one and only one aspect of the electron can be pronounced at given time. That an electron possesses these "complementary" qualities means that an electron, contrary to common sense and even to the known laws of classical physics, is really *two realities in one*: a particle and a wave! This is the essence of the Heisenberg uncertainty principle—discovered by Werner Heisenberg (1901–1976). If having to swallow the unsavory fact that an electron is two realities in one wasn't bad enough, scientists also had to confront the uncomfortable truth that, at the atomic and subatomic level, strict cause and effect has no meaning, and *probability* rules the very structure of basic physical reality. But why is this so? Nobody knows. As with the constant speed of light, we must simply accept that the universe is this way. And again as with the speed of light, we don't notice the probabilistic nature of reality, because it only becomes visible when the very fundamentals of physical reality are glimpsed through special scientific instruments like cloud chambers.

And there is more disturbing news. One of the most cherished ideals of scientific investigation is that a scientist must remain "objective" in his investigation of the outside world; that in order to know what is really happening there, the investigator must remain out of the picture altogether and not influence the outcome of experiments. What Heisenberg discovered is that in the quantum world, objectivity is not possible, because the very act of observation influences or disturbs the system that is being observed. If one were to conduct an experiment on an electron, for instance, the light particles (photons) that are required to see the electron actually bump into it in the process of trying to observe it. This bumping causes the electron to move from its normal course, and so what the scientist ends up measuring is not the objective movement of the electron, but one that has been *altered by the observer*. The real problem is that there is no way to overcome this interference. As a result, quantum scientists have been forced to abandon one of the great pillars of the scientific method. This does not mean that quantum physics is incapable of arriving at real knowledge of the quantum world. It simply means that the effects of the observer must be taken into consideration when conducting experiments. Philosophically speaking, that the observer is always a part of what occurs on the atomic and subatomic level is, in itself, the way that it is—a valuable advance in knowledge that some scientists celebrate. But what happens when there is no observer interfering with the quantum actions? This scenario, although popular among philosophers of science, is not possible, given that the observer does not have to be a human being or experimental equipment. Nature itself—including minute dust particles and particulates of all kinds—is the ever-present cosmic observer that constantly interferes with atomic and subatomic particles.

Similar to the way in which observation prevents objective understanding of the quantum world, language is also a limiting factor in all philosophical and scientific investigations, and not just in phenomenology. By bringing language to bear in philosophical and scientific analysis, philosophers and scientists are constantly "bumping into" and altering the real world with their own ideas and otherwise imposing the convention of organized, human-made meaning onto reality and, as a result, distorting it. Or are they? It's certainly true that language often misrepresents the topics about which it speaks, but is this always the case? Are we stuck in a Heisenberg-like world of fuzzy philosophical uncertainty, where thinking and linguistic expression forever undermine our quest for pure objective understanding?

The notion that truth seekers may be cut off completely from ever understanding what is objectively true, because of unbridgeable human limitations, is the most important issue in all of philosophy and threatens the grand goal of science—to understand the real nature of the material world. This line of thinking received its inspiration from the German philosopher Immanuel Kant (1724–1804). Ironically, Kant had thought that his ideas about the possibility of gaining objective knowledge were going to rescue philosophy, religion, and particularly science from a wave of skepticism that was gaining ground during his time. How his ideas played themselves out over the centuries undoubtedly would have both amazed and disturbed him.

Kant was the last and greatest of the great Enlightenment thinkers. The Enlightenment was the revolutionary cultural movement in eighteenth and nineteenth-century Europe that created the beginning of much that is distinctive about the modern world. Liberal democracy, the rule of law, the market system, human rights and equality, technological optimism, secularism, and our scientific spirit all came to philosophical maturity with the thinkers, writers, and scientists of the Enlightenment. Although one could easily see the Enlightenment as the natural extension of the Italian Renaissance (e.g., Leonardo and Galileo), it went far beyond the Renaissance in crucial ways. For example, it shoved religion, and all forms of superstition, off of the earthly stage and replaced them with a human-based religion that has often been referred to as the "cult of reason." God still had a place in the Enlightenment worldview, but simply as a distant, disengaged onlooker.

Taking the Renaissance idea of the sovereign individual to new heights, Enlightenment thinkers looked to human nature as the source of infinite possibilities. In England, empiricist philosopher John Locke (1632–1704) was promoting the idea that a human being is a "tabula rasa"—a blank slate on which could be composed virtually anything. This means that with the right education and moral tutoring, a human being has the potential to achieve intellectual and moral greatness. In fact, human beings are actually *perfectible* and society itself is a community of potentially perfectible beings. In short, given the malleable quality of human nature, all the moral, social, political, and economic problems that plague humanity could be solved with the proper use, and creative expression, of natural reason. In the

Enlightenment worldview, progress was on the march, and nothing could stop it. Progress is inevitable. Human beings may be blank slates, but from a moral perspective, they are basically *good*, and it was only a matter of time until the good society would emerge and unite all of humanity in liberty, fraternity, and equality—a true brotherhood of humankind! A truly rational and just humanity.

The philosophical orientation of the Enlightenment was *empirical*. Rather than focusing exclusively on general rational principles to explain the world or arguing that all human beings possess innate qualities, Enlightenment truth seekers searched for the particular facts that made up the human reality and strove to describe how everyday experience imprints itself onto human nature. The success of Enlightenment ideals in transforming Western culture represented the victory of empiricism over the philosophy of rationalism—the worldview of philosophers such as René Descartes.

The capstone of the empirical approach to understanding reality was the astonishing successes of the science of Sir Isaac Newton (1643–1727). His laws of motion seemed to have universal application—from predicting with unbelievable accuracy the present and future movements and locations of objects in the universe—from planets to billiard balls—to serving as the fail-proof guide in constructing and operating countless technological devices like steam engines, firearms, and machines of all kinds. The success of Newtonian physics in explaining and predicting what occurs in the world led many to believe that Newton, in his peerless genius, had discovered the very laws that almighty God himself had articulated through the universe at its creation.

Outside of science, Enlightenment ideas and writings about political self-rule, human freedom, natural rights, and a just society for all transformed Western civilization. Most dramatically, they led to the American Revolution in 1775 and provided the philosophical basis for the American experiment in democracy. Unfortunately, in France, where Enlightenment ideals had actually matured, this dynamic cultural movement made a disastrous detour. Overtaxed, disenfranchised, and disrespected citizens finally waged the French Revolution of 1789 to overthrow the corrupt, antiquated, and unreasonable French monarchy; their ultimate goal was to realize Enlightenment, democratic ideals in the political arena. Uncontainable chaos ensued as the King of France—

Louis XVI—who had been removed from power by the revolutionaries, convinced Austria and Prussia to come to his rescue and invade France. In response, the newly elected democratic body, called the National Convention, had King Louis XVI executed for treason. A new army was then drafted, and the Austrians and Prussians were eventually pushed back. In a sort of final phrase of the revolution, bloodthirsty barbarism consumed the revolutionaries. Enlightenment ideals were famously suspended as the revolutionaries carried out the horrific Reign of Terror (1793–1794), in which thousands of people suspected of being enemies of the state lost their heads at the guillotine. Finally, with France in complete political and social disarray, a young Corsican general named Napoleon Bonaparte (1769–1821) came to power in 1799, declared himself absolute "emperor" of France, imposed order, and then ruthlessly proceeded to conquer the rest of Europe. This was not a good ending to the French Revolution—and certainly was not good publicity for Enlightenment ideas, strategies, and programs.

The rest of the world looked on in horror. How could this have happened? Was this where an enlightened society would inevitably lead? Perhaps the chaos, murder, and oppression that emerged in the French Revolution were the natural result of the science-based secularizing of religion, Deism. Maybe human beings are not meant to live in a world of self-seeking individualism, where cold, empirical reason is the exclusive guide, and where an all-pervasive, rational skepticism throws long-held traditions into question. Perhaps we should look to an earlier time for guidance and insight, a time before the artificial creations and alienating philosophies of modern culture dominated and polluted our lives, to a *less rational* time when humanity was *at one* with nature: happy, noble, instinctive, and strong! This was the view of French/Swiss Counter-Enlightenment thinker Jean-Jacques Rousseau (1712–1778). Rousseau has the ironic legacy of both standing opposed to what the Enlightenment stood for while serving to inspire important Enlightenment thinkers and even provoking, to some degree, events in the French Revolution.

"Man is born free but everywhere he is in chains." So thought Rousseau as he laid out his idea of the "social contract"—an agreement *all* citizens must follow that would free them to return to a more natural, ethical, and fulfilling way of life. And why should citizens agree to this contract? Because it was the embodiment of what Rousseau called the "general will"—the reflection of a *higher spiritual self* that all people share as members of the human race. So agreeing to the social contract was agreeing to what everyone really needs, wants, and values anyway, whether they are aware of it or not. Besides, for Rousseau, the social contract was not only in everyone's best individual interests; it was also best for society as a whole. In this way, the personal values of simplicity, honesty, integrity, compassion, self-discipline, selfless devotion, and generosity would become public values.

Rousseau was not merely suggesting that citizens ought to sign onto his social contract. In a stance that caused many subsequent thinkers to consider him a fascist, Rousseau was prepared to argue that people *must* agree to the social contract or risk severe penalties, such as being put to death. Unfortunately, the French revolutionaries seized on this radical interpretation of Rousseau's philosophy to justify their frenzied obsession with the guillotine during the Reign of Terror.

Rousseau is often referred to as the father of what has been labeled the "Counter-Enlightenment." Indeed, Rousseau sparked a tradition that threw into question all the values of the Enlightenment: empirical reasoning, the perfectibility of human nature through Enlightenment's social and educational strategies, and the inevitability of progress, secular philosophizing, and scientism—the unrestrained application of science to all areas of human inquiry and understanding. Actually, this tradition of skepticism was not new with Rousseau but stretched back to ancient Greece, where the Sophists (professional teachers who taught the skills of argument and debate) like Protagoras argued that truth is relative and that values are based more on opinion than objective truth. And we already spoke about Montaigne (16th century), whose whole approach to knowledge, and living generally, was one of skeptical curiosity and suspicious probing. Beginning with Rousseau, though, the tradition of skepticism began gaining solid philosophical support and momentum.

12.2

This skeptical tradition reached a stunning apex in the philosophy of Scottish philosopher and historian David Hume (1711–1776). His particular genius consisted in a cluster of qualities rarely, if ever, found in one philosopher: extreme clarity of thinking; a precise and thoroughly lucid writing style; an intellectual incisiveness that enabled him to focus in, like a laser beam, on the most essential points of a problem, and to unpack, with flawless reasoning, hidden ideas and prejudices; a preternatural ability to communicate very difficult concepts and arguments with creative simplicity; the philosophical boldness to follow a line of reasoning to the absolute end, even if it meant shattering the very foundations of philosophy, science, religion, and ethics; and, last but not least, a cheery disposition toward life, despite his uncompromising skepticism. It's not surprising to discover that he has had a powerful impact on a number of modern intellectual traditions. Outside of philosophy, for instance, physicist Albert Einstein cited Hume's meticulous approach to analyzing what is present in experience as being very important to Einstein's own formulations of his special and general relativity theories.

Hume's reputation as the greatest of all empiricists is based in his brilliant critiques that explain that what we think we know with certainty is often shown to be unjustified once we put the razor-sharp knife of philosophical reasoning to proper use in actual experience. What is a "mind," for instance? What *in actual experience* gives us reason to believe with certainty that it really exists? Hume's answer was: nothing. When we reflect on what we call a mind, we only find a bundle of perceptions. Nothing else. Put another way, a mind, as an integrated, well-defined item that causes our thoughts, is a fiction to which our flawed ways of thinking have given a permanent and stable existence. The same is true of the "self." When we look to experience, we can never find a coherent, abiding self, nor can we ever observe or find a self that is *behind* our experiences of the world. All there is, is one experience followed by another—and even one's reflection on one's alleged self is again just another experience in a lifetime-long series of experiences. Like the mind, the self is a fiction that our non-reason has fabricated.

And Hume did not end here. Even our experience of the outside world is not what we think it is. In advancing a line of reasoning that he borrowed from Irish empiricist George Berkeley (1685–1753), Hume argued that we can't even say with certainty that the something we call "substance" exists independently of our perceptions. For instance, when we experience a red apple, its redness, its taste, its smell, and tactile sensations are how the apple appears to us, and yet these attributes are nothing more than clusters of *subjective* perceptions that we experience and integrate with our thinking ability. If we begin to delete each perception one by one, the apple starts to disappear, until there is no apple left. We can see what Hume was asserting about the mind, the self, and substance: we are being duped by our own psychology and habits of thinking into mistakenly believing in realities that we have no *reason* to believe exist. Was Hume saying definitively that they don't exist? No. He was simply saying that we don't have convincing reasons to believe that they exist.

In his *Inquiry of Human Understanding*, Hume discussed the plausibility of miracles. He understood a miracle as an event that breaks the known laws of nature. He observed that to believe that such events happen without actually observing them is not a reasonable position, and one reason he gave is a wonderful example of his amazing ability in rationally destabilizing accepted truths and so-called facts with easy but penetrating critiques. When considering reports of so-called miracles, is it easier to believe that a law of nature has really been broken or to believe that the accounts and testimonies of eyewitness were flawed for any number of reasons, such as the desire to deceive, or a gross misunderstanding of what actually took place? Hume would say it is much more likely—or probable—that the testimonials are misguided and not true. Hume argued that the report of a miracle is such an extraordinary claim that nothing short of extremely compelling proof would do. This is only reasonable, because this is the only way to give justifiable support to the claim. Such was Hume's position regarding all the reports of miracles in the Bible.

To believe, for instance, that Jesus brought the dead back to life requires more than the reports of fanatical followers. If a stranger told you that your father was a drug dealer and that he knows this with certainty because he saw your father selling drugs on several occasions, would you accept this testimonial as being true, or would you require additional proof? Clearly, you would demand further evidence, and the reason is that a mere claim that your father is a drug dealer is out of balance with the evidence, such as your intimate knowledge of his character and ethics. In other words, there is greater weight in the claim than in the evidence. It's only when an extraordinary claim is supported by sufficient evidence that we can be confident in believing the claim. This was one of Hume's most persuasive arguments against the biblical reports of miracles. Another point that Hume raised against believing in the accounts of miracles was that there is no way to determine if one did *not* take place. This means that there is no acceptable way to distinguish a valid claim from an invalid one, and as a result, *all* reports of miracles lose philosophical plausibility.

Ever since Thomas Aquinas put forth his famous proofs of God's existence in the thirteenth century, many Christian scholars believed that he had provided a comprehensive, philosophical basis for God's existence. In Hume's *Dialogues Concerning Natural Religion* (1757), he challenged these and other proofs of God's existence, and for many, delivered the deathblow to them. One of the most popular arguments in favor of God's existence is often called the "argument from design." If you were walking along the beach and happened to find a watch lying there in the sand, would you be justified in concluding that the watch had a creator, since its construction is so precise, orderly, and purposeful that it could never have assembled itself? The answer is yes. This is the design argument in a nutshell, and it has found modern expression among so-called conservative Christians with the religious notions of creationism and intelligent design. Hume rejected arguments that are based on looking to nature, because he believed that they are misconceived and carry no empirical or logical credibility. It's perfectly fine to assume that a watch has a watchmaker, because we know through experience that watches are the product of human innovation and technological skill; some of us even make watches, or have observed them being created by human hands and human-made machinery. We also understand how and why watches work. In short, since we are the beings that make watches with specific reasons in mind, we are justified to infer that there was a watchmaker who made the watch we found on the beach.

How about the universe? What justification do we have to infer a creator? For Hume, none. The analogy breaks down when we considering the following: we don't make universes and have never witnessed universes being made; since we don't make universes or have ever witnessed one being made, we don't know if the universe that is present was made; since we did not make the universe, we don't even know if there is a purpose to the universe; we also don't know what universes *ought* to be like, since we neither make them nor experience them being made; we don't even know if the universe came into existence, since we have never seen one come into existence, and we know nothing about how this might happen; since we know nothing about its alleged creation, it's certainly possible that the universe was never created in the first place—perhaps it is *eternal*; and we don't even know if the universe that we experience around us is the same everywhere—it's possible that chaos, disorder, and purposelessness are the rule in other sections of the universe. The *mechanical* analogy is also questionable for other reasons: since the universe is vegetative and un-machine-like, perhaps the universe is more like an immensely sophisticated cauliflower (my analogy) than a super-complicated watch!

For Hume, the claim for there being a creator of the universe is much worse when considering the Judeo-Christian God as a possible candidate, because none of God's qualities as recorded in parts of the Bible can be deduced from what we can observe in the universe. The universe is far from moral and just, for instance. In fact, in light of what we know about, and experience of, the universe, the possibility that an all-powerful, all-knowing, and all-benevolent God was its creator seems virtually impossible. In reviewing the evidence that is plain to see, the only God that could be logically inferred from the universe— from a moral perspective—would be a sinister deity, one that either causes or is indifferent to the exceptional suffering and tragedy that assault all life. In simple terms, there is an unbridgeable gulf between how the universe appears and the nature of the alleged God whom some people think created it. And speaking of a creator-God, why is it necessarily true that only one God is being considered as the creator of the universe? Why not, for example, two, twenty-nine, or fifty-eight thousand? How would we know?

Hume, in his philosophical inquiry, fulfilled his duty admirably as the quintessential empiricist by demanding concrete evidence and logical support for arguments in favor of God's existence. For this artful skeptic, the design argument does not provide either, and consequently it is not a defensible position. But there are other arguments in the religionist's arsenal.

The "cosmological argument" states that since all things that we see in the natural universe have *prior* causes, then there also must have been a "first cause" to initiate the causal sequence. Without a first cause to the universe, an "infinite regress" would be unavoidable. An infinite regress ("regress" means "going back") refers to philosophical dilemma of never being able to arrive at a fundamental truth or basic fact, because each attempt to do so requires further explanations, and these explanations also require further explanations, and these explanations in turn also require further explanations, and so forth and so on, endlessly. An infinite regress is a philosophical dead end, because it could never, even in principle, lead to a conclusion. Suggesting that that God did not create the universe is equivalent to saying that the universe did not have a first cause, and without a first cause, the universe would be ensnared in a sort of infinite regress—that is, in a endless backtracking of causes—that would necessarily never arrive at the start of the universe. But the universe *does* exist, and this means that it must have had a beginning and starting point—a first cause. In other words, the existence of the universe becomes incomprehensible without a beginning, and this is why those who deny it are supporting a logically and empirically defenseless position. But in order for there to have been a first cause, the initiator of the universe must itself be uncaused or *self-caused*. For enthusiasts of the cosmological argument, this uncaused first cause is none other than the master universe-creator himself—God!

For Hume, this explanation was flawed beyond repair, thought it does have a certain commonsense appeal. While he agreed that an infinite regress must be avoided, he saw no reason to posit God as a first cause. And the reason is simple: we would also be forced to discover a cause for God's existence. To assert, as subscribers to the cosmological argument do, that God, by definition, is uncaused or self-caused, is merely a convenient, logical ruse that hardly passes the giggle test. Why not avoid all this baseless metaphysics and maintain that the universe itself was uncaused or self-caused? What's the difference? There is no logical or empirical reason why the universe could not possess the creative capacity to be its own first cause, as opposed to an alleged God—and an invisible one at that. It may also be the case that the universe was neither created by another force nor even self-created but is an infinitely repeatable circle without a beginning or end, as some thinkers have suggested. Whatever the answer may be, there is certainly no justification whatsoever for going beyond the physical universe to suggest a nonmaterial, unverifiable, and invisible being as its creator, a being that cannot be shown to have a necessary connection to the universe, either logically or empirically.

But Hume went even deeper into his attack of the cosmological argument. The argument hinges on the "law of causality." Causality is so foundational to the way we think about the world—for example, science—and the way we live in it—for example, technology—that it has never been challenged in a serious way. That is, until Hume. He had a number of profound points to make about causality, which I will take up in detail below. For now, it's sufficient to say that Hume thought that using causality in the cosmological argument in trying to prove that God exists fails, because causality itself is a questionable belief. Yes, in Hume's view, causality is a belief and not a fact! In effect, the cosmological argument is a projection of a mere belief onto the universe, put forward as an undeniable fact. If this is the case, the argument for causality has no legitimacy whatsoever. We will see shortly how Hume backed up his assertion.

In his *Treatise of Human Nature*, the ever-relentless skeptic also launched a devastating attack on the idea of a reason-based, universal morality. Hume believed that moral principles have nothing to do with reason or knowledge of the divine but are based on human emotions, desires, and needs. There are no *moral facts* that can be gleaned from nature: one does not find morality in nature empirically, and there is nothing in nature that logically compels human beings to be moral. For an idea to qualify as knowledge, for Hume, it must either be logically necessary or directly observable in nature. Moral understanding fails on both accounts and therefore cannot be defined as factual knowledge. To think that there is factual, moral knowledge is to be guilty of the "is-ought" error, or as it is more commonly called, the "naturalistic fallacy," which states that what *is* the case, *ought* to be the case. One can describe what is happening in nature—this is "descriptive knowledge"—but one can never derive what one ought to do—"prescriptive knowledge"—from observing nature. "Ought," in other words, could never be a fact of nature.

Hume also attacked our normal idea of morality by questioning the foundation of morality itself—free will. Without the individual being able to choose freely what he or she wants to do, there cannot be true moral choice. Unfortunately, when one observes the world around us and reflects on history, one finds not individual, free choice operating, but *human nature* inclining all human beings to think and act in very similar ways. Belief in individual free will is really an illusion that may be important to how we live and work on a daily basis but is not an accurate reflection of reality. What is true is that we act to reach our goals and to fulfill our desires—all, of course, within the confines of human nature. This is the real source of our moral behavior.

Hume is most famous for his skeptical assault on the foundation of philosophical and scientific knowledge. And it is with his handling of this issue that we find Hume at his most brilliant and philosophically captivating. We noted earlier that Hume saw no justification in using the first cause strategy in trying to prove that God exists, because he viewed this argument as philosophically problematic. He didn't stop there. For him, the belief in cause and effect is just that: a simple belief and far from a fact that could be rationally justified. Let's review Hume reasoning.

First, we must realize what is at stake if Hume is successful in inserting skepticism into the causal machinery. Thinking in terms of cause and effect *is* the foundation of our thinking and actions. The idea is plain enough: each and every event that happens in nature and in the human world is directly connected to, and is caused by, a previous event, and will directly cause a future one. This is not to say that an event may not have more than one cause. On the contrary, the universe is a vast system of causes and effects in constant interaction, where, in some instances, effects follow directly from simple causes, and in other instances, effects follow, both directly and indirectly, from rich confluences of many different causes. Because of the causal links that connect events, the natural and human world is relatively predictable and understandable. Virtually every decision that we make or action that we commit is done in light of its possible causes and effects. And technology is nothing more than enshrining efficiently produced and controlled cause and effect relations within human-made structures in order to make human life easier, safer, or more enjoyable.

And what would science be without the unquestioned belief in, and reliance on, cause and effect? Medical breakthroughs and medical care are made possible through the success of scientific researchers in finding the causes of diseases or physical or psychological disorders. Cures and effective relief, as we all know, can be sought only after causes are found and understood.

Life and earth science would not have been possible without the guiding belief in cause and effect. Newtonian physics, which describes the behavior of objects in space and time, is essentially a mathematics-grounded understanding of cause and effect in relation to the physical world. And technology was born of this mechanical understanding of cause and effect. Even Einstein's theories of relativity were causal and strove to describe the cause and effect connections between, for example, matter and energy or and mass and gravity. (Quantum theories, as we saw earlier, are not causal theories but are based on *probabilistic* mathematics.)

The reliance of science on cause and effect is seen most clearly in the pervasive use of "inductive reasoning" (meaning, from the Latin, "leading into"). In trying to discover what is necessarily true about the physical, biological, and human worlds, scientists try to isolate *local* patterns and discover *particular* facts from which *general* observations and conclusions can be drawn. Inductive reasoning, in this way, tries to discover universal principles about reality. If the sun rose today, and it has been known to rise for as long as it has been observed to exist, then the rising of the sun every day qualifies as a scientific principle of nature. This move from particular example to general statement is inductive reasoning in action, and, as we can see, this form of thinking is not only basic to the scientific pursuit of knowledge but is also a crucial guide to everyday life. As another example, the smell of fire tells us that something is burning, because we have learned from repeated experiences the general principle that a particular kind of smell means that something is burning. It has been concluded that smoking cigarettes can lead to lung cancer, because people smoking cigarettes on a regular basis have been found to develop this disease at a proportionally higher rate than people who don't smoke at all or who smoke very little, taking into consideration all other significant factors.

The essential feature about what we discover inductively is that it is *repeatable*. The sun *always* rises, and a certain smell *always* means that something is burning. And smoking cigarettes *always* results in a greater risk of developing cancer. What, then, is the mechanism for repeatability? Cause. There are physical causes for why we experience the rising of the sun: the rotation and position of the earth relative to the sun at certain times *causes* the sun to appear to rise. And why do we experience a particular burning smell? Because the chemical composition of burning substances *causes* specific gases to be emitted that have certain kinds of odors. And there is a reason why chronic smokers can develop cancer: carcinogenetic effects of tobacco smoke cause the growth of cancer cells in a relatively high percentage of cases.

The reality of cause and effect has always been the first among "self-evident" truths and is a permanent member of the house of unquestioned common sense. What can be more obvious than the belief that what we do has direct consequences? The very meaning of our personal and public lives is thoroughly dependent on the idea of cause and effect—our belief in self-reliance, personal and public responsibility, as well as our sense of moral obligations are all causally defined. And what is our legal system but codified principles of cause and effect? The legal system's laws, rules, regulations, responsibilities, rights, freedoms, and declarations give order and direction to our lives and to society as a whole.

Hume did not believe that alleged self-evident truths, even those that are as basic to our worldview as the idea of cause and effect, automatically deserve the imprimatur of philosophy. In fact, Hume believed that we should be especially suspicious of received wisdom of every kind, for it is there that falsehoods of all types seek refuge. He posed a simple question: can we rationally justify the belief in cause and effect? Notice that he did not ask if there *is* cause and effect; rather, he wanted to know what *evidence* there is for this belief. His shocking conclusion was that there is none. As an empiricist, Hume believed that experience is the source of all our knowledge. For him, it was a natural philosophical reflex to try to observe the presence of cause in the world, but when he looked to experience, he claimed that he could not find cause anywhere. How absurd this conclusion appears! How could he make such a claim when actions causing effects are the defining character of the world? Hume disagreed. In one of the most audaciously brilliant expositions in the history of thought, Hume laid out his case against cause with disarming clarity and persuasiveness in his *Enquiry Concerning Human Understanding*.

What do we really observe when we observe a billiard ball in the process of striking another billiard ball and then see the second ball moving away from the first? For Hume we *only* see:

Ball A moving toward Ball B, with Ball A having *priority in time* in terms of its movement.

We see the *contiguity* of Ball A and Ball B—that is, we see the two balls extremely close to each other.

We see Ball B move away from Ball A.

And this is all! Hume made the startling observation that we never see *cause* in experience. Cause cannot be seen to occur between events, nor can cause be seen as logically necessary between events—this means that, for Hume, cause does not pass the knowledge test. Cause is an *interpolation* of what happens in experience and not a concrete event that we experience as occurring *between* events. What we define as cause and effect Hume calls a "constant conjunction"— two events that always seem to occur together at the same time but are not—according to observation—causally related. He argued that we think causally because of psychological habits: by seeing constant conjunctions occurring time and time again, we come to *expect* these constant conjunctions, and over time we mistakenly define their relationship as causal. But logically and empirically, there are no "necessary connections" between constant conjunctions—no logically binding principle or any observable factual knowledge that suggests, for example, that tomorrow the sun will *necessarily* rise. It all could break down at any moment.

Once again, it's important to keep in mind what Hume was arguing. Hume believed that he, along with the rest of us, ought to live our lives relying on the idea of cause and effect. And besides, we really have no choice but to live this way. Hume's only interest was in pointing out that cause has neither logical nor empirical purchase, and as a result, our ardent belief in a factual reality of cause has no rational or empirical justification. But then, might cause *really* occur in some way that transcends human reason and normal experience?

Hume wasn't concerned with alleged realities that went beyond reason and experience. Remaining true to form, he was a dyed-in-the-wool empiricist until the day he died.

The implications of Hume's skeptical conclusions regarding cause are devastating for philosophy and science. For the layperson, whose daily life is based on the thoughtless belief in cause and effect, it is of no great interest whether or not cause and effect could be justified rationally or empirically; the only thing that matters is that the world continues as always. But for the philosopher and (especially) scientist, whose work and belief systems depend on causal thinking, the debunking of causality could take the heart out of their devotion to philosophical and scientific truth. Philosophical and scientific truth seekers want to believe that through their work they are getting closer to the way that *the world is*, even though they recognize that this process may be never-ending. Pulling the causal rug out from under philosophers and scientists could turn their world topsy-turvy. Hume's reasoning was so well thought out that it was very difficult to disregard him. The only hope was a new solution to the problems that he exposed. The integrity of philosophy and science hung in the balance.

12.3

The philosophy of David Hume marked a dramatic turning point in the history of the Counter-Enlightenment. With him, the skeptical tradition that began with Rousseau reached a remarkable climax. Hume put into philosophical circulation powerful arguments that were disturbing to religious and secular thinkers alike. Hume's philosophical hammer showed no mercy for the ever-growing Enlightenment tradition devoted to the cult of reason, and he had no patience for traditional arguments for God's existence—and he smashed both to smithereens. He was hardly less kind to the belief that universal morality is based on reason. It was right at this moment that Immanuel Kant (1724–1804) rose to meet the skeptical challenges of Hume. He said of Hume that he "woke me from my dogmatic slumber." Hume brought Kant to philosophical life and forced him to stretch his formidable genius to its very limits to devise an adequate response. Kant was in love with Newtonian physics and made his own noteworthy contributions to the field, had a belief in God, and believed in a universal morality. How to rescue science, religion, and morality from the jaws of Hume's daunting skepticism became Kant's overriding passion and reason for being.

Kant assumed a profoundly paradoxical position in the history of thought. He believed that his mission was to resurrect the institutions and belief systems that had been routed by Counter-Enlightenment skeptics such as Hume, yet he is rightly positioned historically as the greatest and most influential of all Counter-Enlightenment thinkers. How do we explain this apparent contradiction? Did he fail in his mission? The answer is no, but ultimately one could easily argue that, in part, his solution turned out to be disastrous for philosophy and for Western civilization itself. There is no question that Kant was the greatest of all modern philosophers to the extent that from his original work sprung all subsequent philosophy, some of which carried on the Kantian tradition, other of which was decidedly ant-Kantian. Kant thought that his philosophy represented a second "Copernican Revolution." As we know, Copernicus was the first modern thinker to assert that the sun and not the earth was the center of our solar system. This was a literal reversal of the prevailing view of the time. The radical shift in thinking from an earth-centered solar system to a sun-centered one was mind-boggling indeed, and it forced the Western mind to rethink many of its hallowed assumptions, truths, and beliefs. Kant made the same claim for his philosophy, in that he believed his philosophy revered our normal ways of thinking about the world and humanity itself. Let's see what he meant by this.

Since it was Hume who goaded Kant on, it is best to have him meet his philosophical nemesis head on. Kant had to admit that Hume had uncovered one of the most profound truths in the history of thought: cause makes no logical or empirical appearance in experience. Hume concluded that reason had been sideswiped by this groundless belief in the factual and logical basis of cause, and that in order for reason to recover from this miscarriage of truth, skepticism had to be adopted as the only respectable philosophical position. Since Hume believed that all knowledge derives only from experience, his skeptical conclusion necessarily followed. From this view, Hume's reasoning was meticulous down to every detail.

In his monumental book *The Critique of Pure Reason* (1787), Kant set out to reinvent philosophy, because he realized that nothing short

314

of its complete overhaul would adequately address the epistemological problems (issues about knowledge) that skepticism posed. Unlike Hume's, Kant's prose is extremely dense and difficult to decipher. Part of the problem was that Kant introduced a radically new way of thinking about philosophy, and his strategy, again unlike Hume's, involved providing solutions to the problems that were raised by skepticism. This often required using new terminology and concepts that were, at best, difficult to express in clear and concise language. On the other hand, it is more likely the case that the quality of Kant's thinking exceeded his writing skills, or that being considerate to his devoted readers was simply not important to him.

Throughout the history of philosophy, great philosophers have always built on the insights of other thinkers. We saw this earlier with Socrates, Plato, and Aristotle. Kant's philosophy also incorporated the insights of many thinkers, particularly rationalists like Descartes and Leibniz and empiricists like Locke and Hume. Kant absorbed all of these insights and reconfigured them with his powerful intellect. Through a number of staggering leaps of his imagination, a new philosophical universe took form.

Both rationalists and empiricists understand the human mind to be relatively uncreative. The former operates on the premise that logic and concepts (especially mathematical ones) derive from the mind alone, and by analyzing and manipulating the logical connections between concepts, philosophical and scientific truth regarding the outside world can be discovered. Empiricists, by contrast, see all knowledge as coming not from the mind but from the outside world by way of *sensations* through the five senses. Kant realized that both traditions contain truth, but he believed that, in themselves, the traditions led the philosophers astray. Both Descartes and Hume were geniuses who made profound discoveries, but Descartes was unable to explain how subjective reason (innate ideas) could arrive at truths about the objective world, and Hume could not convincingly account for the necessity that we undoubtedly find there. Is there a middle way that transcends the limitations of both?

If there is, it must accomplish one goal above all else: it must show that experience is interconnected not simply by psychological habits that one gradually develops through repeat experiences of constant conjunctions, but because of strict laws or rules of experience that *necessarily* result in humans experiencing the world as they do. Without accomplishing this vital task, there is no hope of rescuing philosophy and science from radical skepticism. But how could this be accomplished if Hume had indeed shown, conclusively, that cause and effect could never be discovered in experience? Kant made the startling realization that looking to experience for necessity was looking in the wrong place, and he made the revolutionary declaration that *human cognition* itself supplies the "conditions for the possibility of experience"! In other words, cause and effect is a *category of reasoning* and is not something in the world.

In his *Critique of Pure Reason*, Kant laid out his highly technical philosophy of "transcendental idealism"—his view of how the human mind reconstructs the outside world so that it appears as it does. "Transcendental" means being independent of (transcending) experience, and "idealism" means being completely dependent on the subjective mind. Together they mean that our knowledge of the world results from the human mind taking objective reality and changing it into the various forms that we experience. This *dualistic* conception of reality is clear from Kant's classic formulation of a two-tiered reality: things in themselves—"noumena"—and things for us—"phenomena." The first is the world as it is, independent of our experience of it, and the second is the world after the categories of human understanding have changed it into the world we experience. Kant argued that human cognition produces two ways of experiencing the world: forms of sensibility and categories of understanding.

The forms of sensibility are *space* and *time*. For Kant, space and time are supplied by the mind exclusively and, to use Kantian language, are "*a priori* necessary conditions for all experience." For Kant, a priori means "before experience." What evidence did he offer to demonstrate that space and time are supplied by the mind *a priori*? In one of his more popular thought experiments, Kant observed that if we try to imagine the nonexistence of typical items of experience, such as trees, Germany, and people (my examples), it is easy to do so, but if we try to imagine the nonexistence of space and time, we find that it's not within our intellectual ability. And why? Kant's answer was that space and time are not items *in* experience that can be observed but are "a priori, transcendental conditions" of experience. In other words, space and time *structure* experience, but are not in experience.

The categories of understanding, like the forms of sensibility, are a priori concepts that the mind imposes onto the raw material of experience. Hume was concerned mostly with cause and effect and showed that there is no empirical or rational basis for it. But for Kant, cause and effect was just one of many mental constructs that restructures experience. In the section "Transcendental Logic" in his *Critique*, he outlined what he considered to be all the concepts with which the human mind recreates human reality. And what are these? They are the traditional concepts that make up our understanding of logic, plus a few that Kant added. For example, we think in terms of unity, plurality, totality, reality, negation, limitation, substance, cause, community, possibility, existence, necessity, and nonexistence. These are some of the concepts that the mind uses to create human experience. Kant put these concepts into special categories to reflect how they are used by the human mind in experiencing the world.

It is clear what Kant was after in his philosophical strategy: the forms of sensibility and the categories of understanding are the necessary a priori conditions for the possibility of experience. This way of reasoning—uncovering and focusing on the necessary conditions for something to exist—was another of Kant's innovations and is how he worked his way through the different strands of his philosophy. In fact, his whole project was launched by posing a transcendental argument: how are synthetic a priori judgments possible? Let's quickly explain what this means. Kant broke down logical judgments into five categories:

1. *A priori knowledge*—knowledge that is known to be true independent of experience, such as mathematical statements.
2. *A posteriori knowledge*—knowledge that is reliant on experience but could change, such as knowledge about the weather.
3. *Analytic judgments*—logically self-contained or redundant statements such as "All bachelors are unmarried."
4. *Synthetic judgments*—informative statements that combine observation with reason that can be either true of false such as "All human beings display a similar nature."

317

5. *Synthetic a priori judgments*—statements that are both necessarily true and based on observation/experience, such as "Every event has a cause."

It was precisely the synthetic a priori judgment that Hume thought was illegitimate and the one most valuable to Kant, since the whole edifice of Newtonian physics is built upon it. To overcome Hume's rigorous analysis, Kant deployed his famous "transcendental" form of arguing. Kant asked: "How are synthetic a priori judgments possible?" He then changed the question to: "What are the *conditions* that need to be met in order for these judgments to be possible?" His answer was that the human mind—through the forms of sensibility and the categories of understanding—meets all the conditions for the possibility of experience. This being the case, Kant thought that it is rather simple to account for synthetic a priori judgments and to neutralize Hume's skepticism. Hume was correct in his insight that necessity—cause—could not be found in experience, but he failed to realize that there were many other concepts that also cannot be found in experience. The reason for their absence is that they reside only in the human mind. Without assuming that the human mind supplies mental concepts like cause and effect, Hume's own ideas about knowledge could not be explained. For example, he divided mental perceptions into ideas (thoughts) and impressions (feelings and sensations) and then argued that ideas derive from impressions, and that ideas and impressions differ only in their *liveliness*—for instance, the impression of a flower is more vivid than the idea of a flower. This explanation, however convincing it may or may not be, clearly presupposes necessary connections of various sorts, such as the process of ideas deriving from sensations. In one of the great ironies in the history of Western thought, the very ideas that Hume fought so vigorously to defeat were, in the end, indispensable to his own way of thinking. Hume committed the greatest of all philosophical sins: he fell in love with his own ideas, and his formidable mind became closed off to all other possibilities. At least, this is what a good Kantian would argue.

So what was Kant's final position concerning reality and knowledge, and what did his solution accomplish? There are two forms of reality: 'phenomena" and "noumena"—*things-for-us* and *things-in-themselves*. Human beings have no access to noumenal reality, because the human mind always transforms noumenal reality into phenomenal reality. This means that the idea of a noumenal experience is utterly meaningless—experience *necessarily* implies only phenomenal experience. Human reality is the joint effort of the human mind and the outside world, although we could never know anything about this world. The forms of sensibility and the categories of understanding are the mental transformers of noumena into phenomena and serve as the *necessary conditions for the possibility of experience.* And so what are the benefits of Kant's revolutionary solution?

There are many. For one, by placing cause and effect in the human mind, Kant restored the rational foundation to Newtonian physics—that is, he returned philosophical legitimacy to the synthetic a priori judgment and to inductive reasoning (making general observations from particular facts or examples—both causally determined). Just as remarkable was that Kant also rehabilitated religion after it took an awful beating from Hume, by arguing that religious realities are beyond the grasp of sensibility-bound and category-bound reason and cannot be approached rationally. The extreme limitations of reason mean that there is plenty of space for realities that exist but could never be approached by reason. God, faith, free will, salvation, divine justice, the soul, and miracles—these are *spiritual truths* and, as far as Kant was concerned, are not answerable to the demands of rational inquiry. In this sense, they are equivalent to noumenal reality.

To bolster his case on the limitations of reason, Kant put forth his "antimonies"—two opposing positions that individually seem to be equally rational with respect to an individual judgment. He claimed to show through his antimonies that reason contradicts itself whenever it tries to solve problems that transcend its capabilities—in other words, when reason tries to grapple with the noumenal world. For example, consider these antimonies (my formulations): "The world has a *beginning* and an *end* in space and time, because everything does," as compared to: "The world has no beginning or end, because what could possibly exist outside of space and before time?" And this one: "God is uncaused and is the cause of everything else," as opposed to: "God must have a cause, because everything has a cause." Finally, "There is free will, because otherwise there would be no true morality," as compared to: "There is no free will, because the universe is governed by strict determinism." The point of these antimonies is to show that reason will always fail to be reasonable when it tries to go beyond all possible experience.

Another important contribution of Kant's was in the realm of ethics. Kant went to great lengths to distinguish his idea of morality from that of his great predecessor, Aristotle. If you recall, Aristotle tied moral acts to what he called "eudemonia"—happiness and pleasure that come from a life well lived, a balanced life devoted to excellence. Kant thought that morality based on happiness is a poor guide, because it cannot be *universalized*—that is, it does not necessarily include the welfare of all other people and is not based in a solid, reason-based law. For Kant, moral principles need to be unconditional, or else they can easily be corrupted by situational reason. This is precisely why moral acts based in happiness do not produce unambiguous principles of right and wrong. In the end, moral acts can only flourish in an atmosphere of *freedom*, which for Kant is lost without inflexible, rational guides.

Kant also dealt with Hume's skeptical attack on the possibility of a universal morality. Hume thought that he had put the philosophical nail in the morality coffin when he demonstrated that cause and effect cannot be empirically or rationally justified. Without cause and effect, free will becomes a meaningless idea, because the meaning of free will is based in the individual's belief that his or her particular actions cause particular results. This necessary connection between events means that individuals are morally responsible for their actions. Kant thought that he had disarmed Hume of his free-will argument, since, according to Kant's new philosophy, free will is a noumenal reality and cannot be rationally understood. Free will is one of a human being's most distinguishable attributes, even though pure reason has no way to understand it. Like the other nonrational realities that transcend our possible experience, we must accept free will on faith, since to deny it makes little sense, especially from a moral perspective.

Let's see more completely how Kant recast morality. Kant's goal was clear: to provide a standard of morality that would overcome moral skepticism, moral relativism, and morality based on feelings and the requirements of personal happiness. In his view, morality and human dignity go hand in hand, and to assault human dignity with moral codes based on such arbitrary conditions as feelings and personal views of happiness is to debase the human spirit. The only way to ensure the dignity of each individual and, by extension, the whole of humanity, is for each person to live by moral principles that are *universally binding* and *unconditional.*

In his *Groundwork of the Metaphysic of Morals* (1785), Kant introduced the details of his novel conception of morality: the "categorical imperative." "Categorical" implies *universal* and without qualification, and "imperative" denotes *necessity.* Together, these words mean performing moral acts that are both universally and necessarily valid. With this idea, Kant was making the claim that morality must have a *rational* basis, which means that moral acts need to be logically justified. In fact, this is what his categorical imperative was designed to orchestrate. He contrasted his categorical imperative with the "hypothetical imperative"—moral actions whose value is based solely on *individual* circumstances and personal agendas, goals, feelings, and passions—for example, the moral systems of Aristotle and Hume.

It follows naturally from Kant's notion of a universally binding morality that the *consequences* of moral actions are not relevant to moral worth. Why? Because consequences are always situation-based, and as situations always change, so the meaning of moral actions must change as well. For Kant, ever-shifting moral standards could never be a reliable foundation for moral behavior. Instead, he wanted us to turn our attention first to the particular *motivation* to do what is good—that is, to the "good will" behind particular acts. He proclaimed that it is *only* the moral will that is inherently good, regardless of circumstances, and thereby suited to inspire moral behavior. But here is the crux of the matter: true moral acts result only when good will leads an individual to act morally from a sense of duty. Acting from duty is a supreme expression of human freedom because, in this act, one breaks free from the grip of self-interest, emotional compulsion, and the chaos of fluctuating emotions and states of mind. For Kant, *moral duty is the only legitimate kind of moral action.* But acting from duty makes philosophical sense only if there is a reason-based *moral standard* that supports it. This standard is the categorical imperative. Kant broke down his principle into three parts:

1. "Act as if the maxim of your actions was to become a universal law of nature." Here Kant is asking us to perform a sort of thought experiment: to determine whether or not a particular

act is moral, one must hypothetically make this act a universal law and see if it remains logically feasible. For example, lying is immoral, because universalizing lying results in a self-contradiction: if everyone deceives everyone else continuously, and telling the truth never occurs, then an individual could never lie successfully, because everyone would know that the individual was lying. For Kant, this is self-contradiction, and, as a result, it could never become a law of nature. Telling the truth, by contrast, is moral, because it could easily be universalized and made into a law of nature without self-contradiction. In this case, one can speak the truth freely always out of a sense of duty.

2. "Act in such a way that you always treat humanity, whether in your person or the person of any other, never simply as a means, but at the same time as an end." This idea suggests that each human being is of special moral value and ought never to be exploited in the course of achieving goals. Put differently, human beings are not mere instruments to be used to reach what we might consider to be important ends, but are uniquely valuable among all existent items and beings and must always be treated as ends in themselves. This principle implies respecting—even revering—the humanity in each human being.

3. "So act as if you were through your maxims a law-making member of a kingdom of ends." This final component incorporates the first two but brings morality even more into the public or social sphere. The idea that each person is rationally responsible to act morally from duty, in light of the requirements of reason and the special humanistic value (and "rights") of other people, suggests a human world in which each person is naturally a part of a *moral community of rational wills*—all governed and guided by mutually accepted universal, moral laws.

Kant's theories of knowledge and morality are united in their paradoxical reliance on, and independence of, reason. This mixed estimate of the value of reason threw modern philosophy into a tailspin and was the reason Kant belonged both to the Enlightenment and Counter-

Enlightenment traditions. His groundbreaking views on knowledge and morality were extraordinary attempts to create a philosophical framework in which philosophy, science, religion, and morality could coexist rationally. But the apparent tidiness of his remarkable result belies many philosophical problems that have had long, troubled histories not only in philosophy and science, but also—and even more dramatically—in politics. It's not an exaggeration to say that all philosophy after Kant was a reaction to his reconfiguration of the meaning of philosophy—that is, there was simply no way to think philosophically without having Kant in mind. A number of thinkers carried on the Kantian tradition, while others rejected Kant's overall system of thought in general but nevertheless employed important Kantian insights to create new philosophical universes. The great German philosopher Georg Wilhelm Hegel (1770–1831) belonged to the latter group and was among the first to uncover significant flaws in Kant's theories.

12.4

For Hegel, one of the most obvious problems was Kant's division of reality into "phenomena" (things-for-us) and "noumena" (things-in-themselves). If human beings are necessarily prevented access to things-in-themselves because of the limitations of their cognitive faculties, then how could we be sure that things-in-themselves exist in the first place? How could Kant speak so forcefully about the world that exists beyond all possible experience? An even more conspicuous problem with Kant's dual vision of reality was his argument that the phenomenal world of experience is *caused* by the noumenal one. But how could Kant hold this position, since he argued that cause and effect applies only to things-for-us and is *not* a feature of things-in-themselves? For Hegel, Kant's epistemological division of phenomena and noumena is a false dichotomy that can only be remedied by introducing a seamless conception of reality in which *what is real is rational, and what is rational is real.* There is no necessary separation between consciousness and ultimate reality. Kant was right in discovering that the world is formed and ordered by reason's categories, but he was mistaken in limiting the creative power of reason to the illusionary realm of things-in-themselves. A rational, holistic idea of reality, in which subject, object, mind, and reality are logically interconnected, makes more sense philosophically and takes philosophy into a radically new direction.

Consider what Hegel was saying. His basic premise was that *rationality is the meaning of reality*. This means that our rational understanding of experience (space and time or cause and effect, for instance) makes direct contact with ultimate reality, because ultimate reality, too, is rational. In this way, as long as we think rationally, we are automatically connected to, and in contact with, the truths of the world. For Hegel, once we correct Kant's epistemological error, then we can see what reality really is: *the ever-dynamic unfolding of rational truth in history*. Rationality, then, is not simply a human faculty; it is the essence of reality in which human reasoning is the crucial participant—its driving force, in fact. With Hegel's mind-blowing conflations of subject and object and philosophy and history, Kant's phenomena-noumena division is abolished.

History itself, for Hegel, is nothing more or less than *truth realizing itself* in the increasingly rational thoughts and actions of people, communities, institutions, states, countries, cultures, empires, and civilizations. Kant argued that the function of reason is to organize one's personal reality, but Hegel went far beyond this limited view of reason and saw it as the meaning of the entire cosmos itself: reality is mind realizing itself, step by logical step, moment by moment, day by day, year by year, century by century, and millennium by millennium, until mind comes to full rational awareness of itself. This "teleological"—goal-orientated—idea of mind realizing itself in history was the point of Hegel's massively complicated book *The Phenomenology of Mind*. In this work, Hegel showed all the historical stages that mind goes through on its way to complete and full self-understanding.

One of Hegel's novel conceptions was that the history of mind unfolds by way of *conflict resolution*. Each step along the way to total self-awareness contains within itself a sort of rational contradiction that requires resolution. And the history of every area of human culture contains conflicts that require resolution: philosophy, religion, art, politics and science, for example, represent the various failures and successes of mind confronting and resolving conflicts. Hegel argued that his own philosophy represents the resolution of conflicts that were inherent in Kant's thought, just as Kant's philosophy represented the resolution of conflicts that had existed in Hume's thought. All aspects of reality develop in this *dialectical* way. A crucial component of Hegel's system was that resolutions of conflicts automatically result in a higher synthesis of reason, in that each conflict that is resolved *transfers the truth of this resolution forward to subsequent steps*. This dialectical process of conflict resolution and the resulting advancement of truth continues unabated throughout historical time until the very end of history, when all conflicts are finally resolved, all truth is preserved, and a perfectly harmonized, universal idea blossoms radiantly into full being. History itself will then come to an end, as philosophy will have completed its cosmic mission of total, rational self-discovery!

As bizarre as many of Hegel's ideas were, many important thinkers were seduced by them. If Hegel's fantasy of a goal-oriented, conflict-resolving, historical process that leads ultimately to a utopian-like state sounds vaguely familiar, that is because a young German Hegelian named Karl Marx (1818–1883) took Hegel's ideas and methods of reasoning and refashioned them to construct his own philosophy. What was born out of Marx's remaking of Hegel's philosophy were Marx's own theories of socialism and communism. Marx's whole philosophy was Hegelian in reverse. Marx himself said that he "stood Hegel on his head." In his most influential books, *The Communist Manifesto* and *Das Kapital*, Marx put forth his new ideas. Marx's major innovation was to see reality not as the unfolding of nonmaterial mind but as an earthly, dialectical process in which the physical—"material"—requirements of survival and the economic forces that result move history forward until the very end of history. Marx argued that the physical needs of people determine the ever-changing political, social, and cultural events throughout historical time and that the driving force behind this process is *conflict resolution*. He called this conflict-orientated, historical process "dialectical materialism." He also argued that economic conditions were at the very center of historical change. Marx maintained, for instance, that the economic conflicts particular to feudalism (land-owning aristocracy that controlled the lifeblood of their disenfranchised serfs) led to capitalism (an employer-employee relationship in which employers own and control all equipment and materials, and employees work for a wage), and that the conflicts typical of capitalism will eventually be resolved and result in socialism (government ownership and control of goods and means of production), and finally the conflicts in socialism will be overcome in communism (collective ownership of all property and labor to the advantage of all)—the final stage of history, Marx's answer to Hegel's fully self-realized mind.

In keeping with Hegel's idea of history being a movement toward a higher synthesis of truth, Marx focused on the plight of the working class of society—the proletariat—in its struggle with the bourgeois—the people who own the resources and for whom the proletariat work. This relationship for Marx was one of "exploitation," in which the bourgeois use workers as mere instruments for the bourgeois' own material gain at the expense of the proletariat's economic, psychological, and spiritual well-being. According to Marx, the exploitation of the proletariat by the bourgeois was the conflict within capitalism that will eventually result in the overthrow of the capitalist form of society and result in a higher synthesis in the form of socialism; and socialism itself will ultimately be replaced by the conflict-free, final stage of history: communism.

Marx's ideas about the inevitability of communism not only turned out to be dead wrong, but in the twentieth century, they mutated into corrupt and brutal political ideologies (e.g., the Soviet Union and communist China) that led to the massacre of many millions of people. In the mid-twentieth century, the world was also brought to the brink of a nuclear nightmare because of misconceived Marxist strategies, and even today, at the beginning of the twenty-first century, modern versions of communism still threaten the safety of the civilized world. Clearly, the so-called communist developments in the twentieth and twenty-first centuries would have horrified the idealistic Marx, who was genuinely concerned with the spiritual health of the whole human race.

12.5

Kant's imposing legacy did not stop with Hegel and Marx. His ideas initiated other powerful traditions—one in particular was saturated through and through with even more Kantian ideas. At the beginning of 1820, the great Hegel began delivering a series of lectures at the University of Berlin to enthralled students. In another classroom at the same university, another philosophy professor began a series of lectures, but in this case, there were precious few students present to benefit from his tuition. Arthur Schopenhauer (1788–1860) had scheduled his lectures at the same time as those of Hegel, because he was determined to confront his philosophical nemesis head on and to try his best to undo the damage that he believed Hegelian ideas had wrought. Unfortunately, his scheduling strategy was a pitiful failure, and the university was forced to cancel his courses because of lack of student interest.

What was it about Hegel that Schopenhauer found so objectionable? Everything. Being a great admirer of Hume, he found Hegel's prose ridiculously abstract and confusing—in fact, incomprehensible. He also believed that Hegel's ideas were absurd. His opinion of Hegel the man was consistent with his opinion of Hegel's writing and ideas— he labeled him a "charlatan" and called him "inane, loathsome, and repulsive." For Schopenhauer, Hegel was a pseudo-philosopher who was more concerned with his professional standing within the German academic community than with intellectual integrity and truth.

Hegel's most serious crime, as far as Schopenhauer was concerned, was that he tried to undermine the most important breakthrough in modern thought: the philosophy of Kant. For him, Kant's division of reality into phenomena and noumena was a discovery second to none, and he believed that all genuine philosophy must begin with this fact. Building modern philosophy upon a Kantian foundation, however, does not mean that Kant discovered all of the answers. Far from it. Schopenhauer's own radical ideas, which themselves had a powerful impact on Western culture, were attempts to correct what he considered to be Kant's mistakes. In this sense, Schopenhauer believed that his philosophy was going to complete what Kant had started.

There is no question that human reality is *subject-dependent* in that the way human beings experience the world is necessarily conditioned by their limited perceptions and cognitive abilities. But "limited" doesn't mean that we can only experience a small portion of reality; it means that the specific ways that we experience reality are the *only* ways that we can experience reality. The world can only be seen in space and time and with cause and effect, for instance, because human faculties structure and order our experiences in terms of space and time and cause and effect. In Kantian terminology, the human faculties— forms of sensibilities and categories of understanding—are "the conditions for the possibility of experience." Kant's conclusion, which Schopenhauer fully endorsed, was that human beings are necessarily cut off from the way reality actually is—in other words, we *never*, under any circumstances, experience things-in-themselves—objective reality. Reality is always *structured* by human cognition.

In his attempt to outline what human beings can and cannot know, Kant uncovered a realm that heretofore had been hidden from philosophical awareness: the world of things-for-us—the subjective, phenomenal world. Here is where Schopenhauer set up his philosophical camp, and where he unpacked, piece by piece, a profoundly rich, even mysterious universe, one that even the incomparable Kant had failed to notice. Kant, in fact, made the same mistake that the father of modern philosophy, Descartes, had made over a hundred years before. After Descartes revealed the world of the *cogito*—"I think"— he became so preoccupied with deductively proving the existence of the outside world that he left the cogito far behind, along with all the essential truths that it contained. In a similar fashion, Kant failed to investigate fully and concretely the very place where knowledge is constructed: *subjectivity*. Kant's interest in subjectivity consisted mostly in manipulating abstract concepts and the logical connections between them to account for the necessary conditions for experience. For Schopenhauer, Kant's brilliant, analytical mind fell too much in love with abstract understanding of subjective experience and missed the *personal* and *concrete* basis for subjectivity. That Kant glossed over the essence of subjectivity follows naturally from his intense focus on concepts—for concepts express only general understanding and do not reflect what is particular, specific, or unique. Kant missed the critical insight that the *immediacy of particular experiences* is the very basis of the phenomenal world.

In his book *The World as Will and Representation*, Schopenhauer laid out his entire philosophy. According to Kant, we can know nothing about the noumenal world. Schopenhauer agreed with him only up to a point. To begin with, we certainly can know what the noumenal world *isn't*. For instance, the subjective, phenomenal world of human beings is made up of *things*—plural. But since plurality is a category of understanding created by human cognition, it could *not* be an aspect of the noumenal world. For Schopenhauer, this could only mean that the noumenal world, whatever else it is, must be *undifferentiated*—that is to say, one! He took Kant to task on this very point, for contradicting himself: Kant spoke of things-in-themselves, but what justification did

Kant have in speaking of *things* as a part noumenal reality? Did he not say that projecting subjective categories, such as plurality, onto the noumenal world is a metaphysical error? Using this sort of reverse reasoning, what else could we deduce about the noumenal world?

Schopenhauer pointed out another significant mistake of Kant's, one that Hegel had articulated first: the noumenal world could not be the source of the phenomenal world, as Kant argued, because source implies *causality*, and, again, causality is a category of understanding that cannot be found in the noumenal world. So what does this mean? That's easy—the noumenal world also has to be *cause-less*, and, in fact, without *purpose*. Schopenhauer went down the whole list of Kant's forms of sensibilities and categories of understanding and conducted his assessment of what the noumenal is *not*, in an effort to understand something of what it *is*. Essentially, his conclusion was that the noumenal reality is boundless, undifferentiated, uncaused, unconscious, impersonal, nonliving, purposeless, immaterial, without space or time, and totally indifferent. Schopenhauer wrestled with what to label his replacement for Kant's things-in-themselves and finally settled on what he called the "Will" (*wille*). The noumenal Will is the metaphysical ground for all that is and is embodied as much in a grain of sand as in the center of a star. But what is the noumenal Will's connection to the phenomenal world of human subjectivity?

Schopenhauer described the relationship between the phenomenal and noumenal realities not as a causal one, but as *two aspects* of the same, one reality. In other words, the aspects of the phenomenal world of human experience—its multiplicity, configurations, and causality; its spatial and temporal categories; its living, conscious, and personal components; its substance-character; and its limitations and purposes—are only cognitive *representations* of the noumenal world of the Will. Human reality, in other words, consists only of the various representations of Will—hence the title of his book, *World as Will and Representation*. The idea that two realities are "aspects" of one reality and not causally connected to each other was not new with Schopenhauer, but was used effectively by the great seventeenth-century rationalist and monist Benedict Spinoza, who argued that nature is God and human beings and that, in fact, all things are integral aspects or "modes" of nature and not in any way separate from it.

Schopenhauer was taken aback by an insight he had regarding the world of *material objects*. In accounting for the material world in phenomenal experience, Kant reduced it to the forms of sensibilities and to the categories of understanding, but Kant, once again, missed a crucial element: *each human body is itself a material object in experience*! This means that each person is intimately acquainted with, and knows, at least one material object *directly* and *from the inside*. This is a startling deduction. Schopenhauer admired science greatly, but he recognized the limitations of its empirical strategies and methods. And, of course, he believed in the profound value of philosophical thinking, even though he was fully aware of the many chances for philosophical error. The world is made up of material bodies that are understandable through scientific advances and typical philosophical investigation, but only up to a point. In our attempts to *conceptualize* the material world outside of us, we have been blinded as to the physical object that exists literally right underneath our very noses, and the one material object that our psycho-emotional being knows internally—our body. Schopenhauer concluded that our material bodies provide the opportunity for a sort of *inner knowing* that is qualitatively different from our normal efforts to understand the material world indirectly through abstract concepts or by looking *outward* to the general nature of experience. Moreover, our knowledge of physical objects similar to ours—like other people's bodies—and how and why they do what they do or say what they say is not based on our direct observation of their inner world—this is impossible. Rather, this knowledge derives from our own inner knowledge—that is, by seeing into their very being through the lenses of our own self-understanding and reflective self-awareness.

It's important to note, however, that this inner knowing is not equivalent to having direct knowledge of the noumenal will. Inner knowing is still a phenomenal experience to the extent that this understanding is always conditioned by our cognitive faculties. Knowing the material world from inside of our bodies may be *closer* to the noumnenal will, but it's not a pure experience of it.

Inner knowing consists of becoming aware through self-reflection of what is directly and concretely occurring at the precise moment of reflection. But Kant preferred to focus on abstract concepts like a priori knowledge and determine logically how abstract concepts relate, for example, to the conditions for the possibility of knowledge. While Schopenhauer believed that Kant's thinking represented the major turning point in modern philosophy, he concluded that there is much that this profound thinker missed, namely: *what is present in direct and concrete experience.* Particularly, Kant failed to investigate fully the very realm that he helped to establish, the transcendental dimension— that is, the realm in which *how we experience* the world and *what we experience* is assembled. For Schopenhauer, this realm must include the material body itself, since all thoughts, sensations, and feelings occur within its physical contours, and the transcendental dimension itself performs its creative processes within this fleshy and bony item that exists in space and time.

But there is another awesome implication in the idea that the human body is an individualized material object: if each person is housed in a physical body, then this must mean that from the perspective of noumenal reality, each person is *not* only an individuated, material object, but is also an immaterial, timeless, and undifferentiated aspect of the one. Here Schopenhauer inadvertently stumbled onto what many have considered a quasi-mystical or Hindu/Buddhist—like formulation of human existence and reality. Various philosophical and mystical traditions in both the Western and Eastern worlds have viewed human beings, and material existence in general, as *particularized* manifestations of a primordial oneness. The natural implication of this worldview is that all human beings—and all things, in fact—in their metaphysical essence are a seamless one.

It is fascinating to consider that Schopenhauer came to this metaphysical insight not through studying non-Western spirituality, meditation, or other mystical rituals, but by thinking through, reformulating, and elaborating on the long-standing themes of the great Western philosophical tradition. Beginning with the pre-Socratics and Plato, and continuing down the ages with Augustine, Descartes, Spinoza, Leibniz, Locke, Berkeley, Hume, and finally culminating with Kant, it is easy to trace the philosophical thread that led to Schopenhauer's amazing conclusions. (Actually, at the very beginning of the Western philosophical tradition, the pre-Socratic philosopher Parmenides also believed in the fundamental oneness of ultimate reality, which he thought was *fire*.)

When Schopenhauer finally learned about Eastern thought, it pleased him to no end that his own philosophical conclusions found deep resonance in a world he knew nothing about at the time of his original formulations. But there are major differences between traditional mystical ideas of the oneness of ultimate reality and what Schopenhauer believed. Many mystical traditions, for instance, posit some sort of universal *Mind* or *Consciousness* as constituting ultimate reality, and human beings and all particular things in existence as being individualized manifestations of this primal Mind. This Mind is usually viewed as having a purposeful and cosmic intelligence, as well as possessing a moral component with which human beings are connected. For instance, Buddhism holds that by overcoming negative karma (karma is moral cause and effect) over the course of many lifetimes, the truly enlightened person can shed his or her individual being, and accompanying material body, and become reabsorbed back into the primal Mind. The eventual return of all individual beings to metaphysical oneness, in fact, is a basic spiritual principle of Buddhism. For Schopenhauer, the idea of Mind or God, as well as any idea of purpose, intelligence, or morality, is only a phenomenal manifestation and could have no reality in the noumenal world. In short, there can be no Mind—cosmic or not—because the very idea of Mind, and the qualities typically attributed to it, are based upon phenomenal definitions and descriptions, which have no meaning in the ultimate reality of the noumena. Schopenhauer's noumenal reality, then, is *before* both Mind and material reality and, as such, can have no resemblance to anything in the phenomenal world. To sound a familiar mantra, Schopenhauer believed that the noumenal Will is a nonliving, purposeless, uncaused, immaterial, and *nonconscious* drive that is manifested in the phenomenal world. Let's now investigate another of Schopenhauer's metaphysical insights.

For Schopenhauer, *compassion* is the source of morality; he did not believe in Kant's theory of a universal, reason-based moral system. But what is compassion, anyway? Why do we "feel for" or "suffer with" another person? Indeed, quite often a total stranger? According to Schopenhauer's theory, and again consistent with mystical traditions, the *other* is not really a separate person at all is but really *you* in disguise, as it were. You are recognizing yourself intuitively when you look into the eyes of another person. All human beings, in other words, absent their isolating egos and physical bodies, are noumenally one. In this sense, treating a perfect stranger with kindness is actually treating yourself with kindness, but without your conscious awareness of it. The belief that compassion is the basis for morality found rational support in Schopenhauer's philosophical system and provided renewed credibility for the long-standing tradition of marrying morality with metaphysics.

So what do we find when we look deeply within this material object that is our bodies? Thoughts, memories, feelings, sensations, impulses, desires, and fantasies—real items that are constantly available to us in subjective experience. It is remarkable to think that these incontestable realities cannot be discovered by simply observing them in other physical bodies. This insight alone should give the true philosopher or scientist great pause, for here are undeniable facts of reality that are literally invisible to the usual approaches and methods of philosophy and science.

Despite the vast inner universe that opens up once we begin to focus our philosophical attention on the material object that is our body, there is much that remains hidden. For Schopenhauer, there are certain ideas and desires that will forever remain concealed from reflective view and in fact are actively repressed because they are incompatible with our conscious beliefs of what is right and wrong and decent and indecent. For example, irrational and indecent sexual impulses and violent urges that are intensely loathsome to our normal sensibilities must be psychologically pushed below conscious awareness—that is, they must be repressed so that they never surface and intrude upon our normal ways of thinking and behaving.

These startling observations force us to credit Schopenhauer with being the original discoverer of the modern idea of the unconscious mind, as well as being the first person to define, and give ample examples of, repression. As we know, these concepts have had a rich history in the work of many subsequent thinkers, such as with the father of psychoanalysis, Sigmund Freud (1856–1939), whose whole theory of psychodynamics was based on the notions of the unconscious mind and repression. Although Freud has fallen out of favor with many professional psychologists and scientists, few would argue that the unconscious mind and repression are not real aspects of human psychology.

Schopenhauer's idea of the unconscious mind, in fact, was the culmination of a long tradition in which the idea gradually took shape. The first concrete installment of the idea of an unconsciousness-like reality began in ancient Greece in the fourth century with Plato's theory that all things that exist in the physical world—including notions of beauty, goodness, and truth—are imperfect representations, *ideal forms*, that exist invisibly in a transcendent world somewhere. In the early seventeenth century, René Descartes divided the world into "thinking things" and "extended things," the former being the realm of *subjective* experience and the latter being the outside or *objective* world of material/physical things. With Descartes' idea of subjectivity, as distinct from objectivity, we can see the *thinking and knowing* component of human reality being further isolated, circumscribed, and explored. This development represented the birth of epistemology— the study of how we know what we know—and the birth of the transcendental realm—where the conditions for knowledge are defined. In the modern era, John Locke and David Hume further directed the philosophical gaze to the inner world of the tabula rasa, in Locke's case, and to the psychological realm of unconscious habitual thinking, in Hume's case. It was Kant's idea of a noumenal reality that exists forever outside of phenomenal experience, but nonetheless provides the raw stuff of experience, that really set the philosophical stage for the final installment of the modern idea of the unconscious mind: that there are *inaccessible* levels of the human mind that contain irrational ideas, impulses, and cravings that influence how and what we think and feel and even guide how we behave—all outside of our conscious awareness. This final formulation goes to Schopenhauer.

Despite the psychological barriers that we inevitably meet in reflecting on the inner world of our physical bodies, there is something there of monumental importance that is knowable, the discovery of which was, for Schopenhauer, a critical key in his goal of unraveling the mysteries of human existence. Amid the various thoughts, beliefs, sensations, and impulses that are constantly circulating through our body's inner world, one desire in particular rises most forcefully from the deepest recesses of our very being: the *boundless desire to be*, to exist, to live. In discovering within one's own body the intense desire to be, Schopenhauer believed that he uncovered the most powerful force in the phenomenal world: *the desire to live is a blind and insatiable urge to procreate without limit.*

The net result of this excessive and unquenchable force in nature is that all life is forever frustrated, unfulfilled, distressed, and dissatisfied. In Schopenhauer's view, life is inherently miserable, because it is always being tortured by the ever-restless desire in existence to procreate beyond proportion. To make matters worse, this wicked, natural desire uses trickery of various kinds to achieve its ends. For example, the allure of *love* is one of nature's favorite devices for manipulating unsuspecting people into procreation. In this case, the desire to live manipulates the emotions and minds of two people who are in love and makes them feel and think that their love will last forever and that their sexual passion for each other will never diminish. The disconcerting truth is that nature has duped both individuals into believing lies about love so that they will have sexual relations, promote the life of the species, and satisfy the noumenal Will. The proof is that the initial love and passion that the lovers had for each other begins a slow and painful death and ultimately leaves both people emotionally distraught and heartbroken, often desperate. Many ex-lovers ultimately become very angry at each other, and some exceptionally depressed lovers even commit suicide. So powerful is this drive that even the noblest and most advanced intellects are routinely seduced by the ruses of the will to live and procreate.

But nature couldn't care less, because it got what it wanted: sexual intercourse. And even when individuals act on the urge to procreate, the urge still knows no satisfaction and ends up frustrating and annoying all participants, increasing their stress levels just the same. Living is a no-win situation, because the urge to be can never be truly satisfied, and all attempts to do so end in negative emotions such as frustration, boredom, or misery. And any joy or happiness is either an extreme act of self-deception or, at best, is short lived. This decidedly pessimistic spirit is captured well in one of Schopenhauer's pungent aphorisms: "Never a rose without a thorn but many a thorn without a rose." In the final analysis, despite any happiness that you think that you are experiencing, you can be sure that it won't last, lest you forget that death is always right around the corner and will soon snatch you heartlessly right out of existence The phenomenal world, for Schopenhauer, is an illusion that beguiles all life into participating in it solely for the purpose of satisfying its insatiable desire to be and to procreate. The harsh truth of existence is difficult to confront: life on the phenomenal plane is *nothingness*—literally empty, without content and meaning and with nothing to offer but false promises and expectations, continual disappointment, suffering, and frustration. And at the end, the payoff is even worse: senseless death.

In arguing that the irrational, ruthless desire to be controls the living world, Schopenhauer painted himself into a pessimistic corner that left him with only a couple of options for existential relief and salvation. One was great *art*. Unlike Kant, who reduced art to disinterested pleasure—pleasure not from desire or utility but solely from what we experience as beautiful and for which there is no real purpose—Schopenhauer saw art as useful and as a profound source of truth and relief. Architecture, painting, sculpture, and great literature were for Schopenhauer ways of knowing reality that are more genuine than logical and scientific reasoning. Art captures what is particular and unique, whereas conceptual and logical understanding, while extremely important, can only grasp what is general and typical. Art also can disclose a special dimension of experience that is alien to other forms of understanding: the mysterious. There is a deep mystery to life that escapes logical and mathematical descriptions but is very present in great buildings, paintings, sculpture, and literature. Although representational art is incapable of arriving at unadorned noumenal reality, it definitely comes closer to *what is* than logical and conceptual reasoning. And then there is music.

Schopenhauer placed music in an epistemological category all its own. He viewed music as being the direct manifestation of noumenal reality and actually closer to noumenal reality than other representations in phenomenal reality. This means that music is not expressed *through* the phenomenal world but is a direct emanation *from* the noumenal world. What is distinctive about music is that it is nonrepresentational and abstract—that is, it says nothing about the phenomenal world but reflects a world all its own. It is for these reasons that music comes closest to being the actual *voice of the Will*. And this is why it has such a mystifying effect on the listener. Music is able to strike a resonant chord within the noumenal essence of the human heart. Music in this way is a sort of *phenomenal overture* to the Will that can transport the listener into a quasi-noumenal world of monistic ecstasy.

It is for these reasons that music and all the arts are avenues of escape from the relentless desire to live. When one is caught up in the glory of great art, the desire to live, the desire for sexual relief, is short-circuited, so to speak, and loses its grip on the heart and mind of the individual—at least for the moment. We all know the delightful experience of being so enraptured with the presence of what we see as beautiful that a warm, harmonious calm comes over us, and we feel strangely fulfilled. But this respite is always of short duration, because we can only be enthralled for so long before our normal desire-based consciousness returns, causing the desire to be and all that comes with it to begin imposing its overwhelming power on its unsuspecting victims. But there is a more effective and long-lasting antidote to the misery caused by the desire to live: *total renunciation*.

For Schopenhauer, the only permanent escape from the torturous desire to live, and all its negative trappings, is by severing all contact with the phenomenal world to the point where we are no longer seduced by its empty promises and counterfeit means of gratification. This solution is hardly original with Schopenhauer, but it is essentially the same route the great mystics and saints have taken in the religions of the West and East. Meditation, fasting, and abstinence of various kinds have been successfully employed to break free of the powerful grip of the desires of appetites, which is rooted in our desire to be. Even the focused contemplation of the eventuality of death could serve to neutralize the desire to be and could produce serenity in one's life.

The world is a horrible place—of that there can be no doubt—but it's also the grand theater of heroic action for those spirits who are able to wake up from their phenomenal nightmare, confront their misery honestly, and transform themselves into truly sovereign beings. Suicide as an option is, for Schopenhauer, a "mistake," but it is certainly understandable, and definitely is not a crime. Suicide is cowardly, and—as an act that terminates the flow of philosophical insights into the mind of the person who commits it—it's unacceptable to Schopenhauer. Besides, what do we know about suicide, anyway? It may turn out to be the most unfortunate action of all! It's better to remain stoically defiant and renounce it, rather than to run away from life with our tails between our legs. Suicide is a moral weakness in the face of existence and causes a person to forfeit any chance of living a self-sufficient, noble, and illusion-free life. This idea of how a human being ought to live is, one might say, Schopenhauer's version of existential authenticity.

Schopenhauer's extreme pessimism has inspired either profound contempt or profuse admiration from different people. While some critics have seen his pessimism as the expression of an unbalanced, even perverse mind, others have admired not only his intellectual genius but also his moral and philosophical courage to face what he considered to be the hard facts about reality. Schopenhauer—his ideas as well as his Spartan character—has had a profound influence on Western culture—from inspiring Richard Wagner's greatest opera, *Tristan und Isolde*, to educating many exceptional minds, most notably another philosophical prodigy, Friedrich Nietzsche. But let's not forget other famous beneficiaries of his tuition, such as Darwin, Freud, Jung, and Wittgenstein (the father of "language philosophy"). There are many, many more.

Schopenhauer is a very intimate philosopher, and in reading him you sometimes feel as though he is whispering profound secrets in your ear; without a doubt, he tapped into a rich level of understanding that the honest thinker must take seriously. Schopenhauer's ideas are both fascinating and very disturbing, and it's up to each thinker to decide for him or herself what to make of them. There are always deep insights to be culled from the work of all cultural geniuses. With a radical thinker like Schopenhauer, we have to be especially attentive to our negative reactions to him and make sure that we are not simply fleeing intellectually and morally from ideas that we find too painful to bear. But even when we genuinely disagree with this inconsolable pessimist, his fervent commitment to truth and the countless philosophical and psychological gems that he unearthed can still serve as vital catalysts for our own self-transformation. He was that kind of thinker.

13

The Counter-Enlightenment, the Postmodern, and Meaning-Forms

13.1

Schopenhauer's philosophy is an amazing example of how a great philosopher's thought can fertilize another's and produce an abundance of novel ideas. Without Kant, Schopenhauer would not have been possible. We could go even further and suggest that without Kant, all of modern philosophy would not have been possible. Indeed, all philosophy after Kant was a reaction to his system—some thinkers accepted it fully, others rejected it totally, but in most cases, philosophers accepted certain aspects of it and rejected others. Whatever the case might be, Kant's presence was and still is overwhelming. Even modern philosophy of language contains essential Kantian themes that have been modified and redirected. A prime example is the common notion in modern philosophy that language refers only to itself and has no genuine association to so-called reality; as a result, philosophy's only legitimate concern should be the analysis of language structure and meaning clarification, especially in the service of science. But what this view presupposes is the Kantian idea that reality could never be an object of investigation, since human cognition is necessarily limited to the phenomenal world. Language is a phenomenal reality and is a genuine source of philosophical meaning, so we are justified in studying it.

A few sections back, we spoke about the Heisenberg uncertainty principle and the basic idea that there is a necessary limit to what we can know about atomic and subatomic reality. In philosophy, a similar situation unfolded with the emergence of Kantian philosophy. Kant rightly belongs to both the Enlightenment and Counter-Enlightenment traditions, because he simultaneously recreated philosophy and reinforced the basis for physical science—and, ironically, also compromised both. Kant was a powerful advocate of reason, logic, science, nonrelative law, and universal, reason-based principles of morality. In this sense, he carried the Enlightenment torch for progress through reason into new territories. But the price he had to pay was to limit the reach of reason so radically that the pursuit of truth really became a futile endeavor. What does this mean?

As we noted, Kant's division of the world into phenomena and noumena meant that the noumenal reality is forever out of reach because of the limits of human cognition. The noumena, in other words, could never be an object of possible experience. But do you realize what this means to the very soul of philosophy and science? The pursuit of philosophical and scientific knowledge has always had a quasi-spiritual component, if not actually been propelled by a clear religious motive. The allure of discovering the truth has both enchanted and galvanized the imagination of truth seekers and has sent countless disciples down the difficult road of discovery, disciples who often sacrificed their whole lives and sometimes even jeopardized life and limb for their pursuit of philosophical or scientific truth. But from one Kantian perspective, these sacrifices were all for nothing, because the most one could ever discover is philosophical or scientific knowledge about phenomenal reality, which is not *the truth* about reality—real truth only exists in the noumenal world.

The impact of Kant's idea that ultimate reality is forever beyond human comprehension has been so enormous that new cultural orientations have been created in its wake. The birth of romanticism in the eighteenth and nineteenth centuries, for example, was a direct result of a Kantian worldview (with help from Rousseau). Romanticism was a powerful, reactive cultural movement that affected every area of Western culture and emphasized emotion and instinct over reason, stressed freedom from restraint and limits, and promoted overindulgence in the passionate, the spontaneous, the exotic, and the flamboyant. It was both a philosophical and existential movement *from the objective to the subjective*, where what is real and valuable is grounded in subjective judgments alone, with little regard for the Enlightenment ideals of objective truth, the progress of logical reasoning, and universal principles of any kind. Romanticism was a Counter-Enlightenment movement, and Kant's banishment of objective reality from philosophy and science was the road upon which it traveled.

The effect of Kant on modern culture was subtler than the garish colors of romanticism might indicate. We already saw Schopenhauer arguing that great art has a cognitive dimension—that we can know more deeply about reality through the experience of art, particularly music. But the loss of the rational faculty as a reliable vehicle to ultimate truth also meant that perhaps emotions, passions, instincts, moods, intuitions, or gut-level feelings could be ways to transcend the limits of reason and arrive at a genuine understanding of reality. This model, in fact, was to become a standard strategy for many truth seekers in the Kantian universe. Because of the dominance of Kantian themes, emotion-based philosophizing became a significant force in modern thought, art, and literature. The development of existential thought in the twentieth century, with its emphasis on primal feelings and emotional states of mind as ways of knowing, was also given a tremendous cultural push by the loss of the belief in overarching truths that could guide the rational mind to objective truth and authentic understanding. And the very modern idea of viewing experience from multiple perspectives, without any single perspective being the "right" one, is a natural extension of the loss of objective reality in Kant's shrunken universe.

The most startling consequence of the Counter-Enlightenment's war against the unquestioned belief in the unlimited power of reason and science was not romanticism, however, but the emergence of postmodernism in the late twentieth century. Modernism was the reason and science-based worldview of the Enlightenment thinkers. By stark contrast, postmodernism—as a vision of reality, as a method of philosophical investigation, as a way of designing architecture, as way of creating and judging art, as a way of reading and understanding texts, and as a way of understanding the meaning of culture and history in general—sought to undermine, in the most philosophically subversive ways, everything that modernism represented. In his book *The Postmodern Condition* (1979), postmodern thinker Jean-Francois Lyotard (1924–1998) put forth the view that present history has lost all coherence and that the traditional "meta-narratives," such as religion, humanism, liberal democracy, capitalism, the free market, and traditional philosophy, no longer determine or guide the course of history or the dynamics of culture. Modern civilization, then, is not bound to its *universal stories*, its noble goals, its long-standing traditions, its unifying visions, and its stable cultural paradigms. Instead, modern society is more and more organized around *subcultures* (e.g., feminism and homosexuality) and the ideologies, myths, value systems, and philosophies that spring from them. Moreover, these developments are always in flux and could change drastically with social or political shifts or even with scientific breakthroughs. And this is only the mild side of postmodernism.

Along with Lyotard, other contemporary postmodernists like Jacques Derrida (1930–2004), Richard Rorty (1931–), and Jean Baudrillard (1929–) set out to decimate all Enlightenment ideals and understand the world within the context of modern pop cultures, consumerism, and general cultural uncertainty and chaos. Ambiguity, irrationality, irony, instability, relativism, fragmentation, meaninglessness, and skepticism gained an unprecedented level of respect and credibility with these thinkers. Here is a list of the various postmodern positions:

- There are no ultimate or objective truths.
- Rational descriptions of reality do not lead to deep understanding.
- The idea of ultimate reality is meaningless and absurd.
- Emotions, feelings, and passions disclose more about reality than reason
- Meanings are always conventional and are fabricated by power interests and ideologies.
- Ambiguity is a more authentic mindset than so-called clear thinking.
- The negative is more meaningful than what is positive.
- Thinking that is fragmented is preferred over coherent thinking, because it is a better reflection of how the world is constructed.
- Any notion of a stable identity or a self is an illusion.
- Reality is a social construct that never has any stability, ultimate meaning, or objective significance.

- There is no truth; only relative, subjective perspectives that are based on personal agendas, fluctuating social and power forces, and conventions.
- Language does not reflect so-called reality, but is subservient to social conventions, often rooted in power interests, and the ever-changing cultural rules and principles of the year, day, or hour.
- Crass, lowbrow language and speech, including slang and vulgarity, has more meaning than proper, well written, and spoken language; science and technology are the tools of the elite and power brokers and are used for brainwashing and social control.
- There is no such thing as "progress," only chaotic movements in various directions.
- Written texts and, in fact, anything that is presented as coherent or meaningful, are always ambiguous and always contain conflicting meanings, hidden biases and agendas, and secret ideologies.
- There is no longer any meaningful distinction between high culture and pop culture—both are equally conventional and valuable or valueless. And besides, all cultural expression has been trivialized by crass commercialism and outlandish consumerism.
- "Multiculturalism" is now the only legitimate sociopolitical viewpoint, because all cultural values are, at bottom, of equal worth.

The idea of there being a superior way to think, live, and behave reflects arrogant, power-hungry prejudices that have no place in contemporary society. Even our aesthetic and moral sensibilities are fraught with culturally blind stupidities. From the postmodern perspective, a fat, un-muscled body that has been literally tattooed from head to foot is just as beautiful as Michelangelo's *David*. And why? Because beauty, like any other aesthetic quality, is also an empty idea and reflects only cultural prejudices and ever-shifting frames of reference. Overly moralistic value judgments are also rich sources of misguided and dangerous ideas. Adolph Hitler, Joseph Stalin, and Saddam Hussein, for example, are not really evil men but are the poor victims of an unfavorable upbringing and the misguided sociopolitical events of their times. Sexual/gender distinctions are arbitrary and reflect male-dominated agendas; they have little to do with the nature of sexuality. An astute postmodern citizen knows that absolute judgments of "right and wrong" or "good and evil" must be avoided, because they are nothing but "binary concepts" that reflect the limitations of our conventional ways of thinking, rather than describing anything morally true about people.

The postmodern mentality is the most extreme, but nonetheless logical, extension of the Counter-Enlightenment trends. And the one person who prepared the soil for this strange plant to grow was none other than our great genius Immanuel Kant. The reason is clear: without even the possibility of making contact with an absolute reality, how does one know how, or where, to stand philosophically? Or how to behave? Or how to live? What is beautiful or pleasing? How does one know right from wrong? It all appears to be arbitrary and, at best, unstable. And besides, what good is an interest in truth, anyway, if there is no hope of ever knowing any aspect of it?

Ideas and beliefs are not just invisible playthings of philosophers and scientists: they precede and produce actions, actions that guide the human world. But it's not only individuals who have ideas and beliefs; societies, cultures, and even whole civilizations have guiding ideas and beliefs that mobilize the action of their citizens. What is human history if not the history of ideas: how they emerge and change, how they interact, unite, and break apart, and how they determine the events and course of history? It is for this reason that philosophy—the love and study of ideas—is the most dominant force in human history, with both good (liberal democracy) and bad (Marxism) results.

The more powerful the idea, the more deeply it circulates through the collective mind of humanity and remains there in one form or another. And if a powerful idea is abstract and theoretical, rarely will it remain at that level, but it will eventually re-enter the concrete world of everyday life in the most inconspicuous ways. This is true with Kant, as it was also true of Plato, whose theory of forms (the idea there is a perfect but invisible realm from which all that we see is imperfectly copied) has had numerous incarnations over the centuries in our various religious and philosophical traditions. Kant's powerful ideas are extremely abstract and are not an easy diet for public consumption. In fact, few people outside the worlds of philosophy or academia know anything about this astounding genius or his ideas. And besides, it's hard to imagine that there could be any link between this seventeenth-century German super-intellectual and the bustling life of the modern world. Yet his work in abstract philosophy has entered the consciousness of the modern world and has profoundly informed it in countless ways, with both good and bad results. We need only think of the deep influence that Freud has had on the modern world, with his theory of sexuality or his explosive ideas about the unconscious mind, which have impacted all areas of modern culture, from our educational systems to our over-sexualized pop culture. Without Kant's idea that the material, phenomenal world is all that the rational mind could ever know, and that the noumenal world is permanently *hidden* from human understanding, Schopenhauer would not have discovered the unconscious mind and other key psychological mechanisms like repression and sexual motivations. When Freud developed his theories, Schopenhauer's ideas were "in the air," as were similar ideas from other thinkers such as Nietzsche, who was also greatly influenced by Schopenhauer. Without Kant's philosophy, it's clear that Freud's most important ideas and theories would never have seen the light of day. This is just one of many examples of how Kant's ideas have fertilized the thinking of others over the past three hundred years, and indirectly have led to new, unexpected insights and discoveries.

Kant argued that the rational mind could never make contact with objective reality. This idea could easily suggest that reality, being forever unreachable, is subject to anyone's interpretation, that reality is "up for grabs," as it were. Kant's negative view of the potential of rational thought to know ultimate reality also leaves open the possibility of their being *non-rational* ways to arrive at reality. It's fascinating that both worldviews have materialized and are flourishing in modern pop culture, as evidenced by popular slogans of the "create your own reality" variety. Many of the most successful books that are published today, for instance, are those which offer techniques and strategies that show each person how to bend reality in accordance with his or her own wishes, desires, and even fantasies. But what is the nature of reality *in itself* if it is potentially subject to the whims and passions of each and every person? This is a perfectly reasonable question to ask, and it's one that is Kantian through and through.

Certain liberal views that are being taught in our top educational systems advocate extreme multiculturalism and the "do not judge!" cultural-equivalence ideology. This development could also be understood against a Kantian backdrop, where the guiding light of objective reality has been virtually extinguished, and along with it, objective standards of truth, knowledge, and morality.

The explosion of irrationalism, anti-intellectualism, and philosophical emotionalism in modern pop culture and in our universities must be seen as part of the Kantian legacy. And yet how many people who subscribe to the create your own reality ideology or the philosophy of multiculturism know the origins of their fervently held beliefs?

The association of unfortunate, modern cultural trends with Kantianism would undoubtedly have horrified Kant. After all, didn't he argue in his categorical imperative, for instance, that moral acts must rest on reason-based, universalized principles? Yes, but this idea is not an emotionally powerful one, especially in comparison with his highly sensational and provocative argument against the possibility of making rational contact with objective reality. That his views in favor of a reason-based morality have not captured the popular imagination also suggests that it's difficult to understand in simple, unambiguous terms how there can be universal principles of any kind without the benefit of having a rationally comprehensible, objective reality as a frame of reference. In other words, how could universally rational principles not necessarily imply an objective source independent of subjective experience with which we have rational contact? There are reasonable answers to these sorts of conundrums, but it's all very confusing without a great deal of mind-taxing explanation.

Without a doubt, Kant pulled the philosophical rug out from under Western culture, and sent it down the bumpy road to postmodernism and to the most bizarre forms of philosophical nihilism, where almost anything could be seen as possible within philosophy, morality, and politics. And with postmodernism, all possible alternatives have been, and are still being, explored. If Kant has sent Western civilization into an intellectual and, by extension, existential free-fall, where will it all ultimately lead? Does it depend on whether or not Kant was right? First, let's not forget that he could be wrong, after all, and that philosophical and scientific reasoning are, in fact, in direct contact with realities that are independent of human subjectivity. Certainly many physicists believe this to be true.

But if Kant was right, and reality is necessarily subject-dependent, does this automatically mean that we are condemned to the topsy-turvy world of postmodernism? This question is philosophy's greatest challenge, and one that needs to be met head on without relapsing into the naïve optimism that characterized the eighteenth-century Enlightenment thinkers. A number of current quasi-scientific/philosophical schools of thought that go under the banners of "objectivism" and "secular humanism" are guilty of this mistake. They promote scientific thought and the belief in reason as though Kant had never existed. In fact, many of their most vocal advocates and defenders know virtually nothing of his work or have little understanding of him, and still others who have some awareness of Kant's ideas quite frankly have scant interest in genuinely exploring them. But unless Kant is confronted and either defeated or reconfigured, the noble aim of philosophy and science to understand the true nature of the world cannot be taken seriously. This challenge has been taken up heroically by Nietzsche and others, and it continues today.

Of course, Kant would argue earnestly that a fundamental misunderstanding has corrupted his philosophy—namely, that the phenomenal world is *false*. He would maintain that because the phenomenal world is all that the rational mind could ever know, we are justified in calling the knowledge that we discover there *truth*. In this view, scientists definitely accumulate knowledge about the universe—for instance; Einstein's theories of relativity solved real problems in physics involving space, time, matter, energy, and gravity; quantum physics really did discover that *probability* rules the atomic and subatomic realms; and Darwin's theory of evolution is, in fact, an accurate description and explanation of the development of life on the earth. For many sincere truth seekers, however, this simply won't do. They understand that from a Kantian perspective, all the scientific knowledge in the world only adds up to various configurations of phenomenal knowledge and not noumenal truth. Ultimate truth is what the human spirit craves—not subjective truth, not inter-subjective truth (agreement between people), not phenomenal truth; the human spirit craves truth that is the exact, complete, unchanging, and timeless expression of *what is*!

13.2

What is the invariant item of experience that is present, independent of perspective? Is the invariant item a meaning or a form of physical reality? All experience presupposes a bare necessity, a *ground of meaning*, which is that with respect to which all meanings are related.

13.3

The items of animals' interest are either "ends in themselves" or directly connected to them. In their movements from here to there, they do stop to "smell the roses," but they never do so to find "happiness in the moment" or to justify their very existence.

13.4

Language is possible only for beings for which meaning is the existential fabric of existence.

13.5

Language is a particularly human response to the invasion of freely floating, disembodied meaning-forms.

13.6

Human perception and cognition do not create the items of experience but rather transfer meaning to them with respect to pre-established cultural and natural frames of meaning, and by rare moments of spontaneous recreations.

13.7

We don't experience physical items as sheer material, matter, or energy—or even as units of stimuli; rather, the world always comes to us in meaning-forms, however fragmented, shocking, or confusing.

13.8

Meaning has the same ontological status as a dream. A dream has at least the same intensity of presence as a typical waking experience— the difference is that the meaning-forms in dreams are not connected to the objects, actions, or happenings in the real world, but reside only in fantasy, dissipating—sometimes slowly and at other times quickly— in both intensity and content upon waking.

13.9

The meaning of something is the *perceptual or conceptual aura* that exists around and through a physical or mental item and is not the item itself.

13.10

Nothing—the absence of some thing, idea, or meaning.

13.11

Nothingness—the all-encompassing presence of an absence, void, or vacuum—a cosmic no.

13.12

Fantasies are "thing-less meanings." With the underdeveloped or unbalanced mind, meanings typically remain on the fantasy level and have not "connected up" in a complete or consistent way with items, actions, and happenings in the outside world.

13.13

Thinking and culture mutually create and support each other. In fact, they make each other possible. Thinking requires the input of culture to supply meaning-forms as the content of thinking. Culture needs the creative work of thinking to define, clarify, and harmonize preexisting meaning-forms as well as to introduce new ones.

13.14

The great task of thinking is to guide the bio-ontological shift through the excesses and passions of the imagination, in order to find our ultimate sanctuary in the un-shifting land of understanding—our new dwelling, our new nature.

13.15

The full meaning of thinking evades scientific understanding for the following reason: although brain scientists are able to measure, quantify, and analyze the biochemical/electrical properties of the brain during thinking, as well as describe what occurs in brain activity during specific mental states such as dreaming and emoting, they are unable to answer a critical question: do brain processes strictly *cause* meaning-states, accompany them, or simply express them? Is it possible that brain activity is a necessary but insufficient condition for experience? That *nonphysical,* experiential meanings like fear, joy, and sexual arousal can alter the biochemistry of the brain—that is, affect *physical* states—

forces scientists to reconsider the simplistic idea that the brain action strictly and always *causes* thinking. It's clear that the so-called causal relation between brain action and thinking is, at minimum, a two-way street. But the very nature of psychological causality itself needs to be reconsidered, for it is obvious that the typical mechanistic model is simply not adequate. Although the unexpected world that quantum physics revealed can shed little light on this problem, it has nonetheless pointed to an important fact: there are areas and levels of reality that require counterintuitive methods of thinking and investigation and possess new kinds of understanding that make little sense from a commonsensical or even a typically scientific point of view. Thinking and brain action have interconnections that, at present, transcend our current level of philosophical and scientific understanding. It's likely the truth of the relationship between the brain and mind resides in ideas and theories that, at present, are seen as scientifically and philosophically improbable or ever absurd.

13.16

Language plays a crucial role in the thinking process, but thinking cannot be reduced to language. There is much in thought that is beyond the philosophical and organizational reach of language. Language is a visual, aural, and verbal system of symbols and sounds that is arranged and structured in typically rational ways to communicate ideas, feelings, states of mind, attitudes, and intentions—in this sense, language can be reduced to thinking. But language hides an infinitely complex world of pre-language, quasi-conscious states that is available to each person only obliquely as a jumbled blend of reason, non-reason, and emotion. Language, then, is an emergent property of mental and emotional dynamics, of which we are only partially aware.

13.17

The content of subconscious thinking is so complex and disorderly that, in itself, it is of little use for normal, day-to-day, conscious awareness. Language is the great invisible bridge that carries thought from unconscious confusion and darkness to conscious clarity and light.

13.18

Language is the sine qua non—the essential aspect—of culture; language is projected onto, and installed into, the cultural fabric and is absorbed directly into human nature. And this is why the world has an ineradicable linguistic character to it.

13.19

Language orders, integrates, and simplifies human experience; where language falls into disarray, there follows the deterioration of harmony and stability in all areas of human life.

13.20

Language is both the glue and grease of human reality, continually holding together its contents while freeing the mind to open and explore new frontiers.

13.21

Thoughts are stable and durable meaning-forms that circulate throughout cultural, linguistic life, spreading either health or sickness.

13.22

Which qualities and states of being should we strive to cultivate in ourselves and in others? Physical health; psychological balance; self-esteem; a lust for life; audacity; a sense of humor; an instinct for uproarious laughter, a smiling face; happy eyes; relaxed lips; spontaneous emotion; erect posture; energetic movements; the strength for self-exposing vulnerability; curiosity in the face of the mystery of existence; passion for truth; enjoyment in learning; care for animals; a love for art; talent in a sport; a feel for music and dance; skill in clever repartee; comfort in another's personal space; kindness of heart; courage; fondness for affectionate touching and kissing; an aptitude for free and agile expression of thought; philosophical openness; thoughtfulness; intellectual honesty; self-objectivity; creative self-reliance; trustworthiness; strength of character; patience; focus; expertise in intelligent and thoughtful evaluation; a skeptical but respectful investigation of tradition; a commitment to completion; and a compassion for life that is both familiar and alien to us.

13.23

History spirals forward through time as meaning-forms meander freely through languages and set up, organize, and guide all the cultures of the world in the process.

13.24

Thought is the vital link between human beings; it is for this reason that thinking is the supreme moral act of human existence.

13.25

Action arises out of thinking, and thinking is provoked by action—exactly in that order.

13.26

Thought is the immortal soul of language that is continually reincarnated over the course of human history.

13.27

With proper guidance and education, meaning-forms, and the items, actions, and happenings of experience, eventually become consistently *coupled*—grounding the thinking process into reality.

13.28

What we call consciousness is the *integrated experience of innumerable meaning-forms* at varying degrees of clarity, intensity, and stability.

13.29

There is simply not enough space in the shallowness of conscious experience for the vast universe of the subconscious.

13.30

Thinking is the activity that navigates and misnavigates human beings through the precarious world of the bio-ontological shift.

13.31

Language is a mode of heightened awareness that is shared between or among conscious beings.

13.32

A word tells us something particular and, as such, is necessarily finite. But then how is it possible that even the simplest of words contains an infinite universe of meaning. Consider the easiest word of all: *is*

13.33

Each culture embodies "prepackaged" meaning-forms, and each human—beginning at birth—must learn to connect each meaning-form with particular items, actions, and happenings in the outside world—anew.

13.34

Thinking and language would have no content without meaning-forms; thinking, language, and meaning-forms have a seamless interconnection to the extent that it is impossible to establish thresholds where meaning-forms become thinking and thinking becomes language.

13.35

Language is involved in the general attributes of meaning-forms. This is because conscious thinking in its role of orienting human beings successfully through daily life requires only general knowledge.

13.36

Despite the admirable capacity of linguistic thinking to describe what is occurring in experience, it can never fully reproduce the nuanced hues of meaning that define the dynamic life of meaning-forms. Language is rather like a fuzzy, out-of-focus snapshot that imposes general order onto the restless flux of experience but never captures accurately and with precision the ever-vital life of meaning in experience.

13.37

Language is a secondary aspect of the presence of what is, because it is one step removed from the direct, thoughtful, and raw experience of pure meaning-forms.

13.38

Language can mirror a selective slice of reality, but one that has already receded into the past during the time of its expression. Language is always too late—an ancient relic always and forever in the making.

13.39

The "language of the heart" is ordered by the logic of passions, which does not strive for personal expression or even to be understood, but instead seeks the swiftest ways and means to rapturous, sensual gratification.

13.40

Mystical experience is non-self-reflective awareness that cannot be understood or expressed linguistically, mathematically, or artistically but is understood best as pure, *undifferentiated experience*—that is, as a meaningful presence without separate meaning bits. The psychological effect is that the experiencing person is unable to distinguish between this or that meaning or between himself and what is being experienced. In this case, all meaning and even subject and object become one.

13.41

The human experience of freedom of choice is directly related to the highly dynamic actions of unstable meaning-forms. The key to the experience of human freedom is the capacity of consciousness to detach meaning-forms from their respective items, actions, and happenings in the outside world. By releasing meaning-forms from their host objects, actions, and happenings, we gain the perceptual and cognitive freedom to redirect our interests to other objects, actions, and happenings in the world—this is the meaning of *reflection*, and it represents genuine human freedom in action. Animals, by contrast, possess little capacity to separate meaning-forms from the items, actions, and happenings in the world, and as a result, they are largely perceptively and cognitively stuck to the objects of their interests. This accounts for their limited access to what is occurring in the world and to their highly deterministic behavior.

13.42

If unstable meaning-forms are the connecting points between humans as well as between humans and the natural world, does this not guarantee a certain *arbitrariness and uncertainty* at the very core of human existence itself? And isn't this the more accurate depiction of what many philosophers and poets have called "the human condition"?

13.43

Many of the outstanding issues and problems that arise in connection with meaning-forms can be addressed once we understand the relationship between the individual and the natural world as well as the interrelationship between *natural meaning-forms,* and *cultural meaning-forms.* That natural meaning-forms possess the same meaning across different cultures is the key to gaining insight into the life and work of cultural meaning-forms. The emergence of meaning-forms is best understood by breaking them down into three categories, beginning first with the most primitive life on Earth and then moving onto the subsequent stages of biological evolution.

1. Bio-spasms—Bio-spasms were repetitive, blind, and random *reflexes* that evolved in the first life forms as a first phase of what later would become repeatable, survival-based, instinctive behaviors. Bio-spasms interacted continuously with the outside world but originally had no *necessary* connection to it. As a result, in 99 percent of the cases, these bio-spasms were not beneficial from an evolutionary perspective. Random luck of the draw, however, resulted in a fortunate gathering of conditions in which a bio-spasmotic reflex had reliable survival benefits, and what emerged from the bio-spasmodic soil was a novel form of behavior: *instincts*.

2. *Essential meaning*—With the rise of plant, insect, and animal life, instincts became more firmly fixed to *specific* items, actions, and happenings in the outside world, thereby inaugurating—especially in the case of insects and animals—action-based behaviors for the sole purposes of survival and reproduction. With the evolution of larger brains in animal and primates, particularly in Homo sapiens, and the movement away from instinct-dominant, survival-dominant actions, meaning-forms emerged for the first time.

3. *Meaning-forms*:

A. *Natural meaning-forms*—These are first-generation, nonphysical, universal *essences* that emerged concurrently with animal/mammal consciousness and directly from the newly mobilized survival and reproduction instincts. With natural meaning-forms, meanings arise from *objects* that are found in nature (e.g., sexual organs, food, and water), from typical *actions* from other living beings (e.g., aggressive, life-threatening movements), and from *happenings* in the natural world (e.g., lightening strikes). The meanings that emerged in all three cases remained naturally fixed, even across species and cultural boundaries.

B. *Cultural meaning-forms*—These are second-generation, nonphysical, culture-based essences that emerged in human consciousness, which possessed only culture-dependent meanings. In this phase, meanings arise directly from the objects (e.g., tools), actions (e.g., dances), and happenings (e.g., inter-personal conflicts) in the human-constructed world. Cultural meaning-forms are specific to particular cultures, which means that the meaning-forms—and the objects, actions, and happenings to which they are attached—are meaningful only within the culture in which they emerged, unless or until there is cross-cultural fertilization. Cultural meaning-forms are pure creations of the human imagination, which means that their attachments to the cultural items, actions, and happenings must be learned and relearned with each new generation.

13.44

There is another important category of meaning-form that we must consider. In dividing meaning-forms into their natural and cultural versions—the former derived from nature and the latter derived from culture—I need to make a further designation: a meaning-form that is not derived from either but that originates from the open, prejudgmental awareness of *what is*. Without this further designation, we could never account for philosophical knowledge, artistic truth, and spiritual insight. I call this meaning-form the "meta-form." Unlike the other kinds of meaning-forms, there is only *one* meta-form. And of all three versions of meaning-forms, the meta-form is the most abstract and resists easy comprehension most strenuously. But let's try.

The pure awareness of *what is*—the direct consequence of the bio-ontological shift—cannot be reduced to material hosts or activities in the real world, nor is it locked inside subjective, cognitive processes. Awareness is simply being conscious of what is *present* at any given moment. Awareness is a fact of human experience; it is, to borrow phraseology from twentieth-century existentialists, the "ground" of human experience—the nonmaterial *space* in which experience occurs, so to speak.

But there is a hidden dimension to awareness that must be exposed. Awareness is, at bottom, the intuitive sense of *infinity*—the boundless, limitless, and inexhaustible reality of what is. Another way of saying this is to consider that there is no limit to what could enter our awareness. It is not as though there is a finite amount of knowledge, information, and truth about reality and that as we gain more awareness, the less knowledge, information, and truth there is to discover. Quite the contrary: as our awareness increases, the more we realize that there is even more of which we are not aware. Awareness is open to everything *that is*, as well as to everything *that could be*, and this adds up to *infinite possibilities*—a concept that we can grasp only obliquely.

Awareness, then, is the space where the gain in knowledge *makes no advance* toward ultimate understanding, because in front of every advance of knowledge there still stands an infinity of what we don't know. It's as though the more that knowledge is increased, the more the universe of possible knowledge *inflates*. This is the essential paradox of awareness and is its most profound mystery. Mystery, we can now say, is the meaning of the meta-form; it's always within the infinitely mysterious context of what we *don't know* that there can emerge at least some understanding of *what is*.

Think for a moment about how the darkness of night circumscribes, brings to the foreground, and illuminates the stars that are embedded in it. The darkness represents what is unknown and mysterious, and the stars, small pockets of understanding. And in the same way that night's darkness only expands as we move outward into space and are confronted by the ever-consuming darkness of the infinite universe, the meta-form also becomes even more mysterious as our knowledge of reality increases. *The meta-form is the ever-expanding unknown.* The meta-form is mystery! Since mystery is the ground for awareness, it must also be the source for both natural and cultural meaning-forms.

Philosophy, art, and spirituality of all kinds are particular embodiments of this awareness, because they confront and internalize the meta-form directly—*consciously*, as it were. They are bold enterprises, because, in principle, they could never be successful in comprehending the mystery of existence, but they move ahead with rigor and enthusiasm just the same. The stunning irony here is that the failures and disappointments of philosophy, art, and spirituality represent the most lofty aspirations of the human spirit and have gone a long way in making life good, beautiful and all worth the effort.

13.45

Non-primate, biological life is dominated largely by thoughtless and uncreative biological strategies that are repetitive, oriented toward, and locked in, the past. The human animal, by contrast, is a creative, conflict-orientated work in progress with one foot forever laboring in the past and the other moving inexorably toward an open future.

13.46

It's true that the brain is the "organ of meaning"—the creative engine behind the production of culture. But the brain is also the meeting place where natural meaning and cultural meaning stream into each other, where biological imperatives intertwine with cultural ones, where biological programs serve the purpose of cultural meaning, and where cultural goals serve biological ends.

13.47

Nature has shifted and has brought human nature into existence in the process, and with it new impulses, directions, and programs that serve both the purposes of meaning and those of nature.

13.48

The human brain did not evolve to its present form simply as a biological, adaptive response to formidable environmental challenges. Neither could the brain be understood as a purely cultural innovation, as though its emergence represents humanity's clean break from its biological past. Rather, the brain evolved as a response to the shift *away* from nature, and *this movement away from nature is exactly proportional to humanity's movements into a meaning-based existence.* This new world of humanity occupies a third ground between determinate human nature, on the one hand, and a fabricated culture of meaning on the other. Humanity is thus driven in two directions at once: back into the limited cycles of biological life and forward into the promising world of new and unlimited, meaningful possibilities. This bidirectional antagonism guarantees that there could never be an endpoint or goal that would signal the end to all shifting.

13.49

The connection between an animal's mental states and its behavior is a direct one. The animal has little choice but to act without hesitation and to fulfill its biological imperatives for survival and reproduction. Moreover, the connection between an animal and its environment is a fully engaged one: animals fit easily into specific niches to which they are well adapted, and outside of periodic environmental intrusions, dramatic ecological changes, or lethal attacks from enemies, animals are, on the whole, "at home" in nature.

By contrast, the connection between human mental states and their behaviors is a disharmonious one at best, one fraught with jerks, false starts, inconclusive endings, uncertainty, incomplete actions, and conflicting tendencies. Furthermore, the connection between a human and its environment is always an ambiguous one: human beings live both in nature and in culture, and establishing a lasting balance, while straddling these two radically different worlds, is virtually impossible— one or the other (or both) is always slipping out from under us. A home requires a solid foundation and the promise that tomorrow will not destroy the stability that exists today; such requirements and promises will always remain outside of our mortal reach. Consequently, human beings could never be "at home" in the world, but are forever caught in the middle of two very insistent forces that are moving in opposite directions. Hence, with the bio-ontological shift, a smooth, bump-free ride is the stuff of the imagination.

13.50

Consciousness is the fluid movement of meaning-forms across the ever-expanding landscape of lived experience.

13.51

Cultural meaning-forms are attached to the items, actions, and happenings of the outside world, but these attachments are slippery and unstable, at best. When they are being experienced, meaning-forms are free to move from their hosts to the mind of the experiencing person and become a part of the nonphysical, fluctuating worlds of consciousness and the subconscious. This transmission, however, does not mean that the host items, actions, and happenings are *necessarily* denuded of all meaning. Rather, under normal conditions, the meaning-forms that enter into consciousness are only very closely approximate representations of meaning-forms and not the original meaning-forms themselves, which remain fixed to their hosts. However, mental instability or insufficient education could easily completely dislodge cultural and even natural meaning-forms from their hosts—and then trees could become elephants and a gesture of friendship a malicious action.

Although meaning-forms that are attached to the objects, actions, and happenings in the outside world have an independent existence, they are nevertheless dependent on thinking for their survival, organization, and transmission to other receptive minds. This means that meaning-forms are subject to an infinite variety of modifications—including dividing them into sub-meanings, uniting them with other meaning-forms, and even producing new ones. The movement of representational meaning-forms to consciousness holds the potential for them to be distorted in the process, especially if the interpreting ability of consciousness is insufficient at the moment of perception and conception. Fluctuating states of mind, mood swings, deeply emotional experiences, physical and psychological disturbances, and even creative insights could easily disrupt the transmission of representational meaning-forms—changing, combining, or even destroying them. And it's also not uncommon for consciousness to generate meaning-forms that have no meaningful correlations in the outside world at all but only make sense internally—in *fantasy*.

13.52

The biological strategies that promote survival and reproduction make up the securest foundation of "objective reality"—this will be true as long as human nature retains its biological aspect.

13.53

Natural meaning-forms militate against ways of life that do not promote survival and reproduction. This occurs only when the natural world and human culture collide. For example, suicide is virtually unknown in nature, but is not uncommon in the human world. Nonetheless, because suicide is an assault on the most natural impulse in all of life, it could only have a highly restricted presence.

13.54

The relation between the laws and principles of biology and the principles of cultural meaning-forms is a very complex one—but gaining this understanding is the only real path to knowledge of human nature and human existence as such.

13.55

Young children and people with adolescent or unstable minds typically make mistaken connections between meaning-forms and their respective items, actions, and happenings in the outside world. This is what being "childish" means.

13.56

The evolution of society has given birth to the solitary individual who feels his own isolation and separation from nature and people. This primordial loneliness is not only the source of our greatest fears, but is also the fertile womb in which one's unique destiny is first conceived, energized, and launched. What is the whole of human activity, then, but a collection of unique destinies all moving in as many directions as there are solitary souls?

13.57

1. Cultural meaning-forms proliferate endlessly.

2. Cultural meaning-forms are infinitely fertile, dynamic, and as unpredictable as culture itself.
3. Although they are grounded in mental processes, meaning-forms are *experiential* realities. Meaning-forms cannot be observed or analyzed by typical empirical, scientific (physical, chemical, biological) analysis. Their existence is a *nonmaterial presence*—even though when they appear in the outside world, they are always attached physical objects, actions, or happenings.
4. Meaning-forms constitute the very substance of thinking and are as expansive and infinitely variable as thinking itself.

Meaning-forms are also the substance of the imagination and can have meanings that do not reflect the facts in the outside world.

5. Where nonhuman life responds automatically and thoughtlessly to biological urgings and instincts, human beings think and act with and through meaning-forms.
6. While nonhuman bio/genetic programs and strategies are in place at birth, meaning-forms need to be absorbed, learned, and organized by human consciousness over time before they are connected to the appropriate objects, actions, and happenings in the outside world.
7. Where biological behaviors are *standard* within respective species, human behavior is highly *flexible* because of the relative, culture-based meaning of cultural meaning-forms.
8. Where biological programs and urgings are automatic, cultural meaning-forms require being "set up" by subconscious and conscious thinking processes.
9. Where there is a clear causal relationship between biological and physical events and processes, the connection between meaning-forms is not causal in any deterministic way; rather, the connection is that of a *relation and inter-relation of presences*— where different meaning-forms merge and synergistically produce variations of the initial meaning-forms.
10. Where biological strategies aim toward sheer physical survival and reproduction, meaning-forms aim toward the proliferation of other meaning-forms.

13.58

Meaning-forms exist in a number of ways:

1. As ideas in the thinking process.
2. As logical structures in thinking.
3. As visual essences that engulf the items, actions, and happenings in the outside world.
4. As the substance and form of the thinking process.
5. As images that float freely in the imagination.
6. As images that move freely in dreams.
7. As thoughts, ideas, and concepts in language.
8. As goals and purposes in human life.
9. As images in art.
10. As the content of language.
11. As mystery in the face of existence.

13.59

The bio-ontological shift requires human beings to satisfy three existential needs:

1. The need for a *stable frame of reference* that confers emotional security
2. The need for *answers* to key philosophical questions
3. The need for powerful *calls to action*

13.60

The experience of past, present, and future is directly connected to the contingent and unstable nature of cultural meaning-forms. Each generation is born into a preestablished world of cultural meaning-forms—but their prior existence is not a guarantee of their present or future stability. They still need to be absorbed, organized, and set up so that they are connected to the correct items, actions, and happenings of experience. This whole process is vulnerable to variation, change, distortion, or general breakdown because of the naturally recurring flaws in the actions of perception and cognition, and because the influences of childhood upbringing, education, and typical life experiences can throw received meaning-forms into question. The unstable nature of cultural meaning-forms has several effects: time-senses become especially heightened, because of the constant need to look back to the *past* to try to rescue the stable meanings that have since become unstable and uncertain in *present* experience. But since human experience is future-oriented, there is also the need to look to the *future* to see where one is going, so to speak, and to make sure that there will continue to be a reliable framework of meaning. But the continual problem of bringing past, stable meaning-forms to an uncertain present creates doubt about the future stability of meaning-forms, as well. As a result, the future becomes an object of even greater concern. We can conclude that past, present, and future come into clear view only with an anxious consciousness trying desperately to preserve meaning-forms over time.

13.61

The awareness of the inevitability of my personal death and the deaths of others is also directly connected to the unstable and finite nature of cultural meaning-forms. Cultural meaning-forms pass this way and that; they materialize before our very eyes only to disintegrate into nothing a moment later; and the intensity of their presence can vary dramatically from moment to moment—leaving one always and ultimately with the sense of loss.

13.62

Death is the permanent extinction of all meaning-forms.

13.63

All living things are oppressed by the infinity of what is, whether they "know" it or not.

13.64

In Mia's eyes—what do I see? Innocence? Vulnerability? Tenderness? A cosmic why? A simple yes? A fragile surrender? You, me, and them in the beginning and in the end.

13.65

The unadorned items, actions, and happenings in the outside world are not what engage us, enthrall us; direct us; hold our attention; compel our interests; provoke our passions; satisfy our yearnings; and heighten our moral, philosophical, and spiritual sensibilities; *it is what these items, actions, and happenings mean that really matters to us.* The love of a lifetime, the thrill of seeing Rome for the first time, the expanding sense of liberation after achieving a long-sought-after goal, the feeling of ecstasy that overwhelms us from hearing an astonishing piece of music, and the grief at the death of a parent—these are the works of meaning that drive, orientate, and illuminate human existence.

13.66

Feeling the passage of time derives from being attuned to the endless flux of meaning-forms.

13.67

Time is essentially a feeling of loss and emptiness—we reflect back to the past to try to invigorate or retrieve meaning-forms that have become faint or have disappeared altogether, and we peer toward the future in the hope of filling-in the empty, wide-open spaces of what can be.

13.68

The unconscious coordination and organization of meaning-forms is not the creation of reality but the work of the imagination. The eventual stabilization of meaning-forms as they become attached to the proper items, actions, and happenings of the outside world is where reality begins.

13.69

The fear of the future and the obsession with the passage of time is, at bottom, the feeling of the desperation of not being able to hold onto meaning-forms as they flow capriciously in and out of our awareness.

13.70

What is the past but meaning-forms that have been psychologically *frozen in time*? From this perspective, the past can be superior to the present because it has permanence—that is, as long as teh past reflects accurately what has occurred. As long as our memory doesn't fail us, these timeless meaning-forms remain stable, clear, and poignant. What do these meaning-forms represent? Nothing less than our thoughts, beliefs, decisions, actions, goals, ideals, and values. And what can forgetfulness be, then, but the horrible feeling of the loss of life, the disappearance of what we knew, held onto, and relied on—both psychologically and philosophically?

13.71

Rooted in biology, orientated toward meaning—one mostly regressive, the other mostly progressive—one with clear, realizable purposes and strategies in advance; the other with vague aims and purposes with no necessary end point—this is the human being, a being forever divided against itself.

13.72

Technological creations are like primitive biological organisms: their actions are predetermined and predictable, and their ultimate goals are known in advance. What is the explosion of technology in modern life, then, but nature rearing its biological head in disguised form?

13.73

We must be careful not to think of our orientation toward meaning-forms through culture as a wholesale departure from biological programs and urgings. Culture itself is often used as a means of achieving specific biological ends, e.g., survival and reproduction. Culture, in fact, would not have thrived if it had ignored the requirements of biology. Biology and culture work together in unconscious thinking and emerge in conscious awareness as meaning-forms that serve biological needs and purposes—the countless expressions of human sexuality is a good example.

13.74

Sexual intercourse—originally a simple biological function—was recast by culture and has given rise to a richly complex network of meaning-forms. These include erotic fantasies and accompanying behaviors and traditions, such as dating, romantic language, and marriage. The natural act of mating has also exploded into the complex web of *interpersonal relationships*—a deeply intimate world of highly charged feelings, beliefs, and psycho/physical sensations.

13.75

There is a positive correlation between greater intensity of feeling and the instability of meaning-forms.

13.76

A meaning-form represents a specific quantity of *life-power*. Within a specific experiential framework, the interconnection and interpenetration of all meaning-forms is expressed in a dynamic energy flow between and among all meaning-forms. The total sum of this life-power, along with the psycho/philosophical viewpoint of the experiencing person, regulates which meanings will be manifested in consciousness and with how much intensity.

13.77

As nature and culture intermingle, human reality tends to move toward increasing cultural expression. What is the empirical proof of culture's victory over nature? The proof is humanity's preoccupation with all things unrelated to survival for the sake of reproduction—for instance, music, blue jeans, and gambling. Perhaps the most convincing evidence of the victory of culture over nature, however, is the regular occurrence of human *suicide*—the most extreme affront and contradiction to the most basic principle of the natural world: survival.

13.78

The precise difference between biology and culture is *freedom of expression*. Where biology tends to repetition of biologic processes, culture tends to spontaneous production of more varied meaning-forms and ways of behaving.

13.79

The most baffling issues arise when we consider the shift from pre-human to human life from a biological view. In one sense, the transition is simply another step in a long series of biological adaptations. But the shift to a distinctly human way of being inaugurated a radically new form of life on Earth: one given over to individuality, meaning, consciousness, reason, language, choice, and above all—to *creativity*.

13.80

If human beings are necessarily cultural beings—that is, dependent upon pre-established traditions for their very existence—how could *pre-cultural* human beings have emerged in the first place? Without a cultural world to be *born into*, was prehistoric humanity still under the decisive control of nature? But if so, how could we still consider the very first human beings really human? Human life must have been tenuous at humankind's beginning—still engulfed in nature but yet experiencing primitive, and baffling, cultural meaning-forms for the very first time. Human nature must also have been something quite different then. And it's likely that nascent humanity missed nonexistence by very little when it made its very first baby steps into its alien cultural world.

13.81

It is impossible to imagine the creative power that early humans must have deployed in order to survive the relentless brutalities of nature and establish primitive culture. Creativity is always more difficult when there is little with respect to which to be creative. But it is infinitely more difficult to be innovative when there is virtually no familiar, preexisting, meaningful framework in which to work, no long-standing cultural markers to serve as guides, and no accumulated knowledge that could be criticized, modified, and improved upon. The odds for survival were indeed very, very small for the bungling apelike species. Yet it happened.

13.82

The consciousness of the primitive human beings had to adjust to an unprecedented occurrence: the influx for the very first time of freely floating meaning-forms. Initially, consciousness consisted only of natural meaning-forms since there was little or no preexisting culture. But as culture began to take shape and grow, consciousness began to swell in equal proportion, as cultural meaning-forms became the dominant aspect of consciousness.

13.83

The degree of the inward flow of cultural meaning-forms is the measure of the humanness of the first humans.

13.84

There are four additional subdivisions of meaning-forms:

1. Bio-forms—These are natural meaning-forms that are experienced when we directly observe *natural* items, actions, and happenings in the world—for example, trees, water, and sexual behavior.

2. Fanta-forms—These are both natural and cultural meaning-forms that have become detached from their host items, actions, and happenings and float freely in the imagination, *independent* of their hosts—for example, ideas and images of any kind.

3. Mega-forms—These are both natural and cultural meaning-forms that have some relation to the facts of reality but are creative advances on them—for example, some works and productions of art, philosophy, science, and technology.

4. Super-forms—These are both natural and cultural meaning-forms that are either extreme distortions of the real items, actions, and happenings of reality or *unreal* creations of the imagination—for example, flying unicorns, flying saucers, angels, and nonmaterial gods. The Judeo-Christian God is the most dominant and compelling of all the super-forms—*all*-powerful, *all*-loving, *all*-knowing, *all*-good, *all*-creative, and *all*-just—existing everywhere and all times—the veritable beginning and the end of all creation. God is infinite. God is also the most caring parent (father and mother in one), ultimate protector, and humanity's most devoted lover. This super-form called God—the all-encompassing interconnection of all meaning-forms—is simply the greatest item that has been conceived so far, the most ambitious creation in the history of the human imagination.

13.85

Human culture is an intricately woven fabric of bio-forms, fanta-forms, mega-forms, and super-forms.

13.86

Human creativity arises out of the conflict between nature and culture—that is, between instincts and existential flexibility, between programmed regression and open-ended, spontaneous expression.

13.87

Passive creativity is the automatic cognitive process in which meaning-forms are organized, simplified, and synthesized in the thinking process as they are connected up to items, actions, and happenings in the outside world.

13.88

Human emotion is animal energy filtered through meaning-forms.

13.89

One of the most compelling cases that can be made in support of my theory of meaning-forms involves consideration of the mentally unbalanced. Schizophrenia, for example, is the chaotic movement, and even fantastic intermingling, of meaning-forms in consciousness that are independent of host items, actions, and happenings in the real world. Caught in the maelstrom of meaning-forms, schizophrenic consciousness is unable to see or make the distinction between reality and fantasy—that is to say, fact and fiction, logic and illogic have equal validity, and, as a result, the experience of *what is real* loses all meaning. In this condition, what one thinks—such as "There are sinister people everywhere trying to kill me!" or "I can fly"—is *automatically* believed to be actual facts of reality. Additionally, meaning-forms that float freely and uncontrollably through an unstable consciousness are capable of splintering into sub-meaning-forms or even joining together with others randomly and spontaneously and creating even more fantastic perversions of reality. This development is not necessarily unbalanced in itself; it's believing that these perversions are real that is insane.

13.90

The theory of meaning-forms also suggests a form of psychotherapy, in which a fractured consciousness is trained, slowly and methodically, to reconnect meaning-forms to the appropriate items, actions, and happenings in the real world. Beginning with repetitious exercises involving very simple, natural meaning-forms and gradually advancing to more complex ones, and then following the same procedure with cultural meaning-forms, consciousness would slowly but surely become reconnected to reality. I call this form of psychological intervention "meaning-alignment therapy"—MAT.

13.91

Philosophical answers are connective tissue between humans and the world around them.

13.92

Pain becomes suffering when it's blended with meaning-forms.

13.93

Humans have an intuitive sense—a "vital sense"—that illuminates their contact with the world. The vital sense discerns the quantity and quality of *energy* that inheres in all perceived or conceived objects and actions, and happenings, and this energy is transmitted to the experiencing person through meaning-forms. The experience of energy cannot be reduced to sense-based perception like color or fragrance, but is an overall *psycho/sensual impression* that has either attractive or repulsive power, depending on the meaning-form. Meaning-forms that project strength or virility, such as outstanding athletic accomplishment, have an extremely attractive power, whereas meaning-forms that display feebleness and weakness, such as actions of moral cowardice, are experienced as energetically repulsive.

13.94

Consciousness is the experiential landscape for the vital sense.

13.95

What is needed is power—all else is derivative.

13.96

Reality is intrusive—it impinges on our senses, informs our minds, and frames our awareness.

13.97

In between exquisite pleasure at one extreme and excruciating pain at the other, there are various grades of pleasure and pain sensations, many of which are *dumb sensations* without a clear pleasure/pain aspect. Gripping and maneuvering a steering wheel of a car, for example, provides a sensation of pressure, which is neither pleasurable nor painful but is a sensation just the same.

13.98

History is human culture's answer to biological reproduction.

13.99

Are consciousness and meaning-forms co-equal? Yes.

13.100

Is there consciousness without meaning-forms? No.

13.101

"Psychological Free-Floating" (PFF) is the conscious state in which cultural meaning-forms stream freely through one's awareness and interfere with the ability of consciousness to organize natural meaning-forms, and, in so doing, neutralize the biological strategies for survival and reproduction. This could happen, for instance, if one is caught-up in various hysterias such as the chaos of a riot.

13.102

Understanding the relationships between all meaning-forms, and how they relate to reality, is the ultimate goal of philosophy

Economics, Politics, and Culture Wars

14

14.1

The basic premise and goal of the Western capitalist free market system is to maximize profit for all economic entities that are a part of the system. The defenders of this "hands-off" economic policy point to the dramatic difference in the quality of life between those countries that have more or less followed this economic strategy and those that have not. Western capitalist countries have invented technology—the child of a relatively free and open economy. Technology has transformed the face of the earth and has given humanity so many gifts that human life is unthinkable without it.

It could not be a mere coincidence that Western free market countries are also the most educated, tolerant, and humane in the world, despite the many unwise decisions and brutal acts of violence that have tarnished their histories. Basic human rights—freedom of speech and the press, and freedom of religion, for example—are essential aspects of Western capitalist countries. They also "care for" their citizens, who are protected by the rule of law. The citizens of Western capitalist countries are able to *control* the political process of their countries by the right to vote for the government that they want. And Western capitalist countries also don't go to war with each other. What is the connection, then, between Western free market countries and the various rights, liberties, and actions that define their political and cultural lives? The answer is very simple: *freedom.*

The guiding spirit of Western culture, from its beginnings in ancient Greece, has always been freedom. The first incarnations of the archetype of freedom entered Western consciousness with the Greeks: democracy (freedom to self-rule), science (freedom to investigate the

371

physical universe), philosophy (freedom to think), and art (freedom to affirm the senses and mind and to imitate and idealize the natural world). These ideas are the basis of Western culture. And despite many dark and dismal detours along the way, we could easily interpret the whole history of civilization as a grand march of nations toward increasing freedom. This is not an argument for a teleological theory of human history. It's simply the case that since the time of ancient Greece, Western peoples began defining themselves in terms of various freedoms because of the many benefits that they conferred. Consequently, in so many ways, Western humanity continued striving to realize greater freedom in all sectors of human life. Freedom of thought, belief, and action, freedom from religious and state-sponsored tyranny, freedom of expression, freedom to own property, freedom from unjust treatment, and the freedom of each person to determine the course of his or her life—these are some of the profound rewards for Western humanity's tenacious fight for freedom. The free market system is just another expression of the same cultural aim toward freedom.

Noncapitalist countries lag far behind the Western capitalist ones in all areas and dimensions of freedom. Although poverty still exists in Western capitalist counties, it affects relatively small portions of the populations compared to the dire poverty that characterizes many noncapitalist countries. The fact of the matter is that freedom and mass poverty are inherently incompatible. Living hand-to-mouth day after day, and starving in the meantime, leaves no time to think about the meaning of freedom. In poverty, the human mind is in bondage, with no chance for it to create the wealth that could liberate it. Until a country has reduced its level of poverty to a relatively low degree, freedom, as we have come to understand it in the West, is not feasible. Yet, as history has shown, it's only through a relatively free economy that poverty can be significantly reduced—an unfortunate "catch-22" for poverty-stricken countries.

Non-capitalist countries, such as dictatorships, typically show a blatant disregard for fundamental human rights and freedoms, and they oppress and even murder their own citizens, if the citizens show resistance to the status quo. Nazi Germany under Hitler, the Soviet Union under Stalin, communist China under Mao Tse-tung, Cuba under Castro, North Korea under Kim Jong-il, and Iraq under

Saddam Hussein come to mind. And the economies of these societies are usually designed to favor those in power, who live in opulence, while their citizens often remain at bare-survival existence. Indeed, it's not difficult to argue that Western capitalist countries offer the best possibilities for enhancing the quality of life of *all* people. Yet freedom in the free market system is also dangerous.

The free-market system is inherently *amoral*—and necessarily so. The upshot of this fact is that making profits and human well being have nothing to do with each other. They live in two different universes—one mathematical and the other human. And this is precisely why the free market system is often in conflict with itself—*it uses human agents to try to achieve nonhuman values.* The producers of cigarettes, for example, know that smoking destroys the health of at least one in three users, and they have known this for many years. Has this information caused a crisis of conscience and resulted in the closing down of the industry? Of course not. In fact, the industry has moved to different markets in different countries and is using more clever strategies to entice new smokers. What if it were the case that smoking killed 99 percent of all users? Do you think that the tobacco industry would have a change of heart? Probably so, but not out of moral conviction; with 99 percent of all customers' dead, who would buy cigarettes? The "bottom-line" is all that matters in an economy that is geared solely toward making profits. What's true for the tobacco industry is true for all industries. It's a never-ending battle to try to stop large companies, for example, from poisoning the environment by air or water pollution, causing the extinction of numerous species, uprooting the world's precious forests, and destroying life-sustaining coral reefs. That such ecological destruction may eventually come home to roost does not stop industries from trying to pursue their profit objectives with vigor. Yet, from a purely free market point of view, their utter disregard for human and ecological well-being is not illogical, because the mechanics of the free market do only what they are designed to do: earn a profit. A gun shoots, a hammer hammers, and the free market makes money!

The nonhuman values that fuel the free market economy always run roughshod over purely human concerns not because the free market is evil, but because it is naturally indifferent to any value that does not lead to increased profits. This is why the free market must *not* be absolutely free to pursue profits at all costs: the costs in human and ecological terms are simply too high. The best alternative to the free market economy, and one that is partially in place already, is what I call a "Controlled Market Economy." This is my idea: what drives our economy are what I call "capital-attractors." A capital-attractor is any idea, mechanism, principle, theory, person, organization, or country whose goal is to maximize profits. The underlying premise of capital-attractors is that nothing—neither physical item nor mental construct—has any value independent of its capacity for directly or indirectly making a profit. In the artificial world of capital-attractors, everything is a means to an economic end. This notion is quite frankly the real soul of a free-market system. Corporations, for instance, are immense capital-attractors, and so are productive ideas, inventions, and technologies that lead to the creation of wealth. The spirit of capitalism is a capital-attractor; so too are good businesspeople and financial investors. Mergers and acquisitions are capital-attractors. Applied science for technological development is a capital-attractor. Adjustments and manipulations of our economy—such as changing interest rates—are capital-attractors. The fact that some capital-attractors may actually benefit humanity or the environment is very good—wonderful, in fact—but is actually beside the point. Benefiting humanity or the environment is not the intention of capital-attractors; making money is, and their successes in this area are far outweighed by their potential dangers.

By contrast, a "capital-detractor" is any idea, mechanism, principle, theory, person, organization or country whose goal is to negate, restrict, dilute, or constrain capital-attractors. Its underlying premise is that nothing—neither physical item nor mental construct—has any value independent of its capacity for directly or indirectly promoting human and ecological well-being. In the natural world of capital-detractors, everything is a means to human and ecological ends. Honesty and fairness are capital detractors, and so is morality in general, if being honest, fair, and moral means making less money than you normally would by being dishonest, unfair, and immoral. Authentic religion and spirituality of all kinds are capital-detractors, as are groups and organizations that work to protect and preserve the environment.

Warnings on cigarette packages are capital-detractors. Philosophical thinking about the meaning of life is a capital-detractor. "Family values" are capital-detractors. Poor health is a capital-detractor. Near-death experiences are significant capital-detractors, as are illnesses and the loss of loved ones. Psychological imbalances or breakdowns could be capital-detractors. Civil rights could be capital-detractors. Economic regulation laws are capital-detractors. Picket-lines are capital-detractors. Newspaper editorials critiquing or exposing illegal or immoral industry practices can be capital-detractors. Business scandals are capital detractors. The "rule of law" can be a capital-detractor. Psychotherapy can be a capital-detractor, if the therapist advises his or her patient to relax, take a vacation, reduce the number of working hours, or cultivate other interests besides making money. Artistic integrity could be a capital-detractor. Using the wrong word at the wrong time or even bad moods can be capital-detractors.

Capital-attractors and capital-detractors are mutually antagonistic but can be employed as complementary aspects of the free-market system. An unfettered free market system would ultimately be self-negating because of the damage it would cause to the well-being of humanity and the natural world. Remember, from the point of view of the free market, the *only* value is making a profit, and, given enough time, the profit motive could result in significant damage to the natural world, not to mention the partial or even total destruction of the human race. For example, stripping the world of its natural resources could be very profitable, as could making and selling weapons of mass destruction like nuclear bombs and viruses. On the other hand, overly aggressive restrictions on a free economic life could easily cripple its productive genius and result in economic disaster. Feudalism in the Middle Ages, communism, socialism, and all oppressive dictatorships have failed miserably economically (and in every other way, for that matter) precisely because their economies were not guided by the free and productive powers of human creativity—the real origin of wealth.

The political and economic leaders in modern, Western capitalism intuitively but imperfectly understand the need to control the greedy desire of capital-attractors to make profits at all costs. But capital-detractors are not as successful as they need to be to curb the amoral logic of the market system. What is required is a more conscious effort to implement a controlled market economy. How could this be accomplished? This is one possibility: a general business environment must be created where capital-attractors and capital-detractors meet in intense adversarial combat, in which advocates from both sides fight for their respective interests—financial gain versus the promotion of human and ecological values. Under ideal circumstances, both sides would fight it out using all legal measures at their disposal.

Today, this relationship has been profoundly unbalanced in favor of capital-attractors, because capital-detractors are not well represented and are underfinanced in the economic marketplace. This means that the potential effectiveness of the adversarial approach to business ethics has been unfairly and dangerously compromised. To address this problem, I recommend a Capital Detractor Tax (CDT) of about 0.25 percent to 0.50 percent to be taken from all businesses. This tax money would go to a new self-sustaining, nonpartisan government agency— the Human Ecological Wellness Agency (HEWA). This agency would allocate funds to the qualified people, groups, organizations, and societies that work to promote human and ecological values, that are committed to bringing to light and helping to eliminate destructive business practices through appropriate legal channels, and that lobby for changes in the law in favor of human and ecological well-being. The government must remain neutral with respect to all issues regarding HEWA and function only as an honest broker when government participation becomes necessary.

The key to the effectiveness of this form of controlled market economy is powerfully compelling and informed *adversarial debates* that could possibly lead to change in business practices—this means good representation and adequate financing to HEWA. An important point to keep in mind here is that there is little chance that HEWA would negatively affect the life of our economy, if for no other reason than because of capital-attractors' awesome ability to innovate. Capital-attractors are bound to find new ways to make profits without compromising, or minimally compromising, human and ecological values. Think of solar energy and hybrid cars, for instance. The controlled market economy, guided by effective, well-supported, and well-represented adversarial debates, is the best way to coordinate the vital efforts of both capital-attractors and capital-detractors. This system would prevent the government from interfering excessively, erratically, and ineffectively in the economic life of the country. It would also allow the possibility for crucial control factors to ensure that the economy, human beings, and nature all work together in ways that ultimately minimize the damage to all three but maximize benefits to the human race.

14.2

Circle of Falsehood: believe—intuit—believe.

14.3

Circle of Truth: believe—intuit—think—question—intuit—believe.

14.4

Despite the lip service given to the questionable deterrent potential of the death penalty, the desire for revenge is the more likely explanation for its use. Family members and friends of the deceased often speak of the "closure" brought by the murderer's death. It's clear that closure in this context really means revenge. The official reason why many people support the death penalty, however, is the "eye-for-an-eye" justification. Philosophically and socially, this perspective makes some sense, because it argues for a *measured* approach to punishment. Killing someone for shoplifting, for instance, is not consistent with the logic of an eye for an eye. But killing a person for murdering someone would seem to be a just and proportionate punishment.

The trouble with this line of thinking is that it is based upon a faulty understanding of human nature, one that is grounded in religious thinking.

Here's an example. Many religious leaders view sexual orientation as a *moral* choice. From this viewpoint, homosexuality is a sin, because one "chooses" to be homosexual. The flaw in this argument is that there are crucial biological components to sexual orientation, as well as environmental influences that contribute to sexual orientation. Choice rarely, if ever, comes into play with sexual orientation. However, this fact has fallen upon deaf religious ears. Many prominent religious leaders still insist that sexual orientation is purely a moral choice. The more flexible religionists stray from this hard-and-fast judgment call and insist that homosexuality is a sin only if one *acts* on it. In other words, the homosexual person has one of two choices to avoid living a life of sin: celibacy or changing his or her sexual orientation by psychological or religious counseling, often including prayer. Outside of the grotesque strategy of denying or reconfiguring one's sexual nature, gaining understanding about human sexuality should be the task of biologists and psychologists, not fundamentalist Christians and conservative Jews. Unfortunately, both the Old and New Testaments lend great support to the idea that homosexuality is sinful (e.g., Leviticus 20:13, where "death" is recommended for this "abomination," and Romans 1:26–27, where Saint Paul condemns homosexuality as "dishonorable" and "shameless" and a curse from God). The same kind of religious thinking also colors the question of capital punishment.

My thesis is this: capital punishment cannot be justified, because it's *not* the case that each human being is solely responsible for his or her moral actions. Moral character forms as a result of many factors, including psychological, societal, and genetic/biological ones, and each person represents a unique recipe of these elements. And to what degree does each component contribute to the moral character of a murderer? The psycho/societal/biological dynamics of the person who murders are so complex that disentangling their numerous threads is impossible, except where there are clear organic causes. This much, however, we could say with confidence: socioeconomic factors—such as childhood experiences, parental care, quality of education, economic status, and the quality of neighborhoods—are good indicators of individual performance in many sectors of life, including in the moral sphere. Although all people that are born into poverty, and who may not have the luxury of a good education, may not turn out to be drug addicts, criminals, or gang members, a disproportionate number of them do. If you review the background of the people who populate our prisons, in fact, you will find that a high percentage of them have a great deal in common—including abusive parents, broken homes, little or no education, bio-chemical imbalances, alcoholism, and/or drug addiction. To suggest that criminals simply and freely choose the miserable lives they lead is both naïve and irrational.

Capital punishment enthusiasts will naturally object to the idea that a murderer should be partly absolved of his responsibility for the act of murder. After all, if a person knows right from wrong, then there is no legitimate excuse for his murderous act. Moreover, why should we hold the influences of society responsible to any degree for the actions of a murderer? Most individuals in society are moral people, and they don't commit murder. Why let convicted murderers off the hook? But these questions move past the more important and decisive questions. Why is it that a murderer's moral compass is broken in the first place, and what makes the murderer unlike most other members of society, who are moral? And with these questions, we are back to our original idea that moral actions don't simply follow from so-called free choice but presuppose a complex mix of different causal factors in addition to the individual choice of a person to murder.

Terminating a human life is a moral action that is in a category all its own. And why? Because existing—being alive—is the value of tremendous worth to humans. It is the foundational value upon which all other values rest—for without being alive, no other value could ever be realized. This means that for capital punishment to be acceptable, it must be shown to be an *ultimately* justifiable act—that is, it must have a powerful defense. Clearly this has not been shown. What, then, is a fair and just punishment for convicted murderers?

Life imprisonment without the possibility of parole is the only just punishment for the murderer. This is the only position in which the two guilty and responsible parties—the individual *and* his society—could be reasonably punished (punishing nature for organic-based disorders has no meaning). The criminal is punished with lifelong incarceration, and society is punished by having to bring the defendant to trial, and if he is convicted, keeping him in prison until he dies—which is a considerable financial burden. For mentally handicapped or severely chemically/hormonally unbalanced murderers, other institutional arrangements must be made that isolate them in prison or special institutions, so they will not do additional harm to others.

The death penalty has no justifiable basis when we consider all the factors that influence the moral character of the murderer. The societies and religions that endorse this practice under the banner of justice are acting out an ancient human ritual of revenge, one that has its origins in a less rational, less enlightened, and less compassionate moment in human history. Capital punishment is always murder, but it will never be seen in this light as long as we continue to view human nature through the benighted eyes of religious dogma.

14.5

Television, film, and music have immense power to manipulate a viewer's or listener's thoughts, feelings, and emotions. This capacity derives from the entertainment media's ability to present real or fabricated meaning-forms that are under the complete control of their directors and producers. The result is that the imagination of the viewers and listeners are altered and guided with great precision and finesse. In fact, the value of a television show, film, or CD is based completely on its success in effectively controlling the meaning-forms of the viewers and listeners. As an example, a film is considered of high quality if it beguiles the viewer into believing that dinosaurs are still alive and dangerous, that love conquers all, that the bad guy always gets it in the end, or any other fantasy that is reproduced with the aid of technology and the imagination of shrewd filmmakers. What this means is that filmmakers do their best to determine which meaning-forms to present in order to provoke the desired effect and how best to do it. Success is achieved with a sort of mind control, where the audience experiences exactly what the filmmaker wants them to experience. One often hears that "the suspension of disbelief" is a necessary mindset for the moviegoer to experience the illusion on the screen as real. This suspension could not be achieved without the dramatic alteration of the viewer's normal relationship to meaning-forms.

When consciousness is under the spell of fantasy, its ability to reason and to see reality clearly are effectively shut down; what is fact and what is fiction often become indistinguishable. In television and film, the meaning-forms projected into the viewers' or listeners' awareness are already detached from real items and actions in the world (that is, they are "pre-packaged") and, in this way, possess the status of a waking dream. Like a particularly vivid and viscerally real dream during sleep, we also believe *whatever* we experience on television or film to be true—if that was the intent of the creators. We shouldn't forget about farce and comedy, where the audience is aware at all times that what is being presented isn't real. In these instances, the presence of meaning-forms that intentionally misrepresent reality and make us laugh are welcome experiences. As we all know, there is nothing like a good laugh to shoo away the troubles of the real world. Meaning-forms serve many purposes indeed.

14.6

The *now moment* is not a genuine aspect of time. It is pure illusion. Time is always a bidirectional movement—forever coming and going—constantly moving toward the future while receding into the past. What we call "now" is a perversion of reflective experience that involves an almost instantaneous and indiscernible psychological projection of the *immediate* past onto the *local* future. This means that we don't consciously experience what we call a present moment, because all of our temporal experiences are automatically filtered through the past, which is static by virtue of having already occurred. What results from transferring the immediate past to the local future is the illusion of the present and static *now*. What, then, is movement? Why do we see everything around us in the process of change? Movement and change are the now moment trying to catch up to itself, as it were. Unfortunately, it's always too late to the party, no matter how hard it tries.

14.7

If the *now moment* is the immediate past projected onto the locally moving future, then this must mean that the future is never *consciously* experienced, either. It must also be true that there is always something happening in our locally moving future of which we are never aware—a slice of temporal reality that forever extends beyond, and ahead of, our illusory now moments.

14.8

Being conscious only of the past, but moving relentlessly and blindly toward the future, is the greatest paradox of human experience.

14.9

Platinum Rule: Do unto yourself what you ought to do unto others.

14.10

The only legitimate foundations for morality are pragmatic rules for peaceful coexistence and compassion. The need for peaceful coexistence became evident only with the evolution of culture and significant increases in population. A developing culture and a growing population resulted in the steady accumulation of knowledge about human nature and the requirements for human survival. Humanity learned, for instance, that a sense of existential well-being—what many call "worldly happiness"—is essential to the psychological health of human beings and, as a result, contributes strongly to their continued survival and prosperity. For countless millennia, the mythical mentality was dominant, which meant that the idea of worldly happiness, as an explicit goal of everyday life, was largely beyond human comprehension. Notions of worldly happiness began to emerge only after humanity began to realize that there are facts of human nature—that is, there are typical needs that must be met in order for human beings to live in a truly satisfactory state. Intimate, emotional companionship, mind-body balance, and creative expressive eventually began to be seen as fundamental requirements of human nature and slowly became absorbed into the worldviews of various cultures, including that of ancient Greece. The moral breakthrough occurred, however, with the realization that one's personal happiness required the assistance, not to mention the tolerance, of other people—and not in the hereafter, but right here on Earth.

Survival in large communities confers many vital benefits: help in growing and storing food and managing livestock; assistance in caring for children, the sick, and the old; protection against the whims of nature or unfriendly gods; and protection against common enemies. But all these benefits come with a price: if I require the aid of others, then I must be of service to them, because they also have the same requirements. The idea of the "Golden Rule" emerged in many different cultures with the realization of this sobering reality. It's just another step, morally, to negotiate with others to be tolerant of one's ideas, beliefs, and practices in exchange for the same. As we can see, *quid pro quo* is at the basis of this kind of morality and naturally translates into pragmatic rules for peaceful coexistence. And what are these rules? All the rules of "do not" and "please do" and the many "if you don't mind …" and all the various "if it's not too much trouble, please …" and the ever-popular "let's make a deal; I'll do X if you'll do Y." Morality at this level is entirely practical, and necessarily so.

The emergence of compassion as a source for morality, by contrast, is not as easy to explain. It's interesting to note that compassion, unlike the pragmatic rules for peaceful coexistence, does not necessarily presuppose cultural or historical knowledge. Rather, the source of compassion is a feeling for the *contingent* nature of other living things. Contingent, as it's used here, means that livings being are vulnerable and susceptible to suffering, that their continued existence is not guaranteed, but could easily end tomorrow, today, or even in the next moment. Compassion is a kind of general intuition that all life is tenuous, uncertain, and tragically death-bound. When I see this fragile little bird, or that helpless, stumbling puppy, I *feel for* these innocent creatures; my heart aches for them—I want to help save them from their contingency, but I can't, because their existence is like mine: incorrigibly contingent. From this perspective, I have nothing over any other living being, for we are all in the same existential position: we exist, and we don't know how or why or for what end. They go their way, and I go mine—but our destinies are forever intertwined and ultimately indistinguishable. These sorts of intuitions and feelings are at the source of compassion, even though they are rarely clearly or fully available in conscious awareness. The experience of compassion is far from being understood, but outside of our intelligent guesses and hunches, what we could say for sure is that compassion, as a felt insight, requires above all else the capacity to see beyond one's own needs, concerns, and biases, however briefly, and intuit the existential plight of another.

Moral acts out of feelings of compassion are quite extraordinary, because they are not based on practical concerns, and, as a result, are not easily seduced by moral relativism. One acts morally because "it's the right thing to do," and not because one will necessarily benefit practically or even personally. What is most striking about moral acts of compassion is that they do not require a religious or even a traditionally spiritual basis. The "facts of life" are plain to see, and compassionate actions could be understood as perfectly consistent with these facts. One could easily say, for instance, "Given my thoughtful experiences of the natural condition of life forms in the world, I feel a sense of compassion for them, and I have concluded that it's simply right to treat them morally." Compassion, in this sense, is simply a natural psycho/emotional response to living in an imperfect world.

14.11

What, then, are the conditions that need to be met for compassion to emerge? There is just one: compassion requires moments of concerned reflection on other forms of life independent of one's own self-serving needs and interests.

14.12

Compassion emerged initially within the family unit—where children were cared for *with compassion* by their parents. Compassionate feelings for one's children undoubtedly have a genetic component. When small, tightly knit communities were first created, members of the group were seen as *brothers and sisters, sons and daughters*, and *fathers and mothers*. At this stage, compassion became the common familial bond between all members inside and outside of the immediate family. With the establishment of certain compassionate religions and spiritual traditions, all human beings came to be understood as members of the "brotherhood" of humankind and thus deserved to be treated with familial compassion. From some moral viewpoints, *all* life is spiritually interconnected and should be treated with compassion, including plants, animals, and even insects.

14.13

For the Buddha, the idea of God had no relevance to earthly existence. He saw life as a mystery that, nonetheless, offered certain clues as to its meaning. When the blinders are removed from our perceptions, and when the mind is clear of all biases, pre-conceptions, and delusions, one fact of life stands out above all others: *life is suffering*. It was equally obvious to the Buddha that beings suffer because they are isolated and cut off from each other and from life in general. Human beings are typically guided by the false hopes that grasping for and holding onto material things, discovering philosophical truth, achieving worldly goals, finding gratification in physical pleasure, or experiencing true romantic love will solve the problem of suffering. But these are pure *illusions*, because all accomplishments and experiences of fulfillment—however great or small—are temporary and at best are only superficially rewarding. In the best-case scenario, whatever we have achieved and all that we treasure will ultimately be taken from us at our death.

The Buddha thought it was factually undeniable that the way we see the world has a direct bearing on how we experience it, including determining the quantity and quality of our suffering. In this sense, Buddhism is essentially a psychological discipline. What are perception and thinking but processes that break the world down into unmanageable and incongruent bits and pieces? How foolish it is, then, to try to find happiness within this fractured and fragmented world! The truth is that the world could never be reduced to separate bits and pieces, no matter how convincingly our senses and minds tell us that it can. As we begin to pierce the veils of life's illusions and to see them for what they are—ego tactics that keep all beings disconnected and in conflict with one's self and the world—then we could begin to free ourselves of them. According to Buddhist thought, the process of overcoming the psychological chains that bind an individual to suffering takes many lifetimes. The process is based on the person making the rights choices, committing the right actions, possessing the right emotions, and cultivating the right attitudes—all of which serve to promote greater awareness and experience of the truth of existence. For the Buddha, realizing that *all* life suffers and ought to be treated with compassion is a critical phase in this process, and a necessary step in actualizing the ultimate meaning of existence: nirvana—returning to the bliss of the seamless oneness of reality.

14.14

Abortion is still hotly debated today in America, and for good reason: it's the most profound topic in modern culture. And how the many important issues that abortion involves ultimately impact our society will be one of the most radical watersheds in the history of the human race. With abortion, purely philosophical questions cannot remain in the theoretical realm simply to be bandied about by armchair philosophers in university classrooms; they must be brought down from the clouds and given concrete answers in real-life situations. Here weighty philosophical, scientific, religious, social, and political questions smash head on into each other and become entangled. They demand clear, workable answers. Let's consider a number of the most important questions and possible answers.

When does human life begin? Does a woman have absolute control over her body, including control over the fate of the prenatal life inside her? Is aborting prenatal human life equivalent to aborting a *person*? Are all the distinguishing features of human life *physical* functions such as brain-wave production? The scientific and philosophical answers to these sorts of questions make the abortion problem even more complex, because they raise many more issues and questions. For example, scientists often cite "brain activity"—detectable normally between five to seven months—as the principal sign of human life; but does this mean that the phases *before* there was clear brain activity did not belong to human life? If a very young fetus (a fetus forms at about three months after conception) without brain activity is not human life, then what kind of life is it? All life develops according to genetic programming that is specific to the kind of life that it is; so doesn't this mean that all prenatal life is necessarily human life and that aborting it, even in the first trimester—the first three months of pregnancy—is really murder?

Why do scientists place so much emphasis on brain activity, anyway? All animals have brain activity, and it's probably true that the first sparks of brain activity in a fetus are indistinguishable from those of many animals, and especially the highly evolved, nonhuman primates like chimpanzees. If this is so, then how could we legitimately use brain activity as the primary indicator of human life? If scientists equate brain action with *consciousness*, then they have the problem of defining what consciousness is and what is isn't. How do we know that advanced, nonhuman mammals don't possess a primitive form of consciousness that is similar to very primitive human consciousness? How could scientists ever know the difference? What consciousness could possibly mean in relation to brain activity is a question that scientists have never been able to answer convincingly, and it is still one of the great mysteries of science.

If each human life is created by God and is therefore *sacred*, as is maintained in many religious traditions, and if a fetus is human, then how could God allow even one of his sacred creations to be treated so savagely by being aborted while at the same time permitting other fetuses to go to full term and to emerge healthily into the world? Does God play favorites? Why would God put his sacred creations in the hands of such despicable human beings as aborting mothers and abortion doctors to begin with? Isn't the very fact that abortions occur at all a very compelling argument *against* the very existence of an all-powerful, all-loving, and perfectly moral God?

If there is no God, and the conception of each human life is an *accidental* event of nature, then couldn't a strong case be made that the fetus is not of great value? This position becomes even stronger if we believe that the young fetus is not a person and could *not* be protected by the Constitution. Without the idea that God places ultimate value on each creation of human life, what's to prevent fetuses' survival or termination from being decided in terms of silly *convenience* or *practicality*? And what's to prevent fetuses from being evaluated to be of fluctuating worth based upon varying circumstances, thoughtless judgments, or even the careless whims of an unbalanced mother? Is it really surprising that scientists in biotechnology want to harvest fetuses for their body parts or stem cells? After all, since fetuses are neither human nor sacred, there should not be any moral outrage!

We noted that the arguments in favor of abortion often revolve around the belief that an early fetus is not human; consequently, evacuating it could not be judged as immoral. This position finds justification in science, which maintains that because of the absence of brain activity in the first trimester, a fetus could not be considered human. We mentioned a few of the philosophical problems with this position within science. But there are additional difficulties when we consider that the scientific *threshold* between life and human life has clear social implications. If we are to deem a young fetus as less than human because it lacks brain activity, what does this imply for the acutely mentally handicapped or for those suffering from advanced Alzheimer's disease? In some of the more severe cases, mental and physical abilities are so compromised that the victims are virtually brain-dead and live in a sort of vegetative state with little or no brain activity. Are the brain-dead then no longer human? And some victims have more or less brain activity than others. Does this means that some victims are *less human* than others because they have diminished brain activity?

That these people cannot survive on their own, and must rely totally on technology for their sustained existence, pushes them even closer to the same status as a thoroughly dependent—and from a scientific view—nonhuman, first trimester fetus. If this is true, then what is the reasoning for *not* aborting these one-time, but no longer, human lives? This would seem to be a fair deduction, since possessing *less* of what it means to be human could easily be understood to mean being less human or, in some cases, not human at all.

The abortion issue is usually partitioned into two opposing and highly antagonistic camps: those who support abortion—"pro-choice" advocates—and those who are against it—"pro-life" advocates. In 1973, the United States Supreme Court delivered a controversial, landmark decision in *Roe v. Wade*, in which it maintained that making abortion illegal violated women's constitutional right to privacy. The verdict was also a clear victory for individual rights over collective rights and bolstered the struggle for women's equality and freedom in all arenas of life. A major difficulty in the pro-choice/pro-life debate is that the opposing groups often argue *past* each other. While pro-choice advocates reduce the abortion issue to a simple proposition: *women should have control over their own bodies*, the pro-life advocates move in a thoroughly different direction, adamantly proclaiming that the fetus is *alive*, and therefore abortion is tantamount to murder. Ever since the ruling in favor of abortion, the tension between the two factions has been building and has on occasion even turned violent. The pro-lifers believe that the high court overreached its constitutional authority in *Roe v. Wade*, and they have been relentless in trying to overturn this decision. So far, they have not been successful, even though they have managed to push the enactment of restrictions on abortion, such as requiring parental notification and spousal consent. As far as the status of *Roe v. Wade* is concerned, though, many believe that the 1973 ruling is "settled law" and will not be reversed anytime soon, if ever.

It's been a delicate balancing act for the U.S. government to make rulings on abortion. How does a secular government enter this area without trampling religious viewpoints? After all, the arguments against abortion in America are often based on the Bible. The high court itself has also been severely impeded by philosophical obstacles. For example, it's unable to decide a seemingly very simple but critical question with respect to abortion: when does life begin? Does life begin at conception or at some special time along the path of prenatal development? Without giving a clear answer to this question it's very difficult to justify fully any decision about when, if ever, abortion is acceptable.

The *Roe v. Wade* verdict sidestepped the problem by adopting the "trimester system." In it, a woman's pregnancy is divided into three, three-month segments; abortion could be performed in the first trimester (within three months of conception), but abortions could also be performed in the second or third trimesters if there are health concerns for the mother. In 1992, the trimester model was overturned, and "viability" became the new criterion—that is, an abortion may be performed if the fetus is not potentially able to survive on its own and *outside* of the womb. The viability model has its own problems; fetuses are now able survive outside the womb at younger ages, which means that for pro-choice advocates, the window of opportunity for abortions is shrinking.

An extremely contentious topic in the courts today is partial-birth abortion, a rarely-performed procedure in which a well-developed, prenatal child (late second to early third trimester) is partially extracted from the womb, killed, and then removed altogether. The justification usually given for partial-birth abortions is a health risk to the mother. Despite attempted bans, the high court has upheld this position, even though the evidence seems to show that this procedure may actually pose a greater health risk to the mother than allowing the child to go full term. Critics of partial-birth abortion insist that it's really a gruesome form of *infanticide* and that the term "abortion" does not even apply.

The abortion war has forced onto center stage, in spectacular fashion, some of the most profound issues in philosophy, some of the most intriguing questions in science, some of the most urgent questions in religion, some of the most complex questions in the social realm, and some of most challenging debates in the political sphere. Although many believe that *Roe v. Wade* is settled law, the numerous subjects that abortion has thrown into high relief are far from settled, and they will continue to antagonize our moral sensibilities until there is a philosophical breakthrough regarding abortion. What do I mean by a philosophical breakthrough, and what would it entail? Let's at least offer a beginning.

The abortion issue has underscored one question above all others, and how this question is answered will have deep consequences in all areas of our culture: *when does human life begin?* Many of the arguments in the abortion debate are either directly or indirectly connected to the possible answers to this question. Many pro-life advocates, for example, argue that life begins at conception. By contrast, pro-choice supporters usually rely on brain-function arguments for the threshold for becoming human, such as the point when the fetus shows clear signs of brain activity (five to seven months). The reason why this issue is so fundamental to the abortion argument is that, for many people, how it's answered defines the morality or immorality of abortion decisions. For instance, there appears to be a great deal to lose morally if one decides to have an abortion while believing that a fetus is really an authentic human life. In this case, an abortion could easily be seen as cold-blooded murder. On the other hand, if you believe that a very young fetus is nothing more than reproducing cells and is not yet human, then aborting it would not be seen as murder—but simply as the removal of unwanted cellular growth. The first position is that of the pro-life group, and pro-choice supporters subscribe to the second.

Does human life *begin at* conception, or does a fetus become human when it first shows signs of brain activity? This is my answer: being human is *more* than the capacity for brain activity; and the "more" has no quantitative measurement. This is the main point. Asking the question of when human life begins is not simply a scientific question about brain capacities but is a question of *value*. In our Western tradition, we place extreme value on each human life, and we do so not because specific physical, biological, or cognitive standards are met, but because we believe that *human life is inherently valuable simply by virtue of its coming into existence.* We must confess that the special value that we place on human life is a bias of Western civilization, one that some non-Western cultures don't necessarily share. Nonetheless, this bias is one of the defining features of our moral life, and forces us to an unavoidable conclusion: *human life begins at the moment of conception.* To reduce human life to reproducing cells, and argue that at some point along the path of its development it will qualify as human, is to think *irrationally* from the perspective of our Western value system.

But what if we want to see human life as simply another life-form? Could we still be convinced that *human life* begins at conception? Aside from the argument from the viewpoint of Western values, there is also the argument from what we know about genetics. At the moment of conception, *DNA* that is particular to the human species is mobilized to control and coordinate the growth of the new life that has just come into existence. The brain activity position for abortion is an example of what philosophers call an "ad hoc" argument, which means that it has no convincing, logical connection to the problem at hand. It is a logical tactic that is not necessarily irrational but is not honest. I will go further and say that using this argument to support the pro-choice position is nothing short of philosophical and moral cowardice. *The real motive behind this argument is that it provides pro-choice advocates a way around the accusation that abortion is killing human life.*

Pro-life advocates, for their part, go even further and argue that not only does human life begin at conception, but at the moment of conception, an actual "person" also comes into existence; they believe that this position gives more traction to the idea that abortion is murder. This belief is untenable, however, for the following reasons.

Personhood is not a purely biological state of being, but is a bio/cultural/social state of becoming. This state commences when a child is born. At that precise moment, external reality invades the baby's body and stimulates its physical senses for the first time, and cultural meaning rushes into a baby's immature, but highly receptive, thinking process. Sense stimulation is a baby's first contact with the outside world and starts the process of building its post-natal, cultural nature and existence. Blinding light, loud noises, odd smells, strange tastes, and alien sensations intrude into a baby's body and bring to life its natural powers and capacities to engage and adapt to this new life in the outside world. And what about a baby's thinking process? The brain of the newborn—even though it's highly underdeveloped at birth—is able, at least to some degree, to carry out one of its essential functions: to take in, organize, simplify, and integrate meaning from the cultural world.

The newly born, baby person also begins to participate emotionally, mentally, and physically in the real world. Interacting with the outside world, in fact, is one of the essential activities of personhood.

Although the baby is still dependent on its mother, this dependency is not unconditional. Other caretakers, such as medical aides, family members, friends, or other concerned members of society also assist in caring for the baby. And even though the mother usually remains in possession of her child, this possession is not absolute: besides being the son or daughter of its mother, the baby is also the son or daughter of its father, is a member of society, and by extension, is a participating member of the human race—which is another qualifying dimension of personhood.

Another important dimension of personhood is recognition by others of the baby's individuality: the newly baby person not only *feels* its separation from its mother, but it also *feels recognized* as an individual. This two-dimensional experience is the beginning of what will eventually become the person's self-consciousness of personal identity.

A newly born baby cries immediately upon entering the world; this first sound, and the accompanying initial breaths, represent a baby's first self-generated movements into its new cultural home. With these simple gestures, the baby instantly becomes a communicating participant in its new world, which is an essential aspect of personhood.

Personhood is not a biological characteristic that is automatically present at conception. Instead, it is a way of being that arises only when a baby enters a cultural world. Additionally, once a person comes into existence, he or she begins creating what I call a "legacy of personhood." This means that each individual creates a life-destiny that is unique to that person. At birth, a baby begins emoting and behaving in identifiable ways, and as this person, say, a girl, matures, she begins to think for herself and initiate actions of her own choosing; the consequence of all her emoting, behaving, thinking, choosing, and acting is that her life takes on a well-defined shape, gains substance, and moves forward into its own future. These are the *existential accomplishments* that define an individual's legacy of personhood, and they represent the very core of an existence. And this is the reason why an individual could never lose her person-status—even should old age or disease cause the decline or even the annihilation of her mental function. The person would still survive with her humanity intact, because her legacy of personhood *is* who a person is. What is a person but all that she felt, thought, believed, decided, acted on, lost, gained, suffered, celebrated, created, and accomplished?

So what does it mean to the question of abortion that a human life, and not a person, is created at conception? We have to pull ourselves up by our philosophical and moral bootstraps, come to our senses, return to the fire, and face the heat. Let's accept the situation for what it is: *although abortion does not kill people, it does kill human life.* So how are we to understand the killing of human life in abortion?

Unlike individual people who live in society, prenatal human life is naturally integrated into the nonpublic, internal world of its mother's uterus. This unique biological inner-connection necessarily translates into a unique moral relationship in which the mother is thoroughly and unconditionally responsibility for the new life that lives inside her. This unique moral relationship is best defined by what I call the "Ethic of the Natural Mother." This principle states that: *no authority exceeds that of the natural mother in caring for, or determining the fate of, the new human life that she has conceived.* The mother has earned this supreme right, because this new life lives in and through her—when she eats, the life inside her eats!

Because no authority exceeds that of the natural mother, society control over pre-natal life is highly restricted. The upshot of the mother's exalted position is that she has the exclusive power of life or death over the developing human life that lives inside her. Then what, if any, is the responsibility of society toward prenatal human life? The Ethic of the Natural Mother also maintains that if a mother should decide to carry her fetus to full term, the extreme value of each human life is duly activated, and society must ensure that the mother has the necessary means to care for it. Additionally, society must come to the aid of fetuses whose mothers are ill suited, physically or psychologically, for motherhood. In these circumstances, intervention strategies would be pursued to help both the mother and her fetus until the baby is born, and then the baby would be eligible for adoption.

For her part, the pregnant mother must face the fact that she is carrying human life in her womb, and that deciding to abort it would amount to killing this life. This is a momentous, *moral* choice and should be considered very carefully; the decision to abort a human life should never be taken lightly but should be based on thoughtful, responsible judgment. If a mother does choose to exercise this option, the Ethic of the Natural Mother asserts that her decision must be honored, and all necessary assistance must be available to her in terms of the best medical care to ensure that the abortion is carried out safely and in the best conditions. Abortions should be performed in the first trimester because fetus' nervous system is still largely underdeveloped, which means that the fetus is immune to any sort of pain or suffering.

A partial-birth abortion is an immoral act. "Partial-birth" means the partial birth of a person. *Aborting people is murder*—unethical killing, and should be legally prohibited, unless there is an indisputable danger to the mother's health. Partial birth of a person also means that the absolute authority that the mother had over her prenatal life is neutralized, and the life of the person is now protected by civil liberties as guaranteed by the United States Constitution.

The Ethic of the Natural Mother is the best solution to the abortion debate. It achieves two important goals: it upholds the right of the mother to make decisions about the prenatal human life for which she is absolutely responsible. It also permits society to retain its guiding ideal of the special value of human life, provided that the authority of the natural mother does not suspend it. This position is based on the idea that human life begins at conception—philosophically and scientifically, the most convincing and defendable position. This view focuses on the unique biological and moral relationship between the mother and the human life that she carries. The right of the mother to kill prenatal human life, therefore, has no moral implication for the treatment of post-natal human life—people. In other words, the fear of the so-called "slippery slope" has no philosophical traction.

The proposition that I have outlined is decidedly secular, and will not be received with open arms by our so-called religious culture. Despite the aggressive rise of Islam in a number of European countries, the total secularization of modern Western civilization is well on its way, even in America. The strong polarization between religious and secular camps that we observe in early twenty-first-century America, for example, is a typical stage that cultures travel through on their way to a complete secularism. As modern civilization comes to its philosophical senses, there will be radical shifts that will recast human existence in a different light. The idea that the natural mother is the ultimate caregiver and sustainer of her indwelling, prenatal human life—and not an alleged supernatural being in heaven—will then be seen as an unquestioned article of common sense, as will the doctrine of the Ethic of the Natural Mother.

14.15

The complex philosophical, scientific, moral, religious, and political issues that swirl around abortion are closely connected to another highly explosive and related topic: stem cell research. In the interest of curing diseases, reducing human suffering because of physical injury and/or genetic/biologic defects, and improving the quality of human life, biologists have begun to focus on the possibility of utilizing human cells, particularly very young cells, as a means to rejuvenate and repair dysfunctional biological parts and functions and even to replace them with newly created ones—at least this is the fantastic dream of many stem cell scientists.

Stem cells are found in early stages of newly embryonic development, and later in bone marrow, brain cells, the digestive tract, skin cells, liver cells, pancreas cells, blood vessels, skeletal muscle cells, and in blood taken from umbilical cords. All stem cells, wherever they may be found, derive from the body's master cells—*embryonic stem cells*, which are the richest in human growth potential. In fact, if the creative power of embryonic stem cells were ever fully harnessed, human immortality, or something resembling it, could actually become a reality. At the time of this writing, stem cell biologists have had very limited success in extracting embryonic stem cells successfully and making use of them in fruitful ways. However, it's clear that it's only a matter of time and research money until they will achieve the breakthroughs that will revolutionize medicine and health care and will transform life on Earth in many ways. Not the least of these transformations might be that human disease and permanent disabilities because of injury would become consigned forever to the past, and vibrant human life could easily be extended to well over one hundred years.

Although the other form of stem cells—adult stem cells—are also valuable biological enhancers, they don't have nearly the reproductive and creative muscle as do embryonic stem cells. *All* the body's tissues and functions develop from embryonic stem cells; adult stem cells are older and have become more specialized along specific biological channels—therefore, they have dramatically limited creative potential. In fact, stem cells become progressively more specific and limited the older they become. This is why five-day-old embryonic stem cells are ideal: they have not yet begun to specialize. Aging, adult stem cells are of much less interest to researchers, who are looking for the ultimate recipe for unprecedented, vibrant health, which they believe can be found only in the cells extracted from very young embryos. But the obstacles to unlocking the secrets of embryonic stem cells are formidable.

Like the pro-choice activists for abortion, embryonic stem cell researchers have been forced to grapple with complex philosophical, moral, religious, and political perspectives. Unfortunately, current stem cell technology (in the first years of the twenty-first century) is unable to extract embryonic stem cells from an embryo—a process carried out between five to seven days after fertilization—without destroying it; this will likely change soon. In the meantime, embryonic researchers have to contend with the accusation of murder that is frequently leveled against them; after all, the anti-embryonic stem cell activists maintain, a human being is being killed with the destruction of each embryo. Supporters of the process usually discount such interpretations. They argue that a five-day cluster of about 150 cells—what scientists call a "blastocyst"—sitting in a Petri dish hardly constitutes a human being. (A Petri dish is a shallow, round, and transparent dish with a lid that is used for such things as growing microbes or fertilizing eggs.)

A couple who has been unsuccessful conceiving may utilize the services of a fertility clinic, in which a female egg is extracted, placed in a Petri dish, and fertilized by male sperm and then "implanted" back into the female. The process of fertilizing an egg in this way is called in-vitro fertilization. Typically, at least twelve embryos are produced in this process to ensure that there are extra embryos, in case pregnancy fails to occur with the initial implantation. The extra embryos are frozen to keep them viable.

When we consider the possibility of eliminating cancer, diabetes, Alzheimer's disease, spinal cord injuries, and countless other human illnesses, would it not be a veritable crime against humanity to ignore an avenue that offers so much promise? But this is not the basic problem.

For many, embryos are *human beings* that deserve the high value that all human beings are traditionally accorded by Western moral perspectives. Manipulating embryos that have been created in fertility clinics for purposes of scientific research—and killing them—is, in this view, an appalling moral aberration, one, in fact, that is reminiscent of the awful Nazi crimes during the Second World War. It also points to the further debasement of humanity and the secular world's thorough abandonment of all moral sensibilities. Conservative thinkers believe that, with embryonic stem cell research, the secular moral compass has finally been broken beyond repair.

Others argue that we cannot honestly equate a cluster of human cells in a Petri dish with a breathing/thinking/feeling human being. And how could we not utilize these cells to try to improve the quality of life for human beings who are suffering, physically impaired, or dying of terrible diseases? How could we claim to be a moral and decent people and not pursue an avenue that could help so many in need? Supporters of embryonic stem cell research point to fertility clinics, where many embryos have been created and frozen, most of which will go unused and ultimately will be incinerated. Why allow such a rich source of life-enhancing cells to go to waste? Unfortunately, fertility clinics, even given the possibility of unlimited access to their embryos, simply don't have the quantity of frozen embryos that is necessary to meet the needs of scientific research. In order for this new scientific endeavor to bear fruit, many new embryos need to be created specifically for the purpose of research, but *harvesting* embryos, which is what this practice amounts to, is morally unacceptable to many and distasteful to all.

Nevertheless, stem cell research is here to stay, even though progress has been stifled in all countries worldwide by a lack of funding and sufficient governmental support. To be clear, the problem is specifically with embryonic stem cell research and not with adult stem cell research. Unfortunately, at the present moment, only the former holds the promise of leading science down the royal road to revolutionary medical and healthcare breakthroughs. On the other hand, this situation could change if, for instance, scientists were to discover a way to manipulate adult stem cell biochemistry in a way that would cause them to *regress* to younger, more "creative" phases. In such a case, the regressed stem cells could function, at least to some degree, like embryonic stem cells and provide the sorely needed stem cells.

To shed some light on this cultural/moral dilemma, we must consider the essential questions around which the conflicting positions revolve. Does a five-day-old cluster of growing cells in a Petri dish qualify as human life? Is an embryo a person? What is the difference in value between an embryo that is created naturally in the uterus and one that is produced artificially in a Petri dish? Is a person more valuable than an embryo? Are there religious implications in the creation of embryos for purposes of scientific research and killing them in the process? Should the government fund embryonic stem cell research? These are a few of the main questions that need to be confronted and answered. Let's try to answer each one briefly.

Does a five-day-old cluster of dividing cells in a Petri dish qualify as human life? Yes. A young embryo develops by virtue of genetic programming that is specific to the human species.

Is an embryo a person? No. Personhood can only emerge within the cultural world where an individual—even a baby person—is able meet the conditions of personhood, such as the requirement of interacting with the outside world physically, emotionally, and mentally.

What is the difference in value between an embryo that is created naturally in the uterus and one that is produced artificially in a Petri dish? If an embryo is conceived naturally in the uterus, it is subject to the Ethic of the Natural Mother, which gives the mother absolute control over the human life developing inside her. If a woman utilizes a fertility clinic for reproductive purposes exclusively, the same condition as above holds. If, however, a mother decides to *give over* her eggs to science, she forfeits her authority over them, and scientists can then use these eggs to produce embryos for embryonic stem cell research.

Is a person more valuable than an embryo? Yes. Despite the special value that we place on human life, a person's appearance in the world is of deeper concern and value for society and the reason is clear enough: a person's beliefs, decisions, and actions have consequences that directly and indirectly affect the lives of other people.

Are there religious implications in the creation of embryos for purposes of scientific research and killing them in the process? Yes. Stem cell research presupposes that an alleged God does not create each human life and that an embryo has no spiritual essence that should be preserved or respected. However, the secular viewpoint does not mean that human life cannot be seen as precious. Quite the contrary; this view maintains that thoughtful, informed choices with respect to this sort of biological research is an enthusiastic movement toward a greater humanism, precisely because it could result in the elevation in the quality of life for the human race.

Should the government fund embryonic stem cell research? Yes. One of the principal purposes of the government is to promote the well-being of its citizenry. Stem cell research will ultimately lead to breakthroughs that will dramatically improve the quality of life for all human beings. Governmental funding of embryonic stem cell research, therefore, is not only a "good" for society, it's also a moral responsibility.

14.18

Be suspicious of a person whose power of conviction does not vary with his power of reasoning, for he is being guided not by the love of the truth, by a passion for the facts, or even by the desire for what is just and fair, but by the endless cravings of a power-hungry spirit and the person will sacrifice anything and anyone to satisfy his need for self-inflation—even his own life and the lives of people he loves.

14.19

Animals—where instinct goes, there goes meaning.

Humans—where meaning goes, there goes instinct.

14.20

Existence has no meaning apart from nonexistence; this can only mean that they both *are* in different ways.

14.21

Meaning-forms are expressions of existence and as such are repositories of energy. When they lose their energy, they lose their meaning.

14.22

Before compassion is possible, the ground must be prepared, if even for a brief moment, by one party being capable of *recognizing* another.

14.23

Music is beauty's most devoted lover: intrusive, seductive, and intoxicating. The greater the music, the more irresistible are its entreaties and the more insatiable are its appetites.

14.24

Why does Puccini's music tug and tear at the heart? Why do his lovely melodies and exquisite harmonies cause us to feel so much joy *and* so much suffering? His is the most tender music ever written—youthful, innocent, and fragile—music of the first kiss, but tragically, also of the last.

14.25

The ability of great art to capture the heart and overwhelm the mind is rooted in its mysterious presence: astonishing, unexpected, inexplicable, and even unjustified. Might we say the same of love?

14.26

Human beings know existence from the *inside*, from the cravings and compulsions of individuality.

15
Nietzsche: Destroyer and Visionary

✳

"Courageous, untroubled, mocking, and violent is what wisdom wants us to be. Wisdom is a woman and always loves only a warrior."
FriedrichNietzsche (1844–1900)

15.1

Friedrich Nietzsche's ideas rarely remained floating harmlessly in abstract, theoretical space, but instead they smashed violently into the cultural terrain of modern Western civilization. They were invasive, disrupting, disturbing, destructive, and surging with energy. They caused philosophical earthquakes and upheavals and announced the beginning of a new phase of world history. Nietzsche said as much when speaking about himself in 1888 toward the end of his short life: "I am no man, I am dynamite." Here was a philosopher of a different sort: a luminous thinker, a literary genius, and a cultural revolutionary. We would have to go back well over two thousand years—to Plato—to find someone of comparable gifts. Nietzsche's preternatural mind also exposed the false optimism of his time, gazed prophetically into the future, and saw, with startling clarity, the spiritual, political, and social cataclysms that were right around the historical corner. He presented his famous diagnoses in some of the most beautiful and brilliant prose of any thinker—sometimes shocking, scathing, and incendiary, but rarely without piercing relevancy and daring insight. And his solutions were hardly less beautifully conceived and described. They were sensational—and seductive.

Since his untimely death in 1900, Nietzsche's fame has grown steadily as it became more and more evident that not only was his thought characterized by profound depth and richness, but it also speaks directly and urgently to many critical issues in today's culture.

Nietzsche himself predicted that great fame would come to him only after his death: "some are born posthumously," he said famously in his autobiography, *Ecce Homo*. Even now, we are only beginning to comprehend what this lonely genius had to say to us. There is no doubt that he is still in the process of being born and will continue to do so for many centuries to come.

Nietzsche simply didn't have thoughts and insights; *they had him*—they possessed him body and soul. At times they came like a thief in the night, ambushing and disarming him, and even disorienting him. In other moments, they emerged quietly from thoughtless silence only to gain complete mastery—at least temporarily—over his thinking and understanding of the world. Many of his ingenious ideas, shocking intuitions, and amazing epiphanies came into existence first like precious little babies crying out for nourishment, and he nurtured them with the selfless care and patience of a proud and loving mother until they were strong, flexible, and resilient. But all this is not surprising for a man who was continuously pregnant with philosophical insight. As a result, the world lit up for him, and he was enraptured by it.

His love for his ideas was, nonetheless, never unconditional. Once they gained strength and sovereignty, he provoked, challenged, and even attacked them. And what was his standard of judgment? Does a thought exult or betray the earth? Does an idea lead to an overflow or depletion of life's energies? Nietzsche's heart was deeply embedded in the everyday world, where, for him, all that really mattered in life exists. His love for worldly truth was so uncompromising that he was even willing to sacrifice his own beloved firstborn truths for its sake. And he often did. His thinking was unmasking, subversive, and destructive; but it was also revealing, affirming, and creative—both aspects of his thinking were complementary and indispensable. Since thinking was for him an *entering into* the world and not a retreat or abstraction from it, his ideas and writings were naturally saturated with feelings, moods, and passions.

One of his noteworthy literary achievements, in fact, was that he could make his *thoughts emote* just as he could make his *feelings think*. This poetic capability is quite extraordinary for a philosopher, but in his view, incorporating this dimension into philosophical thinking is really what genuine philosophy requires; it is a more *truthful* means to reach reality. Ideas are nothing if not ways to express some truth about the world. But for ideas to be truthful, they must be *inclusive*. For Nietzsche, the mechanics of the world may appear to be logical and orderly, but if we probe more deeply, we will discover that the world has a domineering, frenetic, unpredictable, explosive, and random component to it. In his view, our natural feelings, passions, and instincts are not stupid or empty; they *register* these facts of reality. They *know* something! To put it succinctly: our emotions, passions, and instincts are *ways into* the world. Feelings of courage and fear in the face of real-life challenges, our passion for adventure and excitement, and our sense of wonder at the fact of mere existence point to the genuine risks, opportunities, and realities that make up normal human existence. Imagine the overwhelming emotions of joy, elation, excitement, and gratitude that you would experience should you discover that your father and mother survived a horrible car crash with hardly a scratch. Wouldn't these emotions deepen your sense of being alive, make you realize a richer meaning of love for your parents, and even lead to a clearer understanding about your own purpose?

Although emotions like joy and gratitude may possess important knowledge of existence, it's in compulsions, cravings, and instinctual drives that human beings truly come face to face with reality. Where reason is distant, detached, and general, the passions are intimate, engaging, and particular. Sexual experiences, for instance, can go to a deeper, more revealing level of the real world, where our superficial thoughts and culture-based biases and judgments are left far behind. One might call knowledge of this sort *lived knowledge*, where life discloses its meanings through a human being acting instinctively— that is, naturally. And what is the nature of the knowledge that one discovers in lived experiences? One sees more keenly, and one hears, smells, tastes, and feels more intensely—my body is no longer a clumsy, insensate lump of flesh, bone, and muscle that makes itself known to me only when there is some sort of imbalance or irritation or when its petty needs cry out for satisfaction. Rather, in powerful, lived knowledge, my body comes alive; it quakes, it quivers, it feels itself to its very core. Now the world is no longer simply *out there*—obtuse and barely touchable, but is *in here, in me*, trembling under my skin. My whole body feels its textures and swelling power. The world—nature—

is now pulsating *in me*. And what comes of thinking? Analyzing, dissecting, compartmentalizing, and objectifying are circumvented altogether. In lived knowledge, the power of thinking to divide the world into artificial parts is duly neutralized and now works only to incorporate, unify, and harmonize all that is. Lived knowledge is a very different kind of knowledge. But there is yet another dimension to lived knowledge.

Nietzsche viewed creativity as the power that is most extraordinary and best about human beings. The reason for his lofty estimate of creative expression was that, for him, *an act of creativity is natural, spontaneous knowing,* an essential aspect of a life well lived. Where does creativity originate? In the conscious mind? Certainly not. Creativity originates well below our awareness, where logic has no reach whatsoever. It's in a vast, dark, and tumultuous realm of the unconscious where creativity is birthed and where it derives its sublime power to bring something new into existence. And that something new is knowledge—knowledge about how to apply paint to canvas, build a ship, smash an atom, design computers, or remodel a house. Although study, experience, and talent are helpful preconditions to creative output, there is something altogether different about the actual process of true creative expression: it transcends our accumulated knowledge, experience, and even talent and takes us into the realm of the unknown. We become the effortless, thoughtless vessels through which new knowledge passes and is manifested. It's precisely because creative actions are natural and unlearned and possess profound knowledge that Nietzsche believed that through them we come closest to understanding the meaning of the world. It's for this reason that he says that creative expression is our *noblest instinct.*

It's clear that, for Nietzsche, pure reason alone could never get to the core of existence, and this is why he often argued so strongly for the importance of lived knowledge and passionate experience. This did not mean that he abhorred rational thinking, however—only rapacious, life-negating versions of it. His whole life as a philosopher was dedicated to the art of thinking, and he experimented constantly with its various forms in the effort to make thinking speak the truth of existence. Nietzsche was, nonetheless, suspicious of cold, feeling-less logic, because he believed that, on its own, it does not does serve authentic philosophical thinking. In fact, when taken to an *irrational* extreme, logical thinking was for him a sort of insidious virus that short-circuited the truth-seeking process. So what was Nietzsche's recipe for discovering truth?

Only reason *dynamically interacting* with our feelings, passions, and instincts could approach the truth of *what is*. In this approach to philosophy, the conflict and tension that may naturally arise when the restraint of reason openly engages the uninhibited life of feelings, passions, and instincts offer a philosopher the fortunate opportunity to penetrate more deeply into the truth of the world. In fact, the genuine seeker of truth must be able to sustain considerable psychological and philosophical imbalance and discomfort during the quest for knowledge. As Nietzsche said, it is only out of "chaos" that real insight into *what is*, is born. Insight was what Nietzsche was ultimately after, and he was perhaps the most insightful philosopher of all time. Micro-visions of all kinds often came to him in flashes—frequently when he was hiking in the Swiss Alps or strolling thoughtfully along the seaside in Italy. The intensity of these sudden flashes of insight and the fact that they seemed to come out of nowhere always astonished him. There is no question that there is a direct connection between his unrivaled capacity for penetrating insight and how he carried out his art of philosophizing.

Nietzsche's writings show in extraordinary detail his philosophical strategy for gaining insight: he was continuously shifting perspectives. He was experimental, inventive, probing, suspicious, brutally candid, confrontational, intrusive, explosive, and audacious. In this sense, he was the Leonardo of philosophers—his restless and infinitely curious mind moved from one realm of existence to another and deployed a rich variety of approaches in the effort to understand virtually every aspect of existence. Nietzsche preferred the *aphoristic* form of philosophizing above all others, because it allowed him to penetrate a subject matter quickly and incisively and to extract, in untarnished condition, many precious philosophical gems. Additionally, the aphoristic approach represented his opposition to grand *systems* of thought, which Nietzsche believed did more to obscure and bury truth than to reveal it. When a philosopher creates a philosophical system, his primary concern quickly turns to ensuring that all his ideas and lines of thinking are logically compatible. In this effort to think systematically, revealing the truth of what is could easily be sacrificed; philosophical systems also house biases and hidden agendas of all kinds that are easily disguised by clever and dishonest reasoning. In contrast, by registering insights in aphorisms, the philosopher's loyalty is only to the insight that is now entering his consciousness. As a result, there is a greater chance of capturing real understanding, with a minimum of logical and ideological distortions and tricks.

What drove Nietzsche in his relentless pursuit of reality was his belief that philosophy should never be content with itself or what it *thinks* it has accomplished; rather, it must continue doing what it does best: unmask and reveal what is false, deceitful, and truth-negating, as well as bring *into the open* what something really is—that is to say, *to let be* what is. He opposed any measure that artificially constrained or narrowed the philosophical process, because the pursuit of truth, knowledge, and wisdom has no endpoint. It's for this reason that philosophy must employ as many ways of knowing as possible. The expunging of emotion, passion, and instinct from most of traditional philosophy is, in this sense, a strategic mistake, a failure of philosophical nerve, and the sure recipe for error. This is why Nietzsche saw the usual practice of philosophy as largely untrue, deceitful, degrading, corrupt, diseased, and anti-life affirming—in a word: *nihilistic*.

Nietzsche has had many labels attached to his name—atheist, revolutionary, optimist, pessimist mystic, pagan, visionary, fascist, prophet, militant, elitist, materialist, racist, and nihilist—the list could go on and on. In fact, all these descriptions are reflected in his philosophy. That a genius could embody contradictory qualities is nothing unusual—think of the lonely, brooding, and volatile Beethoven who was famously misanthropic, but whose immortal *Symphony No. 9* was a clarion call to universal brotherhood. What is significant about Nietzsche's contradictions, however, is that they are conspicuously present throughout his writings. Philosophy in the West has traditionally been described as the *rational* pursuit of truth and wisdom. Implicit in the idea of rational pursuit is logical consistency, and the greatest philosophers have always self-consciously aimed at presenting their ideas or theories with logical necessity. The whole history of philosophy is largely the long story of how the ideas and theories of great thinkers were changed or overthrown because of their failure to meet their logical commitments and obligations. Nietzsche thought that this whole tradition of logical philosophizing was a profound failure that needed reformulating. Logic is indispensable to philosophy as long as it serves to reveal *what is*. But what Nietzsche diagnosed in the long Western philosophical tradition was that logic had been employed more as a tool to confuse or hide what is the case rather than to reveal it. Why would logic be put to such disgraceful use?

Nietzsche's astonishing answer was that *behind philosophy stands psychology*. The notion that there is a connection between psychological states and philosophical ideas flies in the face of a cherished principle of philosophical analysis, which says that the validity or truthfulness of an idea or theory must stand or fall on the merits or demerits of the ideas or theories alone. In short, psychology has no relevance to philosophy. Although Nietzsche agreed that truth claims need to be rationally justified, he also believed that ignoring the psychology behind the different forms of thinking was naïve, misguided, and even dangerous. The logical justification for separating philosophy from psychology is a prime example of how reason could be misused to inhibit what was for him beyond dispute: how one sees, judges, and understands the world, what one values, and even how one feels about life in general indicate varying degrees of physical, philosophical, and emotional health or illness. Nietzsche put forth two psychologies that he believed embody these states of psychological being in very specific ways: master morality and slave morality.

Nietzsche advocated both a holistic and naturalistic approach to understanding all aspects of human reality. Philosophies and worldviews that compartmentalize the human mind and body into mutually independent boxes are as misguided as is trying to explain human experience through supernatural sources. For example, thinking is not simply a mental activity but is a natural aspect of the biological life of the body, and, as a result, it also expresses the quality of life of the body. If thinking is not *pure mind*, then the body is not only purely physical sensation and actions, either, but is naturally animated, vitalized, and even devitalized by thoughts, feelings, and orienting viewpoints. In short, the mind and body *interpenetrate* each other in both simple and complex ways to the point where it is philosophically illegitimate to focus on one aspect to the exclusion of the other. But Nietzsche offered us a new understanding of the mind and body and their relationship that led to startling conclusions.

For Nietzsche, all life, whether in its various physical forms or in its psycho/emotional forms, has two distinct orientations—one toward increasing health, expansive power, and greater levels of self-sufficiency, and the other toward illness, impotence, and increased levels of dependency. Life is a never-ending struggle between these two antagonistic forces. In human life, particularly, this struggle plays itself out in spectacular fashion. Additionally, these orientations do not operate on the biological level alone but also enter freely into the psychological, emotional, philosophical, and even cultural realms and are expressed through these dimensions in numberless ways. One of Nietzsche's most provocative and influential ideas was that not only is the orientation toward health, strength, and self-sufficiency an *aggressive* force that invades and informs human nature, but, paradoxically, the orientation toward sickness, impotency, and dependency also strives for domination, control, and command in human life. A favorite Nietzschean technique for understanding a particular human being's state of health was to pose the question as to which of the two powers was on the *ascent* in the person: did strength or weakness, life affirmation or life negation, claim his spirit? The implications of this theory are many, but Nietzsche was particularly interested in the effects that these contradictory energies have on moral behavior.

Nietzsche asked us to consider a person with a strong, disciplined, self-reliant, and domineering nature; who engages life passionately; who enjoys the many challenges of existence and approaches them joyfully and with vigor; who says "yes" to life; who enjoys his bodily passions and delights in the world of the senses; who has immense self-esteem and self-respect; who takes pleasure in thinking for himself; who endures well the hardships of existence; who prefers to lead and command rather than follow and be commanded; who judges what is strong, confident, and proud as good and what is weak, submissive, and meek as bad. Nietzsche called this mindset "master morality." People guided by master morality are also distinguished by having created their own values—in effect, they live by their own rules, rules that serve to nurture and augment their self-sufficiency, strength of character, and ability to act in the world with creative resolve, wisdom, and authority. Master morality is the morality of legislators, leaders, heroic warriors, and creators of all kinds—especially artists. In master morality, the two antagonistic forces of life have reached a finely tuned balance, in which the orientation toward health, expanding power, and self-sufficiency has gained the upper hand over the powers of sickness, impotency, and dependency. As a result, the vital energies of life in an individual are able to control and even utilize their antipodes to promote even greater spiritual health as well as strength and depth of character.

Contrast this person with someone with an existentially supine, spiritually anemic, and self-loathing nature; who looks upon sensual pleasure and the body's natural desires with snarling suspicion, guilt, and disgust; who says "no" to life; who is racked by guilt, insecurity, and self-hatred; who suffers from a sense of physical, emotional, and psychological powerlessness and impotency. Nietzsche called this mindset "slave morality." Those guided by slave morality have little interest in thinking for themselves and typically look outside of themselves, often to higher authorities, for guidance and meaning. Their values are those that they thoughtlessly adopt and defend not by honest reasoning or deep conviction, but by defensive and superficial rationalizing. In contrast with master morality, in slave morality what is sick, deteriorating, and weak has overcome over what is healthy, progressive, and self-sufficient.

These two moral types of people served as psychological archetypes for Nietzsche, as each reflects the results of the power struggle between life's two conflicting forces and define two radically divergent ways of living in the world. Whereas in master morality the *affirmation* of earthly existence is the guiding spirit, Nietzsche argued that the dominant force in slave morality is the all-consuming emotion of *resentment.* In the mentality of resentment, Nietzsche believed that he had uncovered a profound truth about human psychology. Operating on his premise that the two antagonistic forces of nature necessarily express themselves aggressively in and through the human realm, he reached the conclusion that the expressions of resentment in slave morality signal the crushing victory of life-negating weakness over life-affirming strength. Resentment is a form of psychological anger that is consumed by revenge and malice toward whatever stands opposed to it:

battle with resentment

people who are strong, healthy, self-sufficient, self-loving, passionate, and life-affirming—in other words, those who are guided by master morality. How did Nietzsche arrive at his ideas about morality?

Nietzsche's approach to moral questions was "genealogical"; that is, he sought to understand the *historical* circumstances from which different moral codes emerged. He argued that the earliest version of master morality was the original moral code of primitive humanity in the West. Warrior-like, *noble* savages at this time proclaimed a primary moral division between "good" and "bad" actions. Good actions follow from physical and emotional toughness, courage, self-reliance, pride, swelling self-esteem, and an overflowing joy at being alive. For these masters, the good life is an *active* one, because action engages, promotes, and provokes human abilities, draws on human potential, and encourages boldness of thought and behavior in everyday life. In this sense, good and noble are equivalent.

On the other hand, the ancient masters judged bad actions as those that follow from weakness of character, from a lack or depletion of vital energy, from a sense of inferiority and inadequacy, and from a willingness to submit rather than to lead. In this context, bad is equivalent to common or ignoble. And what group of people embodied these bad moral qualities? *Slaves.* This primitive master/slave relationship was Nietzsche's key for uncovering the moral character of Western history and, particularly, the emergence of resentment as a motivating cultural force. Nietzsche focused on the psychological relationship between these two antagonistic but complementary factions.

The first savage masters subdued and enslaved people and ruled over every aspect of their existence. The masters had contempt for their slaves, whom they viewed as lowly, nonhuman animals—mere *beasts of burden*—that deserved neither respect nor dignity. The masters addressed their slaves only from the "pathos of distance"—that is, by looking down on them with great disdain. The slaves, in turn, despised their masters but, nonetheless, secretly harbored deep feelings of envy and jealously: *how they wished that they, too, could be powerful and in command of the world around them!* The psychological effect of being treated as powerless and degenerate non-people was devastating to the slaves' psychology and resulted in the poisoning of their character. To add additional damage to an already badly beaten self-image, the slaves believed privately that their masters' low estimate of them was, in fact, true—and they *hated themselves for it.*

The slave now saw the world only through the blood-gorged, bulging eyes of rage and revenge. Nietzsche located the birth of resentment at this precise moment and argued that this mentality accomplished a feat that resulted in the most radical turning point in the moral history of the West. The "spirit of resentment" represented a particularly malevolent synthesis of nature's two antagonistic orientations and signaled the triumph of death over life, disease over health, and of a morality of life-negating vindictiveness over one of life-affirming passion. Resentment, in short, became "creative" and gave birth to a new moral code. Nietzsche called this moral birthing out of resentment the "transvaluation of values."

In resentment, the powers of sickness, impotency, and dependency gained sway over the orientation toward health, strength, and self-sufficiency. Nietzsche asked us to consider what a morality would look like if the person moralizing was being guided by resentment. This was the essential moral question for Nietzsche, and his answer was straightforward. The "slave revolt" in morality turned master morality on its head: the original division of "good and bad" in master morality had now changed to "good and evil." What was now considered "good" for the slave was the opposite of master morality: submission, humility, chastity, self-pity, selflessness, and self-sacrifice. And not only were these moral qualities good, but so too was the slave who embodied them.

Furthermore, what was now evil was what the master morality had originally judged as good: pride, self-confidence, sensual expression, worldly ambition, love of life, self-love, and bold independence. Following suit, the person who embodied any or all of these moral qualities was *evil.* Master morality, from the perspective of this new moral code, was decadent and morally depraved. With this moral flip-flop, the slaves repressed their self-loathing and their sense of impotence; now their *feeling of power* surged, and they looked upon their former masters with contempt and the uncontainable desire for revenge. But where did resentment emerge in the first place, and under what precise conditions? Nietzsche's genealogical quest to understand the origin of resentment led him to the cultural soil of Judaism and Christianity.

Nietzsche's great admiration for the Jews—who he thought were exceptionally intelligent and morally tenacious—did not stop him from seeing in their harsh historical circumstances the conditions that first gave rise to the philosophy of resentment in the Western world. This "nation of priests" was the first to institutionalize resentment in reaction to their long history of servitude at the hands of ruthless masters. It was in their rituals, customs, and especially in their strict moral code that resentment took its various forms. Even more remarkable was the new psychology of guilt, fear, and punishment that developed among the Jews. According to Nietzsche, these emotions had a long pre-history, in which ancient economic relations of owing debts in primitive business transactions (and all the guilt, fear, and punishment that attended this) became transferred over time, and through the mythical imagination, to the supernatural realm—to God. Thus, God became the one to whom the Jews had to repay endlessly for *his* infinite generosity. The transvaluation of values that resulted in the new Jewish morality, coupled with the psychology of guilt, fear, and punishment, all came together to produce, most notably, the religious conscience (self-imposed responsibility), altruism (sacrificing oneself for others), and asceticism (repressing instincts and denying oneself pleasure). All three of these are forms of psychological self-punishment that were the consequence of not repaying sufficiently well one's debts to God. Nietzsche called this way of living "herd morality."

Nonetheless, Nietzsche's wrath was not aimed toward the Jews. In fact, he not only heaped praise on famous Jews like Jesus and Spinoza, and was profoundly moved by the Jewish people's relentless will to survive under the worst conditions, but he also held much of the Old Testament in very high esteem and lauded its heroic spirit and powerful personalities. Although Nietzsche's ideas unintentionally but clearly stoked the flames of anti-Semitism, he had no tolerance for that prejudice, and he even broke off with his great mentor, composer Richard Wagner, at least in part because of Wagner's rabid anti-Semitism.

15.2

About Christianity Nietzsche had no mixed feelings whatsoever. Although he thought that Jesus had gone astray with his emphasis on the value of an afterlife, Nietzsche respected and admired the man, who he believed was a true cultural revolutionary and moral genius. Nietzsche argued throughout all his writings that one crucial indicator of individual greatness is the extent to which a person lives by values of his own creation. Jesus was for Nietzsche this kind of elevated person. His moral radicalism greatly appealed to Nietzsche, as did Jesus' unwavering commitment to his own beliefs. Nietzsche once said famously of Jesus, "There was only one Christian—he died on the cross." On the other hand, Nietzsche did not feel nearly the same enthusiasm for the religion that grew up around Jesus' name.

If Judaism originally gave birth to resentment, it was in the radical Jewish sect of Christianity where resentment was transformed into an all-consuming monster. And the aim of its voracious appetite? Nothing short of devouring all of Western culture. Nietzsche felt that Apostle Paul was the true culprit in Christianity's insidious rise to power. He had perverted the teachings of Jesus and turned Christianity into a revengeful, life-negating religion. It was because Christianity wreaked havoc on the spiritual well-being of Western culture that Nietzsche waged war on it. He knew what he was up against. A force that had dominated Western culture for nearly two thousand years would take super-heroic measures to defeat. Yet it had to be done, for in his view not only is Christianity the darkest lie in Western history, but it's also a malignant disease, one that has ravaged Nietzsche's beloved Earth far too long.

Much of Nietzsche's philosophy dealt with the cultural implications of atheism. But unlike Enlightenment thinkers like David Hume, he wasn't much concerned with the illogic of believing in God. He believed that Western culture had moved past this issue—at least philosophically. If Nietzsche were alive today and was asked to comment on the topic, he probably would say something like, "Offering reasons against believing in God would be analogous to giving reasons why the Tooth Fairy or Santa Claus does not or could not exist. The belief in God and the reasons for this belief are likewise ridiculous and below philosophical dignity."

Despite his strong stances against untruth and Christianity in particular, Nietzsche wasn't necessarily opposed to belief in illusion. On the contrary, he believed that great illusion made life richer and more beautiful; illusion serves us best when it inspires heroic action and compels us to go beyond ourselves, beyond our natural limitations, to achieve greatness. In this sense, he would say that illusion is indispensable to human life. The important question was whether or not a belief, idea, or worldview exalts and affirms this world or degrades and betrays it. As we will see, he attacked Western philosophy and especially its founder, Socrates, for destroying the power of myth to inspire greatness in true thought and action. Because of his deep belief in life-inspiring illusions, it's easy to understand why Nietzsche adored Greek mythology (before Socrates) and even called himself a devoted disciple of Dionysus, the god of wine, abundance, and fertility.

That the Christian religion is untrue was not the essential issue for Nietzsche; what mattered to him most was that, according to the New Testament, the Christian values of pity, self-denial, anti-passion, anti-reason, and selflessness were the expressions of resentment, the mentality of *anti-life*. Nietzsche thought that one of his greatest achievements was that he had "unmasked" the hidden psychology of Christianity and brought to light its secret ambition: to gain power and advantage in the world by scheming and plotting against powerful, life-affirming people—in effect, to control the destiny of the Western soul. And what was the Christian strategy? To use every form of rational trickery and psychological manipulation to subvert honest, healthy thinking so the world is seen as sinful through and through. And for most of Western history, the guiding spirit of Christian revenge has been successful and is still very much with us; the important thoughts, actions, and aspirations of Western humanity still reek of Christian virtues and sensibilities.

The most immediate inclination of the Christian type is to *pull back* in the face of existential realities of life and to relinquish his autonomy to his religious group. The Christian eagerness to live a servile existence produced a specific way of thinking. Christian thinking is not aimed at discovery or probing into the mysteries and uncertainties of life as much as it is a *weapon* for moral criticism, mind and behavior control of Christians and non-Christians alike, and conflict resolution within the Christian community. Thinking used in this way is reactive, defensive, deceptive, cunning, and manipulative—in short, it's a pragmatic strategy for maintaining the status quo. As a purely intellectual process among its leaders, Christians try to convince both believers and nonbelievers that Christianity alike that their exclusive value system is the only good and proper way to live, and that all other ways are misguided and evil.

New Testament Christianity also wages a systematic, psychological war on the passions of the body in an attempt to eradicate all natural desires that cannot be steadfastly controlled. For example, sexuality is typically sanctioned only within a clearly prescribed context—in other words, in ritualized marriage—and in these instances there are usually rigid regulations as to which sexual practices are acceptable and which are not. The general rule is that sexual intercourse is to be carried out exclusively for the purpose of reproduction and not for sensual pleasure. Following scriptural sentiments, sexual intercourse only for the sake of pleasure is typically judged as soiled, impure, and disgusting. Further, sexual practices that could not possibly result in pregnancy are strictly forbidden.

For Nietzsche, the whole tradition of Christianity had an appallingly sadistic basis to it. For instance, self-mutilations, self-flagellations, and morbid self-sacrifice were promoted as the highest forms of spiritual practice during the Middle Ages. Extreme physical and psychological pain and suffering were also seen as good for the *soul*. And who were the greatest promoters of Christian sadism? Priests! They were psychological experts in convincing their congregations that they were, as Saint Paul put it, "as filthy rags" and, by nature, unworthy of dignity or respect.

Filled with sin, desires, and lustful thoughts, human beings are lost and—without "salvation through Christ"—are bound for "eternal damnation" in a place designed to punish them for their darkened natures: hell. Human beings are naturally attached to the "things of this world," and as such, they are in direct contact with the "Prince of Darkness"—Satan—the evil angel who was cast out of heaven for rebelling against God. Now Satan, along with his demonic underlings, roams the earth looking for humans to seduce into turning away from the Gospel of Jesus Christ. And how do Satan and his servants carry out their mission of seduction? By using temptations—such as sexual craving—to keep human interests focused exclusively on the "desires of the flesh" and by obstructing their spiritual vision so they cannot see the truthfulness of Christianity. During the Middle Ages, Satan and his demons were believed to populate the world and were seen as the source of countless calamities, from physical and mental illness to every form of disagreeable and sensual-based behavior. The earth was Satan's playground; he was everywhere and in everything, and he was always ready to take full demonic advantage of even a moment of moral weakness in order to steal someone's soul and salvation. Life was terrifying: one could easily end up in hell suffering for an eternity if one was not careful.

Let's not forget about the tens of thousands of girls and women in the Middle Ages who were slowly tortured and brutally murdered by the church in the most gruesome ways, simply for being accused of being *witches*—Satan's female servants. Is it any wonder that many terrified and guilt-ridden Christians routinely engaged in self-mutilations and self-flagellations—both literal and psychological—to try to neutralize their nasty thoughts or misdeeds? And who were the heroes during this time in Western history? The many Catholic saints, like Saint Anthony, who were glorified as cultural icons for their horrific acts of self-torture and appalling lifestyles of self-deprivation—such as fasting to the point of death, drinking laundry water, and using rocks for pillows. But as Nietzsche pointed out, pain, agony, suffering, torture, and bloodshed are important elements of a religion possessed by the most perversely violent form of resentment. Let's not forget that, according to the New Testament, Christ's life ended with unspeakable torture and then was terminated with one of the most painful kinds of death: Roman crucifixion. And of what does Christian "Communion" consist? Ritualistically drinking the blood and eating the body of Christ! For Nietzsche, this ceremonial form of cannibalism was the natural expression of a death-oriented psychology.

If Nietzsche were alive today, he would undoubtedly find it amusing that even modern-day fundamentalists and committed evangelicals rarely bring up Satan, hell, eternal damnation, demon possession, and the whole Christian exhortation to extreme self-negation—all of which are clearly chronicled in New Testament Christianity. Is this *deception through omission* just another ploy in resentment's arsenal to keep the real soul of Christianity hidden from the critical thinking that dominates Western culture, so it can continue to influence the life of Western civilization? After all, even the most devout Christian would find it hard to justify many of the beliefs and practices outlined in the New Testament (not to mention in the Old Testament), such as the view that life on Earth should be repudiated or the view that to live a genuine Christian life, one must endure suffering patiently, live in poverty as did Jesus ("Pick up your cross and follow after me"), and endure this evil, Satan-dominated life by focusing on life after death.

But resentment's lust for revenge still rears its ugly head even in today's comparatively diminished religious culture. Who does the death penalty really benefit, for example? Nietzsche would likely say that putting someone to death is rarely done out of a true sense of justice, but is a pure and simple act of *revenge*. In fact, he would go further and say that the death penalty is just a convenient excuse for killing someone and that the executioner and those looking on actually derive perverse gratification from seeing someone die—and many of them would prefer to watch a slow, painful death. It's interesting to note that death by lethal injection, compared to death by hanging or death by the electric chair, is a relatively humane form of carrying out the death penalty and is for this reason less desirable for some death-penalty advocates in Christian America. This is not to suggest that only Christians enjoy a good death, but simply that deriving pleasure from watching an execution has a special poignancy and irony for an alleged religion of love and forgiveness. Is it a mere coincidence that the death penalty is still in place in America (and in other hyper-religious cultures, such as those in the Muslim world), the most self-proclaimed religious country in the Western world, while all European countries have abandoned it long ago—along with their religiosity? There is no doubt that Nietzsche would have predicted the continuation of the death penalty in America had his prescient mind fallen upon the subject.

As we noted, Nietzsche believed that understanding a belief system required unmasking the psychology that stands behind it. Western culture has two traditions and corresponding psychologies that have guided its history: Greco-Roman and Judeo-Christian. Each represents a radically different worldview, including mutually antagonistic value systems. Nietzsche held that the Greco-Roman tradition is life-affirming and joyous, while the Judeo-Christian tradition is life-negating and depressing. These two psychologies together represent a sort of *collective unconsciousness* of Western culture, with each psychology gaining dominance over the other at different historical moments and even battling it out in one culture at particular times. For example, the Judeo-Christian tradition reigned supreme during most of the Middle Ages, while the Greco-Roman tradition of paganism regained considerable power and influence during the Italian Renaissance, even though the Italian culture was still Christian. And during the French Enlightenment in the eighteenth century, Christianity was finally pushed to the outskirts of cultural and intellectual life altogether as the pagan worldview moved to center stage. (Nietzsche would probably say that the violence that characterized French culture during the Enlightenment resulted more from the irrational fanaticism of competing groups than from cultural resentment.)

The centuries-long dominance and influence of Christian resentment had a particular irony for Nietzsche and brings us to one of his most fantastic and audacious proclamations. In the middle of his notorious aphorism "The Madman," in his book *The Gay Science*, Nietzsche declares: "God is dead."

"God is dead. God remains dead. And we have killed him." Why would Nietzsche, who made his atheism no secret, make such a claim? How could God be dead if he never existed in the first place? Nietzsche deliberately employed this provocative language to call attention to his belief that the existence or nonexistence of God is beside the point; what really matters is whether or not God's existence is believable. During the Middle Ages, God's existence was accepted unconditionally; in fact, atheism as a meaningful concept had no place in the mindset of the time. Compelling philosophical arguments for atheism had yet to be formulated, and the scientific revolution was still in the future—and, along with it, the rationale for a totally material, godless universe. The result of the unquestioned belief in God was that every aspect of medieval life was completely informed by the mores, rules, and regulations of the Christian Church. And thinking itself was forced into the very narrow framework of Christian dogma.

15.3

Beginning in the Italian Renaissance (fifteenth century) and culminating in the Enlightenment (seventeenth century), European culture underwent significant changes with the rediscovery of the pagan cultures of Greece and Rome. Science, philosophy, literature, and art from the ancient world came back to life. Building upon the Greek and Roman accomplishments in these areas, modern philosophers, scientists, writers, and artists laid the foundation for the modern world. Thinking was finally liberated from the straitjacket of religious dogma. It was in this cultural setting that atheism finally became a meaningful concept. The philosopher David Hume and scientists like Isaac Newton opened up worlds of understanding and put in place both directly (Hume) and indirectly (Newton) the logic for a godless universe. Hume showed that the traditional arguments for God's existence, such as the idea that we can look to the design of the universe as evidence for God's creative handiwork, were logically flawed.

For his part, Newton showed the whole universe to be bound by physical law, which meant that many of the responsibilities of running the universe that had once been in the omnipotent hands of God were now embodied in mathematical laws that seem to operate on their own without any sort of assistance. In 1859, Charles Darwin published his revolutionary book *On the Origin of Species*, in which he made his case for a thoroughly naturalistic understanding for the biological evolution of life on Earth.

Darwin's theory of evolution by natural selection does not require an appeal to any force or intelligence outside of the natural universe, and, as such, it has done more damage to the belief in God than any other doctrine in science or philosophy. Nietzsche was very much aware of Darwin's theory and even took exception to what he believed to be its overemphasis on stronger life forms—the "fittest"—always surviving at the expense of weaker ones. For Nietzsche, Western history shows the opposite, namely that the weak, fueled by resentment, have subdued the strong. Nietzsche was wrong, however, about Darwin's theory. The fittest and the strongest are not synonymous in Darwin's idea of natural selection; the fittest, in fact, could actually be the physically weakest if being weak confers adaptive advantages, such as inclining a life form to remain hidden from possible predators and therefore contributing to its ability to survive and reproduce. That a biological theory that required no belief in God was conceived in the early nineteenth century was a clear sign of the times. But for Nietzsche, the realistic possibility of atheism in the philosophical and scientific worlds was only half of the story—actually, less than half.

Nietzsche believed that the Christian God died from a sort of suicide. The Christian emphasis on seeking the truth eventually resulted in Christianity itself becoming the object of scrutiny; it was only a matter of time before Christianity bled to death from the piercing wounds of rational investigation, on the one hand, and simple, reasonable curiosity, on the other. During the Middle Ages, free inquiry was kept under house arrest and was only permitted limited expression when it directly served the needs of the church. But with the slow awakening of the modern mind in the late Middle Ages, and with its full blossoming in the Italian Renaissance and the Enlightenment, thinking could no longer be effectively controlled. Although philosophical investigation into scripture began in earnest in the nineteenth century—revealing disturbing inconsistencies, if not downright contradictions, as well as problems of author-authenticity—simple common sense began absorbing the skeptical spirit of the time and losing its capacity to believe supernatural ideas without reason.

It's in the very nature of freethinking to expose and reveal, and for Nietzsche, once dispassionate reasoning was applied to Christianity—both formally in the biblical scholarship as well as through simple, honest questioning—it was only a matter of time before the myth of Christianity would begin to die. Who wrote the Bible? How do we know that it is true? What evidence is there that the events recorded in the Bible really occurred? What evidence do we have that Christ really existed? Given that, according to the Bible, there can only be one truth, what version of Christianity is the correct one? After all, different denominations of Christianity have grave differences among them. A good example of this is something as essential as what is required for salvation: "good works" in Catholicism or "faith" in Protestantism. Which denomination is the right one? Both cannot be right. And are those with the wrong version of Christianity really going to hell to suffer for an eternity? And how about honest truth seekers in other religions? Are they going to hell, as well? And are we to believe that any other religion except Christianity is doomed spiritually? How could God be good, just, and loving and yet stand by and watch large segments of the human race lose their souls, often for no other reason than being born in the wrong part of the world and into different religious traditions? Is there really a devil? Is the world really the stage for the devil to steal the souls of humans? Are the desires of the flesh really sinful? Are we to believe that God gave human beings the ability to think and yet required that they not ask important questions about the nature of God and Christianity and demand answers? More and more, scholars and laypeople alike began to ask questions like these, and the glib answers provided by religious authorities became increasingly shrill and difficult to accept.

A couple of centuries earlier, Copernicus and Galileo had helped loosen the grip of dogmatic Christianity on the European mind by giving strong evidence that the sun and not the earth, as the Bible suggests, is the center of our solar system. If the Bible was wrong about the solar system, about what else might it be wrong? The investigation of the unknown world by courageous explorers like Marco Polo in the thirteenth century (the Venetian explorer who discovered the advanced civilization of China), Christopher Columbus in the fifteenth century (the Italian explorer who discovered America), and Ferdinand Magellan in the sixteenth century (the Portuguese explorer who was the first to lead an exploration around the entire world) also played no small role in shaking the Europeans out of their cultural and religious narcissism. It was shocking to find that there were highly developed, non-European cultures thriving with little in common with Europe; this knowledge was very difficult to fit into the narrow Christian interpretation of the world, which saw non-Christian cultures as cultures as barbaric, sinful, and incapable of civilized living. Be that as it may, the mind-blowing discoveries in science and world exploration only served to create the context for Christianity's suicide. The decisive process of inner erosion of belief occurred at the hands of modern Christians themselves: little did they realize that the natural desire to understand the truth about their religion would result in the killing of the Judeo-Christian God. It's easy to conclude that once philosophy entered Christianity—starting in the thirteenth century with the synthesis of Aristotle and Christianity by Thomas Aquinas and others—it was the beginning of the end. In other words, with the advance of secular culture, it was inevitable that the belief in God would totally collapse.

Nietzsche believed that Christianity itself delivered the mortal blow to God and that, unlike Lazarus, God will remain dead. But then, isn't Nietzsche clearly wrong? How would he have explained the various cycles of religious resurgence in modern times, such as in America? Historical events often need time to manifest their consequences. God's death happened—about that there can be no doubt. For Nietzsche, it was simply the case that this event had cultural implications that were not immediately clear but, nevertheless, inconspicuously affected all areas of culture. The various instances of religious resurgence are really the opposite of what they appear to be: they are evidence that God has died. It's nothing short of an exotic form of self-deception that aims to foster religious belief.

If Nietzsche were alive today, he would likely argue that all the lip service that Americans pay to their apparent belief in God is essentially a hoax and is another indication that God has died. Statements of belief are one form of evidence for religious devotion, but committed, unwavering actions of devotion are quite another—and are also much more persuasive. Christian Americans provide abundant evidence for the former but are sorely lacking in the latter. One would be hard pressed to find in the New Testament any justification for the lifestyle of modern American Christians with their general lust for the good life, their obsession with material possessions, and their overriding goal of financial gain at all costs, including spiritual costs. The irony about modern Christians in liberal, capitalist countries is that their lifestyles and cultural values have precious little in common with that of their standard bearer—Jesus Christ, who warned against pursuing material possessions and giving any significance to the "ways of the world." According to the Gospels, Jesus chose to live in relative poverty, gave much of what he had to the poor, and preached the values of a simple, humble, and devoted life given over to prayer and extreme self-sacrifice—his life, in short, was a bitter rebuke of liberal, capitalistic values and ideals.

Nietzsche might even suggest that modern American Christians—despite their regular church attendance on Sunday, their evangelical proselytizing, their daily prayers to the Almighty, their warm feelings toward fellow Christians and strangers, and the many verbal blessings that they offer to God on a daily basis—are not really Christians at all, but live more like earthbound nonbelievers. One could take it further and argue that these Christians are just as qualified as their atheistic, heathen brethren to suffer the fate of eternal damnation as it is graphically described in the Gospel of Jesus Christ. Finally, Nietzsche would have probably concluded that modern Christians don't really believe in God at all, and that their actual values and lifestyles prove it; in this sense, ironically, they are living testimonials to God's bloody death.

When Nietzsche pronounced the death of God in the late nineteenth century, he did so with both exhilaration and trepidation. Nietzsche believed God's demise made room for a sort of renewed innocence for the human race, where love of life, self-love, and boundless creativity would replace the horror of Christian rule. But he did not think for a moment that this wondrous new age was going to emerge spontaneously and painlessly from the cosmic void that was left in the wake of God's death. On the contrary, Nietzsche anticipated, almost with a sense of dread, a radical transition period where Western civilization was going to struggle desperately to come to terms with a godless universe. He saw era this transition period of as the era of "nihilism." The importance that Western culture had placed on an all-powerful, all-knowing, and all-moral God was such that the very meaning of life for Western people was inextricably interconnected to this conception of God and the accompanying Christian worldview. God—both literally and metaphorically—was the embodiment of objectivity—that absolute, universal, and ideal standard against which our actions are to be judged, as well as the unwavering frame of reference against which what we believe and know are to be scrutinized. Although we could never possess absolute truth or moral perfection, God does, and this means that we should strive to realize, as much as possible, these Godly virtues. The ideals of absolute truth and moral perfection have served as the critical guiding principles of Western Christian culture for centuries. This guidance seemed to have led Western culture in the right direction; after all, Western humanity has certainly gained insight into what is universally true and good, and although this understanding is limited and imperfect, it seems to be taking us closer to what God knows in fullness. Nietzsche called the so-called values and truths upon which Western culture was based "noble lies."

The belief in noble lies was the faith of Western Christian civilization, a faith that has been thoroughly shattered by God's demise—at least according to Nietzsche. The death of God meant nothing less than the absolute collapse of the moral and intellectual framework of Western civilization. And the reason is clear: this framework was constructed on the metaphysical foundation of God, a foundation that has always been tentative and shaky at best. It was only a matter of time until the foundation began wobbling under the gathering weight of the Christian lies, deception, and misdeeds that had been piled upon it century after century for over two thousand years. The final, cosmic toppling came in the modern era from the frontal assault of critical thinking on all things Christian, and especially from within Christianity itself. Nietzsche argued that the death of God was the natural consequence of Western Christian metaphysics. Put another way, the radical emptying of Western values—both intellectual and moral—was inevitable. This is nihilism pure and simple.

Nietzsche believed that he was witnessing before his very eyes the fateful moment of European culture giving birth to nihilism, and he sensed the cultural vertigo that was about to grip European civilization as a consequence. What would happen to our cherished standards of decency and good moral behavior without absolute standards of right and wrong? Without the traditional metaphysical underpinning, how would we know what truth is? Wouldn't objective reality collapse into relativity and subjectivity without a permanent, universal frame of reference against which we could measure what is true or false? Wouldn't nationalism grow, take a sinister turn, and have devastating effects? Nietzsche died in 1900 after a severe brain disorder that left him without his mental faculties for ten years, so he never lived to observe what many believe was his prophetic understanding of Western civilization in the twentieth century. The rise and history in the early part of the twentieth century of Nazism in Germany, communism in Russia, and fascism in Italy all bear testimony to a civilization that had lost its way and spun out of control.

The godless universe seemed to have opened the way for the justification for unbridled aggressive nationalism and the sheer, ruthless will of power-intoxicated, self-proclaimed demigods: Germany's Hitler, Russia's Stalin, and Italy's Mussolini. They all exploited a spiritually lost, socially confused, and economically devastated Europe to realize Nietzsche's worst nightmares. The sheer loss of human life at the murderous hands of these dictators was the supreme indicator of nihilism's rise to dominance. Beside the massive killing of human life in the various battles and campaigns of the Second World War, there were also tens of millions of innocent men, women, and children who were tortured, experimented on, and murdered in the concentration camps of Western Europe and in the gulags of Russia. That human life lost its inherent value and was treated with such sadistic disregard was nothing new in human history; but it was truly beyond belief that it occurred in the twentieth century, in the very heart of Western civilization, and with such inhumane intensity by, in many cases, educated and cultured people. Yet it happened. The abuse of modern technology to make genocide more efficient only adds to the incomprehensible absurdity of these horrors.

Resentment has had a long, unfortunate history. Christian resentment expressed itself through its rituals and traditions, and it was highly destructive to Western civilization, even though it was held in check to some degree by the life-affirming values of ancient Greece and Rome that began infiltrating European culture in the late Middle Ages. With the death of God and the cultural vacuum that followed, resentment was freed from all constraints and became a natural part of the spirit of nihilism and the chaos and carnage that followed. Nietzsche believed that the seeds of nihilism were planted with the first installments of resentment in ancient Judaism and Christianity. This meant that the surfacing of nihilism was the unavoidable consequence of the logic of resentment as it unfolded over the course of Western history. Western civilization was, in this sense, doomed from the outset. It is now in the hands of modern humans to intercede and save their deteriorating culture.

To Nietzsche, the annihilation of resentment must become the primary goal of modern civilization. How to overcome this powerful force that has held Western humanity in its crushing grip for so long became his passion. What is going to take the place of the false metaphysics that has led humanity down the road to so much misery? Could the death of God prepare the ground for the rebirth of the immortal spirit of life? This exhilarating thought began to orientate Nietzsche's thinking as he continued his philosophical task of unmasking and revealing. He was filled with boundless hope at the idea of retrieving Western humanity from the merciless jaws of a sadistic God and of reversing Europe's movement toward nihilism. The answers that he sought to achieve this end indeed began coming into view, but he still needed to probe deeper, and to continue smashing to smithereens one life-negating idea after the other. He had to be relentless in his strategy to "philosophize with a hammer"—for it's only by this destructive act that a new philosophical/cultural space could be cleared, one in which a fresh vision of humanity could be manifested—and one that could lead the way to the West's own self-transformation.

As Nietzsche thought deeply about the psychology of resentment and the battle of the strong and healthy orientations against those of the weak and sick, he had an insight that ultimately revolutionized his philosophy. How could both strong and weak orientations strive to dominate each other? Why wouldn't the strong always subdue the weak? What's in the orientation of weakness that makes it so powerful? Nietzsche realized that what both kinds of inclinations possess is the desire to dominate and control the other. Could Nietzsche have unearthed a tendency in the human psyche that is actually deeper than its two antagonistic orientations? What is this tendency to dominate, and is it limited only to the human psyche? One of Nietzsche's most notorious brainchildren was born out of such considerations. What motivates human behavior, what fuels all its actions of whatever kind, what stands behind and below our conscious ways of thinking and emoting, what determines the choices that we make, what determines how we operate in the world, and what guides our dealings with other human beings and entities in the world is the "will-to-power." Nietzsche didn't stop with human beings: all of life—every aspect of existence, both animate and inanimate—*is* a will-to-power!

The will-to-power is not a sort of Freudian instinct for self-preservation or the sexual drive, and it's not a Schopenhauerian compulsion for procreation; neither is it an organic striving for excellence, an orientation toward health, or a natural tendency toward sickness and death. Nietzsche recognized the existence of such natural processes, but he realized that they were mere surface manifestations of a deeper force of nature, one whose object was to increase in power, control, and dominance in whatever form it is expressed. In approaching the meaning of the will-to-power from a slightly different angle, Nietzsche also used the concept of "self-overcoming" to describe the continuous tendency of something to go over and beyond its current state of being. Whatever is strong is naturally inclined toward greater strength, whatever is weak is naturally inclined toward increased weakness, whatever is healthy is naturally incline toward greater health, and whatever is sick is naturally inclined toward greater illness. Whatever exists in the universe—plants, animals, energy, diseases, human psychologies, emotions, cultural traditions, philosophies, and moral behavior—are all will-to-power and nothing else. The overall picture that rudely comes into focus from Nietzsche's theory of the will-to-power is that reality is the brutal clash of wills, forces, drives, and tendencies—all striving for increased power and dominance over each other. Nietzsche was unwilling to back away from this harsh assessment of reality. All that exists strives to spend itself freely without reserve, to move toward excess, to squander its energies in the attempt to arrive at higher states of power, control, and dominance.

The will-to-power is the final organizing principle of Nietzsche's philosophy. His ideas of master morality versus slave morality, for example, and his penetrating insights into the psychology of resentment and its millennia-long dominance in Western culture all achieve a greater cohesion and meaning once we put them in the context of the will-to-power. Nietzsche returned to this theory many times, just as we will, as he explored the many areas of human and cultural reality.

For Nietzsche, the elimination of resentment is modern humanity's greatest aim and must become its destiny. God's death has not eradicated resentment but merely driven it into more inconspicuous and equally destructive channels of expression. Something had to be done. For his part, Nietzsche wanted to initiate a new beginning for Western humanity, one where resentment was eradicated and where the horrors of God were wiped from the face of the earth. But there was another problem that Nietzsche had to address before he offered his remedies, one that shared center stage with Christianity as the other cultural evil: the rationalism of Socrates.

Nietzsche has been rightly accused of worshipping great individuals. He even went so far as to say that the whole purpose of history is to produce a handful of geniuses. For example, his fondness for the great thinkers, artists, literary figures, and leaders who thrived in ancient

Greece and Rome knew no bounds, and he also adored a number of creative geniuses from the modern era. He devoted a great deal of his writing to exceptional personalities like Heraclites, Sophocles, Euripides, Plato, Caesar, Jesus, Raphael, Dante, Shakespeare, Spinoza, Napoleon, and Goethe, and he elaborated on their personal qualities as a way to describe what greatness means and what it doesn't. But among all the exceptional people who occupied Nietzsche's interests, the one person whose personal and cultural greatness intruded on his thinking the most was the philosopher Socrates (470–399 BCE). It might be more accurate to say that he was afflicted by the thought of Socrates; if ever there were a case of pure ambivalence in the history of great thinkers, Nietzsche's feelings for Socrates was the one.

Nietzsche truly loved Socrates, the founder of Western rationalism, and yet he battled with him throughout his entire life. Socrates appeared, on the one hand, to be the incarnation of what one might call Nietzschean virtues: emotional and physical toughness, self-mastery, psychological resilience, mental independence, self-sufficiency, self-determination, moral courage, intellectual audacity, philosophical creativity, and an unconditional commitment to the higher principles that he actively incorporated into the way he lived.

There is no question that Nietzsche was in awe of Socrates and saw in him that the will-to-power achieved a uniquely potent configuration. Nietzsche also deeply identified with him and saw himself as a sort of modern-day Socrates. Like Nietzsche, Socrates challenged all the received wisdom of the day, insisted that knowledge is useless unless it elevates the quality of one's life on a daily basis, and even said that the purpose of life is self-development along the path of discovering truth. Socrates viewed himself as the conscience of Athens, unrelenting in his quest to reveal the hypocrisies and untruths masquerading as truth. Socrates aim was to force his culture to arrive at a greater level of spirituality. Likewise, Nietzsche's self-proclaimed mission was to unmask and reveal the lies and deceptions that have poisoned the spirit of Western humanity and to show the way to a radical spiritual transformation.

Socrates was a master dialectician who took on all challengers in free, open debate and was very adept at logically disarming his philosophical combatants. This was a warrior-like ability that Nietzsche highly esteemed and also cultivated for his own wars against Western culture.

That said, the quality that Nietzsche revered the most in Socrates was his unfaltering intellectual conscience. Socrates was committed—body and soul—to philosophical investigation, and contrary to the habits of many so-called truth seekers, he was able to put aside his own biases in his debates. He also managed to dispense with the need to win at all costs and focused exclusively on trying to understand the truth of what was being discussed. There is no greater proof of his devotion to his calling than what transpired during and after his trial in 399 BCE.

As we discussed earlier, Socrates was found guilty of corrupting the youth of Athens by using his truth-seeking method of cross-examination to cast doubt on sacred Greek ideals, beliefs, and traditions. When given the choice of either ceasing to philosophize or be put to death, Socrates, without hesitation or regret, chose to die for philosophy. While he was in jail, he was offered a means to escape and save his life, but he refused to do so, because he viewed such actions to be unlawful and philosophically immoral. Instead, and while remaining in good spirits, Socrates drank the poison hemlock and died, even as his friends and students looked on in horror. Such nobility of character has rarely—if ever—been equaled. Socrates' unwavering love of the truth, his dedication to elevating the spiritual life of humanity, and his supreme act of sacrifice for the cause of rational inquiry created—along with Christianity—the spiritual context in which the Western culture flourished, and this is why Socrates has generally been regarded as the highest symbol of philosophical virtue that the West has ever produced.

On the other hand, it was at this point where Nietzsche had something of a panic attack. While he could not help but agree with much of this estimation of Socrates, he also saw Socrates in another light, one that stood in stark contrast to this viewpoint. Nietzsche's commitment to his search for truth compelled him to attack, time and time again, the traditions, beliefs, and "idols" that he believed had poisoned the spirit of humanity. To "philosophize with a hammer" was never an easy task for him, and one could only conclude that in repudiating Socrates, the thinker whom he deeply loved and venerated, he experienced an extraordinary degree of anguish. And yet he could not turn from what he understood to be Socrates' high crimes against Western culture. The essence of Nietzsche's allegation is the following: Socrates introduced an aggressive form of rationalism into the very heart of Greek mythical world—"dialectical reasoning," that undermined the great contributions of the ancient Greeks. In Nietzsche's view, the Socratic method of inquiry subsequently became the mode of thinking that has come to define of Western civilization as a whole, and the result has been equally destructive.

Nietzsche began his assault on Socrates in his first book, *The Birth of Tragedy*, in which he developed his theory of the origins of Greek art and high culture. Nietzsche was in agreement with all scholars of antiquity that the ancient Greek civilization represented a moment in history when human creativity reached almost miraculous expression. It's not an exaggeration to say that much of what we value in Western civilization began in ancient Greece. In the arts alone, for instance, the Greek contribution was stunning: Greek sculpture, architecture, literature, and drama still rank among the greatest productions of the human spirit. And the same could be said about their contributions to philosophy, mathematics, science, sociology, and political science.

Nietzsche's theory of the emergence of Greek high culture was one of the most audacious and ingenious attempts to address the wonder of the Greek achievement; his insights here also served him well as touchstones for many of the brilliant ideas that he formulated throughout his productive life. Ancient Greece was a polytheistic culture in which gods were believed to be the items, elements, and processes of nature—specific gods were identified with each particular aspect of nature. Even abstract ideas like chaos, order, wisdom, prophecy, justice, and fortune were concretized in gods, as were life, death, and fertility. War and peace each had corresponding gods; so did the underworld, heaven, and earth. The life of the Greek gods was a very dynamic one in which they played, toyed, strategized, conspired, and battled with each other. They also had extensive, even outrageous, sexual relations. The sexual encounters between the gods—which were often exploitive, revengeful, violent, incestuous, and even cannibalistic—gave birth to new gods, who in turn repeated the scandalous lifestyles of their immortal parents. The gods were also believed to have had amorous relationships with human beings that produced offspring who were partly mortal and partly immortal.

For Nietzsche, Greek mythology's humanlike deities were reflective of the ancient Greeks themselves, and rather than standing as contrasting, superior spirits who were forever beyond human comprehension and contact, the gods were often seen as ideal reflections of human nature. In that way, they seemed to be understandable, close at hand, and viscerally present. The belief in the gods, in fact, gave spiritual sustenance, inspiration, and guidance to Greek life precisely because these supernatural/human beings were thought to embody mortal temperaments as well as human virtues and vices. It was Nietzsche's idea that the Greek gods were a profound boon to living in the world passionately, as they promoted personal and collective strength, courage, creativity, heroism, a sense of destiny, and the love of life. The Greeks lived and loved with gusto! They also played, laughed, cried, schemed, competed, challenged, adored themselves, accepted the inevitability of what was to come, and worshipped greatness in action and thought, as did their gods. The mortals learned from their immortal brethren and identified with them. In this sense, they saw the gods as higher aspects of their own mortal being. Nietzsche would say that the capacity of the ancient Greeks to affirm life—to say "yes" to life in thought and action, in the present and in the unknown but destined future—was due, in no small measure, to the cultural habit of looking to their gods as tangible examples of what they could be.

As we noted earlier, Nietzsche was not primarily concerned with whether or not supernatural beings exist. He was interested in the effect that an idea, belief, or tradition had on the quality of human life—that is to say, whether an idea, belief, or tradition was life-affirming or life-negating. In a word, what Nietzsche valued most was the *psychology* behind a belief or belief system, for it is in psychology that spiritual health or illness flourishes and fashions behavior. Nietzsche was an atheist, but he loved Greek mythology nonetheless, because it reflected a people wholly committed to the art of living in the world happily with exuberance, acceptance, and creative expression.

Nietzsche's treatment of Greek (Athenian) culture stood in stark contrast to the Greek scholarship at the time in Germany, which was concerned mostly with questions of traditional philology—the study of the relationship between languages in connection to their cultures and the study of original texts, which involved analyzing Greek grammar and syntax. Although Nietzsche was considered the most gifted philologist of his time, he called his fellow philologists "scholarly oxen." It was blasphemous, he thought, to debase ancient Greek culture by reducing it to the technical understanding of its texts; this was nothing short of stripping the Greeks of their spiritual essence. The Greeks breathed the crisp, energetic air of Homer and the great tragedies. Their values and view of themselves, and of life in general, were informed by the passions of these literary traditions. In Nietzsche's view, the real task of the truth seeker in this context is to discover how these works of art provoked and galvanized the Greek spirit, how they helped to elevate the Greeks to unparalleled greatness. In a play like *Oedipus the King* by Sophocles, for instance, fate, curses, incest, self-mutilation, and patricide—issues that seem absurd or grotesque to modern sensibilities—were confronted by the Greeks and played out unflinchingly before their very eyes in popular performances. Even the average Athenian took art very seriously. The way that the Greeks used tragedy, in particular, to embrace what is most horrible, absurd, and cruel about life was to Nietzsche the key to unraveling the mystery of Greek genius. Here were a powerful people for whom daring, nobility, and heroism had real, concrete meaning, who saw cowardice and compromise as the ultimate evils. The Greeks affirmed life—and their interests, beliefs, and actions proved it.

For Nietzsche, the life-affirming lifestyle of the ancient Greeks was itself an artistic creation and not a natural state of being. It is here that Nietzsche began his famous dissection of the Greek accomplishment. The extraordinary spirit of the ancient Greeks originated in their acute awareness of the horror and suffering of existence. They were acutely aware that the ominous forces of nature had the power to overwhelm them at any moment. The Greeks were also exquisitely sensitive to the knowledge that life is death-bound, uncertain, and riddled with pain and misery. This is a fact of life that most people, and even whole cultures, largely ignore. And much of human life is devoted to devising creative ways of avoiding thinking about it. Yet this fact of reality is the greatest spiritual challenge in life, and how well it's dealt with is decisive to the final value of human existence. Nietzsche called the awareness of this dimension of life "tragic" awareness. The tragic awareness of life is deep, profound, intense, inward-looking, passionate, and emotional. Above all other people, the Greeks had the psychological and spiritual fortitude to embrace the tragic aspect of existence rather than closing their hearts and minds to it. And this amazing capacity, in Nietzsche's view, raised the Greeks above all other cultures before or since.

15.4

Nietzsche associated the tragic Greek sense of existence with Dionysus, the god of wine, dance, destruction, rebirth, orgiastic passion, and excess. It was his idea that the "Dionysian spirit" was one of the two primary forces that streamed through the Greek collective psychology and partly shaped the Greeks' cultural and spiritual sensibilities and orientations. Nietzsche discerned another force that also helped structure the psyche and culture of the ancient Greeks—the Apollonian. This was a force that ran counter to, and conflicted with, the Dionysian. The Apollonian power was named after Apollo, the god of individualization, reason, illusion, clarity, form, and appearance. As far as Nietzsche was concerned, Dionysus and Apollo were not merely gods of convenience or convention to be dealt with occasionally and casually at a distance; they became dynamic archetypes in Greek consciousness, and they created ways of understanding reality and prescribed ways of thinking and acting in the world. The ancient Greeks could not have survived, much less have produced their glorious civilization, if the Dionysian was the only force guiding their thinking and actions. Had this been the case, their culture would likely have destroyed itself or spun hopelessly out of control because of excessive decadence and debauchery. The Apollonian force alone would also have been insufficient to produce the glory that was Greece, because the power of imposing order or form, in itself, makes little sense unless there is something to be ordered or formed; an Apollonian sculptor, for example, is a nonsensical idea because such an artist would have the impossible task of creating a statue that was pure surface! But even if one could imagine such a sculpture, how would such a work of pure surface appear? It would be hopelessly boring and pointless—without the power to inspire the imagination, provoke the passions, induce heroic action, or reveal the depth and soul of existence. For Nietzsche, pure Apollonian power is cut off from life's vital energies; it's an illusion through which emptiness is all that is seen more clearly; it's a barren dream signifying nothing; it's dead, morbid.

The contrasting energies of Dionysus and Apollo flowed openly through the cultural life of the ancient Greeks and were constantly colliding and interpenetrating into each other. Frenzy and restraint are dysfunctional bedfellows, and the immense tensions that arose in their relationship could have crippled the vitality of the ancient Greeks and spelled disaster for their culture. But they solved the problem magnificently by discovering a way of integrating and balancing both the Dionysian and Apollonian forces; this way was perfected in the creation of tragedy. A tragedy is a literary work that emphasizes the fragility of human beings who suffer—often excessively—because of their actions and the actions of the gods. A tragedy typically focuses on the main character, who—despite episodes of great heroism and nobility—is ultimately brought to ruin or extreme sorrow because of a "tragic flaw" or a character/moral weakness. Greek tragedy was a natural development from the ancient Dionysian cults, in which approximately fifty men or boys (perhaps dressed as satyrs—half-human and half-goat beings) performed dithyrambs at each performance. Dithyrambs, which date to around 700 BCE, were wild, ecstatic hymns sung by dancing participants to honor Dionysus. The object of the dithyrambs was to compel the participants to *lose themselves*—their individuality— and to unite with the all-consuming spirit of Dionysus. During a dithyramb, the god would enter each participant and invoke frenzied, animal-like, uninhibited behavior. The modern word "enthusiasm," it's interesting to note, comes from the ancient Greek word *entheos*, which means to be filled with, or to be possessed by, a god.

The first Greek tragedies evolved from the dithyrambs around 500 BCE. Nietzsche believed that Aeschylus (525–456 BCE) and Sophocles (497–496 BCE) were the greatest authors of Greek tragedy. Popular works include respectively: The Persians, Prometheus Bound, Antigone, Oedipus Rex. It was through the structural elements and the plots of the plays (Aristotle said that the "plot was the soul of tragedy") that the Dionysian and Apollonian forces engaged each other, battled it out, and came to some resolution—all in front of the audience. But the people in the audience were not disengaged onlookers, as they are in modern plays; they participated emotionally and spiritually in the world unfolding in front of them. How was this accomplished? The tragedies incorporated what was called a "chorus." The chorus was composed of twelve to fifteen men or boys who sang, danced, narrated, and interacted with both the actors in the play and the audience. The singing, dancing, and narrating chorus represented Dionysian excitation. The people in the audience became so engrossed in the Dionysian passion of the chorus that they were inclined to shed their individuality and be absorbed into the fervor.

The loss of a sense of individuality—ecstasy—that is felt during extreme emotional discharge, and the feeling of oneness with the uncontrolled energy of the universe, was the essence of the Dionysian experience. The audience experienced this critical psychological exercise through the emotional interaction with the chorus and, by extension, the actors and actions. Through the Dionysian experience, knowledge of the truth of existence was not an intellectual exercise—which is always very limited and shallow—but instead was an experiential revealing. One comes to know the ecstatic truth of the Dionysian because one participates in, and becomes one with, this truth.

But pure Dionysian vitality would soon have wasted itself without the constraint, guidance, and nuance of its Apollonian complement. This was provided by the language, poetry, illusions, actors, actions, costumes, masks, and physical props that made up the performance. These elements of tragedy represented the many ways that the Dionysian force could be shaped and focused to achieve gratifying psychological results. The Apollonian power to create illusion was an especially important function of tragedy, because illusion gave necessary form and context to unruly Dionysian forces.

The notion that art could save a culture from self-destruction became a guiding theme in all of Nietzsche's philosophy. That Greek tragedy achieved a fruitful—that is, creative—integration and balance of the Dionysian and Apollonian forces was to Nietzsche an accomplishment second to none, and one that should have revolutionized all subsequent culture. But this was not to be. The fanatical truth seeker Socrates walked onto cultural center stage and murdered tragedy, or more precisely, reasoned it to death.

Plato told us in his dialogue "The Apology" that the Oracle at Delphi had told a friend of Socrates that Socrates was the "the wisest of men." The Delphic oracle was a priestess through whom the god Apollo allegedly spoke, often in riddles, to express some truth about a variety of topics from politics and war to philosophy. The Greeks often sought oracular knowledge at difficult times when particular decisions had great weight. When Socrates heard about the oracle's statement, he was mystified, because he always thought that he didn't know anything—and he often said as much in his daily discussions with his friends. The oracle's statement launched his mission to discover what the oracle meant. He began interviewing anyone in Athens who would talk to him—using an aggressive and prolonged form of rational cross-examination—to try to learn what others knew in the hope that this information would help him understand why he was so wise. What he uncovered astounded him. His rigorous method of rational enquiry exposed countless falsehoods, pretensions, and deceptions in many supposedly knowledgeable people. Socrates was forced to conclude that he, along with everyone else whom he interrogated, suffered from a lack of knowledge. Finally, the oracle's message became clear: Socrates was the wisest of men because he was the only one who knew that he knew nothing!

As we saw, his relentless and disturbing questioning created many enemies who wanted him silenced. Eventually, he was put on trial for the trumped-up charge of corrupting the youth of Athens, creating general skepticism about Athenian traditions, and encouraging disbelief in the gods. The death penalty would be carried out if he were found guilty. When the time came for Socrates to defend himself in front of his fellow Athenians, he gave no defense at all, but instead insisted that under no circumstances could he ever remain silent, because seeking what is good, truthful, and wise was not only divinely inspired, but was also essential for the health of both one's soul and the state. "The examined life is not worth living," he proclaimed, and he encouraged his judges to sentence him to die, arguing that it was, in fact, his patriotic duty to die for the right to seek truth and wisdom.

The death of Socrates gave philosophy its greatest martyr and catapulted him to mythical stature. Beyond his celebrity status, however, what Socrates stood for and died for became emblematic of the intellectual tradition of Western civilization. And what were the messages that Socrates' life and death bequeathed to the West? All of *what is* must be investigated rationally, and what cannot be investigated rationally is irrelevant and not real; rational knowledge is power; knowledge is virtue; where there is no rational knowledge, power is also lacking; there is a reason for everything; if one knows rationally what is good, one cannot act contrary to this knowledge; what is bad is ignorance; all goodness springs from knowledge; all bad actions spring from ignorance; for something to be beautiful, it must be rationally intelligible; illusion is bad; overcoming illusion is good; becoming conscious of all that is, is the supreme goal of reason and is humankind's highest calling; all creativity comes from conscious awareness; unconscious reality is false; instinct lacks insight and knowledge, is false and misleading; becoming more conscious necessarily means becoming better; and becoming less conscious always means becoming less good.

These are some of the messages that Socrates transmitted to us. And considering to what extent his ideas have molded Western culture, it's not surprising that our civilization has often been called Socratic. What are science and technology—the hallmarks of Western civilization—but so many ways of codifying and applying Socrates' heroic call to reason! And are we not a logical people, always looking for the reasons that underlie how we feel, what we think, how we act, and how nature and the human world function? Does not every day present us with an endless series of personal, professional, social, moral, and political problems that are best solved by applying rational analysis, the ultimate "problem-solver?" Today—with science and technology consuming increasingly more sectors of human reality—the grip of Socrates on Western culture is stronger than ever. What a testimony to an ignorant species to have gained so much knowledge, and control, of reality with only the power of rational thought! But Nietzsche didn't see things that way.

Rather than viewing the ubiquitous presence of Socrates in Western rational culture as a gift, Nietzsche saw it as a curse on humanity, one that has destroyed much of what is of real value in life. The life and death of Socrates cast a spell on Greek civilization and altered it from a society based on mysticism, passion, and instinct to one guided largely by rational/logical thought. In Nietzsche's view, the first and most consequential victim of Socrates' rational madness, was Greek tragedy. Socrates' rationalism struck at the heart of Greek culture through the tragedies of Euripides (480–406 BCE). His most noted works are Alcestis, Medea, Electra, and Bacchae.

If the original purpose of tragedy was to integrate and balance both the Dionysian and Apollonian forces, the plays of Euripides radically changed all that. Tragedy had served the critical psychological function of offering the audience a transforming Dionysian experience, by inducing it to become one with the chorus, which celebrated the Dionysus spirit of intoxication, excess, and ecstasy. Euripides transformed the chorus into the moral, narrative voice of the play, as though it were just another rational actor on the stage instructing the audience, no different from the average person on the street.

Euripides thought that desire in the soul should be under the command of reason. The poet must shun the unconscious mind and access only the conscious mind to create his ideas and images. Because of Euripides' innovation, the transforming power of tragedy was systematically eliminated from the play, and the audience was left emotionally neutralized, passionately unfulfilled, and as alienated from the untamed Dionysian forces of nature as they were before the performance. Having not participated in the ecstatic passions of the performance, the audience was left with only dim recollections of what it learned in the performance, rather than a profound, experiential insight into the very nature of existence.

The tragedies of Sophocles and Aeschylus, by contrast, find their meaning in the unconscious mind, in the mysteries of existence, in natural instinct and suffering, in passion and ecstasy, and in dreams and illusions. The first insight of Dionysian awareness is that life is wasteful, wild, ecstatic, filled with suffering, and overflowing with energy—no amount of Socratic analysis could ever reach this understanding. As hungry as Socratic thinking is to arrive at higher levels of truth, it is, nonetheless, powerless to get to the core of existence. Socrates' world is one of surfaces, of superficial meanings, of distorting logical analysis, and broad generalities. Dramatic art, by contrast, is deep, particular, invasive, and exposing. What truly great tragedy highlights is the profound wonder of existence. It points to the depths of life that lie beneath the veneer of logic and rational formulations. It embraces the non-rational instincts as the most direct and authentic contact that human beings have with the forces of life.

Nietzsche also accused Euripides (and Socrates) of undermining a basic truth of human existence: human life requires illusion in order to survive. All people possess a sizable aptitude for experiencing enormous mental and emotional pain. The brutal facts of life—suffering, destruction, injustice, and death (especially one's own)—are often too difficult to bear without the natural reflex of the mind to look away from what is unbearable in life and, through the prism of illusion, see instead beauty, goodness, hope, and justice.

The worldview of Socrates and Euripides was a strategy for the philosophical and moral improvement of humanity: knowledge leads necessarily to truth and virtuous behavior, because reality and desire, at their base, are logical. Socrates preached it, and Euripides scripted it and produced, not inspiring visions in the viewer, but calculated "psychological effects." By employing reason in all areas of human existence, life itself can be reduced to a series of logical formulas and rational recipes for living. Improving humanity was to Nietzsche an affront to the health of the philosophical spirit, subversive of the wonder of *what is*, and grotesquely dismissive of the Dionysian energy that creates, supports, and promotes life. Improving humans really means nothing more than domesticating or taming the human animal by means of rational control and restriction—in other words, corrupting and diffusing the power of the human spirit, which is naturally in communion with its Dionysian source. Here we see how Nietzsche's reputation as a pure, materialistic atheist is both misleading and unfair. He had profound reverence for the earth and believed that living in the world artistically—with passion, strength, courage, creative self-expression, and honest openness to the truth of what is, as well as being in intimate contact with life's natural instincts—was the only authentic form of spirituality. This is what he learned from his beloved Greeks.

Socrates was a traitor to the cause of philosophy and to humanity in general, because he militated against this form of spirituality. In this sense, Socrates, the great advocate for critical thinking, helped to set the stage for the ascent of the worst of all possible treasonous worldviews, the Christian one. Nietzsche found it very revealing that before his death in prison, Socrates allegedly said to his attending disciples, "I owe a cock to Asclepius"—who was the god of health. Nietzsche took this comment to mean that, for Socrates, life is a disease and that death is the only cure. This sarcastic comment by Socrates in the final hour of life underscored, in Nietzsche's view, what his philosophy was fundamentally concerned with: escaping the truth of what is by an act of negation—critical thinking. But the indictment continues. Socrates' deathbed confession also supports Nietzsche's idea that Socrates, in annihilating his opponents through his dialectical form of argumentation, was motivated more by resentment than by genuine philosophical passion. By paralyzing the intellects of Athenian noblemen with his bloodthirsty logic, Socrates, the plebian, struck back sadistically at the noblemen whom he secretly admired. We can see here the counterpart to Nietzsche's idea of the slave/master dialectic that produced the slave morality of Judaism and Christianity.

It's not surprising that Socrates' particular view of reason was taken up and developed into a more formal philosophy by his brilliant student Plato, who more self-consciously focused attention away from the earthly plane to a world of ideal forms, of which all items in the everyday world are imperfect, degraded, and defective representations. For Nietzsche, the seed of existential loathing first planted by Socrates and then cultivated by Plato eventually found even more fertile soil, from which it grew to monstrous proportions: Christianity—the most pernicious doctrine of earthly hatred ever devised by humankind. Despite Nietzsche's adoration for his mentor, he regretfully had to conclude that Socratic rationalism is a heartless and vicious attack on life and on the life-affirming energy that resides in instinct, passion, and creative power. Socrates, in other words, said "no" to life, and for this ultimate betrayal, Nietzsche would never forgive him.

What is the purpose of existence? What makes life worth living? Since the belief in God was only a passing episode in the dramatic story of humanity, how do we now justify life without the belief in the greatest lie in human history—God? These questions preoccupied Nietzsche's thoughts throughout his life, even though in his very first book, *The Birth of Tragedy*, he offered his general answer, which he never repudiated: "It is only as an aesthetic phenomenon that existence and the world are eternally justified." Justifying existence and the world aesthetically meant to him embracing life as unconditionally beautiful—that is, living joyfully and exuberantly—by affirming, without reservation, its natural powers, overabundant energies, passions, and instincts. Reason could never be self-justifying, because it's merely a tool for dissecting small portions of *what is*. It accumulates knowledge, certainly, but only the most superficial and limited kind. Primal feelings, cravings, fantasies, and dreams are non-rational, philosophical portals into what is. They expose and reveal deeper realities that pure, rational thought has little capacity to capture because of its requirements of defining the world exclusively through abstract, logical understanding. Socrates no doubt had the passion to know what is, but by discrediting the power of myth and the Dionysian reality, he systematically eliminating profound inroads into truth of what is. He reduced his quest for truth to the rationalization of all of reality and tragically failed to realize that the source and context of reality is not rational.

Nietzsche's indictment of Socrates was not a wholesale rejection of reason, but only the Socratic version of it that says that every dimension of reality is a legitimate object of rational thinking and that what is not susceptible to logical analysis does not qualify as real or of genuine value. For Nietzsche, this form of philosophizing misled Western philosophy at almost every turn: rationalism/idealism (reason is the fundamental reality) and materialism (matter is the fundamental reality) are opposite sides of the same metaphysical coin, because each view contorts, distorts, and restricts *what is* to suit the rational biases of its particular viewpoint. And what of science, the greatest, most successful application of rational thought? Nietzsche had great respect for science and praised the selfless commitments that scientists show in their efforts to gain knowledge of the physical universe. But science goes far astray when it listens too attentively to the Socratic-like directive that insists that science can know all the secrets of existence only through the rational methods of science, and that other approaches are misguided, foolish and unscientific.

15.5

In the book of which he was most proud, *Thus Spoke Zarathustra*, Nietzsche indulged in his most experimental writing by juxtaposing and harmonizing aphorisms, poems, and parables in a quasi-biblical phraseology. He called it "the deepest book ever written." Here metaphor and clear, rational assertions dance energetically with each other, requiring the reader not only to think philosophically, but also to feel and intuit artistically. And in addition to bold philosophizing and oracular pronouncements, the book is filled with playful puns and paradoxes. In *Thus Spoke Zarathustra*, Nietzsche put forward his case for nihilism finally being overcome by a new, earthbound, Dionysian spirituality, one that is based in a profound vision of unconditional love. He believed that by reigniting the Dionysian spirit, he might help bring into existence a radically new kind of human being, one who would transcend humanity's "human-all-too-human" legacy and live a passionate life of continual self-creation. *Thus Spoke Zarathustra* features the Persian prophet Zoroaster—here called, in German, Zarathustra. Nietzsche chose the Persian prophet as the mouthpiece for his radical ideas because Zarathustra was the first to establish a lasting monotheistic religion, and to assert that the universe is the cosmic battleground between the forces of good and evil. Nietzsche thought that since Zoroaster created this worldview, it would be only appropriate for him to annihilate it, as well.

After ten years of solitude and freedom, Zarathustra decides to come down from his mountain to pass on to humankind the wisdom that he has gained. Since the death of God, Western civilization has been in the grips of nihilism—the collapse of objective values and meaning. Nihilism has produced a spiritual vacuum that has undermined European culture, since the belief in God, and the moral and philosophical thinking that it implies, have been its organizing principle for hundreds of centuries. How is Western culture going to cope with the cultural wasteland that has emerged in the wake of nihilism? This was the question that Zarathustra had to face and answer.

During Zarathustra's spiritual journey, he delivers a series speeches and lectures, in which he offers his diagnoses and insights regarding the current state of modern civilization, as well as his solutions to its cultural/moral bankruptcy. Modern humans have fallen into a nihilistic stupor in which "wretched contentment" defines the quality of their lives. And for what does the "last man" live? To be content and satisfied with the status quo, to seek out petty pleasures, and to avoid discomfort and frustration at all costs—in short, to be happy. "We have happiness, says the last men, and they blink." Happiness is seen by the last man as a place of rest, of peace, a place where all striving and stress come to an end. In happiness, the last man retires spiritually, and loses his desire to live creatively with passion and burning curiosity. But for Zarathustra, the happiness of the last man is a disease that is consuming what is highest in humanity: the natural tendency to become stronger, healthier, more excellent and self-sufficient, and above all—more creative. The last man does not challenge himself but stagnates perpetually in mediocrity; his goals and aspirations amount to little more than acquiring more comfort items that reinforce his mindless herd existence. And in the last man the bloodless knife of nihilism plunges deeply into his inner being and paralyzes his capacity to feel intensely, think creatively, act freely, and celebrate life with exhilaration.

Zarathustra's strategy for combating nihilism is to teach humankind his doctrine of the "overman"—in German, *ubermensch*. The overman is a new form of human being that Zarathustra argues must emerge out of the cultural morass of Western, nihilistic culture. With God dead and decaying, the overman must now become the "meaning" of the earth—the noble goal toward which all cultural activities must aim.

> I teach you the overman. Man is something that has to be overcome. What have ye done to suppress man?
>
> All beings hitherto have created something beyond themselves; and ye want to be the ebb of that great tide, and would rather go back to the beast than surpass man?
>
> Ye have made your way from worm to man, and much in you is still worm. Once ye were apes, and even yet man is more of an ape than the apes.
>
> Even the wisest of you is only a disharmony and hybrid of plant and phantom. But I do bid you become phantoms or plants?
>
> Lo I teach you the overman!
>
> The overman is the meaning of the earth!
>
> I conjure you, my brethren, remain true to the earth, and believe not those who speak unto you of super-earthly hopes!
>
> Poisoners are they, whether they know it or not.
>
> Despisers of life are they, decaying ones themselves, of whom the earth is weary: So away with them!

Zarathustra says that "Man is a rope tied between beast and overman, a rope over the abyss." In other words, modern man is a bridge between the animal and overman, and as such he is a mere transitional phase in humanity's evolution toward the overman. There have been a few extraordinary people in history—like Caesar, Jesus, and especially the German poet, writer, and scientist Johann Wolfgang

Goethe—who represented tantalizing hints of what the future overman might be. But even our great geniuses have been mired in human-all-too-human qualities; even they were not able to reach Nietzsche's ideal. What, then, is the overman, and what are his exceptional qualities?

The overman is the next and ultimate step in human spiritual evolution, and the appearance of overman was made necessary because of the cultural earthquake of nihilism. Nietzsche wasn't clear about how the overman is to emerge; certainly his coming into being could be the result of "luck accidents," but it is most likely that the overman will emerge when his appearance is seen collectively as a cultural necessity. The overman would then be willed into existence.

And what are his qualities? The overman never reclines in a satisfied state of pure being but is constantly becoming more of what he is—he is always overcoming himself, always reaching higher, and always seeing his dreams and fantasies as within his creative reach. His higher self is his guide, mentor, and master, and the overman's ears are constantly attuned to his master's voice that says in no uncertain terms: "Become who you are!" This Dionysian affirmation means that the overman's primary existential project is self-creation. A human being is an infinitely rich womb of possibilities, of potential ways and means of engaging the world physically, emotionally, psychologically, and intellectually. And what percentage of people ever realizes even a modicum of what they are capable? The overman, by contrast, is a genius in self-realization. The blocks that typically prevent growth in normal human beings—whether they are psychological, intellectual, or moral—are not present in the overman. He is free! Free to become who he is and free to create at will.

The overman is a Dionysian artist of the first rank, whose greatest, and most original creation is himself. Nietzsche said that the overman would be distinguished by his natural inclination to create his own values and meaning and to live in defiance of the status quo, if the status quo is stagnant, uninspiring, and not fertile soil from which novel creations could emerge. The overman is concerned less with individual moral acts than with the energy and character from which moral actions emerge. Because the overman is spiritually and mentally strong and healthy, what he does will naturally reflect this state of being. His actions, in this way, will tend to be the right ones The overman is a passionate man of action who feels, thinks, and acts out of excess or overflow of life's energies. His potential for loving is immense, because he loves from strength and surplus rather than from weakness and deficiency. The overman loves because he wants to, and not because he has to. That he gives out of abundance means that in giving he loses nothing and in fact gains all the more; in giving himself so completely, he merges with explosive forces of nature that know no limit and are forever squandering themselves. In this sense, he is instinct incarnate, but an instinct directed and expressed through creative thought and action.

The overman is free to destroy at will but chooses not to, because for him, destruction must always lead to greater freedom, power, and creativity. He has no desire to hurt the weak or subdue what is inferior; what would be the sense of it? How could he experience his own strength and aliveness if what he confronted did not strongly resist and challenge him? Without a worthy adversary, how would he know who he is; how would he be able to feel his distinction, his difference? Besides, his love of life and all that is necessary in it would not be served well by injuring the innocent and vulnerable. Better to nurture them and prop them up so they, too, can know the glory of overcoming their all-too-human limitations. Help prepare them for battle; drive them to be courageous and worthy warriors to be respected and feared—this is true love, the love of the overman.

The overman is a being, whose will-to-power is under his absolute command, and he uses his power as a great painter or sculptor would use his paintbrush or chisel to produce a beautiful work of art. Like a great Renaissance artist, the overman sees the world as beautiful and is committed to making it even more beautiful by his transfiguring touch. And what is ultimately beautiful to the overman? All that is necessary in life, including its inherent suffering, excess, and tragedy.

The overman does not strive for happiness. He *is* happy. And he is naturally happy, because he is always becoming who he is; he is continually realizing his full potential, because he is *in* life—in the flow, so to speak. The overman does not act from need; he is not needy. Because he is filled with the Dionysian spirit, the overman gives of himself gratuitously without expectation—he is rich enough for that. This is another way of saying that generosity is a natural aspect of his nature.

The Dionysian force in Nietzsche's mature philosophy naturally incorporates within itself the Apollonian component, which means that the overman possesses the inherent capacity to form *creatively* the energies of Dionysus—that is, to organize the chaos swirling around inside of him—and he becomes in this sense an expert in self-mastery: his awesome will-to-power is effortlessly at the service of his goals and aspirations.

In lecturing about the possible evolution of the overman, Zarathustra discusses the "Three Metamorphoses"—three stages, spiritual transformations—that one must pass through on the way to becoming the overman. The three stages unfold cyclically, as three distinct realities are met and eventually transcended. The first is the *camel*. The camel is a beast of burden who lives under the control of external authority and performs his difficult work out of a sense of duty. The camel, at first, is incapable of independent thinking, but does what he ought to do. But such selfless work begins to teach the camel discipline and builds his character. The camel starts to take pride in his hard work, but he also starts to question the meaning of his life, because its labor is not fulfilling. He begins to suspect that the eternal truths upon which he relied to justify his difficult existence may turn out to be fleeting and insubstantial. The camel soon realizes his most onerous burden: having to endure the reality that life does not possess objective, unchanging truth, but rather is always in a state of *becoming*—reality is not stagnant but is forever changing. The camel now flees into the desert to be alone and ponder how to live in a world of constant becoming. Although the reality of incessant becoming weighs heavily on the camel's spirit, this psycho-emotional turmoil ultimately becomes the engine of its own spiritual transformation. A great self-overcoming occurs when the camel goes beyond himself and becomes a lion.

If the camel was the beast of burden, then the *lion* is the beast of prey. The camel changed into a fearless and noble warrior who lives to kill. Killing is his most natural instinct. And why does the lion kill? For freedom. And what threatens that freedom above all else? The all-consuming "dragon" of "thou shalt" and the feelings of guilt that the dragon wields like a deadly sword. The dragon believes that it possesses the one eternal truth and that God watches over a transcendent realm of absolute ideas and verities that is knowable through rational thought.

445

The dragon will not tolerate opposing viewpoints and insists that one either conforms to its demands or be crushed. The lion refuses, exerts his will, and kills the dragon, but he is left without the guiding hand of God or absolute ideas and truths to orient his life. The lion is now responsible for himself, but he lacks the creative ability to create new values to replace the old ones. He is a destroyer and not a creator. Another self-overcoming is at hand as the lion reaches to his highest nature and transforms himself into a *child*.

Unlike the camel or lion, the child is innocent, new, and fresh. The child does not have the memory of the burdens and duties of the camel; or the struggle, destruction, and guilt of the lion—"thou shalt" does not exist for the child. The child is a new day, an effortless beginning—in Nietzsche's words, "a sport, a self-propelling wheel, a first motion and a sacred Yes." The child creates out of joy and natural curiosity; the child is the constant state of realizing its potential; and she does so by playing endlessly. Having forgotten all that came before, the child is free to do what he wants without reservation or censorship. He lives for the moment, for that's all he has. But eventually what the child has created—new values and truths—will themselves become stale and lifeless, and so the spirit of the camel and lion must return— and so must a new child, as this cyclical process starts over again and repeats itself endlessly. *Becoming* knows no ending or cessation.

With the emergence of each new child, new values and truths will also emerge. The child plays, investigates the world, discovers problems, and invents solutions given his particular circumstances. The child has no awareness of anything outside of his immediate interests, so the idea of a God or transcendent realm of absolutes never emerges in his daily activities. The child acts, plays, and creates new values and truths by virtue of his will-to-power, which is a natural expression of his life. The camel was caught in stagnant being, but by questioning it, the camel changed into the lion, who then slew being and made space for the child to rise to live a life of creative becoming. The Three Metamorphoses is the life cycle of the overman, of one who is always overcoming himself, of one who is in love with becoming. This is Zarathustra's teaching.

But Zarathustra has a great deal more to say to those who are interested in his ideas. He instructs his listeners to be "faithful to the earth." Those who teach that there are transcendent realities that are more valuable, truthful, or real are "preachers of death" who destroy the reverence for life. Zarathustra is a staunch monist. He teaches that the traditional philosophical and religious metaphysical dualisms—such as mind versus body or appearance versus a "higher" reality—must be rejected out of hand. *Appearance* is reality, however varied appearance may be. There is no world behind the one that is present to our physical senses; Plato and Christianity were wrong to teach otherwise.

Zarathustra is also a kind of materialist. As an example, he advocates analyzing physical behavior and not the abstract mind to discover the truth about human nature. A human being is an integrated whole and not part body and part mind—and the mind itself is a fiction, anyway. Repeating a theme from *The Birth of Tragedy*, Zarathustra says that the body is the source of what is good—for instance, works of philosophy and art that are born in the unconscious, from passion and instinct, are of much greater value and are more truthful than those that arise solely from intelligent reflection or rational analysis.

Zarathustra teaches that only an aggressive individualism will be able to stem the tide of nihilism. Values that promote peace and tranquility, either culturally or socially, are not healthy, because they operate against the natural dynamics of life which have a will-to-power that continually promotes change and conflict. In this regard, Zarathustra cautions his listeners to beware of overly moral, good, and just people, for they are merely following the rules of herd morality and are devoid of real integrity—and are even dangerous to the healthy individual. The basic conflict is that what the herd sees as evil is really the source of greatness and nobility of character. Zarathustra says, "With a person it is as with a tree. The more he aspires to height and light, the more strongly will his roots strive earthward, downward, into the dark, into the deep—into evil." The "evil" that Zarathustra is talking about is the passion, the instincts, and the dark, subterranean world of the unconscious. Only a person who is deeply rooted into the earth is capable of true virtue and excellence.

Zarathustra's judgment is final: morality, as it has been conceived and applied so far within its Judeo-Christian framework, has crippled the collective body of the human race and has forced it to grow crooked, brittle, and frail. Zarathustra wants his followers to grasp the profound truth that all greatness occurs "beyond good and evil," beyond the narrow and stifling confines of traditional morality. Those who preach otherwise will punish you for your virtues and condemn you for your love of life.

Zarathustra's philosophy is not for the timid or faint of heart. He admonishes his listeners: "The secret of the greatest fruitfulness and greatest enjoyment is: to live dangerously. Build your houses on the slopes of Mount Vesuvius." If life is at its base an irrepressible will-to-power, then to negate this power is to reject life itself—the source of all that is. The consequence of affirming life—of saying "yes" to life—then, is to engage in the natural power struggle of existence and compete with opposing forces in order to feel and measure one's resilience, strength, and distinction—in short, to do battle with challenging wills. It's easy to misunderstand what Zarathustra is talking about. While it's clear that he is encouraging a warrior-like mentality, he is not sanctioning violent behavior or endorsing an aggressive military strategy. As we noted previously, the will-to-power has both healthy and unhealthy expressions, and sheer violence or cruelty for its own sake demonstrates a will-to-power either diseased or improperly channeled. To think otherwise would mean that Zarathustra is putting forward as the ideal for the overman a violently sadistic human monster. This is ludicrous and runs contrary to the very essence of the "over" in overman. Zarathustra also says in a section called "On the New Idol": "Only where the state ends, is where the individual begins who is not superfluous." Statism, and the militaristic support system that typically accompanies it, is for Zarathustra anathema, because it forces one to betray one's individuality and one's creative self-reliance. He thinks statism is nothing short of alienation.

The death of God ripped a gaping hole in the spiritual fabric of Western civilization and left it without cohesion, purpose, and meaning—that is, without sovereign power. God was the ultimate power source who placed all items in the universe in their proper place and context and gave them unchanging meanings. His death could only mean that human beings themselves must now become centers of power and creators of meaning—actual forces of nature who give purpose to existence.

It is from this perspective that we must understand Zarathustra's call to the fearlessly powerful individual and to the warrior-like mentality. Living in a universe that has been stripped of its meaning, purpose, and caretaking responsibility is, at first, difficult to embrace with open arms. Coming to terms with pain, suffering, and ultimately death without the security blanket of an all-powerful, all-protecting, and all-loving God requires developing new ways of seeing the world and oneself. As far as Nietzsche was concerned, to live well in a godless world, one must be strong, resilient, and creatively self-reliant. One must be practiced in the high art of wielding power productively, both for one's benefit and for the benefit of others. To fall back into archaic or extinct belief systems, and to try to ignore the death of God by pursuing a vulgar form of happiness, as the last man tries to do, is a cowardly betrayal of the human spirit. Zarathustra wants his followers to embrace reality and to take creative responsibility for the meaning of their lives. Life is will-to-power, and each person living powerfully and passionately is an admirable demonstration of this fact.

The profound truth is that God's death means the death of many long-standing articles of faith. Not only are objective and unchanging standards of right and wrong wiped away, but so is the rational character of the universe, insofar as rationality has always been accepted as necessarily interconnected with the greatest rationalist of them all—the supreme mathematical wizard and architect, God. With God out of the cosmic picture, the universe could now be seen for what it really is at its most basic level: chaos. What humanity did with morality, it also accomplished with rationality: imposed it on the universe to the point where its real essence became hidden. To see reason in every crevice and corner of the universe is to be blinded by surface trimmings and artificiality.

One of the most misguided articles of faith is the belief in static being. As an ardent admirer of the pre-Socratic philosopher Heraclitus, who believed that change is reality, Nietzsche/Zarathustra argued that *becoming* is the basis of *what is*. Life, people, and physical processes are not static states of being, but are always moving dynamically into something else—"becoming" something else. Nietzsche believed that embracing *being* over *becoming* was another sign of moral corruption, since it's based in fear: fear of the unknown, fear of the mysterious, and fear of life's will-to-power. Affirming *becoming* with authentic power, on the other hand, means engaging the chaos of existence and creating order or beauty out of it. The great artist was, for Nietzsche, the great genius of becoming—she courageously confronts the endless flow of becoming and transforms it into timeless beauty.

Since there was no God who created the universe or what's in it, death must take on a whole new meaning. If God is not responsible for each person coming into existence, going *out* of existence is each person's responsibility. Zarathustra's admonition is to "die at the right time." Not too soon or too late, but at the right time. The natural death is foolish. Why would we want to die when we are worn out and when the diminishing life force is slowly enfeebling us? Rather, we should want to die when our strength has reached its highest expression and after we have realized our life's goals. This is a "free death," and Zarathustra believes that dying freely is best accomplished in "battle."

In contrast with Christian thought, Zarathustra praises sexual expression, selfishness, and the lust to rule. Sex is a celebration of the body and of life. Selfishness is based in self-love, pride in one's creative accomplishments, and the freedom to enjoy life. The lust to rule is merely the will-to-power expressing itself in a healthy form. This general attitude is part of Zarathustra's program of overcoming the "spirit of gravity" that has been squeezing the life out of Western humanity. "Zarathustra is a "dancer," Nietzsche tells us. She is light on her feet, but capable of the most astonishing movements, both physically and creatively. He also laughs and sings. Philosophy up until now has been heavy and ponderous, and for this very reason fraudulent, decadent, and silly. Zarathustra could have said, leave your burdensome beliefs and convictions behind, and rise to the level of simple joy and celebration. And if one cannot sing and dance, one has missed the truth about existence!

One of Zarathustra's principal teachings—one opposed to Christianity—is the requirement not only for students to vigorously challenge their teachers and mentors, but to subsequently leave them to pursue their own truths and life path. "Now I bid you lose me and find yourselves; and only when you have all denied me will I return to you," he instructs. The idea that modern humans must break free of all authority and create lives of radical independence was an important theme throughout Nietzsche's writings. He even urges his readers to question Nietzsche's own status as a speaker of truth and wisdom. Nietzsche wants his most passionate admirers to develop their own values and worldviews, even if they contradict his own. After all, Nietzsche could be wrong!

As Zarathustra's spiritual journey unfolds, he begins wrestling with his own thoughts and even questions their value. He comes to realize that singing and dancing may have more truth-value than philosophy itself. He concludes that he needs to go deeper into the unknown— into the Dionysian underworld; his doubts still won't leave him, and he wonders whether his antidote to nihilism is just another senseless answer. Zarathustra's grappling with his value as a truth seeker forces him to go off on his own and plunge even more deeply into his unknown and darkest self, in order to discover why he feels his philosophical project as the "spirit of gravity" that weighs heavily on his shoulders.

Finally, an idea that has been percolating for some time right below his awareness begins to emerge in the light of day. The full implications of this idea take Zarathustra aback and disturb him. The idea comes to him that the universe is governed by the "eternal recurrence" of the same. The universe, and time along with it, are cyclical: every item that exists (both inanimate and animate), and everything that occurs, has already existed and happened an infinite number of times in the past. Further, all of these things are destined to repeat themselves an infinite number of times in the future. In this sense, the future and the past have the same history. "All truth is crooked. Time is a circle"—so says a dwarflike being, who had been on Zarathustra's back, pressing down on him. (Nietzsche's speculative, quasi-philosophical/scientific underpinning for eternal recurrence is that since time is infinite, and matter or energy is finite, the precise matter/energy configurations that are now manifested in the universe must repeat themselves over and over again ad infinitum.)

Thinking about the eternal recurrence is nauseating to Zarathustra. This idea means that there is no real progress in the universe and that the overman, if he does emerge one day, will eventually have to give way to the worst examples of humanity's past. Christianity will return one day, as will the last man, and so will every deplorable episode of humanity's unfortunate history, and all innumerable times. Zarathustra's distress causes him to have a vision of a shepherd who is choked by a black serpent that has crawled into his throat. The shepherd fails at removing the serpent until Zarathustra screams at him to bite off the serpent's head, which the shepherd does. When the shepherd spits out the serpent's head, he is instantly a new man: he is free from what distressed him most, and he accomplished this himself. Zarathustra now understands that gaining this form of liberation must be his goal.

Finally, Zarathustra not only recovers from the nausea and distress, but also has an epiphany that reverses his understanding of the idea of eternal recurrence. Up to this point, Zarathustra was fixated on the past, with its corroding effect on the health of the human spirit. He was also focused on the future that he saw as belonging to the overman and to a higher culture. But these preoccupations came at a great price: he forgot the present moment and the requirement to live passionately in the *now*. Zarathustra's blindness caused him to miss the fact that once the idea of eternal recurrence gains possession of one's mind and imagination, each moment is then seen as "eternity." Since everything returns without end, "Being begins at every moment. The center is everywhere." So says Zarathustra's two companions, his snake and eagle. The paralyzing effect of this idea is thereby neutralized, and one gains the freedom to *be* at every moment. This occurs when one understands that one must exercise his own commitment to the earth—body and soul—at every moment, because that is all that there is. Is there any more profound affirmation of life than to embrace each moment with gusto and to love it without restriction, without reservation, and with all the love that one is capable? And wouldn't this be the ultimate gesture of the overman? In light of this revelation, singing and dancing take on even greater importance for Zarathustra; he sees them as the highest forms of affirmation.

Zarathustra's mission to spread wisdom to all those who would listen took an unexpected twist when he realized that teaching truth requires remaining a student of life. In preaching the need for humanity to bring into existence the overman, Zarathustra had to undergo a radical transformation, a "self-overcoming," in order live up to his ideal of being an unconditional lover of the earth. The overman, as Zarathustra envisioned him, is the natural replacement for the loss of belief in God. And he will have to distance himself from all that has come before him, including, for instance, Western humanity's sick obsession with Christianity and its ill-conceived mania for rationality at all costs.

Zarathustra's "self-overcoming" has recast the meaning of the overman and has redefined his essence. The overman is a human being become light, power, discipline, and purpose; he is a self-creator who is forever going beyond himself, and he is a formidable will-to-power who is devoted to the loving affirmation of life. This means that the overman must also embrace the darkness, the mysterious, and the irrational; he must be fearless in the face of what is most bleak and distressing. Total affirmation means loving every aspect of life and desiring that nothing be subtracted from it. This is the new lesson that Zarathustra has learned and the most profound of all his insights:

Be aware, o man!
What does the deep midnight declare?
I was asleep. From a deep dream I awoke.
The world is deep—
Deeper than day had thought.
Deep is its woe.
But ecstasy is deeper than agony.
Woe says: Be gone!
But joy aims at eternity—
At deep, deep eternity

Living by the standard of eternal recurrence, however, does not mean that the overman should suppress his will-to-power, diffuse his creative passion, or fail actively to realize his full potential. Instead, it means that the overman continues to overcome himself out of the full and loving acceptance of reality. For Zarathustra, this is the most sublime expression of unconditional love. The overman does not strive for happiness; *he is happy*, and then he does what he chooses. He realizes that all *that is*, is inextricably interconnected with everything else. To affirm fully even one joy implies wanting all that is—in whatever form—to come back again and again, forever. To commit an act, however insignificant, is to commit an eternal act—it is to will eternity!

The overman, the will-to-power, and eternal recurrence—the three main concepts in *Thus Spoke Zarathustra*—together deliver a comprehensive message, the essence of which was already present in Nietzsche's first book, *The Birth of Tragedy*. I have summarized what I think is the essence of Nietzsche's thought. I have labeled this summary, "Nietzsche's Creed":

> Say YES to life; love the natural world with all your heart; exalt each moment by offering it your highest and happiest thoughts and heroic efforts; cultivate a warrior's spirit so you are able to overcome all obstacles that stand in your way to victory and to all the victories after that; have reverence for your body and be attentive to its needs, moods, and wisdom; allow your passions and instincts guide you to a deeper experience of life and give them necessary expression so you can celebrate the joy that they can bring; face up to chaos, uncertainty, ugliness, suffering, and irrationality and use them as fuel for your creative expression; employ your reasoning ability to unveil, investigate, and proclaim what is; challenge what you have been taught and compare what you think you know against opposing thoughts and conflicting ideals. Create your own meaning and purpose; confront your thoughts, beliefs, feelings, and actions with unconditional honesty; decide for yourself when your life's purpose has been fulfilled; face death with courage; see the world for what it is independent of human interests and biases: guiltless, shameless, sinless, and innocent—pure becoming.
>
> Place no value in so-called transcendental/supernatural realms or other-worldly philosophies and truths; discover what has ultimate value for you by recognizing your native talents and interests and developing them to their fullest potential; forget what is unnecessary and burdensome from your past and be mindful of the thoughts and instincts that propel you forward to who you are becoming; create your values be experimenting with different values systems and ways of thinking, feeling, and acting; understand yourself as an integral part of the natural world and spend time communing with it; find answers to your most pressing questions be looking to experience, reflecting on your inspired ideas and heartfelt intuitions, and by listening closely to the suggestions and insights of exceptional teachers.

Love others by helping them become self-sufficient, emotionally and mentally strong, more creative, honest, and open to, and accepting of, what is; nurture the habit of keeping promises; seize everyday with boldness and audacity to break through to more freedom, to go beyond yourself, to create yourself—in Nietzsche's words—to "become who you are"; probe daringly—heart and mind—into the mysteries of existence and let what is, be; love yourself as one who is becoming a higher, richer, and fuller being; stay attuned to the normal pleasures of life such as cherishing friendships.

Moralize from the power that naturally flows from enthusiastically affirming the world and your place in it; make your life beautiful by giving free rein to creative thoughts and emotions as well as to well-crafted actions; think and act not from obsessive needs or feelings of inadequacy, but from principles that register the overflow of your unconditional love of life; don't flee from unpleasant feelings and thoughts, but listen to what they are saying and use them to your advantage; validate your highest principles with concrete action; think of yourself as a priceless work of art that is in a perpetual state of increasing excellence—of endless creation—and YOU with chisel in hand forming the being that you want to become; learn to sing, dance, and laugh habitually; live life with gusto; be happy and then do what you want.

Nietzsche called himself the first "tragic philosopher." He awarded himself this honor because he claimed that he was the first thinker to base a philosophy upon the full, complete, and enthusiastic acceptance of life—including its Dionysian component. Seeing what is ugly, cruel, and chaotic as *necessary antagonisms* to what is beautiful, wonderful, and harmonious is not only to love life in totality, it is to redeem the past. We typically feel regret for former misdeeds, horrible decisions, or unfortunate experiences; to make matters worse, regret often turns into guilt, anger, resentment, and even despair and can afflict us in our everyday lives.

Zarathustra acknowledged that human beings couldn't *will in reverse* and change what has occurred. This means that the immense weight of a problematic past could easily crush any hope for total life affirmation. How the overman could be rescued from the past became a critical issue for Zarathustra. He concluded that once the insight of eternal recurrence overtakes the overman, the past would be redeemed naturally—that is, once the world is seen through the eyes of unconditional love for all that is, then even what was experienced as horrible can be understood as intimately and inextricably interconnected to all joy and happiness. Along with the absolute acceptance and interpenetration of the present and the past, the future too is bathed in the loving glow of total affirmation. Nietzsche called this attitude "amor fati"—love of fate. This term describes the state of mind that the believer in eternal recurrence possesses. In his autobiography, *Ecce Homo*, Nietzsche wrote: "My formula for greatness in man is *amor fati*: that a man should wish to have nothing altered, neither forward, nor backward, nor in all eternity. Not merely to endure necessity, still less to conceal it—all idealism is falsehood in the face of necessity—but rather to love it."

The doctrine of eternal recurrence has been the most difficult of all Nietzsche's brainchildren to understand. Did he really believe it? Or was it a sort of theoretical litmus test to determine the value of our actions? In the latter case, we could pose the following question before each of our actions: is this action desirable enough to want to experience it again and again for all eternity? If not, then it's not worth pursuing. The sarcastic response could be that nothing is really worth repeating eternally, which may very well be right. It seems to me that this was not the role that Nietzsche wanted his theory to fulfill, anyway. He had great disdain for moral imperatives—that is, the practice of judging human behavior by rigid moral standards. How, then, are we to understand his theory?

The truth-value of an idea, philosophy, or worldview was important to Nietzsche, but it wasn't what mattered most. As we noted, he was in love with pagan mythology not because it was truer than other worldviews, but because it illuminated and elevated the real world, the powers of nature, and human beings—which it often cast in *heroic* characters. And conversely, his loathing of Christianity was based in his belief that it darkened and degraded the real world and made human beings into helpless, pathetic, and benighted sinners.

456

Although Nietzsche thought that there was some philosophical and scientific evidence for eternal recurrence, the idea itself was born out of an elevated mood of existential affirmation and not from rational analysis. The philosophical underpinning to which Nietzsche gave some attention was an afterthought rather than a first premise. In *The Gay Science*, the book that he published right before he wrote *Thus Spoke Zarathustra*, Nietzsche introduced his radical insight. The aphorism is called: "The Heaviest Weight."

What if some day or night a demon were to steal with you into your loneliest loneliness and say to you: "This life as you live it and have lived it, you have to live once more and innumerable times more; and there will be nothing new in it, but every pain and every joy and every thought and sigh and everything unutterably small or great in your life will have to return to you, all in the same succession and sequence even this spider and this moonlight between the trees, and even this moment and I myself. The eternal hourglass of existence is turned upside down again and again, and you with it, speck of dust!"

Would you not throw yourself down and gnash your teeth and curse the demon who spoke thus? Or have you once experienced a tremendous moment when you would have answered him: "You are a god and never have I heard anything more divine."

If this thought gained possession of you, it would change you as you are or perhaps crush you. The question in each in everything, "Do you desire this once more and innumerable times more?" would lie upon your actions as the greatest weight. Or how well disposed would you have to become to yourself and to life to crave nothing more fervently than this ultimate confirmation and seal?

Nietzsche believed that eternal recurrence was a crucial component to his yea-saying philosophy. He took such pride in this conception because, like so many of his brilliant ideas, it was born not from detached, rational reflection but from engaged, visceral experience— from, one might say, a *Dionysian moment*. In his autobiography, *Ecce Homo*, he wrote:

The fundamental idea of my work—namely, the Eternal Recurrence of all things—this highest of all possible formulae of a Yea-saying philosophy, first occurred to me in August 1881. I made a note of the thought on a sheet of paper, with the postscript: 6,000 feet beyond men and time! That day I happened to be wandering through the woods alongside of the lake of Silvaplana, and I halted beside a huge, pyramidal and towering rock not far from Surlei. It was then that the thought struck me. Looking back now, I find that exactly two months previous to this inspiration, I had had an omen of its coming in the form of a sudden and decisive alteration in my tastes— more particularly in music. It would even be possible to consider all Zarathustra as a musical composition. At all events, a very necessary condition in its production was a renaissance in myself of the art of healing. In a small mountain resort (Recoaro) near Vicenza, where I spent the spring of 1881, I and my friend and Maestro, Peter Gast— also one who had been born again—discovered that the phoenix music hovered over us, wore lighter and brighter plumes than it had done theretofore. Nietzsche was what I call an "epiphanist"—a thinker who is repeatedly bombarded by philosophical insights. This was the essence of his genius and explains a great deal about his style of philosophizing and even the content and quality of his philosophy. This is nowhere more evident than in his revelation of eternal recurrence. As we can see from his description above, the idea "struck" him; he had an "omen" of it; he refers to eternal recurrence as an "inspiration." He also stated that his Zarathustra could be viewed as a "musical composition." Music was, to Nietzsche, a Dionysian phenomenon in that it originates in the depths of the unconscious, where animal instinct and human passion commingle.

15.6

The truth-value of Nietzsche's theory of eternal recurrence makes for an interesting philosophical discussion, although philosophers generally have never thought that it possessed the logical necessity that Nietzsche occasionally attributed to it. More importantly, though, the idea emerged out of Nietzsche's Dionysian experience of total life affirmation. From this view, its literal, philosophical credibility is largely irrelevant. As we noted earlier, the actual truthfulness of an idea, belief, or worldview was not of primary importance to Nietzsche. In fact, he gave utmost value to life-affirming illusions and fantasies; he believed that they were necessary to the spiritual and psychological well-being of individuals and cultures as a whole—but to receive Nietzsche's imprimatur, an illusion or fantasy must promote the incomparable value of the earth and its powers, and above all else, it must be a boon to passionate self-expression, human-centered nobility, and unfettered creativity. Does this not mean that Nietzsche thought that his idea of eternal recurrence was pure fantasy? Nietzsche was clearly undecided about the ultimate truth-value of his idea. He certainly toyed with the idea that it had a scientific basis. In the end, however, he was unsure of its status purely as a scientific phenomenon. That being said, he believed, without question, that his idea conferred a deeper and vaster dimension to life-affirmation. But even if eternal recurrence were not literally true, the idea still served Nietzsche very well. For instance, it integrated and crystallized a crucial aspect of his philosophy, and gave it a compelling, cosmic presence and power without having to transcend the physical universe.

The meaning of the eternal recurrence should not be seen as separate from the overman—the purest embodiment of his amor fati—love of fate. The overman is, for Nietzsche, a qualitatively different kind of human being, almost a new species: he has no desire whatsoever for so-called transcendental truth or realities; the overman is not victimized by typical, all-too-human needs and motivations, such as the impulse to follow herd morality, or to submit thoughtlessly to herd authority, or to think, act, and moralize out of resentment; he is a veritable fount of creativity whose immediate instinct is to go beyond himself and to incite others to do the same. Most characteristically, the overman loves unconditionally everything that is necessary in existence—including what is painful and unfortunate.

We could understand the eternal recurrence as a sort of a philosophical myth (a "noble lie," if you like) that symbolizes the boundless love for life—its Dionysian mantra could be "once more and infinite times more." Unlike other kinds of myths, such as those in the New Testament, it is *nontranscendental* and life affirming, and, as such, it glorifies nature, natural powers, and human creativity. Amor fati is neither a reasoned position nor a quantifiable, empirical one; rather, it is an *experiential reality*—that is, a psycho-emotional state of mind that emerges out of the overflow of creative energy—"out of the yea-saying spirit." Amor fati is a natural expression of energy overflow in the same way that resentment is the natural expression of energy depletion: both reflect will-to-power moving in opposite directions.

After *Thus Spoke Zarathustra*, Nietzsche continued developing, refining, and clarifying his ideas in a number of ingenious books: *Beyond Good and Evil, The Genealogy of Morals, Twilight of the Idols, the Dawn, the AntiChrist,* and his autobiography, *Ecce Homo.* Despite the unsystematic, spontaneous nature of his thinking, he never deviated from his goal of exploring, by experimenting with many ideas, the new world that has been opened up as a result of the death of God. Nietzsche has often been accused of inconsistency and even contradicting himself—and these allegations are not unjustified. What many of his critics have failed to realize, however, was that he was both an experimental thinker and an epiphanist. With this form of philosophizing, thinking systematically and consistently could easily become impediments to the free, open, and creative investigating into *what is.*

Experimentation of any kind is based upon the attitude of "let's try a variety of approaches and see what happens." And if contradictions do come to light, the investigator has the choice to try to resolve them or to let them be. But Nietzsche the epiphanist was unwilling to repudiate an individual insight if he thought that it might contain a kernel of truth, even if the insight appeared to be inconsistent with other insights. By letting contradictions stand on their own, Nietzsche was respecting the integrity of each insight; in his view, logic should not be permitted to destroy a meaningful viewpoint. He applied logic within the context of individual insights, but not necessarily between *different* insights. And when his insights were mutually consistent, as they sometimes were, then at least he had achieved consistency without having to compromise the thoughts' significance. He did all this in the spirit of exploring the mystery of what is.

Rational thought is a critical tool for understanding reality, but it knows more about itself than about what is unknown. This is why logic must be employed carefully to make sure that it does not interfere with the power of insight; sometimes the value of an idea is not clear at first, but becomes obvious only after the idea bumps up against contending ideas and takes on a different meaning. And, in some instances, insights are worlds unto themselves that necessarily stand in stark contrast to other insights. Did Nietzsche believe that all his insights would *ultimately* lead to a supreme insight that incorporated all others? Apparently, he said as much at least once. But his body of philosophical work said the opposite: reality is much too complex and multidimensional to be reduced to one overarching perspective.

But beyond that, reality, for Nietzsche, is not just resting there in front of us. He believed that the seeker of truth is also an artist who *participates creatively* in the experience of truth. But unlike one of his great nemeses, Immanuel Kant, he did not hold that there was an objective world that exists out there beyond our senses and thinking apparatus. What is present to us in normal experience *is* what is objective, and it is all that there is; the seeker of truth has no choice but to see reality through as many creative perspectives as possible; this is the only path to real understanding. Why? Because of the imbalance between the radical finitude of human understanding in contrast to the infinity of what is. If there were an infinite God, then one comprehensive insight could embrace the totality of what is. Since human beings are devoid of such a cosmic intelligence, we are left with finite perspectives in trying to understand reality—and an endless number of perspectives at that.

As significantly, human beings are not detached subjectivities observing the outside world from a distance. Instead, we are intimate parts of the natural world and participating aspects of it: *human creativity and the creativity of the universe go hand in hand and together are caught up in the becoming of what is.* In this sense, Nietzsche's overman is a veritable force of nature that continuously *goes with the flow* of becoming. The philosopher/artist has the amazing power to pose questions and to find, and sometimes even create, answers that illuminate what is. This creative action is what Nietzsche sees as the future role of the philosopher. Philosophical knowledge, in this way, does not consist of unchanging, frozen descriptions about something out there or up there, but instead, is a portal into the multidimensional nature of reality, in the here and now, which the philosopher not only discovers but also helps create.

That is to say, the philosopher of the future must not only be a discoverer of reality but also a creator of reality. Philosopher and artist must become one. This union of philosopher and artist is a good example of an idea that conflicts with other Nietzschean ideas. He argued for open and free creative self-expression while at the same time maintained that free will is a fiction. Who we are, what we think, how we behave, and what we value are the result of countless influences that fall outside of our conscious awareness and control. It is sheer foolishness to believe that we navigate our lives by virtue of free will; after all, look how clumsy, error-laden, and *unconscious* our decision-making is. There is a whole universe of determining forces that shape all aspects of our lives, about which we have very little awareness. Nietzsche held that belief in free will was just another insidious article of faith in the repertoire of resentment-thinking, a belief invented by our religious traditions to create guilt and shame for purposes of controlling human thought and action. Yet Nietzsche was perhaps the most profound advocate for creative expression. What was the overman but the very essence of personal freedom?

These sorts of inconsistencies pepper all of Nietzsche's thought, and many brilliant philosophers have darkened countless pages to try to explain them away. But harmonizing Nietzsche's thought is hardly possible, since many of the inconsistencies were the result of one of the most ingenious minds in history experimenting with different ways into the truth of what is; incompatible versions are to be expected. That Nietzsche was an experimental philosopher does not mean, however, that his ideas should be taken lightly. On the contrary: it's because he had no allegiance to any system of thought, and because his thinking did not strive for absolute, logical consistency, that his ideas have an additional power, poignancy, and credibility. This accounts, at least in part, for his infectious appeal: the reader never knows what amazing insight might show up in the next aphorism, or what shocking revelation will hit her like a thunderbolt in the next section or book. Nietzsche always keeps his readers sitting anxiously on the edge of their philosophical seats. He wanted his readers to wrestle with him and his contentious and unruly ideas and insights. In his view, the tension that results from the conflict of antagonistic ideas, or versions of reality, could only lead to deeper insights and greater philosophical overcoming. And he indeed puts his readers in the philosophical corner time and time again and compels them to respond; Nietzsche, of course, would prefer his readers to come back at him with an all-out frontal assault.

Many of Nietzsche's ideas—not to mention his writing as a whole—are of such sublime quality that one is sometimes tempted to give up fighting with him altogether. But the inconsistencies in his thinking, and controversial nature of many of his arguments, make this impossible, so we do battle with him—and a great deal of crucial philosophical debate today remains locked in a sort of Nietzschean dialectic. Nietzsche would have been delighted. Nonetheless, some serious philosophical difficulties naturally arise in his thinking. Despite the depth and scope of its penetrating vision, Nietzsche's philosophy is very poor in solutions to the many problems that he exposes, discusses, and explores.

For example, what a Nietzschean society would actually look like is difficult to ascertain in totality. He had no patience for democracy, because he thought that it neutralizes individuality and creative expression. He seemed to have little awareness of the liberal versions of democracy with their rule of law, civil liberties, and freedom to vote. He preferred an aristocratic form of government with its natural antagonisms between classes, which he viewed as spiritually healthy. The world today, however, is heading more and more toward liberal democratic rule, despite holdouts from Muslim cultures and lingering socialistic/communistic states. The chances of liberal democracies voluntarily reverting (Nietzsche would say "advancing") to aristocracies appear to be slim to none. He was also oblivious to economic reality and how strongly it influences all aspects of cultural life.

Nietzsche believed that the only hope for humanity to regain its health and vigor would be for powerful individuals to emerge who have the creative talent to create their own values and meaning and to gain control of civilization. But how would a society survive meaningfully when only a minority has the aptitude to create its own values and meaning? The majority cannot turn to the myth of God anymore. He's dead. And how are they to acquire their values and the meaning of their lives? From the creative elite? How this is to be accomplished, and what should be done to prevent fascism from arising from such cultural conditions are questions that Nietzsche never answered. He believed that reality is made up of wills-to-power continuously clashing with each other, and the winners of these battles simply gain sway over the others. This is very risky business. The Christian religion, for example, had a stranglehold on Western culture for thousands of years because resentment's will-to-power dominated all other contenders.

How is this kind of pernicious takeover to be prevented from a future will-to-power free-for-all? Nietzsche never addressed this question. In fact, he appealed to *power* as the ultimate frame of reference for what is good and bad. Generally, what is strong, self-sufficient, creative, and self-actualizing is good, and what is weak, dependent, static, and deteriorating is bad. But how this is all sorted out in actual sociopolitical circumstances is a mystery that Nietzsche never deployed his ingenious mind to solve.

And that's not all. All his remarkable ideas suffer from similar limitations. What it comes down to is that philosophical *insight* is one thing, and adequate philosophical *justification* is quite another. Nietzsche is the greatest genius in Western history with respect to the former, but seriously deficient with respect to the latter. This is true despite his brilliant excursions into more extended philosophical prose, such as in *The Birth of Tragedy* and *The Genealogy of Morals*.

Many critics of Nietzsche point to what they view as his many misstatements, exaggerations, historical errors, and scientific misunderstandings. A number of his contentions were unnecessarily inflammatory and offensive, such as his occasional comments about the inferiority of women, his relentless ad hominem attacks, and his many racist statements, particularly against the Germans and the English. Apparently, he also believed in a kind of Lamarckian evolution in which behavior patterns could be passed onto subsequent generations if they were repeated enough times. We now know that only "genes" and not "acquired characteristics" are passed on to subsequent generations. Nietzsche has also been harshly attacked as one of the principal fathers (if not *the* principal father) of postmodernism, with its fruitless denial of reason and morality and its emphasis on irrationality, anti-intellectualism, and violence. Nietzsche's critics have, moreover, pointed to a number of careless remarks that appeared in his books that made it easy for immoral interpreters to make Nietzsche into a Nazi prophet and sympathizer. There is validity to all these charges. In fact, we could go on, pointing to the human-all-too-human Nietzsche, exposing his many philosophical and rhetorical blemishes.

Unfortunately, these sorts of criticisms of Nietzsche, however valid, can easily cause us to misunderstand what kind of thinker and man he was. Nietzsche once said of his work: "to make the individual uncomfortable, that is my task." In fact, Nietzsche was less interested in solving philosophical and political problems than in destroying a worn-out and diseased worldview and replacing it with a new, life-affirming *vision*, one that he believed humanity desperately needed. He left it to other geniuses to work out the details and strategies of a new humanity. Again, we must always keep in mind that Nietzsche was a visionary and an epiphanist above all else. He did not want to become preoccupied with answering philosophical questions to the point of losing sight of what philosophy was all about, at least for him: *creative participation in the becoming of what is*. This is not a justification for ignoring philosophical details and not offering well-thought-out solutions; it's simply that these valuable philosophical functions were not his primary interest. Nonetheless, Nietzsche did think that being overly focused on philosophical minutiae was mostly a ridiculous game for the intellectually and morally impotent.

Again, it's important that we understand his position. Philosophical inquiry is, without a doubt, a noble endeavor; what is ignoble, however, is misusing philosophy to further psychologically deranged agendas, like satisfying the wretched needs of personal resentment. As we saw, Nietzsche accused Socrates of this crime. Nietzsche viewed his philosophy as a dramatic turning point in Western culture. He believed that he was the only one who saw the nihilistic thread that had been menacingly weaving its way through the West's philosophical and religious traditions from their inceptions. Nietzsche saw progress, optimism, perfectibility, peace, and brotherhood—the watchwords of the Enlightenment—as dangerous illusions that camouflaged the growing pessimism, anxiety, and uncertainty that he believed were about to explode into conspicuous view.

The death of God that he so vociferously proclaimed was, in his view, the literal and symbolic sign of a culture that had emptied itself of meaning, rationality, and purpose. Nietzsche also saw himself as the only thinker who had the philosophical capability and courage to obliterate the lies, deceptions, and myths that had dragged Western culture down its destructive path. Finally, he saw himself as the one creative genius with a vision so majestic and awe-inspiring that it could lead Western culture out of the cesspool of Christian and Socratic resentment and point the way it to its own self-overcoming.

How will Western humanity turn out? In the short run, Nietzsche saw with awesome clarity the cultural mayhem that lay right down the road, right around the corner, and just out of sight. However, his belief in chance and randomness was too strong for him to be able to hazard a guess about Western culture's long-term prospects. What he did know for certain was that humanity was in dire need of powerful ideas and a transforming vision to redeem it from its pathetic history, and to point the way to a "higher" form of existence.

15.7

Interestingly enough, that Nietzsche showed himself to be less than perfect has always had the effect of endearing him even more to many of his readers. It's almost a relief to know that this profound visionary was also a flawed human being. Here was a man of matchless philosophical and literary ability who was also honestly and unabashedly human-all-too-human! One gets the sense when reading his work that his brilliance was such that everything that he said—despite our possible disapproval—must be considered and considered deeply. And why? *Perhaps in the back of our minds, we know that he could be right after all!* And we must be courageous enough to face him, even though we may be gripped with outrage or even fear. And this is an aspect of Nietzsche that sets him apart from all other thinkers. His genius was unpredictable: it could emerge in a flash, seize, disarm, knock you back on your heels—perhaps in the next phrase or with a solitary word.

Nietzsche has also been claimed by modern schools of philosophy, such as language philosophy, because he anticipated their emergence. For example, he blamed the misunderstanding and misuse of language and grammar as sources of metaphysical fictions. The belief in cause and effect, he argued, had one of its sources in how grammar is employed in language. The modern preoccupation with language by philosophers, in fact, began, at least in part, with these sorts of Nietzschean insights regarding traditional metaphysics. Clearly, his thinking was philosophical will-to-power to an extreme.

Despite the many unknown twists and turns that civilization may take in the future, it will never free itself from the protean grasp of Nietzsche's formidable mind. As the pivotal turning point in modern philosophical history, he created the cultural framework in which humanity will have to come to terms with itself—for better or worse.

Nietzsche once famously said that "what doesn't kill you will make you stronger." This was Nietzsche's faith, and one that he fearlessly defended throughout his career. Whether or not he was ultimately right remains to be seen. His dream of the astounding and joyous overman, who loves unconditionally all of existence with his endlessly creative, life-affirming will-to-power, floats ambiguously in front of the human race both as a ridiculous illusion and as a glorious, breathtaking possibility. Will humanity enact the ultimate self-overcoming and initiate a new age of beauty, nobility, and creative power? Or will the *last man*—with his passionless culture of convenience, pseudo-spirituality, and consumerism—proliferate endlessly? The latter is Nietzsche's nightmare scenario. And the former? Well, perhaps it's just the exotic fantasy of a worried genius hopelessly in love with life. But maybe not. History is abundant in hidden variables, and it's certainly possible that at least some of them have Nietzsche's name on them. After all, history has shown more than once that he is not a man to be underestimated. At the very least, for those of us who are intoxicated by the mystery and wonder of what is, we have no choice but to keep our hearts and minds open to Nietzsche's thoughts and challenges—even to his most disturbing insights and accusations—for what is most likely hidden inside: pathways to deeper experiences of life, and a greater intuition of who we are and what we ought to become. Let's permit Nietzsche have the last word about what he thought and what he hoped for:

The Meaning of our Cheerfulness (*The Gay Science*)

The greatest recent event—that "God is dead," that the belief in the Christian God has become unbelievable—is already beginning to cast its first shadows over Europe. For the few at least, whose eyes—the *suspicion* in whose eyes is strong and subtle enough for this spectacle, some suns seem to have set and some ancient and profound trust has been turned into doubt: to them our old world must appear daily more like evening, more mistrustful, stranger, "older." But in the main one may say: the event is far too distant, too remote from the multitude's capacity for comprehension even for the tidings of it to be thought of as having *arrived* as yet. Much less may one suppose that many people know as yet *what* this event really means—and how much collapse now that this faith has been undermined because it was built upon this faith, propped up by it, grown into it; for example the whole of European morality. This long plenitude and sequence of breakdown, destruction, ruin and cataclysm that is now impending—who could guess enough of it today to be compelled to play the teacher and advance proclaimer of this monstrous logic of terror, the profit of gloom and an eclipse of the sun whose like has probably never yet occurred on earth?

Even we born guessers of riddles who are, as it were, waiting on the mountains, posted between today and tomorrow, we firstlings and premature births of the coming century, to whom the shadows that must soon envelop Europe really *should* have appeared by now—why is it that even we look forward to the approaching gloom without any sense of involvement and above all without any worry or fear for *ourselves?* Are we perhaps too much under the impression of the *initial consequences* of this event—and these initial consequences, the consequences for *ourselves*, are quite the opposite of what one might perhaps expect: They are not at all sad and gloomy but rather like a new and scarcely describable kind of light, relief, exhilaration, encouragement, dawn.

Indeed, we philosophers and "free spirits" feel when we hear the news that "the old God is dead," as if a new dawn shone on us; our heart overflows with gratitude, amazement, premonitions, expectation. At long last or ships may venture out again, venture our to face any danger; all the daring of the lover of knowledge is permitted again; the sea, *our* sea, lies open again; perhaps there has never been such an "open sea."

The Great Health (*The Gay Science*)

Being new, nameless, hard to understand, we premature births of an as of yet proven future need for a new goal also a means—namely a new health, stronger, more seasoned, tougher, more audacious, and gayer than any previous health. Whoever has a soul that craves to have experienced the whole range of values and desiderata to date, and to have sailed around all the coast of this ideal "Mediterranean;" whoever wants to know from the adventures of his most authentic experience how a discover and conqueror of the ideal feels, also an artist, a saint, a legislator, a sage, a scholar, a pious man, a soothsayer, and one who stands divinely apart in the old style—one needs above everything else: the *great health*—that one does not merely have but also acquires continually, and must acquire because one gives it up again and again, and must give it up.

And now, after we have long been on our way in this manner, we argonauts of the ideal, with more daring perhaps than is prudent, and have suffered shipwreck and damage often enough, but are, to repeat it, healthier than one likes to permit us as if, as a reward, we now confronted an as of yet undiscovered country whose boundaries nobody has surveyed yet, something beyond all the lands and nooks of the ideal so far, a world so overrich in what is beautiful, strange, questionable, terrible, and divine that our curiosity as well as our craving to possess it got beside itself—alas, now nothing will sate us anymore!

After such vistas and with such a burning hunger in our conscience and science, how could we still be satisfied with *present-day man*? It may be too bad but it is inevitable that we find it difficult to remain serious when we look at his worthiest goals and hopes, and perhaps we do not even bother to look any more.

Another idea runs ahead of us, a strange, tempting, dangerous ideal to which we should not wish to persuade anybody because we do not concede *the right to it* to anyone: the ideal of a spirit who plays naïvely—that is, not deliberately but from overflowing power and abundance—with all that was hitherto called holy, good, untouchable, divine; for whom those supreme things that the people naturally accept as their value standards, signify danger, decay, a debasement, or at least recreation, blindness, and self-oblivion; the ideal of a human, superhuman well-being and benevolence that will often appear inhuman—for example, when it confronts all earthly seriousness so far, all solemnity in gesture, word, tone, eye, morality, and task so far, as if it were their most incarnate and involuntary parody—and in spite of all of this, it is perhaps only with him that *great seriousness* really begins, that the real question mark is posed for the first time, that the destiny of the soul changes, the hand moves forward, the tragedy *begins*.

Vita Femina *(The Gay Science)*

The Greeks, to be sure prayed: "Everything beautiful twice and even three times!" They implored the gods with good reason, for ungodly reality gives us the beautiful either not at all or only once. I mean to say that the world is overfull of beautiful things, but nevertheless poor, very poor when it comes to beautiful moments and unveilings of these moments. But perhaps this is the most powerful magic of life: it is covered by a veil interwoven with gold, a veil of beautiful possibilities, sparkling with promise, resistance, bashfulness, mockery, pity and seduction. Yes, life is a woman.

Life is No Argument (*The Gay Science*)

We have arranged for ourselves a world in which we live—by the postulating of bodies, lines, surfaces, causes and effects, motion and rest, form and content: with these articles of faith no man could manage to live at present. But for all these are stilled unproved. Life is not argument; error might be among the conditions of life.

For the New Year (*The Gay Science*)

I still live. I still think. I must still live, for I must still think. Sum (I am), ergo (therefore), cogito (I think): cogito ergo sum (I think therefore I am). Today everyone takes the liberty of expressing his wish and his favorite thought: well, I am also mean to tell what I have wished for myself today, and what thought first crossed my mind this year—a thought which ought to be the basis, the pledge and the sweetening of all my future life! I want more and more to perceive the necessary character in things as the beautiful—I shall thus be one of those who beautify things. *Amor fati*: let that henceforth be my love! I do not want to wage war with the ugly. I do not want to accuse, I do not want to accuse the accusers. Looking away, let that be my sole negation! And all in all, to sum it up: I wish to be now and all time afterwards only a yea-sayer!

Image of Torture *(The Gay Science)*

Let me proceed like Raphael and never paint another image of torture!

One Thing is Needful (*The Gay Science*)

One thing is needful—To "give style" to one's character—a rare and great art! It is practiced by those who survey all the strengths and weaknesses of their character and then fit them into an artistic plan until every one of them appears as art and reason and even weakness delights the eye. Here a large mass of second nature has been added: there a piece of original nature has been removed—both times through long practice and daily work at it. Here the ugly that could not be removed is concealed; there is has been reinterpreted and made sublime. Much that is vague and resisted shaping has been saved and exploited for distant views; it is meant to beckon toward the far and immeasurable.

Human, All Too Human

The visionary lies to himself, the liar only to others.

Human, All Too Human

The irrationality of a thing is no argument against its existence, rather a condition of it.

Human, All Too Human

There is not enough love and goodness in the world for us to be permitted to give any of it away to imaginary things.

Untimely Meditations

Human beings who do not want to belong to the herd need only to stop and not be comfortable. Follow your conscience that cries out "Be yourself! What you are now doing, thinking, desiring is not who you are—your educators can only be your liberators."

Human, All Too Human

The surest way to corrupt a youth is to instruct him to hold in higher esteem those who think alike than those who think differently.

Thus Spoke Zarathustra

That a man be delivered from revenge, that is for me the bridge to the highest hope and a rainbow after long storms.

Thus Spoke Zarathustra

But thus I counsel you, my friends, distrust all in whom the impulse to punish is powerful.

Thus Spoke Zarathustra

This is my way; where is yours? Thus I answered those who ask me "the way." For "the way"—that does not exist.

Beyond Good and Evil

Whoever fights monsters should see to it that in the process he does not become a monster. And when you look into the abyss, the abyss looks into you.

Beyond Good and Evil

The degree and type of the sexuality of a man extend all the way to the ultimate peak of his spirit.

Beyond Good and Evil

In love and revenge women are superior to men.

Beyond Good and Evil

What? A great man? I always see only the actor of his own ideal.
Beyond Good and Evil

What is done out of love always occurs beyond good and evil.
Beyond Good and Evil

A philosopher is a human being who constantly experiences, sees, hears, suspects, hopes and dreams extraordinary things; he is one who is struck by his own thoughts as if from the outside, as if from above and below, as if by his own kind of lightning bolts; who is perhaps himself a storm pregnant with new lightnings; a fateful human being around whom there are constant grumblings, growlings, and uncanny doings. A philosopher: alas, a being that often runs away from himself, is often afraid of himself—but is too curious to stay away from himself.
Twilight of the Idols

Which is it, is man one of God's blunders, or is God one of man's?
Twilight of the Idols

Without music life would be a mistake.
The Anti-Christ

Morality is the best of all devices for leading mankind around by the nose.
The Ant-Christ

A casual stroll through the lunatic asylum shows that faith does not prove anything.
The Anti-Christ

What is good? All that heightens the feeling of power in man, power itself. What is bad? All that is born of weakness. And what is happiness? The feeling that power is growing, that a resistance is overcome.
Ecce Homo

I do not by any means know atheism as a result; even less as an event; it is a matter of course for me, from instinct. I am too inquisitive, too questionable, too exuberant to stand for any gross answer, an indelicacy against us thinkers—at bottom merely a gross prohibition: you shall not think!
Ecce Homo

I know my fate, one day my name will be associated with the memory of something tremendous—a crisis without equal on earth, the most profound collision of conscience, a decision that was conjured up against everything that had been believed, demanded, hallowed so far. I am no man, I am dynamite.

Thus Spoke Zarathustra

Now I go alone, my disciples, You, too, go now, alone. Thus I want it.

Go away from me and resist Zarathustra! And even better: be ashamed of him! Perhaps he deceived you.

The man of knowledge must not only love his enemies, he must also be able to hate his friends.

One repays a teacher badly if one remains nothing but a pupil. And why do you not want to pluck at my wreath?

You revere me; but what if your reverence tumbles one day? Beware less a statue slay you.

You say that you believe in Zarathustra? But what matters Zarathustra? You are my believers—but what matters all believers?

You have not sought yourselves and you have found me. Thus do all believers; therefore all faith amounts to very little.

Now I bid you lose me and find yourselves; and only when you have all denied me will I return to you.

Ecce Homo

At the bridge I stood
lately in the brown night.
From afar came a song:
as a golden drop it welled
over the quivering surface.
Gondolas, lights, and music—
drunken it swam out into the twilight.
My soul, a stringed instrument,
sang to itself, invisibly touched,
a secret gondola song,
quivering with iridescent happiness.
—Did anyone hear it?

Ecce Homo

Has anyone understood me? Dionysus versus the Crucified.

Thus Spoke Zarathustra

No, life has not disappointed me. On the contrary, I find it truer, more desirable and mysterious every year—ever since the day when the great liberator came to me: the idea that life could be an experiment of the seeker for knowledge—and not a duty, not a calamity, not trickery.—And knowledge itself: let it be something else for others; for example, a bed to rest on, or a form of leisure—for me it is a world of dangers and victories in which heroic feelings, too, find places to dance and play. "Life as a means to knowledge—with this principle in one's heart one can live not only boldly but even gaily, and laugh gaily, too. And who knows how to laugh anyway and live well if he does not first know a good deal about war and victory?

16

Existentialism, Phenomenology, and Final Thoughts

16.1

What is comes into being in five ways:

Occasionally—0–24 percent

Often—25–49 percent

Frequently—50–79 percent

Mostly—80–99.999999 ... percent

Absolutely—100 percent

Examples of occasional truths: stubbing your toe; winning a contest; receiving a traffic ticket; being in a car accident; catching a cold; having an intuition about a future or distant event that turns out to be true.

Examples of truths that occur often: telling untruths; people committing unjust acts, misplacing personal items; creating mishaps in verbal communication and social interactions.

Examples of frequent truths: casual friends calling to say hello; being treated fairly by police officers; being served delicious food at good restaurants; becoming irrational when being harshly criticized harshly.

Examples of truths that occur in most instances: enjoying good physical health until approximately age sixty; having typical personality characteristics; having specific emotional responses to either good or bad news; feelings of romantic love changing over time; human beings always preferring the company of people whom they like; loving parents being concerned for the well-being of their children.

Examples of absolute truths: mathematical truths, analytic truths (e.g., all bachelors are men); physical/materialistic/biological truths (e.g., gravity, evolution); human beings being born into a cultural world of meaning; hunger; death; what is, is.

With the exception of the last category of absolute truth, the other four categories are highly flexible and could easily switch from one to the other. In fact, they are often altered by particular circumstances, individual personality traits, and unexpected or random occurrences. Absolute truths, by contrast, are categorical and universal—absolute. Western thinking, being grounding in the mathematical/materialistic/ biological worldview, sees *what is* from the perspective of the absolute version, and while it recognizes other aspects of reality, it nonetheless places them on a less than absolutely true category. For instance, while most people agree that good restaurants typically serve delicious food, they would also argue that there is a greater chance for a good restaurant to serve a bad meal than for the sun not to set this evening. In this sense, the former is not as reliably true as the latter. Without question, there is good reason for placing elements of *what is* on different levels, and reliability is the best indicator.

The problem, however, is that what we might classify as less than reliably true could also be true nonetheless—but just not in a scientific sense. Scientists argue that claims to truth must stand up to the high standards of science. What is true should have a foundation in carefully designed experiments that are repeatable by other scientists. Physicists maintain that the truth of the universe must be described with mathematics. Of course, in other sciences like biology, mathematical application is mostly inappropriate, because organic life is much too complex for simple mathematical descriptions. But in the nonphysical sciences, other forms of rigorous standards are implemented, such as the genetic understanding of human life and development.

Considering the multifaceted nature of what is, it's more accurate to argue that what we call scientific truth is particular to science and does not necessarily exhaust all the possibilities of *what is*. That is to say, it's not unreasonable to think that perhaps some dimensions of *what is* are not amenable to empirical, repeatable experimentation. It's possible that what we call psychic phenomena, for example, are real and true, but only *occasionally* so, and that an aspect of their truthfulness is that they are erratically and unpredictably manifested in the world because of complex conditions in the universe about which we currently have no understanding. From this view, there should be no final judgment on psychic realities except to say that such possibilities make little scientific sense from what we know at the present time, and that such claims don't stand up to our current standards of scientific verification and experimentation. Are psychic phenomena therefore necessarily unreal? No. In the true spirit of science, we must suspend final judgment in consideration of our limited understanding of what is.

Let's not forget that the so-called truths of quantum physics—for example, the probabilistic nature of ultimate physical reality and non-local connectedness to local ones *instantly*—did not fit into our classical understanding of the physical world when they were first discovered at the beginning of the twentieth century. For this reason, even the immortal Einstein would not consider the quantum reality as ultimately true. Today, we know better and have to say with regret that the great professor was wrong and that his judgment was ill founded. Twenty-first-century physics discovered, and continues to discover, ways to incorporate quantum reality into the bigger picture of the physical universe. In other words, science had to alter its philosophical and mathematical understanding of the physical universe to accommodate the deeper truths of physical reality that it stumbled upon. And there is no reason to believe that this process of scientific discovery and self-discovery will not continue as long as there is scientific progress. In this sense, science is not only uncovering truths about the physical universe, but just as importantly, it is discovering truths about how it must transform itself in order to accommodate greater apprehensions of *what is*.

16.2

What is—objective reality—necessarily includes subjectivity as a genuine category of what is objectively real. To be sure, there are distinctions among the various aspects of what is, and it's important that we recognize where these different aspects fit into the general scheme of things. Subjective ideas, feelings, moods, intentions and inclinations, for instance, are not physical things, and, therefore, do not have the same ontological status as, say, trees, fire engines, and air, *but they are just as real* and, I might add, they are at least just as important.

16.3

The centuries-long pursuits of truth and knowledge in philosophy and science have been projects fraught with countless mistakes, false starts, and destructive stupidities. This tainted record, nevertheless, should not be held against philosophers and scientists. That humanity has unearthed much that is true about existence, and has built vast mountains of reliable knowledge, have to be seen as small miracles when we consider that the human beings are naturally irrational, inclined toward error, and pathologically forgetful.

16.4

What then are missteps, falsehoods, and self-deception to the lover of ideas, but unavoidable steppingstones on the uncertain path to knowledge and wisdom.

16.5

The genuine truth seeker learns to brave the turbulent waters of human fallibility with practiced, athletic skill and a heroic spirit, even as the land that seemed ever so near always manages to recede just beyond his most praiseworthy reach.

16.6

Existentialism is a philosophy that aims to illuminate *what is* necessarily true about human existence, from the perspective a person experiencing, firsthand, himself, other people, the world, and the universe. Existentialism is not concerned with traditional rational, philosophical, or scientific understanding of human life, because, according to existentialists, these forms of understanding are abstract, detached, disengaged, and "unlived." Existentialism, by contrast, strives to explore what is most personal and alive in *immediate* experience: the instincts, passions, feelings, moods, and the intuitive ideas and emotions that typically color—and give meaning to—day-to-day existence. Existentialism also focuses on "inter-subjective" experience: by their very nature, human beings are social beings, and this fact frames how we experience ourselves, other beings, the world, and the universe in which we find ourselves. Existentialism represents a wide range of thoughts and thinkers because it derives from different sources and traditions. Questions of meaning, purpose, free will, morality, ethics, suffering, alienation, and many other existential themes are important in all literary traditions, and have had a long history. But for the existentialists, these ideas took on radically different meanings from what they had meant in the past.

Western philosophy during the nineteenth century, especially the philosophy of Georg Wilhelm Friedrich Hegel (1770–1831), was taken to task by thinkers like Soren Kierkegaard (1813–1855) for systematically deleting from its areas of interest the importance of *subjectivity* in the human experience, and, particularly, its significance to the pursuit of truth and human meaning. The typical feelings, intuitions, and passions that populate subjective experience were viewed by Hegel and his followers as nonobjective and unworthy of philosophical attention, and were cast aside as having no value to genuine thinking; at best, they are the substance of poetry and art—certainly, in their view, inferior kinds of knowing. Authentic knowledge, by contrast, is discovered only through logical reasoning and not by way of feelings, passions, or emotions, because they simply have no philosophical truth-value—and, in fact, they distort and cloud the rational mind and make it difficult, if not impossible, for the mind to see what is true. For Kierkegaard, however, without subjectivity there is no *individuality*, and without individuality the true meaning of being human is forever lost. Authentic truth could never be discovered within such an artificial context. Human passions and emotions are not necessarily stupid or ill-attuned to existence but are the very substance of subjectivity—of individuality. It's for this reason that Kierkegaard viewed "passionate inwardness" as fundamental to how human beings know themselves, the truth of the world, and the meaning of life. For Kierkegaard, a human being *exists*—that is, *stands out* as a *solitary* and *passionate* individual, an individual who experiences the world from her own *subjective* reality.

In his most famous books, *Either/Or*, *Fear and Trembling*, and *Sickness Unto Death*, Kierkegaard approached subjectivity from the perspective of his deeply held religious beliefs. He saw human beings as naturally *conflicted*—part human and part divine—with the two components actively moving in opposing moral directions; each individual is caught up, body and soul, in the struggle for the realization of personal selfhood, ethical righteousness, and spiritual connectedness to God. This struggle is a highly emotional and deeply felt process—an inward process—in which unsettling feelings like anxiety, melancholy, loneliness, uncertainty, and even despair challenge each human being to move closer to God and to an ethical life.

If Kierkegaard's inwardly passionate human being is struggling to integrate his partly mortal and partly divine nature, Friedrich Nietzsche's meaning-seeking human is struggling to abolish all remnants of God. By announcing the death of God in the late nineteenth century, Nietzsche, in *The Gay Science* and *Thus Spoke Zarathustra*, proclaimed the dawn of a new era for humanity. But the loss of God came at a weighty price: the very fabric of meaning that has kept Western humanity safe and warm and protected for over two-thousand years has been ripped to shreds, both from inside Christianity itself—through self-doubt—and from the outside—through breakthroughs in secular understanding. Meaninglessness, nothingness, lostness, and total self-responsibility are now staring humanity right in the face; they are the frightening, new truths of existence that require direct engagement. What is humanity to do? How is it going to wield this newfound freedom? Western humanity had been under the sadistic heel of Christianity, as it systematically extirpated the West's healthy instincts and passions and replaced them with a diseased, nay-saying culture. But the lies of Christian morality, and the lie that was God itself, are no longer believable. Mustn't humankind now embark on a new journey of self-creation in which it generates its own values and meaning for living? With Nietzsche, the loss of religious belief meant that each human life becomes *personal and psychological*: my instincts, passions, and thoughts are now the foundation to my life; I am now on my own; I have to live with myself and create my own meaning; I have to come to terms with my desires for power and control. Since much of *what I am* exists below my awareness, how do I embrace my mysterious, dark sides to ensure that my existence is forever life affirming? How do I now say "yes" to life and reclaim the earth as beautiful, my own, and of ultimate value?

In Nietzsche's view, even Western humanity's philosophical tradition became corrupted almost as soon as it began, by Socratic rationality, which destroyed the natural belief in life and undermined the organic desires of our instincts and passions. By subjecting every aspect of human existence to the cold knife of rationality, our life-affirming beliefs and myths have been cut to pieces, and even the deep, dark, and wondrous mysteries of life have been rationalized out of existence. In short, the very conditions that make life beautiful and profoundly meaningful have been nullified by a rationality that possesses neither joy nor wisdom. For Nietzsche, modern humanity must face the harsh reality that its long-esteemed tradition of rationality was fueled more by a hatred for life than a love of, or ecstatic wonder about, it.

In the twentieth century, existential thinkers such as Heidegger and Sartre absorbed Kierkegaard and Nietzsche's insights into human existence and modern culture, and they continued the bold investigation into subjectivity, opening up this mysterious world in new and provocative ways. What, then, is distinctive about twentieth-century existential thought? One answer is the following: existentialism is a prime example of how powerful ideas could gain power and prestige because of sociopolitical developments. The two world wars in the twentieth century had a devastating effect on the European mentality, and for many thinkers, they crushed once and for all the cherished Enlightenment ideals of unstoppable cultural progress, belief in the absolute goodness of human nature, faith in the eventual "brotherhood of man," and confidence in the unlimited power of reason to solve all of humankind's ills. And traditional, religious thought did not fare any better. "Where is God in all of this unmitigated destruction and loss of life?"—heartbroken Europeans asked as the grotesque consequences of the wars became clear. "What God?" some existentialists famously replied.

With the unimaginable physical destruction and loss of human life that the wars wrought, many thinkers and artists in the early twentieth century sought ways to comprehend what had occurred and to explain the philosophical implications. It was in this sociopolitical soil that existential thinkers cultivated their ideas, many of which opened up fresh and uninvestigated areas of study. A number of these ideas were borrowed from philosophers like Kierkegaard and Nietzsche and were expanded and refocused to come to terms with the European spiritual crisis. Questions about the nature of irrationality, evil, nihilism, human nature, free will, and the meaning of existence took on a ferocious intensity with existential thinkers, and for the first time in the history of ideas, these highly charged themes moved to philosophical center-stage. After World War I, and continuing through and after World

War II, existentialism grew into a formidable cultural force that had a significant impact not only on European philosophy but also on political and social thought. Existential thinking, for instance, brought to light original approaches to psychological theory and therapy.

16.7

But there was another critical ingredient in this rich and diverse existential mix, one that, ironically, had nothing to do with European literary traditions or sociopolitical events but became the foundation and guide for most of the important existential thinkers in the twentieth century. Edmund Husserl (1859–1938), a Moravian-born mathematician/physicist turned philosopher, created a new discipline, which he understood as the science of describing the essential "structures" of meaning in experience: phenomenology.

But what are structures of meaning, and why are they so important? For Husserl, the way the world *appears* to a perceiving subject in experience is through "meaning," and each meaning has *invariant attributes*—that is, defining qualities that separate one meaningful item or experience from another. The reason that we can distinguish a tree from a basketball, for example, is because each has distinct, invariant structures that make them identifiable or meaningful to a person observing them; it's not simply that trees and basketballs are shaped differently and are of different sizes; it's that their different shapes and sizes *mean* something very specific. Husserl's "scientific philosophy"— phenomenology—is the systematic method for investigating the ways in which the structural meanings of experience appear to a person or people experiencing them, or, in phenomenological language, how meaning is "constituted" in consciousness. Husserl was so confident that his brainchild could describe, *objectively*, how meanings show themselves that his motto was "To the things themselves."

Even bolder was his claim that his phenomenology was a "presuppositionless philosophy." By presuppositionless, he meant that his scientific philosophy did not require *untested* first premises, which virtually all sciences and fields of intellectual pursuit possess. As an example, scientists always prefer simple or elegant theories and explanations to more complex and bulky ones, if both can account equally well for the same phenomena. This was the reason why, at least initially, the heliocentric theory—sun as the center of the solar system—replaced the geocentric theory—earth as the center of the solar system; the former was much simpler and therefore more efficient than the latter. To scientists, this meant that it was the better theory. But scientists cannot test to discover if simpler, in fact, has greater truth-value than more complex; rather, it merely *appears* to be so. Thus, the first premise that simpler is better is always accepted as true, because it seems to make sense.

Husserl made the audacious claim that in looking to the "things themselves," first premises are simply not required. But his argument is far-fetched for many reasons, not the least of which is that phenomenology, too, presupposes the untested first premise of simplicity. And then there is the problem of the *language* that is employed in phenomenology, which, like all kinds of language, contains biases and untested premises. Nonetheless, we could still appreciate the fact that Husserl's scientific philosophy strove to go directly to "immediate experience" and describe the invariable meaning structures that are found there; and the enormous influence that phenomenology has had on ingenious thinkers, in itself, clearly indicates that his new science uncovered new truths about consciousness and its relationship to meaning.

Husserlian phenomenology is first and foremost a method of investigating human consciousness rather than a body of knowledge about consciousness and meaning. Husserl put forth his most key technique of investigation, the "phenomenological reduction," as a way to isolate what is most *essential* about the experience of objects in the outside world—from the perspective of an observing consciousness. The phenomenological reduction is carried out by an observer suspending or "bracketing" all preconceived ideas, beliefs, judgments, theories, biases, expectations, and habitual ways of thinking about what is being observed, including—and most radically—leaving aside the question of whether or not the object being observed really exists. We are typically caught up in the "natural attitude" in which we see before us—for instance, cars, birds, and coffee cups—and we expect that the things we see are interconnected in a complex web of cause and effect relationships. With Husserl's reduction, the natural attitude is temporarily put aside, so that cars, birds, coffee cups, and cause and effect relationships are not granted any existential status. Questions as to *the very existence* of these objects and phenomena are "put in brackets"—suspended. By reducing an object in experience to its bare, unadorned appearance, Husserl thought that the phenomenologist would be able to isolate, see, and describe what is really *present* in experience. And what Husserl believed is revealed in this denaturalized viewing of experience are the necessary "essences" that make up the item or items under investigation. Husserlian phenomenology, then, could be understood generally as the systematic search for the essences in experience. This was Husserl's version of getting to the "things themselves."

Husserl's insight that an observer could imagine even the *nonexistence* of an object was to have profound consequences for all subsequent existential thought. And the reason is simple, but profound: the phenomenological reduction naturally inserts a *skeptical wedge* between an object and its meaning. If objects can be stripped of their meaning by a simple manipulation of the imagination, this must signify that there is no necessary connection between an item and its meaning. Meaning then is, at best, unstable. Jean-Paul Sartre (1905–1985), in particular, seized upon this idea and expanded it by suggesting that not only is meaning unstable, but it is also fleeting, and random, often an illusion, and frequently a fabrication, as is most vividly evidenced when we project fanciful meanings onto fictions like God and the self. As we will see, the fact that Husserl saw consciousness as an activity that constitutes meaning also added significantly to the undermining of the idea of a stable, cohesive, and meaningful objective reality, toward which people orientate their thinking, feelings, and actions.

The centerpiece of Husserlian phenomenology is the idea of "intentionality"—that "consciousness is consciousness of." Husserl borrowed this concept from one of his teachers, psychologist Franz Brentano (1838–1917), who saw it as a key to understanding psychological activity. In this view, consciousness is, by its very nature, *bipolar*, in that it must always have an object, real or imagined, toward which it is directed. Husserl reformulated Brentano's version to mean that consciousness is always in the process of constituting the meaning of the *real* objects that it is experiencing. Here, "constituting" does not mean creating the object that it experiences (this was the basic criticism of Brentano's meaning); it means assembling in consciousness the meaning that already exists in the outside world in the form of the meaningful items that consciousness actually encounters. The notion of consciousness without real, intentional objects was sheer nonsense to Husserl. How could consciousness carry out its essential function of constituting meaning if there were no objects whose meaning it could constitute? The concept of intentionality was put to abundant use by subsequent phenomenologists and existentialists.

In Husserl's last and unfinished work, *The Crisis of European Sciences*, he introduced his notion of the "lebenswelt"—or life-world. All science and all our natural activities rest upon a concrete reality that is given to our senses. This pre-given world is there at birth; we are born into it, as it were, without our awareness of it. We typically don't experience directly the lebenswelt, because we naturally cover it up with our ideas about how we think the world should be. Science, in particular, has lost sight of the lebenswelt because of its requirements of "idealizing" nature in mathematical descriptions. Husserl cites the scientific idealizing of nature as beginning primarily with physicist Galileo in the late sixteenth and early seventeenth centuries. Galileo started this tradition by recasting all of nature in perfect, geometrical forms so that it could be easily investigated and tested mathematically. But nature is not precisely geometric; it only appears that way because of the "garb of ideas" that has been imposed onto it. And this distortion of basic reality is not only a scientific activity; everyday human life is also characterized by human beings thoughtlessly suppressing and distorting what is naturally before their very eyes. We may say, for example, that a particular road is straight, when in reality the road isn't straight at all; it just appears that way because we have been trained to thinks in terms of straightness and because it's convenient to think and speak imprecisely. Once we *go below* what we normally think, however, a truer, more fundamental reality begins to emerge.

16.8

Husserl's most famous student and successor in phenomenology, Martin Heidegger (1889–1976), developed and radicalized Husserl's idea of the lebenswelt to the point that it caused a philosophical rift between the two men. Heidegger's own version of the life-world was destined to become the ground for a new philosophy that had a greater impact on existentialism than even his teacher's.

Heidegger departed from Husserlian phenomenology because he thought that it was idealistic—that is, was overly focused on questions of consciousness and meaning independent of the real world. Nonetheless, he borrowed Husserl's descriptive method of systematically observing experience and a number of Husserl's key insights, which he reformulated in fascinating and in, one might say, breathtaking ways. He focused deeply on Husserl's ideas about meaning and developed a new phenomenology that was concerned less with *epistemology*—or, questions of knowledge and how meaning is constituted in experience—than with *ontology*—or, questions of existence, especially human existence. Why human existence? *Because the nature of human existence creates the context in which knowledge and meaning are possible.* Husserl made the error of beginning his scientific philosophy in midair, so to speak, without accounting for what meaning is and how its emergence was possible in the first place. What this meant to Heidegger was that rather than inquiring into the nature of consciousness and how it constitutes this or that meaning in experience, phenomenology should be concerned with describing what he called "Being"—the very source of all meaning.

Let's try to explain Heidegger's abstract reasoning and simplify his difficult ideas. Questions about how meaning is constituted in consciousness are, for Heidegger, going in the wrong direction and presuppose fragmenting human reality into mutually conflicting parts—subject over and against object, and natural consciousness over and against phenomenological consciousness ("transcendental ego"). By contrast, what philosophy needs to do is investigate the larger, holistic context from which all meaning arises. This larger context is "Being." His notion of Being is among the most difficult ideas to understand in all of philosophy and requires, first of all, separating *beings* from *Being*. Beings are the various physical items that exist in the world that we experience both directly (through normal experience) and indirectly (through scientific study). Being, by contrast is the *nonphysical presence of all that is*—the "is-ness" of all individual beings. Heidegger called the difference between physical beings and non-physical Being the "ontological difference." Despite the fact that there are many items or beings in the universe, and that there are physical differences between them, they all have one common feature in equal measure: they all exist! And their existence cannot be reduced to this or that feature, because existence is not a *quantitative* quality. If we pose the question "Who exists more: a thin person or an obese person?" the point becomes clear. The obvious answer is that thin people and overweight people have the same level of existence, because existence is not measurable—*it just is*! This is-ness is what Heidegger was talking about with Being. Let's take a different approach to make the same point.

Each being or item that we encounter in experience *means* something—chairs, the moon, and airplanes, for example, are physical items to which we have assigned meanings and names. These meanings and names exist as nonphysical ideas, concepts, and labels. But in addition to these individual, nonphysical meanings and names, there is also the general, nonphysical, nonspecific *ocean of meaning from which all individual meanings emerge*. This boundless, nonmaterial ocean of meaning is Being.

Another illuminating metaphor is music. (This is my metaphor, not Heidegger's.) When we hear a beautiful love ballad, we hear an aesthetically integrated whole and not simply the individual parts of the song, such as the melody line or isolated, particular notes; if we did, we could easily lose the benefit of a genuine musical experience. If we think of the parts of a song in Heideggerian terms, and imagine each part as individual *beings*, with the whole song itself as Being, we can begin to understand what Heidegger was after. In the same way that we could focus in on a particular musical element—such as the melody—and, in so doing, become deaf to the musical experience as a whole, we can also focus exclusively on the particular beings experience and forget their source—Being.

A significant part of the glory of music is its mystery: that mere sound waves can transform our personal feelings and thoughts in such profound ways is indeed one of the most amazing occurrences in human experience. Music certainly seems to involve more than mere sound waves vibrating our eardrums and causing us to feel pleasant sensations; there appears to be something more to music than particular instances of it. This is why it's almost impossible to think about the power of music without pondering its source and wondering what music means. Heidegger thought the same about Being. Experiencing an object not only calls to mind the existence of the object itself but also calls to mind the question as to what existence, as such, *is*. For Heidegger, this question is the most profound question that one could ask, because in asking the question, we enter the nonphysical realm of being, which is the real source of all meaning. This is why, in his view, it took a high degree of cultural brainwashing to erase Being—the very ground of all meaning—from the memory of Western consciousness, but this is exactly what Western science and technology have done.

Heidegger argued that the general awareness of the nonphysical is-ness of material items, despite its importance to the spiritual health of Western culture, is virtually gone. Why? Because science and technology have taught modern humans—virtually independent of their awareness—to see reality only in terms of what is measurable and quantifiable. That is to say, our capacity for experiencing the rich diversity of *what is* has been effectively reduced and limited to materialistic interpretations—to the point that modern humans have lost the intuitive awareness of nonphysical Being. Heidegger called this condition the "forgetfulness of Being." Philosophy itself has forgotten Being and has been seduced by materialism, and for this reason it has gone astray. This wasn't always the case, however, according to Heidegger. Some ancient Greek philosopher/scientists—before the rise of Socratic thinking—had some awareness of Being, as is evidenced in the thinking of, for example, the pre-Socratic astronomer and philosopher Anaximander (610–546 BCE), who sought to discover the meaning of *what is*.

Heidegger inferred that the possibility of experiencing meaning in our everyday lives, in any form, derives from the implicit presence of the is-ness of things—of Being. What do meaning and Being have in common? They both exist, and both are nonphysical realities. To Heidegger, this insight was the royal road to understanding what meaning is and how it relates to human consciousness. Consciousness knows meaning because of its capacity of recognizing—of seeing and being attuned to—Being. The task that lay before Heidegger was to describe phenomenologically his idea of Being, and the result was his revolutionary phenomenological study of Being in his epochal but incomplete book, *Being and Time*.

Whereas Husserl began with a description of experience and meaning through his abstract phenomenological reduction, Heidegger started by describing the natural conditions that make human meaning possible. The "existential turn" in Heidegger's work began when he realized

488

that the study of Being must begin with describing the "ground" from which questions about the meaning of Being arise in the first place. This ground is the human being himself, which Heidegger called *Dasein*— German for "there-being." By exploring Dasein first, Heidegger thought that he was laying the foundation for the larger study of Being. Until the meaning of Dasein is understood, the ultimate meaning of Being will remain out of reach. Unlike Husserl, who focused mainly on a disengaged consciousness as the focal point of meaning, Heidegger saw not consciousness, but Dasein's "being-in-the-world" as the proper place where meaning and experience arise. Heidegger, in elaborating his ideas of Dasein, was intentionally trying to undermine the traditional notion of what a human being is as a simple object that can be investigated and understood using typical materialistic/scientific and philosophical descriptive methods and categories.

In *Being and Time*, Heidegger redirected the phenomenological eye away from consciousness and Husserl's abstract manipulations of consciousness, to Dasein, where he set out to describe its "necessary structures"—those essences that constitute the being of Dasein. Heidegger's preoccupation with the structures of human existence, of Dasein, and his startling elaboration of what they mean, provided crucial building blocks for other existential thinkers. The most important of Dasein's structures are its: "being-in-the-world" without its choosing; Dasein's "care" or concern for his existence; Dasein's "loneliness" and "lostness" in a strange, alien world; Dasein's living anonymously among countless other anonymous Daseins; Dasein's "call of conscience" to realize its "authentic self"; Dasein's "anxiety" in the face of death; the necessity for Dasein to make choices that have unknown consequences, and yet being totally responsible for itself; Dasein's "being toward death"—that is, its unstoppable movement forward through time toward certain extinction—these are the universal structures that existentialists put to their own creative, and sometimes flamboyant, use.

By designating Dasein as a being-in-the-world, Heidegger had hoped to fracture the materialist, Western, scientific/philosophical mindset about what human being is, and what it means for human beings *to be*. Dasein is not a mere thing that sits motionlessly and statically on top of the earth like some inanimate rock. Rather, Dasein is a self-propelling, future moving, "historical" being, who is born into, and forever "dwells" *thoughtfully* in, a cultural world. At birth, Dasein begins its temporal journey forward in historical time until it reaches its final termination point: *its own unique death*—Dasein *is* "a being toward death." But Dasein has two possible ways of being: Dasein could dwell "inauthentically"— that is, Dasein could live "anonymously" among the "they"—among other inauthentic Daseins, without thinking for itself, without formulating its own ideas and beliefs, and without acting from its own decision-making processes. It could live without consciously realizing its unique identity, but instead seeing itself only in general, impersonal terms, such as an engineer, a mother, or a member of the human race. Dasein could also move into its future according to the detached, mechanical, and lifeless tick-tick-tick of clock-time on the wall, or the anxious wristwatch-time on its wrist, or according to the monotonous time-schedule at work. Because inauthentic Dasein lives only in general time, it does not have its own personal time, and consequently, it also does not consciously create its own past or project itself into its own future; instead it moves passively and thoughtlessly along detached time trajectories—the very same ones that other inauthentic Daseins move along. By living inauthentically, Dasein is indistinguishable from other Daseins, and as a result, *individuality* has no real meaning to inauthentic Dasein. The tragic irony for inauthentic Dasein is that it will die a death that is uniquely its own, without ever having possessed a life that was uniquely its own.

Dasein's other possibility is that it could choose to respond to its "call of conscience" to live "authentically"—where it forms its own thoughts and beliefs; where it decides its own actions; where it experiences its past, present, and future—as *personal*—as its own, and where it embraces honestly, thoughtfully, and courageously its own personal movement in time toward its own, unique death. Because authentic Dasein has retrieved itself from inauthentic existence, it's able to understand its individual life—the one-of-a-kind temporal course that it has traveled throughout its lifetime—as distinguishable from that of all other Daseins who have ever lived or whoever will live.

16.9

Heidegger's exotic definition of Dasein, and the descriptions of its structures, provided all subsequent existentialists with an endless supply of existential inroads and insights. One thinker who was swept away by Heidegger's philosophy, and who became the quintessential existentialist, was Jean-Paul Sartre (1905–1980). His existentialism was an ingenious blend of, and expansion on, not only the ideas of Heidegger, but also those of Husserl and Hegel. Sartre wrote philosophical treatises (*Being and Nothingness*), plays (*No Exit*), and novels (*Nausea)* to teach his existentialism. As an ardent student of both Husserl and Heidegger, Sartre enthusiastically took up the cause of phenomenology and eventually developed it into his own remarkable brand of existentialism. He argued that both Husserl's and Heidegger's voyages into consciousness and into human existence, although revolutionary, did not go nearly far enough. For instance, in uncovering the role of consciousness in constituting meaning, Husserl unknowingly exposed the core of human existence—freedom—and did not realize what he had brought to light. "Free acts of consciousness," in fact, became for Sartre the essence if what it means to be human.

Sartre, borrowing Hegelian terminology, described a human being as a "being for itself" as opposed to a physical item in the world, which he called "being in itself." He argued that while the latter is determined by physical causes, the former—defined by consciousness and self-awareness—is not. By understanding consciousness as a series of free, uncaused acts, he abandoned the notion of the *self* altogether. For Sartre, this meant that there is no preceding "causal agent" determining the act of choosing. He believed that this position was a logical extension of phenomenological analysis—that he was simply following the phenomenological principle of not adding anything to experience that was not—in essence—there. When we reflect on ourselves, for instance, we do not find a self or agent. Rather, we discover simply the act of reflection itself. As far as Sartre was concerned, the inability to find an abiding, causal self is simply the result of doing good phenomenology.

Sartre considered that even emotions are free acts of consciousness—choices—that do not determine our behavior. In this sense, "losing control" over our emotions is a false description, because we always freely choose how we act. If we become very angry at not being promoted at work, for instance, this is because we *choose* to give importance to receiving a promotion, and becoming angry is the way that we *choose* to express our displeasure. Moreover, attributing bad behavior to being "swept away" by emotions, or blaming someone, something, or circumstances for our behavior, or even blaming "who we are"—these are all, in Sartre's estimation, immoral acts. He calls these thinly disguised justifications "bad faith." In the final analysis, they are nothing more than pure escapism—conscious choices not to take full responsibility for our actions.

He goes so far as to say that people even use emotional outbursts to induce in themselves the *illusion* that they had no choice other than to act as they did; in effect, they "magically transform" reality so as to *appear* that they cannot assume responsibility for their actions. The compulsion to act in bad faith is so intense in humans that Sartre said rather poignantly, "Man is a useless passion," desperately trying to exist as though he were a victimized "being in itself," rather than being what he really is: a totally free and responsible "being for itself."

Sartre was even more provocative when he said that not only is there no self but that a human being is a "nothing" seeking to find existence. Sartre extended Husserl's notion of intentionality in his book *Being and Nothingness*, in which Sartre says that if a human being is nothing more than free acts of consciousness, and if consciousness is always and necessarily intentional—that is, always-dependent, then it must be the case that *consciousness is what consciousness intends*. In other words, human beings are, by their nature, empty, and they need to rely on what they are conscious of, on what they intend—for the content of their being. A thoroughly empty consciousness is not possible, but there are degrees of being filled with intentional objects. The basic maxim is that the more one intends, the more one exists.

For Sartre, the biggest and most filling intentional object is acquired when we absorb (in love, for instance) into our consciousness another "being for itself," another person, for not only will we have another item to fill our empty consciousness, but it will have also inherited the intentional objects of person that we have taken in. We can see Sartre devising a whole theory of human nature and human relationships based on Husserlian-like themes. Sartre even defended atheism on phenomenological grounds by arguing that God—as pure, infinite consciousness—is not possible, because all consciousness is necessarily dependent on intentional objects: a dependent God is a contradiction in terms; therefore, God cannot exist.

Sartre's most famous quip is that "existence precedes essence." This simply means that a human being is not born with a specific or general purpose—the way, for example, a chair was created for the purpose of sitting or a hammer for nailing. Rather, human beings must create their purpose and meaning through their choices. Since God does not exist, there is no pre-established plan or design for human life. Sounding a quasi-Heideggerian chord, Sartre believed that we are alone in this mysterious universe and left with only our free choices to create meaning and purpose in our lives. Thus, we are, as Sartre says in one of his startling phrases, "condemned to be free." This understanding of human existence may sound absurd, but it is, nevertheless, true. Sartre's idea of freedom followed naturally from Husserl's insight that meaning is not a necessary aspect of an object but can be suspended at will. Sartre filled in the existential blanks: if meaning could be suspended at will, then it could be added, as well. Meaning in this sense is a pure creation of the imagination, and not a permanent fixture of human experience.

As we have seen, Husserl's descriptive method and his focus on intentionality, in addition to Heidegger's exploration of the structures of Dasein, came together in Sartre in fascinating, even shocking ways. Another example is a notion that Sartre borrowed from Heidegger (who glimpsed it from Kierkegaard and Nietzsche): emotions and moods are not empty, meaningless feelings, but speak to us deeply about dimensions of human reality that are inaccessible to purely rational understanding. Heidegger spoke about the "anxiety" that each and every Dasein experiences in the face of its eventual death. This anxiety is not a fear of this or that threatening situation or nemesis; it is a nonspecific, general emotional unease about our personal death-bound life and our intuitive awareness that our life will be cut short at some unknown moment in the future. Sartre went further than Heidegger and incorporated Hegelian themes, saying in his book *Being and Nothingness* that human beings are aware, however vaguely, of the "presence of nothingness" and that the anxiety that this presence evokes accurately reflects the incorrigible emptiness and essential meaninglessness of life. This presence of nothingness also feeds into our own existential condition of being an empty consciousness. For Sartre, each human life necessarily consists in anxious people erecting makeshift worlds of meaning in order to try to keep nothingness at bay, lest nothingness rushes in uncontrollably and flattens their flimsy constructs of meaning. We can see that Sartre's ideas about existence and about human reality represent what is most exciting and disturbing about existentialism.

The startling insights into consciousness and human existence that came to light in the works of phenomenology and existentialism will always stand as a dramatic turning point in the history of a humanity struggling to understand itself. And their contributions to the history of ideas represent philosophy's most compelling arguments for what humankind must do, not only in order to survive, but also to live well—that is, with passion and meaning.

16.10

Philosophy is constantly wrestling with definitions. For instance, the traditional definition of "essence" with respect to the "nature" of something implies permanence and unchangeability. Driving is the essence of a car, for instance; nailing is the essence of a hammer; playing tennis is the essence of a tennis racket. In all such cases, it's always true that the items in question were created with their essences in mind, and their essences determine the nature of their existence. But Sartre's meaning of essence when applied to human beings is radically different.

For him, human essence is not determinative but is highly flexible and could change as quickly as a decision, for instance, to become a writer rather than a computer engineer, or to be gregarious rather than reclusive. Human essence comes and goes with the twisting, staccato-like course of everyday living and thinking, where the chaos of decision-making confers upon the whole decision-making process enormous uncertainty and tentativeness. An unsure and undecided human essence naturally follows There are no "structural essences" in human beings simply waiting to be actualized, as it were, but the very opposite: there is an unvarying existential void that is in constant in need of being filled through free acts of choosing. In this sense, an individual life is a testimony to the essences that its author has created through his choices. What we have done, what we have created, the works that we leave behind, and the various paths that we have taken—all reflect the interconnected web of our essences that, in total, represent the concrete evidence of a meaningful life.

In a Sartrean world, our choices create a sort of *ontological inertia* to the extent that they send us on our way from moment to moment and from one point in our personal time to another. Although human essences could disappear when we are not in the act of choosing, our memories of our choices and our habitual ways of thinking, feeling, and behaving keep our essences alive, powerful, and moving forward. That is, at least until new decisions are made, which either reinforce our past essences or send us off into different directions with new ones. Essence is not a thing or feature of a human life that is there at birth; it comes into being and is sustained through each individual action of free choice. We are constantly in jeopardy of losing our essence if indecision paralyzes our decision-making capacity. Without choosing, one is set adrift in the void—one is *a nothing adrift in nothingness.*

Essence is real only in choosing, because choosing propels us into the future—and it does so in very specific ways: as teachers, philosophers, murderers, car manufacturers, and so on. Choosing always involves realizing future possibilities, and this is why essence is future-orientated. Essence structures our thoughts, feelings, and activities and gives meaning to the moments in which it is mobilized. Essence organizes, focuses, and directs our movement through time. A hammer is made for hammering; it comes into existence and realizes its essence because it was designed by a creator to do just that. A godless universe provides no such assurance to human beings. It's the height of absurdity that insentient, metal-and-wood tool has, as its birthright, a lasting essence, while the so-called highest of all of nature's creations has *no choice* but to spend the whole of his or her precious few years of existence in the frustrating and often painful effort of trying to find a fixed and lasting essence—and never really succeeding. At least this is what Sartre would likely say.

16.11

What is reality-in-itself? Reality-in-itself is all the potential and actual psychological, emotional, sensual, intuitive, physical, and intellectual states, insights, and experiences that accurately reflect *what is.*

1612

What is real? What does this mean? What is it now? What was it then? What is it that will be? These questions are the philosophical portals through which objective reality—the "whats" and "its" of existence—rushes through.

16.13

That each of us must die one day is tragic enough, but that many of us will die not by accident, murder, or even from natural causes, but gradually from suicide, is what is most unfortunate.

16.14

Why do we lose that cheerful twinkle in our eyes and easy smile as we age, as well as forfeit our keen mental agility and creative muscle? Are these diminishing qualities nothing more that the unavoidable consequences of our atrophying instincts and our bodies and minds slowly becoming depleted of life's vital energies? The answer is that advancing age often diminishes what in youth was there in abundance. Fortunately, unlike all other species, humans are able to put up the "good fight" and knock nature back on her heels. There is no doubt that improving the "quality" of our lives through proper diet, sufficient exercise, preventive health regimens, caring relationships, life-embracing worldviews, and intellectual stimulation can go along way is keeping our mortal coffers overflowing with invigorating life-energy, even as the years pass.

For the exceptional individual, however, living a quality life has an even richer meaning than simply staying in good physical, emotional, and intellectual health. It also means learning how to create new avenues to a more thrilling sense of being alive, as well as cultivating deeper capacities for self-love, for loving other people, and for loving life itself. And what does "a more thrilling sense of being alive" mean to the exceptional individual? It means nothing less than to challenge heroically the natural limitations of the body, to intensify the capacity to feel the world around us, and to explode closed-minded thinking. With these self-liberations, the exceptional person is free to be "born again," and to relive with passion, the glories of youth. And what about love?

There is much talk in popular culture today about the need for all of us to love each other "unconditionally." Unfortunately, to love everyone unconditionally means destroying the very essence of love, for love has real meaning and power only in distinction from what we could never love—such as unjustified acts of violence and immoral individuals. Indeed, learning how to love includes developing discerning judgment in order to know what is, and what is not, worthy of being loved—and for those who are not naturally endowed with this wisdom, this is the most difficult challenge of all to living an exceptional life. But what about loving oneself? Should we not strive to love oneself unconditionally? Certainly not. In the same way that I should only love people who are deserving of love, I also should love myself only if I am worthy of the profound compliment, or else I could easily run the risk of never being truly loved by anyone else.

16.15

Human freedom emerges only when it's guided by constraining factors—this is the paradox that many lovers of freedom fail to realize. I am reminded of the meaning of a "technique"—say, a technique for playing tennis, for instance. A tennis player learns specific ways of gripping and moving a tennis racket, for example, of moving around a tennis court, of making contact with the ball, of moving to the net, of serving, and of returning tennis balls from an opponent. The more *consistently* a tennis player carries out these activities, the better the person will be at playing tennis. These consistent ways of playing tennis, taken together, make-up the player's technique. And what does a great tennis player experience and demonstrate when her technique is serving her especially well? Greater command and control, as well as the *freedom* to express her amazing skill creatively. And yet, she is able to achieve such excellence only because her technique requires that she play tennis not in just any way, or in many ways, but rather, in very precise, limiting ways. The mastery and creative freedom that she experiences, in other words, results directly from her technique that tells her not only what to do, but just as importantly, what *not* to do. The relationship between freedom and the restrictions of technique is such that the better the technique, the greater the constraint—and, as a result, the freer and even more creative the performance. Freedom by way of technique, then, is not freedom *from* constraints, but the freedom *to* constrain; and this logic applies not only to sports—it's the very core of human freedom whenever it's expressed. The rule-of-thumb is very simple: Human freedom requires placing proper limitations on its expressions or else it will turn into its opposite: chaos and bondage.

16.16

Great art requires great restraint, for it's only in great restraint that the artist can manifest freedom of choice—the hallmark of all creative genius.

16.17

And what is beauty but the infinity of *what is*—shining forth brilliantly in the here-and-now—in this or that beautiful presence!

16.18

The presence of what is beautiful is the most profound of all experiences because of its mystifying ability to transform how we see the world—it becomes brighter, warmer, and more joyful—happier. The beautified world has a natural necessity to it: everything is in its proper place; everything feels just right; everything tickles my fancy—this smile and gesture, that tuft of hair flowing in the breeze, those bodies lost in passionate embrace—all are present to delight and please me. And even my own thoughts become messengers of what is beautiful, as every idea, belief, and judgment is good, truthful, and indispensable. But beauty has more than one face and effect: it also has the power to draw me out of myself, to unmask my feigned emotions, to force me to see through my miserable thoughts and misconceived actions, and to bring to mind a vision of *what I could be*. In this way, the presence of what is beautiful is not only an incomparable source of pleasure, but it's also useful—a veritable spur to my own self-beautification, even as it employs the radiant glow of illusion to light the way.

16.19

"Live and know life!"—has been whispered in my ear since I was a little boy. I know this voice well—its distinctive tone, inflections, and feeling. But whose voice is it? And how could it have stayed so pure, bright, and youthful over all these years? Forever the springtime? Forever the morning?

Lightning Source UK Ltd.
Milton Keynes UK
22 March 2010

151725UK00001BA/274/P